The Ghost of Equality

The Ghost of Equality

*The Public Lives
of D. D. T. Jabavu
of South Africa,
1885–1959*

Catherine Higgs

OHIO UNIVERSITY PRESS
ATHENS

DAVID PHILIP
CAPE TOWN & JOHANNESBURG

MAYIBUYE BOOKS
UNIVERSITY OF THE WESTERN CAPE

Ohio University Press, Athens, Ohio 45701
© 1997 by Catherine Ann Higgs
Printed in the United States of America
All rights reserved

Published in southern Africa by
David Philip Publishers (Pty) Ltd.,
208 Werdmuller Centre, Claremont 7700
South Africa
and Mayibuye Books
University of the Western Cape
Private Bag X17, Bellville 7535
ISBN 0-86486 305 5 (David Philip and Mayibuye Books)
Mayibuye Books History and Literature Series No. 69

The Mayibuye Center for History and Culture is based at the
University of the Western Cape. Focusing on all aspects of apartheid,
resistance, social life, and culture in South Africa, its aim is to help
recover the rich heritage of all South Africans and to encourage
cultural creativity and expression. The Mayibuye History and
Literature Series is part of this project. The series editors are Barry
Feinberg and André Odendaal.

Ohio University Press books
are printed on acid-free paper

01 00 99 98 97 5 4 3 2 1

Library of Congress Cataloging-in-Publication Data
Higgs, Catherine.
   The Ghost of Equality : The Public Lives of D. D. T. Jabavu of
South Africa, 1885–1959 / Catherine Higgs
      p. cm.
      Includes bibliographical references and index.
      ISBN 0-8214-1169-1 (cl : alk. paper). —
      ISBN 0-8214-1171-3 (pa : alk. paper)
      1. Jabavu, Davidson D. T. (Davidson Don Tengo), b. 1885.
      2. South Africa—Race relations. I. Title.
DT1927.J34H54   1996   96-13506
305.8′00968 — dc20   CIP

For my father, Robert Wilson Higgs

and in memory of my sister, Laura Jean Higgs

Contents

ILLUSTRATIONS

Photographs

Map

ACKNOWLEDGMENTS

This book grew out of my graduate work in the Department of History and in the Southern African Research Program (SARP) seminar at Yale University. I thank the participants in the SARP seminar, and I especially thank the members of my dissertation committee, including Diana Wylie (now of Boston University) and Leonard Thompson, who kindly commented on the revisions to chapter four of the manuscript. I am particularly grateful to my thesis adviser, Robert Harms, who generously read the entire revised manuscript. I also owe a deep debt of gratitude to Moore Crossey, the curator of the African Collection at Yale University, who has tracked down numerous obscure details for me over the years.

My studies and research were funded by a doctoral fellowship from the Social Sciences and Humanities Research Council of Canada, by the Marty Memorial Scholarship Committee of Queen's University at Kingston, Ontario, and by the Friends of Queen's University of New York City.

In South Africa, I would like to thank the staffs of the University of South Africa's Documentation Centre for African Studies, the Central Archives Depot, the Cape Archives Depot, the South African Library, the J. W. Jagger Library of the University of Cape Town (especially Leonie Twentyman Jones), the Cory Library for Historical Research at Rhodes University (especially Sandy Rowoldt), the Howard Pim Library of Rare Books at the University of Fort Hare, the Division of Historical and Literary Papers at the University of the Witwatersrand Library (especially Anna Cunningham and Michelle Pickover), and the Library of the South African Institute of Race Relations. Many South African academics generously advised me, including Tim Couzens, Rodney Davenport, Johan and Jeanette Groenewald, Richard Haines, Peter Kota, and Bill Nasson. In the United States, I thank the librarians at the Library of Congress, Swarthmore College, Tuskegee University, and the Yale Divinity School and Yale University libraries.

To Cecil Wele Manona, who translated D. D. T. Jabavu's works in Xhosa into English, and to Sipo Makalima, who showed me D. D. T. Jabavu's eastern Cape, I owe a special debt of gratitude. I am also deeply grateful to D. D. T. Jabavu's two daughters, Helen Nontando Jabavu Crosfield and Alexandra Jabavu-Mulira, who graciously shared their memories of their father. I cannot begin to thank the other fifty people who granted me interviews and made the South Africa of the 1930s and 1940s come alive.

Robert Shell first recommended the manuscript for publication, and I am grateful to him and to Patrick Furlong, who offered many thoughtful suggestions for revisions. I also thank Gillian Berchowitz of the Ohio University Press for her guidance in preparing the manuscript for publication.

Among the friends who have provided much-needed encouragement over the years, I thank Leslie Bessant, Jill Bleakley, James Francis, Elizabeth Johanson, the late Arthur Keppel-Jones (who first introduced me to South African history when I was a student at Queen's University), Jack Lane, Chris Lowe, John Mason, Michelle McKenna, Karin Shapiro, Harrison Wright, and especially Sean Redding and Lynn Berat, both of whom have read many versions of this manuscript, and who have individually set standards for scholarship which I can only hope to emulate. I also thank two colleagues in the Department of History at the University of Tennessee: Elizabeth Haiken, who proofread the text, and Bruce Wheeler, who helped index it. In the Program in African and African-American Studies, I thank Jonathan Reynolds and Angelia Roach, who insisted I take a break occasionally, and Andre Dean, who infused the office with good humor, and diligently photocopied endless pages.

I thank Martin Legassick of the University of the Western Cape for permission to quote from his two unpublished articles: "The Making of 'South African Native Policy,' 1903–1923: The Origins of 'Segregation'" (1972) and "The Rise of Modern South African Liberalism: Its Assumptions and Social Base" (1972). Similarly, I thank the Central Archives Depot for permission to cite from vol. 63 (Native Legislation, 1932–1939) and vol. 80 (Coloured and Native Representation) of the J. B. M. Hertzog Collection; the British Broadcasting Corporation for permission to quote from the transcript of the "Picture Page" television interview with D. D. T. Jabavu on September 15, 1937; and the United Church Board for World Ministries for permission to quote from the "ABC: Biographical Collection" file on D. D. T. Jabavu in the American Board of Commissioners for Foreign Mission Papers, which are stored in the Houghton Library at Harvard University.

The photographs accompanying the text are from the D. D. T. Jabavu Collection at the University of South Africa (UNISA), the Jabavu Family Collection at the University of Cape Town (UCT), the Helen Nontando Jabavu Crosfield Collection (in the care of Harrison Wright), and from the private collection of Harrison Wright. Brian Williams of the Geography Department at the University of Tennessee drew the map.

Finally, I thank my father, Robert Wilson Higgs, who has always encouraged me to pursue my interests. This book is dedicated to the memory of my sister, Laura Jean Higgs, who never got to tease me about finally finishing.

Catherine Higgs

Abbreviations

AAC	All African Convention
AAC (WP)	All African Convention (Western Province)
AME	African Methodist Episcopal [Church]
ANC	African National Congress
Anti-CAD	Anti-Coloured Affairs Department
APO	African People's Organization
CAD	Coloured Affairs Department
CNVC	Cape Native Voters' Convention
CPSA	Communist Party of South Africa
DRC	Dutch Reformed Churches
ICU	Industrial and Commercial Workers' Union
LMS	London Missionary Society
NAC	Native Affairs Commission
NAD	Native Affairs Department
NEA	Native Educational Association
NEUM	Non-European Unity Movement
NFA	Native Farmers' Association
NFRA	Non-Racial Franchise Association
NP	National Party
NRC	Natives' Representative Council
PAC	Pan Africanist Congress
SAIC	South African Indian Congress
SAIRR	South African Institute of Race Relations
SANC	South African Native Congress
SANFC	South African Native Farmers' Congress
SANNC	South African Native National Congress (later renamed the African National Congress)
SAP	South African Party
TCA	Teachers' Christian Association
TTGC	Transkei Territories General Council

Note on Terminology

Many of the words commonly used during D. D. T. Jabavu's lifetime to describe the peoples of southern Africa are now considered pejorative. *Native*, *Bantu*, *Non-European*, *Coloured*, and *Indian*, are used here only in direct quotation, or where clarity—particularly with reference to the terms *Coloured* and *Indian*—demands their use. Variations of the terms *Native* and *Bantu* appear with reference to official legislation and institutions; in all other instances, the word *African* is used. In Jabavu's day, *black* was used in reference to Africans only; *Non-European* referred collectively to "Natives," "Coloureds," and "Indians"—that is, to people who were not European, or of direct European descent. Here, the term *black* is used in place of *Non-European*; the term *white* replaces the antiquated *European*.

THE GHOST OF EQUALITY

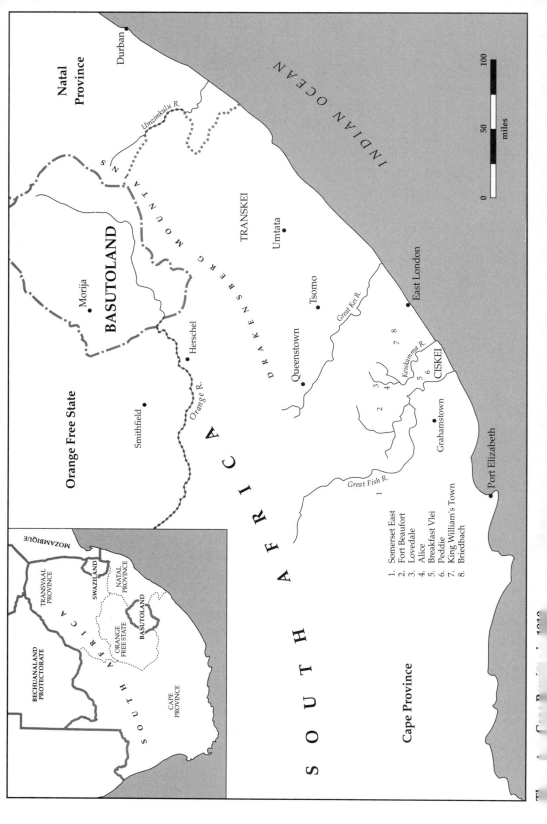

Introduction

Davidson Don Tengo Jabavu was born in the Cape Colony in British southern Africa on October 20, 1885, when a few African men could vote and the prospects for black equality with the ruling whites seemed promising. He died on August 3, 1959 in the Cape Province of the Union of South Africa,[1] eleven years after the apartheid state had begun stripping blacks of their rights and exorcising the "ghost of equality" with a completeness unparalleled in the country's history. The "ghost of equality" was the last vestige of the Cape liberal tradition—itself best summed up by the dictum "equal rights for all civilized men"—finally erased in 1959 with the passage of legislation that would, the following year, remove from parliament the last elected white representatives of Africans.[2]

Educated in southern Africa and the United Kingdom (where he was among the first black South Africans to attain a university degree), D. D. T. Jabavu was a college lecturer, an advocate for teachers and farmers, a Methodist lay preacher, and a political activist. He lived an extraordinary life; he traveled to the United States, the Middle East, and India; he conferred with politicians, missionaries, and scholars; he sought always a more equitable dispensation for black South Africans.[3]

The quintessential "Cape liberal" of his generation of African politicians, he was a strong advocate of a "common citizenship" for all South Africans—albeit one defined in Western terms and rooted in "the meritocratic Christian values of the late Victorian era, in which race was supposedly no criterion for citizenship."[4] This worldview had little validity in the racially exclusive Union of South Africa created by the South Africa Act of 1909. Nevertheless it was a vision to which Jabavu—a child of the nineteenth century—held fast, even as it left him increasingly marginalized, especially in the political sphere.

If D. D. T. Jabavu's life reveals anything about South Africa's political history, it is that this history was not monolithic. It was not simply a lengthy confrontation between a black elite represented by the African National Congress (ANC) and the white segregationist state. Rather, there was a range of black political opinion and activity, of which Jabavu, an active participant in virtually every government-sponsored and every major extraparliamentary conference between 1920 and the late 1940s, represented one prominent historical strain.

This book, however, is about more than D. D. T. Jabavu's politics; it is about his public life, or perhaps more accurately, his public lives. The book is arranged thematically, divided according to the parts Jabavu played: student, teacher, Methodist, and politician. This is an admitted conceit; we do not, after all, live our lives thematically. Yet the documentary evidence does support this compartmentalization. As a lecturer in African languages and Latin at the South African Native College (now the University of Fort Hare), Jabavu's politics rarely intruded onto the campus, even at the height of the protests he led in 1935 to retain the franchise for those Cape Africans who exercised it. Similarly, while he did lecture to the Students' Christian Association at the College, most of the sermons he gave and lessons he read as a Methodist lay preacher were delivered off campus; indeed, he was perhaps most publicly Christian in his published writings, and in his speeches delivered to international religious conferences.

To write about D. D. T. Jabavu's life in such a fashion, then, is not to suggest that all the various threads ran parallel courses, but rather to attempt to make sense of the tangled web they wove. Chapter one provides an overview of Cape liberalism, and a brief history of the Jabavu family, but its main focus is Jabavu's education in the Cape Colony, Basutoland (modern-day Lesotho), Wales, and England, and his absorption of a Western model of civilization. The focus of chapter two is how he passed those values on, both to his students at the South African Native College and to African teachers and farmers in the wider community of the eastern Cape. If education in Jabavu's estimation was essential to the definition of a "civilized" man, so too was Christianity, and chapter three examines his religious beliefs, and the manner in which he used them to give voice to African concerns both nationally and internationally. Chapters four and five trace Jabavu's rise to and fall from political prominence, and suggest that while his embrace of the Cape liberal tradition helped explain his political activism, that same tradition also contributed to his failure as a politician. Jabavu's final years, and his own assessment of South Africa in the 1950s, are the subject of the concluding chapter.

If the central question the biographer asks is, "What did this life mean?"[5] Jabavu is a particularly accessible subject, for he seemed to wear no mask, no public face for the white world and private face for the black.[6] D. D. T. Jabavu knew the meaning of his own life. He self-consciously defined himself as a role model for other, less fortunate Africans; his goal in life was to educate them, to help them progress, so that they too might claim their equal rights as civilized men.[7] Education for Jabavu was the great leveler of both class and race differences. His embrace of Cape liberalism was for the most part without irony,[8] though this is not to suggest that he was so enamored of the West that he did not also define himself as an African.[9] He spent his professional life teaching African languages, and his political career promoting African rights. He wrote and published throughout his life in Xhosa as well as in English, and near the end of his life published a collection of Xhosa clan names acquired over the course of thirty-five years of traveling in the eastern Cape.[10] D. D. T. Jabavu fit very well the model of the "New African,"[11] able to function in two worlds without apparent conflict. What conflict there might have been is largely lost to the biographer, for very little of Jabavu's private correspondence, which might have revealed such insights, has survived.[12]

What has survived are his published works: books, pamphlets, and articles, concerned primarily with political, educational, and religious issues. Supplemented by interviews with former students and colleagues, they reflect, with a few noteworthy exceptions, a very consistent worldview from the 1910s through the 1950s. Included among these works is D. D. T. Jabavu's biography of his father, John Tengo Jabavu, published in 1922, the year after his death. An accomplished and often controversial figure, John Tengo Jabavu founded the first African-owned newspaper in the Cape Colony, *Imvo Zabantsundu* (African Opinion), and was himself a prominent political figure in the late-nineteenth and early-twentieth-century eastern Cape. His son's biography of him falls firmly into the late Victorian "great men" school of biographical writing,[13] and though not completely uncritical, it does, in its celebration of his life and downplaying of his mistakes, border on hagiography.

Though D. D. T. Jabavu's biography of his father is not an isolated example of a biography written by and about a black South African, there is no great tradition of biography of either blacks or whites in South African historical writing.[14] In English, T. D. Mweli Skota's biographical dictionary, *The African Yearly Register*, published in 1930, stands out as a record of early black achievements.[15] In his 1943 survey of African literature, D. D. T. Jabavu identified one biography written in Northern Sotho,[16] and five biographies written in Xhosa, including the novelist S. E. K. Mqhayi's biography of the Presbyterian minister John Knox Bokwe, and Bokwe's biography of the Xhosa prophet of Christianity, Ntsikana.[17] Published mainly by mission presses keen to promote Christianity, and concerned to remove any contentious material,[18] these early biographies were, in D. D. T. Jabavu's opinion, "small and undistinguished though valuable as humble records of lives worthily lived."[19]

More common, and of more recent vintage, is a tradition of autobiographies in English by black South Africans.[20] The most recent contributor to this genre is Nelson Mandela—one of the most prominent world figures of the late twentieth century—whose autobiography, *Long Walk to Freedom*, was published in 1994.[21] Mandela's personal story adds texture to a well-documented public record of his life. This is true too of the autobiographies of other prominent ANC leaders, including Albert Luthuli's *Let My People Go* (1962), and Z. K. Matthews's *Freedom for My People* (1968).[22]

But autobiography is not reserved only for the politically prominent, as recent autobiographies by Ellen Kuzwayo (1985), Mark Mathabane (1986), Emma Mashinini (1991), Phyllis Ntantala (1993), and Frieda Matthews (1995) testify.[23] While it should be noted that Ntantala and Matthews are the widows of famous men (Ntantala of the novelist and political commentator A. C. Jordan, and Matthews of Z. K. Matthews), they were as effectively hidden from history as less well-known autobiographers, not only by their spouses, but by being—as the historian Shula Marks has argued—black and female.[24] What all these autobiographers share is a need to "set the record straight," in a society in which an official white history has distorted historical understanding for all South Africans.[25] Yet as the historian Jane Starfield has noted, "in at least one important way, autobiography is not quite history; it is limited by being a 'personal' view."[26]

Historians have sought to overcome this limitation by marshaling evidence (both written and oral) to document the lives of black South Africans.[27] These scholarly biographers share with earlier biographers, and with those who have written their own life stories, a particular compulsion to get the story right, given that the history of South Africa, as the historian Brian Willan has observed, has for so long "been highly selective in its recall."[28] What Willan in his biography of the ANC leader Sol Plaatje (1984), and Tim Couzens in his study of the playwright H. I. E. Dhlomo (1985), and Shula Marks in her two biographical studies, *The Ambiguities of Dependence* (1986) and *Not Either an Experimental Doll* (1987), have all tried to do is to restore to South Africa's history voices muted by race, or by class, or by gender.[29]

D. D. T. Jabavu's own historical voice has been muted by race, and also by a political philosophy now dismissed as misguided. Thirty-five years after his death, it was the significantly modified and egalitarian vision of "equal rights for all citizens," rather than for "all civilized men," which triumphed with the election of Nelson Mandela as president of South Africa in 1994. Yet Jabavu's younger contemporaries were generous in their assessment of him. A. P. Mda, a leading theorist of the African National Congress Youth League in the 1940s, remembered Jabavu in 1988 as a "classic liberal," who believed in "the oneness of the human race . . . despite differences in colour, language, . . . cultural background and so on. . . . As human beings we are one."[30] This vision of South Africa proved beyond D. D. T. Jabavu's grasp, but it remains an ideal within the reach of the people of a free South Africa.

1 Southern Africa and the Wider World, 1885–1914

At the time of D. D. T. Jabavu's birth in 1885, the Cape of Good Hope had been a British colony for more than eighty years, and South Africa, as a distinct political entity, did not yet exist. On the eastern coast of southern Africa there was another British possession, the Colony of Natal. In the interior, two independent republics—the South African Republic and the Orange Free State— had been founded by the descendants of the Dutch and the French who had first settled at Cape Town in the mid to late seventeenth century.[1] Of the original African peoples of the region, only the Venda, occupying territory north of the Limpopo River on the northwest border of the South African Republic, and the Mpondo, located south of the Umzimkulu River on the east coast, remained independent of European rule.[2]

British colonists had first arrived in the Cape Colony in substantial numbers in 1820. The British government's intent was to settle them as farmers in the eastern part of the colony, south of lands historically claimed by the Xhosa. Most 1820 settlers, however, lacked the skills and experience to farm the arid land of the eastern Cape effectively; instead they settled in the town that grew up around the British fort at Grahamstown, or in Port Elizabeth. Those who remained on the land eventually achieved a degree of prosperity by turning to sheep ranching. Thus British settlers remained a presence in the eastern Cape, periodically clashing with the Xhosa and encroaching further into their territory.[3]

British settlers also clashed with the earlier European settlers (initially called Boers, from the Dutch word for farmer, and later, Afrikaners).[4] Beginning in the mid-1830s and continuing to 1840, Afrikaners opposed to the British administration, and particularly to Britain's decision to abolish slavery in its colonies in 1833, began to migrate into the interior in a movement called the Great Trek. The Cape Colony lost about one tenth of its white population, or about 6,000 people.[5] Afrikaner trekkers first established the Natal Republic in 1839, to the north of the Mpondo, and south of the Zulu kingdom. Continued friction between the Africans and the Afrikaners led the British, concerned with stability on the eastern frontier, to annex the Natal Republic as a British colony in 1842.[6] Many Afrikaner trekkers responded by moving into the interior, where, ultimately, the British would acknowledge the independence of the South African Republic (also known as the Transvaal) in 1852, and of the Orange Free State in 1854.[7] Both were racially exclusive states in which blacks had no rights.[8] The Afrikaners, however, continued to battle the African peoples whose lands they occupied, and the British government remained concerned about this continued unrest on the borders of its colonies. In 1853 the British granted representative government to the Cape Colony; three years later the Colony of Natal was granted the same privilege.[9]

With respect to the Cape Colony, the historians Stanley Trapido and Rodney Davenport have argued that the introduction of representative government was largely a pragmatic decision, intended to stabilize a territorial frontier which had expanded too rapidly and on which the military was often the sole source of authority.[10] From 1853, the Cape legislature was empowered to frame domestic policy, though the British government retained a veto.[11] The new arrangement in the Cape also included a franchise based not on color but on salary and land ownership, and which defined "private land ownership as a civilizing agency."[12] This was a nod to mid-nineteenth-century British liberalism, a concept which, as the historian Phyllis Lewsen has pointed out, was "wide and blurred at the edges, but at its core," stressed "the value of the individual and his right to freedom."[13] Modeled on the expanding franchise in Britain, the Cape franchise excluded women, but included any adult male who earned £50 a year or owned land with a building on it with a combined value of £25.[14]

The nonracial franchise embodied the "equal rights for all civilized men" at the heart of D. D. T. Jabavu's idealistic interpretation of the Cape liberal tradition. Yet the author of that phrase was none other than the mining magnate Cecil Rhodes, who made his fortune exploiting African laborers in the diamond fields and gold mines of southern Africa.[15] He served as prime minister of the Cape Colony in the 1890s, and was more concerned with the rights of British miners than with those of Africans.[16] That D. D. T. Jabavu's political philosophy should paraphrase a man whose definition of civilization included only white men was thus more than a little ironic.[17] "Equal rights for all civilized men" nevertheless became Jabavu's creed, and he would, throughout much of his career, consistently interpret the granting of the franchise as evidence of the British spirit of magnanimity and fair play.[18]

In practice, however, the property and salary qualifications of the franchise meant that the number of black voters in the Cape would be quite small, consisting, as Trapido has observed, of "the propertied peasantry and the skilled artisans."[19] When the number of African voters threatened to become too large, and whites began to fear "that unless they changed the electoral rules they would one day lose political control of the Cape legislature," qualifications for voters were simply raised. Under the 1892 Franchise and Ballot Act, for example, the property qualification was raised to £75 (although the salary qualification remained the same), and a simple literacy test was added.[20] While the Cape liberal tradition was thus subject to modification by the more immediate concerns of white politicians, it theoretically retained at its core a vision of a society in which—at some point in the very distant future—all men would be civilized, and all would be equal partners in the political arena.

The Jabavus

D. D. T. Jabavu was born into a family that exemplified the "missionaries' axiom, that to be Christian was to be civilized, and to be civilized was to be Christian."[21] His mother, Elda Sakuba Jabavu, was the daughter of the Rev. James B. Sakuba, one of the first African Wesleyan Methodist ministers. His father, John Tengo Jabavu, was the son of Ntwanambi Jabavu and Mary Mpinda, converts who were, respectively, an itinerant laborer and a washerwoman.[22] By 1885 Tengo Jabavu (as he was more commonly known) had become a noted journalist, editor of the Xhosa-English weekly *Imvo Zabantsundu* (African Opinion), and an ardent supporter of the Cape liberal tradition.[23]

Yet D. D. T. Jabavu was also deeply aware of his family's history before their conversion to Christianity in the mid-nineteenth century. In his biography of his father, D. D. T. Jabavu outlined the origins of the family name, explaining to his readers that his great grandfather

> belonged to the Kuze clan of the Ama-Zizi tribe that formed the Intlangwini section settled to this day near Riverside on the Umzimkulu River bordering Natal. He claimed to belong to chief Msingapantsi of the house of Lusibalukulu among the Aba-Mbo or Fingoes, (a migratory people of Zulu extraction), with the clan appellation of Jili of the 'Ama-Singawoti,' the 'Mawengwas,' the 'Qabububendes,'

forbidding but favourite names of African ancestry. His father says that their true name 'Citywa' had been lost because 'Jabavu,' (which signifies 'battle champion,') was an acquired war-cognomen given to his progenitor on account of his fighting prowess.[24]

The Jabavus were "Fingoes" or Mfengu (as were the Sakubas), descendants of peoples displaced by the Mfecane,[25] the expansion of the Zulu kingdom in the early nineteenth century, in the area which would become the province of Natal.[26] Moving south, the Mfengu began settling as clients of the Gcaleka Xhosa[27] in the Transkei region[28] of the eastern Cape in the 1820s,[29] and soon took advantage of existing trade networks to prosper as tobacco and grain farmers, as sheep and cattle ranchers, and as traders.[30]

The Mfengu would also bring new pressure to bear on the Xhosa by realigning themselves with the British. In 1835, 16,000 Mfengu, with 22,000 cattle, migrated again, this time into the Ciskei (the area southwest of the Kei River).[31] They did so at the invitation of the governor of the Cape Colony, Sir Benjamin D'Urban, who envisioned the Mfengu as a buffer between the colony and the Xhosa, with whom a war had just been concluded. The Mfengu were settled near Grahamstown and Fort Peddie, on land so poor that D'Urban described it as "worse than useless," though he remained confident that Mfengu diligence would turn it into a "flourishing garden."[32] In a ceremony in May 1835 at EmQwashwini, a milkwood tree halfway between Peddie and Breakfast Vlei, representatives of the Mfengu made three promises to the Methodist minister, the Rev. John Ayliff, who was representing the colonial government. They pledged to "be truthful to God and support the missionaries . . . be truthful to the British king and the government," and to "educate their children."[33] Such sentiments put them at odds with many of the Xhosa, and in the Frontier Wars of 1846, 1850–53, and 1877–78, the Mfengu fought for the colonial government against their former hosts.[34]

Historians have traced Mfengu willingness to change sides to a variety of factors, including their lower social and economic status within the dominant Xhosa community, their early exposure to missionaries, and the absence of strong leaders among the Mfengu.[35] While it is thus tempting to trace D. D. T. Jabavu's embrace of the Cape liberal tradition and a Western model of civilization to the seemingly ambiguous identity of the Mfengu, to do so would be misleading. The historian Jeffrey Peires has linked some of the Xhosa-Mfengu antagonism not to a lack of identity on the part of the Mfengu (who spoke Xhosa and practiced the Xhosa customs of circumcision and initiation in modified form),[36] but rather to Mfengu unwillingness—once they had recovered from the dislocation of the Mfecane—to abandon their identity completely and be fully absorbed into the Xhosa polity.[37] The promises they made to the British in 1835 may thus be seen as a redefinition of Mfengu identity and a reassertion of independence, rather than as an uncritical embrace of Western values.[38]

The precise nature of the relationship between the Xhosa and their Mfengu clients would nevertheless remain a subject of occasionally intense debate for more than a century. In *I-Nkulungwane yama Mfengu 1835–1936 ne si-vivane: Fingo Centenary 1835–1935 and Centenary Fund*, D. D. T. Jabavu wrote of the Gcaleka Xhosa leader Hintsa, "He was gracious to us, he enabled us to grow crops and rear stock. Some of us worked for him."[39] Jabavu hotly denied the notion—implied by the missionaries John Ayliff and Joseph Whiteside in their history of the Mfengu,[40] and revived during the 1935 centenary celebrations—that the Mfengu had been slaves of the Xhosa.[41] Though he did not deny that the Mfengu had made their pledge to the British in 1835 in return for land, Jabavu considered the Xhosa-Mfengu rivalry an artificial construction, a classic case of divide-and-rule tactics invented by "white 'benefactors' and historians with interested motives."[42] Jabavu himself traced the tension back to "at least one missionary," who "was on unfriendly terms with Hintsa,"[43] and in league with the Cape colonial authorities hounding the Gcaleka Xhosa. Together, Jabavu asserted, they sought to discredit Hintsa by manufacturing the story of his oppression of the Mfengu.[44]

Jabavu did not identify the offending missionary, but it was probably John Ayliff (to whom the Mfengu had made their pledge in 1835).[45] Ayliff, who was stationed at Butterworth in the Transkei, had become a hero to the Mfengu and an enemy of the Xhosa when he gave refuge to Mfengu sought by Hintsa.[46] If Ayliff was the culprit, then Jabavu was effectively rewriting Ayliff's and Whiteside's version of Mfengu history. In Jabavu's account, the Mfengu were not emancipated by the British in 1835; rather, they left their Xhosa patrons in search of land for their cattle. With respect to the alleged slavery of the Mfengu, Jabavu argued "that certain Fingoes [Mfengu] had been misled into using it [slavery] by their missionaries and other White mentors for the purpose of gaining new land—an understandable desire, in itself." In their quest for land, the Mfengu became, in Jabavu's recounting, "innocent dupes"[47] of a colonial "policy of *divide et impera*,"[48] as much victims as the Xhosa.

Yet insisting that the Xhosa-Mfengu divide had been invented by the British would not make it go away. Indeed, a certain distance persists between the Xhosa and the Mfengu to the present day, particularly in rural areas.[49] Although he consistently downplayed the antipathy between the Xhosa and the Mfengu, Jabavu was aware of the potentially negative effect of the tension on his local power base in the rural eastern Cape. From 1920 he made a point of attending both AbaMbo Day—the yearly celebration commemorating the Mfengu pledge to the British—and the rival Xhosa celebration memorializing the Xhosa Christian prophet Ntsikana,[50] using each as an occasion to argue for an unqualified Xhosa-Mfengu unity.[51] Writing in *Imbumba yamaNyama* (Unity is strength), which he published privately in 1952, he even went so far as to proclaim, "I am a Xhosa proper because I was born in the Ntinde chiefdom in King William's Town in the land of the Ngqika."[52]

In protesting a bit too much against the "Fingo Slavery Myth" in 1935, Jabavu was clearly attempting to remove any doubt about his own legitimacy as a spokesman for African interests in the eastern Cape.[53] Recasting the motive for the Mfengu pledge to the British as an "understandable desire" for more land minimized the specter of Mfengu disloyalty to the Xhosa. Significantly, however, Jabavu's rewriting of Mfengu history did not require the Mfengu to reject their three-part pledge to embrace Christianity, to remain loyal to the government, and to educate their children. For Jabavu had a broader agenda in attempting to quash the slavery myth and ease the tension between the Xhosa and the Mfengu, which the Mfengu pledge at least partially supported:

> The duty of us Blacks, on both sides of this artificial . . . line, is to combine spiritually to cultivate a new amicable rapprochement and mend the error of the past. Those of us who are intelligent, Christian, and loyal to all that is best in humanity, should agree openly to utilise all celebrations of the AbaMbo Day and the Ntsikana Day as glorious opportunities to teach the truth, and call upon our people to develop a friendly spirit. If there be any rivalry, let us impart to it a new orientation to produce the maximum in furthering the cause of Christianity, education and the social betterment of our backward brothers.[54]

In place of the ethnic (or, in the language of the time, "tribal")[55] rivalry represented by the Xhosa-Mfengu divide, Jabavu advocated a wider black, or African, consciousness rooted in the values of the Cape liberal tradition.

In taking this position he was not alone; the historian André Odendaal has argued that among the educated African elite to which Tengo and D. D. T. Jabavu belonged, ethnic identifications were consciously downplayed, and African unity emphasized.[56] There were exceptions to this general rule; when Tengo Jabavu supported the Afrikaner Bond (which had long opposed the African vote but was then courting it), in the pages of *Imvo Zabantsundu* during the 1898 Cape colonial election,[57] his opponents urged African voters to "'abandon Jabavu, for he is only a Fingo and is taking you to the Boers.'"[58] By contrast, when D. D. T. Jabavu erred early in his political career by joining

Selope Thema (a Pedi)[59] in supporting the 1923 Native Registration and Protection Bill (which would have required all African men to carry passes),[60] Henry Tyamzashe (a Xhosa)[61] censured both men for their youth, their ignorance, and their disloyalty to the "race."[62]

Tyamzashe went on to praise D. D. T. Jabavu as "a student, a gentleman, and a genius," but added (prophetically, as it turned out), "one almost feels inclined to say: 'Like father, like son.'"[63] While this latter comment may have been an allusion to Jabavu's Mfengu heritage, there is scant evidence to suggest that being Mfengu had any tangible effect on his career as a teacher, a Methodist spokesman, or a politician, in either the national or international arenas. As the anthropologist Cecil Manona has observed, "ethnic rivalries were temporarily subsumed under the politics of African nationalism from the 1920s until after the 1950s,"[64] a period that corresponded almost exactly to that of D. D. T. Jabavu's greatest prominence. In this context, of far greater significance in shaping the course of D. D. T. Jabavu's public life was his political inheritance from his father—the Cape liberal tradition.

FATHER AND SON

When his first child was born, Tengo Jabavu was twenty-six years old.[65] He had graduated from the Healdtown Missionary Institution in 1875,[66] taught school for five years in Somerset East, apprenticed as a printer, and earned a matriculation certificate (necessary to gain entrance to university)[67] at the Lovedale Missionary Institution.[68] Between 1881 and 1884, he had edited Lovedale's journal, *Isigidimi Sama Xosa* (The Xhosa Messenger), leaving only when the Lovedale authorities objected to him including political commentary critical of the Cape parliament in *Isigidimi*.[69]

While casting about for career options,[70] Tengo Jabavu canvassed for King William's Town lawyer Richard Rose Innes, who was running his brother James's campaign for the Victoria East parliamentary seat. The Rose Innes brothers supported the Cape liberal tradition and the nonracial franchise embodied by it; in Tengo Jabavu, they found a powerful political ally and mobilizer of African voters.[71] For the young African journalist it was also time well spent, for after the election (which James Rose Innes won),[72] Richard Rose Innes along with King William's Town businessman James Wilson Weir[73] decided to back Jabavu financially in setting up his own newspaper, *Imvo Zabantsundu*. Published in Xhosa and English, the first issue appeared on November 3, 1884.[74]

In the late-nineteenth-century eastern Cape, *Imvo Zabantsundu* became the vehicle for the expression of "African opinion," particularly the political opinions of those individuals who wanted to "develop the nation"[75] by forcing the boundaries of the missionary education which had produced them. They were the members of what Odendaal has described as an "old boys' club" for the African educated elite, made up of graduates of the Healdtown and Lovedale Missionary Institutions. The club counted among its members Meshach Pelem and Walter Rubusana (both founding members of the South African Native National Congress, later the African National Congress), Pambani Mzimba (founder of the independent African Presbyterian Church), Richard Kawa (an author and historian of the Mfengu), and Isaac Wauchope (a poet who wrote under the name I. W. W. Citashe).[76] They were, in Odendaal's words, "young men with a mission in life,"[77] a mission captured by one of Wauchope's poems: "Leave the breechloader alone/ And turn to the pen./ Take paper and ink,/ For that is your shield."[78]

Rather than becoming teachers, clerks, or ministers, these men aspired to a greater role in colonial society as businessmen, lawyers, journalists, farmers,[79] and even as politicians. In 1879 members of this school elite founded the quasi-political Native Educational Association (NEA), the goal of which was "the improvement and elevation of the native races" and the promotion of "social morality and the general welfare of natives through education."[80] In 1882 they established Imbumba Yama Nyama (known in English as the South African Aborigines Association), an explicitly political organization with the goal of uniting Africans "in fighting for national rights."[81] These aspirations, however, were hampered by the contradictory nature of Africans' relationships to their white mentors and sponsors. Tengo Jabavu, for all his assertions of *Imvo*'s editorial independence, was financially dependent on his white backers and, at least initially, on the presses of the white-owned *Cape Mercury* in King William's Town.[82] He also did not, as a general rule, support the idea of blacks sitting as members of parliament, on the grounds that it would be unnecessarily divisive and distract attention from issues of concern to Africans.[83] In 1884 Africans as a group did not in any event possess the financial wherewithal or experience to launch a political party.[84]

The ambiguity of Tengo Jabavu's own relationships with white liberals was aptly illustrated by one of the early causes publicized by *Imvo Zabantsundu*. In January 1885 Wilhelm Pelzer, an Afrikaner farmer at Burghersdorp, shot and killed an African, Zachariah Gqishela, for trespassing. When Pelzer went unpunished, the Rev. John Davidson Don, a Presbyterian minister living in King William's Town, wrote a letter to the editor of *The Cape Mercury* denouncing the government's refusal to prosecute Pelzer as a miscarriage of justice. The government instead prosecuted Don for criminal libel, but he was acquitted in November 1885.[85]

Tengo Jabavu paid tribute to Don twice, naming his month-old son Davidson Don Tengo Jabavu, and publicly thanking the minister at a posttrial reception in King William's Town. Jabavu praised the Rev. Don for allaying "our suspicions as to the soundness of the Government . . . and . . . re-establish[ing] the faith of the wavering, who had begun to fear that even religion itself was but a political dodge intended to weaken the minds of men into submission,"[86] a veiled reference, perhaps, to Tengo Jabavu's own disagreements with the missionary administrators of Lovedale's *Isigidimi Sama Xosa*. In his study of the Pelzer case, the historian Neville Hogan has suggested that Tengo Jabavu's comments reflected "a pattern of dependence and trust which is discernable in any group who have undergone a process of dispossession and colonisation."[87] Tengo Jabavu did ally himself throughout his career with white politicians whom he perceived to be "friends of the natives"[88]—defenders of existing African rights, including the franchise, and advocates of the extension of those rights—individuals who were, by Tengo Jabavu's definition, liberal. His eldest son would follow a similar path.

Davidson Don Tengo Jabavu, the name Tengo Jabavu gave his firstborn son, reflected the reality of the late-nineteenth-century Cape Colony for the senior Jabavu. It was a name filled with destiny and history,[89] a South African mantle in two parts, passed from father to son. *Davidson Don* embodied Christianity and civilization, and the liberal ideal of justice for all men. *Tengo Jabavu* represented the groundbreaking accomplishments of the father and invoked the warrior legacy claimed by the grandfather. Tengo Jabavu clearly expected great things of his eldest son.

As a young boy, however, D. D. T. Jabavu showed little prospect of matching his father's accomplishments. In *The Ochre People*, a memoir of her eastern Cape childhood, Noni Jabavu recorded that her father was not considered a particularly "promising child"; his younger brother Richard (Dick) was the clever one, and "people often used to say: 'Pity Dick is only second-born; has more personality, brains than your *izibulo* [firstborn].'"[90] Volatile and temperamental as a child, D. D. T. Jabavu would nevertheless benefit from his position as the firstborn son.[91]

He spent much of his early childhood with his mother's parents at Peddie (thirty miles south of King William's Town), where he learned to herd cattle, hunted small animals in the nearby woods, and played with his brothers Richard and Alexander. In the pastoral calm of the small village, the young Davidson was free of the social constraints of King William's Town, and the propriety demanded of him as the son of the editor of *Imvo Zabantsundu*.[92]

This idyll ended around 1892 when his father enrolled him at a Methodist mission school outside King William's Town.[93] By the early 1880s, about 20 percent of the Africans—or about 17,000 people—living in the King William's Town district had had some schooling.[94] The majority of Africans (mainly Xhosa, but including some Mfengu), however, regarded mission education as a threat to an existing and still predominant way of life centered on cattle herding and mixed agriculture.[95] "School" people, by contrast, had converted to Christianity, adopted European dress, and embraced Western education.[96]

The Mfengu were in general more open to this process of change than were the Xhosa;[97] Sir Langham Dale, the Cape Commissioner of Education, noted in his 1891 report that "the monetary value of school-instruction is appreciated by the Fingoes and hence more than 100 schools are regularly maintained among them." Yet in an era when few white children had easy access to education, the political climate did not favor education for Africans. Most schools for Africans were still run by missions,[98] governmental financial support was minimal, and Dale himself opposed standardizing African education: "if some system of obligatory school-attendance were introduced and thousands of Kaffirs were leaving school year by year with sufficient school instruction to set them loose from tribal customs and modes of savage life, what would you do with them?"[99]

What Tengo Jabavu intended to do was have his eldest son join him as a journalist for *Imvo Zabantsundu*.[100] To that end, his goal was to secure for D. D. T. Jabavu the best education available. In 1898 he sent him to the Training College at Morija in Basutoland (modern-day Lesotho), so that he could study Sesotho.[101] Morija had been established in 1868 by missionaries of the Protestant Paris Evangelical Missionary Society. Though courses were taught in Sesotho rather than in English, the college's goals (like those of Lovedale, on which it was modeled), were "the training of *good native teachers*," and "if practicable, Evangelists."[102] It also offered courses in agriculture, masonry, carpentry, and a variety of other trades, and boasted one of the earliest presses in southern Africa, dating from 1862.[103]

D. D. T. Jabavu spent two years at Morija, struggling to learn Sesotho, and very likely, studying printing. The kindness and the linguistic skills of the French and Swiss missionaries—who preached and taught in Sesotho—impressed him, but what captured his heart were the Basuto ponies. He spent his free time riding·in the mountains around Morija, and had his father not had grander plans for him, he might well have become a horse breeder.[104] He left Morija in mid-1900, when the nine-month-old war between the British and the Afrikaner republics began to threaten Basutoland.

At its crudest level, the South African War was about who would control the gold discovered on the Witwatersrand in the Transvaal in 1886. The war pitted Transvaal officials against the foreign miners and mine owners (mainly British, and backed by sympathetic imperial officials), who had settled in the mining city of Johannesburg and threatened to outnumber their Afrikaner counterparts. Between 1899 and 1901, Transvaalers, joined by their fellow Afrikaners in the Orange Free State, fought a losing battle to maintain their independence.[105] In the Cape Colony, prominent critics of the war included the liberal politicians John X. Merriman and Jacobus Sauer, and their longtime African ally, Tengo Jabavu.[106] In August 1901 *Imvo Zabantsundu* was banned by the Cape Colony's wartime military government because of its editorial policy, which favored the Afrikaners over the British in the ongoing conflict.[107] Crossing the devastated Orange Free State a year earlier, the young D. D. T. Jabavu had acquired a deep sympathy for the Afrikaners, which echoed his father's sentiments: "Farm after farm was wrecked, Boer homesteads looted, burning, going up in smoke . . . the greedy English red-jackets pillaged . . . stole, helped themselves to Boers' belongings or broke up what they didn't take, oh, it was senseless, ugly!"[108]

Chastened by the suffering and brutality he had seen, D. D. T. Jabavu was nevertheless delighted to be back in the Cape. Freed from the need to speak Sesotho, he immersed himself in Xhosa, and found that his trek across the war zone had made him a hero among his playmates, whom he regaled with stories of his adventures.[109] At home, he also found a new baby sister, Nozipo, and encountered, probably for the first time, personal tragedy. Elda Sakuba Jabavu died on July 4, 1900, fourteen days after giving birth to her tenth child, and shortly before her thirty-sixth birthday. Nozipo died shortly thereafter, and of the four surviving brothers, Davidson, at fourteen, was the oldest; Richard was twelve; Alexander was ten; and Wilson was seven. Within six months of his first wife's death, Tengo Jabavu married Gertrude Rachel Joninga.[110]

D. D. T. Jabavu would have had little time to contemplate this rapid turn of events; the November 1900 report of the Cape Department of Public Education listed him as a student in standard five (grade seven) at the Lovedale Missionary Institution. Though there is no key to deciphering his grades, it would appear that he received marks of "good" (g) in reading and dictation, and "fair-to-good" (fg) in arithmetic in 1900. In 1901 he earned a "good" (g) in reading, a "very good" (vg) in dictation, and a "fair-to-poor" (fp) in arithmetic, and passed into standard six (grade eight).[111] Thus, despite what must have been a stressful year, filled with dislocation, loss, and separation, D. D. T. Jabavu seems to have flourished at Lovedale. The school itself was set amid the rolling hills of the Amatola range in the eastern Cape, across the Tyumie River from Alice, the small town that had grown up to serve the surrounding farms. In this relatively isolated setting, by most accounts, an easy tolerance existed between blacks and whites.[112] Yet when that tolerance was tested, it proved to be—like the Cape liberal tradition itself—rather shallow.

DALE COLLEGE AND COLWYN BAY

In August 1901 Tengo Jabavu tried to get D. D. T. Jabavu admitted to Dale College,[113] a government high school for white boys in King William's Town. Though Tengo Jabavu had matriculated at Lovedale, and would send all his sons there,[114] he was on the whole critical of the mission institutions, observing that "the education given in them is not fixed by statute as is the case . . . in Public Schools." More important, "the Education Office" did not "countenance work on the lines prescribed by the university even from the very start; and it is here that the shoe pinches."[115] Tengo Jabavu's goal for his eldest son was a university education.

The senior Jabavu's actions sparked a lively debate in the pages of the King William's Town English weekly, *The Cape Mercury*. Though Tengo Jabavu claimed that he had intended the application to remain a private matter,[116] it seems likely that he hoped to set a precedent, the very grounds on which the Dale College committee rejected the application: "we cannot look upon your son's case as exceptional and isolated, or assume that your application is unlikely to be followed by others. . . . if we admit him, we must be prepared to receive other applications of the same kind. Thus the whole question of mixed schools is introduced."[117] In 1901 Tengo Jabavu found himself blocked by the tacit segregation of the Cape Colony's schools.[118] A decade earlier, in his 1891 report on education in the Cape Colony, Sir Langham Dale (for whom Dale College was named)[119] had advocated the "separation of European and coloured children" in Cape schools; his successor as Commissioner of Education, Sir Thomas Muir, favored the segregation of white and African schoolchildren.[120] That Cape liberalism, as Lewsen has observed, "was never, in practice, as completely 'colour-blind' as it was in theory"[121] was aptly illustrated by the response of the Dale College board to D. D. T. Jabavu's application. The civilized son of a civilized man was rejected because he was black.

In his confrontation with Dale College, Tengo Jabavu acquired an unlikely ally in the form of his chief competitor, the Xhosa-English weekly *Izwi Labantu* (The Voice of the People).[122] Though opposed to Tengo Jabavu's support for the Afrikaners in the ongoing war, on the issue of Dale College *Izwi Labantu* thanked him "for going to the root of the question and exposing the rottenness of the European position."[123] David Hunter, the new editor of *The Christian Express* at Lovedale,[124] also entered the fray, dismissing *Izwi's* assertions that Africans had to travel to the United States to gain access to higher education, and observing that few students took advantage of the matriculation course at Lovedale. He also dismissed the controversy concerning African students' desire to study Greek and Latin (necessary for access to the legal and medical professions) with the comment that they should first master English before "lumbering their minds with a superficial knowledge of one or two dead languages."[125]

Hunter's assertions reflected both a concern with the growth of African separatist churches and with the nature of African education itself. Most of the approximately 200 students who would leave South Africa for the United States and the United Kingdom between 1898 and 1908 were supported by separatist churches,[126] whose growth challenged the mainline European denominations, and the education offered by schools like the Glasgow Missionary Society's Lovedale. The second issue—the debate over whether Africans should be permitted to pursue a literary or "book" education, or whether they should be taught practical skills like carpentry and agriculture, better suited to the roles whites expected them to play in the colonial economy—had begun when the first school for Africans was opened.[127]

While Hunter favored practical education for most Africans, he was not opposed to higher education for a select few, as his publication of the Rev. J. D. Don's letter to *The Christian Express* indicated. Like Hunter, Don was concerned by the anti-European stance of many African separatist churches, and disturbed by the illiberal attitude of Dale College, which was, after all, a government school. On the issue of higher education for Africans, he argued:

> Justice demands that we consider them, and I may add, self-interest. . . . It will be better for us amid discussions and struggles which lie before us in this country that the leaders of the native people should be men whom a liberal education of the best kind has enabled to form a just estimate of the facts of history and life, to take a sane view of any situation and bring a sound judgment to bear on questions that may emerge, instead of being blinded by passion and prejudice and incapacitated by ignorance and narrowness of view for recognising their own true interests, and those of the whole country.[128]

Since it seemed unlikely that Africans would be permitted to attend government schools, the best solution, in Don's opinion, would be for the government to establish a separate "College for the higher education" of Africans. He thought, however, that the solution was a long way off,[129] and in this he was correct—the South African Native College would not open for another fifteen years.

In April 1903 Tengo Jabavu effectively sidestepped the issue by sending his seventeen-year-old son to the African Training Institute in the resort town of Colwyn Bay on the southern coast of Wales. The institute had been founded in 1889 by the Welsh missionary William Hughes, who had served with the

Baptist Foreign Missionary Society in the Congo in the early 1880s.[130] Hughes's aim was to "civilize" and Christianize young Africans, and return them "to their native land either as missionaries, schoolmasters, or useful handicrafts-men."[131] Though the majority of the institute's students came from the Congo and Cameroon, Hughes was familiar with Lovedale.[132] Tengo Jabavu probably learned of the institute from Hughes's 1892 monograph, *Dark Africa and the Way Out; or A Scheme for Civilizing and Evangelizing the Dark Continent*. D. D. T. Jabavu spent three years at the institute, where the training was "partly industrial, but chiefly educational and spiritual."[133] Students were, however, apprenticed to local chemists, carpenters, blacksmiths, and printers,[134] and it is likely that D. D. T. Jabavu, following his father's model, was apprenticed to one of the local printers.

Black people were not an uncommon sight in Wales in the early twentieth century; a small community in Cardiff, composed mainly of sailors and their families, dated from the 1890s.[135] Still, D. D. T. Jabavu found that he was enough of a novelty that he could earn pocket change performing the cake-walk[136] for tourists on Colwyn Bay's boardwalk.[137] Such seemingly harmless fun was not universally appreciated; one theater critic reviewing the play *Williams and Walker in Dahomey*,[138] which opened in London on May 16, 1903, and which featured the dance, dismissed the cakewalk as "a grotesque, savage, and lustful heathen dance, quite proper in Ashanti, but shocking on the boards of a London hall."[139] By doing the cakewalk on Colwyn Bay's boardwalk, D. D. T. Jabavu was inadvertently reinforcing British stereotypes about Africans, the very stereotypes he would spend his adult life fighting, both in South Africa and abroad.

In his study of the black community in Cardiff, the sociologist K. L. Little linked the hardening of racial attitudes in Britain in the late nineteenth century to both emancipation and colonialism. The emancipation of slaves in British-held territories in the mid-1830s made the black man an equal of the white, legally if not socially.[140] The imperatives of late-nineteenth-century colonial-ism, however, demanded that Africans be by definition an inferior people to be conquered in the name of civilization.[141] To complicate these contradictory racial attitudes further, African students appear to have encountered less prej-udice than black Britons, apparently because they were temporary visitors, and had accepted the ideal of civilization through education.[142] Still the African Training Institute's place in Colwyn Bay was not secure; the school closed in 1911 after the magazine *John Bull* printed a story suggesting that one of Hughes's African students had fathered a child by a local white woman.[143]

What the young D. D. T. Jabavu thought of Colwyn Bay, and what he might have experienced there, is for the most part a mystery. He concentrated on his studies, and in December 1905 earned a first-class certificate in "10 subjects with Scripture and Book-keeping" by correspondence from the London-based College of Preceptors.[144] In June 1906 he received his University Matriculation Certificate,[145] and that October, at age twenty-one, headed for London to complete his schooling.

LONDON AND BIRMINGHAM

London had a long-established black population—it was estimated at between 14,000 and 20,000 in 1770—and African students, mainly from the West African coast, had been studying there since the eighteenth century.[146] At least three other South Africans were in England in 1906: Pixley Seme, newly graduated from Columbia University with a B.A., was studying law at Jesus College, Oxford; Richard Msimang was studying law at Queens College, Somerset; and Alfred Mangena was studying law at Lincoln's Inn, London.[147] Whether Jabavu contacted Seme, Msimang, or Mangena, or sought friends among the African students or the broader black population in London remains unclear. He most certainly felt some degree of isolation, and in the home of liberalism, he also encountered racism. The hurt was abundant in his recollection that "in England, where I was always a social monstrosity to be gazed at everywhere by every mortal, I had got brazen to being stared at and learnt to expect it everywhere."[148]

Sympathetic Britons were sensitive to the issue of racism; in July 1913 the Aborigines' and Anti-Slavery Protection Society sponsored a conference in London to address the question of the hospitality extended to the approximately seventy Africans studying in the city. To counter the isolation and prejudice experienced by African students, the conference committee appealed to the Colonial Office for funds for an African students' club, a request that was turned down in 1913 and again in 1914.[149] In the absence of such organized fellowship, it was a testament to D. D. T. Jabavu's resilience that he nevertheless managed to enjoy his sojourn in London, visiting museums, studying violin and piano, and attending concerts and cricket matches.[150]

Only the barest record of Jabavu's six years in London has survived. He took up residence at 57 South Hill Park, Hampstead N.W., under the guardianship of J. A. North,[151] and enrolled at the University Tutorial College on Red Lion Square.[152] In 1908 he sat the Intermediate Examination in Arts of the University of London as an external student and failed, but his University Matriculation Certificate from the College of Preceptors apparently proved sufficient to allow him to enroll in the University of London's University College for the 1908–9 session. He took introductory courses in English literature, French, and logic, earning third-class certificates across the board and passing the Special Intermediate Examination in Arts in June 1909.[153] Over the next two years, he continued his study of English literature and, significantly, took on Latin as a subsidiary subject. In 1911 he registered for the B.A. Honours program in English, which included courses in Gothic, Old and Middle English, and English literature, and failed.[154] He enrolled again in 1912 and obtained a third-class pass, as did seventeen of the forty-two students who earned degrees in English in 1912.[155]

The accomplishment made him part of the exclusive group of black South Africans who held university degrees. From 1912 on, he styled himself D. D. T. Jabavu, B.A. (London), in a mixture of pride and arrogance from which his colleagues and students inferred the superiority of a British degree over a South African one.[156] He would also claim for himself a place as the first black South African to earn a degree from a British University. Strictly speaking, this was true; he was the first to earn a British degree after the proclamation of the Union of South Africa (uniting the Cape, Natal, Transvaal, and Orange River colonies) on May 31, 1910,[157] made him a South African.[158]

The claim was a tacit acknowledgment of the passage of the South Africa Act, which his father and others had traveled to London to protest in 1909.[159] Under the act, blacks were barred from sitting in parliament (though none had actually ever done so),[160] and the pre-Union franchise laws of each former colony were continued in the new provinces of South Africa. Africans in the Transvaal and the Orange Free State had never had the vote, and the number of registered voters in British Natal was tiny.[161] Cape liberal politicians did manage to retain the nonracial franchise in the Cape, and were successful in securing a clause in the South Africa Act that required a two-thirds majority of a joint sitting of both houses of parliament to agree to any modifications to the Cape franchise.[162]

Though Cape Africans retained the right to vote, their numbers were never large; in 1910 there were 6,663 African voters and 121,346 white voters in the Cape Province,[163] a ratio of one to eighteen.[164] In several eastern Cape districts, however, African votes continued to determine which white candidate was elected to parliament,[165] and so a semblance of power—a "ghost of equality"—remained. For all intents and purposes, however, the Cape liberal tradition died in 1909 with the passage of the South Africa Act,[166] which quashed the prospect that the Cape franchise might be extended to Africans in the other provinces,[167] and circumscribed the roles educated Africans could hope to play in the new country.

How aware D. D. T. Jabavu was of these limitations is difficult to gauge, but an article he wrote for the *Kent Messenger* in December 1912 suggests that he was still thinking more like a subject of the British Cape Colony—with its promise of "equal rights for all civilized men"—than as a marginalized citizen of the racially exclusive South African state. Indeed, South Africa did not completely sever its ties with Britain until it declared itself a republic and withdrew from the British Commonwealth in 1961, two years after Jabavu's death.[168] Thus throughout much of his public life, British justice would remain Jabavu's lodestar, even if he learned not to expect tangible assistance from Britain itself.

After completing his courses at the University of London in June 1912, Jabavu undertook a three-month course in business and journalism at the Kensington Business College, followed by a three-month stint working for the *Kent Messenger*.[169] No records of the Kensington Business College have survived,[170] and Jabavu appears to have written only one bylined article for the *Kent Messenger*. Entitled "Christmas in South Africa and Other Topics," this first available sample of D. D. T. Jabavu's writing appeared on December 28, 1912.[171]

Though the article began on a light-hearted note, contrasting how Britons and South Africans passed Christmas day, Jabavu's real goal was to rid his English readers of their notions of Africans as "a people without a law or god," and Africa as "a jungle with a scantily clad black man, a lion and the ubiquitous snake." This he did by stressing the capacity of Africans for civilization, evident in educated Africans' knowledge of that most civilized game—cricket[172]—and contrasting it with Europeans' capacity for brutality: to "obtain the wealth they are after . . . their civilization strangely undergoes a metamorphosis into the most ferocious savagery: witness the Congo atrocities," a reference to the Belgian King Leopold II's exploitation of Africans to harvest rubber in the Congo Independent State.[173] If part of the definition of civilization meant acting in a moral manner, Jabavu argued, then it was clear that the savage white man could not claim superiority over the black man because of the black man's supposed proximity to his own savage past.[174]

That D. D. T. Jabavu himself was an educated African who had absorbed the best aspects of Western culture (in keeping with the Cape liberal tradition, which assumed the superiority of European civilization over any variant of African civilization) would have been clear to readers of the *Kent Messenger*.[175] His article included references to the geographer Richard Hakluyt, the poet John Milton, the historian George Otto Trevelyan, the statesman and Labour Party leader Ramsay MacDonald, and the explorer and former colonial administrator Sir Harry Johnston.[176] It was as an educated, Westernized African that D. D. T. Jabavu included in his article a solicitation for funds for a future South African "Native college," a project to educate Africans locally to university degree level.

Tengo Jabavu had brought the issue of a "South African Native College" before an international audience when he returned to London in 1911, this time as a delegate to the Universal Races Congress.[177] The congress attracted scholars, politicians, and religious figures from Europe, Africa, Asia, and the Americas. Their goal was "to discuss, in the light of science and the modern conscience, the general relations between the peoples of the West and those of the East, between the so-called White and so-called coloured peoples, with a view to encouraging between them a fuller understanding and a heartier consideration."[178] To this self-consciously enlightened audience, Tengo Jabavu argued that there was much to be admired in the African past, that the indigenous peoples of South Africa were in their own way as civilized as the European conquerors who had encountered them. He conceded, however, that black South Africans had indeed been conquered, and then often subjected to extreme racism and exploitation. Like other delegates to the Universal Races Congress, he argued that a universal brotherhood of man should replace claims of racial superiority,[179] a theme echoed by D. D. T. Jabavu in his 1912 article in the Kent Messenger. In Tengo Jabavu's opinion, the way to achieve this in the South African context was to level the racial playing field by "instructing the masses in the vernacular, while concentrating on the few who are to be the leaders and uplifters of the rest." For the "talented few," who had already "made a favourable impression not only on their fellows, but also on their European neighbors," there should be a university.[180] Here was the implicit hope, that even in the new, racially exclusive South African state, whites might be persuaded to concede "equal rights for all civilized men."

That D. D. T. Jabavu was meant to be one of the "uplifters of the rest" went without saying, and the next step in his education took him to Birmingham, where in 1913 he registered at Kingsmead College. The college had been established in 1905 by the Foreign Mission Association of the Society of Friends (the Quakers) as a missionary training college for Quakers and members of other denominations.[181] Kingsmead attracted students from all over the world, many of whom, like Jabavu at the time, were not Quakers. The college offered no set program of courses; students could study the history of Quakerism, anthropology, comparative religion and theology, or pursue diplomas in social service from the University of Birmingham or secondary school teaching from Cambridge University.[182] Between March 1913 and July 1914, Jabavu took courses in religion, social work, and education at Kingsmead College,[183] strengthening the moral component he had deemed in his Kent Messenger article as essential to the truly civilized man.[184]

His studies at Kingsmead appear to have been supported by the London-based Westminster and Longford Monthly Meeting of the Society of Friends.[185] The Jabavu family's connection to the Quakers was a long one; though they became lifelong Wesleyan Methodists, Mary and Ntwanambi Jabavu's first

minister in the 1850s (an H. Impey) had been a Quaker.[186] Tengo Jabavu encountered the Quakers again in early 1901, when Joshua Rowntree, sent by the
society on a three-month tour to observe war conditions in South Africa,
visited the offices of *Imvo Zabantsundu*.[187] When the newspaper was closed
later that year because of Tengo Jabavu's antiwar stance, Rowntree donated £12
to the journal.[188] Tengo Jabavu stayed with Quakers when he visited London
in 1909, and applied to become a member of the society when he returned in
1911 to attend the Universal Races Congress.[189] He was accepted in 1912, and in
his 1922 biography, D. D. T. Jabavu recorded that his father often wished that
"he could transport these people [Quakers] to his land to be used as a Christian leaven in so-called Christian South Africa,"[190] a sentiment shared by his
eldest son, who would join the society in 1914.[191] For both father and son, the
attraction seems to have been the Society of Friends' nonracialism and
pacificism. Though the theologies of Methodism and Quakerism differed
significantly, they shared a commitment to community service embraced
wholeheartedly by both Tengo and D. D. T. Jabavu.[192]

In 1913 the London Meeting arranged for D. D. T. Jabavu to study for a
Diploma in Education at the University of Birmingham beginning that September. The career move, from newspaper publishing to teaching, reflected the
declining fortunes of the Jabavu family. Joshua Rowntree's £12 was but a drop
in the bucket,[193] and Tengo Jabavu decided that Davidson would not join his
brother Alexander on the staff of *Imvo Zabantsundu* as originally planned, "as
the burden on it would be too heavy."[194]

TUSKEGEE

Having decided to support D. D. T. Jabavu's studies at the University of Birmingham, the Society of Friends next contacted Booker T. Washington, principal of the Tuskegee Normal and Industrial Institute in Tuskegee, Alabama,[195]
to inquire whether Jabavu might spend the summer at the institute observing
its methods for educating African-Americans.[196] Tuskegee had opened its
doors in 1881 as a school for training teachers, and while it offered students a
wide range of academic subjects, including English, mathematics, economics,
natural sciences, and music, its main focus was agricultural and industrial (or
trade-based) training.[197] Washington himself had gained international recognition with the 1901 publication of his autobiography *Up from Slavery*, which
documented his rise through self-help and industrial education.[198]

The historian Joel Williamson has argued that in the increasingly segregated atmosphere which prevailed in the southern United States following the

period of post–Civil War Reconstruction, Washington succeeded in building Tuskegee into a feudal fiefdom, of which he was lord.[199] His policy of accommodation with whites, which entailed safeguarding "family, farm and education" for African-Americans while withdrawing demands for political rights, ensured the survival of Tuskegee in the face of white hostility to any advancement by African-Americans. With his Atlanta Compromise speech in 1895 — in which he declared: "In all things that are purely social we can be as separate as the fingers, yet as one hand in all things essential to mutual progress"[200] — he set the tone for black-white relations for the next decade and became the principal spokesman for southern blacks.

Washington's status was threatened by the Atlanta riots of 1906, when African-American businesses were destroyed by white mobs, and by the ascendancy of W. E. B. Du Bois, who with the publication of *The Souls of Black Folk* in 1903, began advocating that African-Americans confront rather than accommodate oppressive whites.[201] The Tuskegee model, in the view of Washington's critics, was "essentially an educational blueprint for black subordination."[202] Du Bois, who held a Ph.D. from Harvard University,[203] was particularly dismayed by the cultural implications of Washington's emphasis on industrial education. For Du Bois, "higher education was not merely a passport to social and professional standing but the master key to collective empowerment as well."[204] As one of the "talented few" (or in American parlance, the "talented tenth")[205] determined to uplift his own people, D. D. T. Jabavu could identify with this position. He met Du Bois briefly in New York in 1913, and though he did not record what transpired at the meeting, he was aware of Du Bois's disagreements with Washington.[206] At the time D. D. T. Jabavu visited Tuskegee in the summer of 1913, two years before Washington's death, the American educator nevertheless remained an influential figure. Though not uncritical of Washington and his methods, Jabavu clearly felt that the Tuskegee model had much to offer black South Africans.

D. D. T. Jabavu's journey in July 1913 from Southampton to New York City and then south to Tuskegee marked the first time he had visited the United States. He titled the diary he kept of his visit "My Tuskegee Pilgrimage 1913,"[207] an evocation perhaps of John Bunyan's religious treatise, *The Pilgrim's Progress*,[208] which Tiyo Soga had made a standard work in Xhosa when he translated it as *Uhambo lomhambi* in 1866.[209] More directly, the diary's title reflected Jabavu's decision "to rough it" on the eight-day voyage across the Atlantic, and "go 'steerage' (—3rd class) rather than lose the pilgrimage."[210]

As a young man of education and refinement, however, he found himself thoroughly unsuited to the steerage compartment. His cabin was tiny, service nonexistent, and the food so unpalatable that he gave up eating.[211] His opinion of his fellow passengers was equally low; he described them as "the scum and dregs of European capitals washed out by the Balkan war tide . . . and into our boat."[212] Despite his long English sojourn, or perhaps because of it, he professed a slightly higher opinion of the Irish passengers, but was wary of the women, whom he felt had "no reserve and [we]re ready to make friends with any and all." He resolved "to avoid their friendship and kept strictly either to myself or to the men, to be on the safest side—a good rule in travelling."[213] It was with a sigh of relief that he arrived at Ellis Island, New York, on July 10, 1913.[214]

From New York, he boarded a train for the three-day, thousand-mile journey south to Tuskegee.[215] The trip was notable for two reasons. First, for the first time in a decade, Jabavu came into contact with large numbers of black people. A three-hour stopover in Washington, D.C., gave him the opportunity to tour the city by streetcar, where he observed with delight, "At the different stops coloured people going to business or elsewhere keep coming in and a strange thrill seizes me and I feel as if I am in Africa again."[216] Second, south of the capital, he encountered segregation, American-style. African-Americans, Jabavu discovered, were packed into "the second carriage from the engine marked 'coloured', known as the 'Jim Crow' car."[217] Speaking with his fellow passengers, he concluded that what they objected to was "not the enforced separation from whites but . . . the bad and crowded accommodation for equal fares."[218] For the recent graduate of the Kensington Business College, such a policy indicated "a lack of perspicacity on the part of the Southern Railway Co.,"[219] a lapse that Booker T. Washington and his Tuskegee Institute promised to redress.

Jabavu's first meeting with Washington on July 12, 1913, proved, however, to be somewhat of a disappointment. Washington, Jabavu observed,

> talks little. If he has anything like the average American loquacity he saves it for the platform and more serviceable spheres. Asked a question now and then; and off and on discussed with me some South African topic or other for his information. I reminded him of my meeting him in England, but all my cajolery and wiles to get him to expatiate on any theme were of no avail. The man seems buried in his colossal schemes and work for his fellow men and . . . in maintaining his influence, social relations with the venomous Southern Whites who might, on any false step of his, any unguarded utterance, not hesitate to blow up the Tuskegee Inst. with bombs, and lynch him and his students in a single night and demolish and annihilate the whole industrial city.[220]

Jabavu's assessment of the obstacles facing Washington was astute; that southern society in the early twentieth century was racist and violent was a reality to which

Jabavu was particularly sensitive. In "My Tuskegee Pilgrimage," he recorded nineteen incidents, gleaned from local newspapers, of racial or interracial violence, including six lynchings, between July 28 and September 1, 1913.[221]

Washington's ability to survive in the racist and hostile environment of the South had earned him the title the "Wizard of Tuskegee."[222] In 1895, shortly before his Atlanta Compromise speech, that wizardry had led him to deny sanctuary at Tuskegee to Tom Harris, a black lawyer wounded by a white lynch mob offended by his "airs of superiority," and intent on driving him out of town. Washington's public stance earned him white praise, but privately he arranged for Harris to receive medical attention.[223] Of Washington's private politics, Jabavu was unaware; he criticized the older man for standing "outside the conflicts of the political arena," adding that "men of purely political pursuits can hardly look for his active guidance and participation."[224] On a public level, this was true and in line with Washington's accommodationist policy. Privately, however, Washington led what his biographer Louis Harlan has termed a "secret life," supplying "money and leadership for an assault on racially discriminatory laws in the courts."[225]

If Booker T. Washington personally proved a disappointment to Jabavu, Tuskegee did not. With the sympathetic if somewhat skeptical support of the registrar—a Mr. Palmer—Jabavu threw himself into learning "the basis of the whole machinery of methods employed in running the Institute."[226] He set himself an ambitious reading schedule of Washington's books, reserving his greatest praise for *The Future of the American Negro*, a collection of Washington's newspaper articles and speeches outlining the principles of industrial education (published in 1899), and for *Working with the Hands* (1904), which the university-educated Jabavu considered "in some ways a refutation to the charges that the author preached labor education to the neglect, if not exclusion of higher education,"[227] a veiled reference to Du Bois's rift with Washington. Jabavu also attended Washington's daily lectures to teachers studying at the summer school, accompanied registrar Palmer to a meeting of the local farmers' association, and delivered a lecture on life in England and Africa at the Baptist Church in Tuskegee.

A large proportion of his activities, however, appear to have been of a social nature. He gave several impromptu concerts for students and teachers,[228] and one formal concert, which was clearly the highlight of his visit, for he devoted five pages of his fifty-seven-page diary to describing it.[229] The concert, which included selections from Chopin, showcased Jabavu's singing voice and his skill with violin and piano. That he was both vain and a natural clown was clear from his response to the audience's applause: "I bow with a mock-modest smile, as much as to say 'It is too good of you, but I do not deserve it all.' I return to the stage and accidentally arouse merriment by colliding with the low-suspended electric lamp. . . . the girls . . . laugh with an unrestrained joy to which I must confess giving encouragement."[230] Yet here, as with his newspaper article, "Christmas in South Africa," his goals went beyond mere entertainment:

> My Recital:—Full House all expectant—especially after what they had read of 'Dark Africa' and many irresponsible magazine articles and pamphlets, which by laying great stress only on the worst side of the African, had not only damaged the prestige of the potential powers of the [American] negro, but had left a patronising, if not actually a contemptuous attitude towards the native African. Today it was my duty to discount this.[231]

Jabavu's aim—by virtue of his own civilized example—was to rid his African-American audience of any notion that Africans in particular, or black people in general, were by definition "primitive."

His concert a success, he was planning his departure when a cable for Washington from the Minister of Native Affairs arrived, inquiring "whether Davidson Jabavu suitable person furnish report adaptability your education system this country."[232] Tengo Jabavu had made the suggestion,[233] and Native Affairs Department (NAD) officials, agreeing that "existing methods of native education in this country admittedly leave a good deal to be desired and a good report would be of real value," awarded D. D. T. Jabavu a £50 grant to offset his expenses.[234] Washington acceded to the NAD request, provided that Jabavu extended his stay by one month to observe Tuskegee in operation during the regular term.[235] Jabavu delayed his entrance to the University of Birmingham by two weeks and sat down to write "A Report on the Tuskegee Institute," based on the institute's catalogs and Washington's writings. Remarkably, he completed the 300-page report, the bulk of which was a narrative of the academic and industrial courses offered by Tuskegee, within the month.

In discussing the suitability of the Tuskegee program for South African students, Jabavu stressed the "important differences between the circumstances of black people in the two countries concerned."[236] African-Americans, he noted, had access to over one hundred academic and professional schools, and over four hundred agricultural and industrial schools specifically catering to their needs. They also had access to northern colleges, where they were judged (at least theoretically), by the same standards as white students.[237] Black South African students had no comparable advantages. There was no college of higher education for African students in South Africa and while institutions like Lovedale had long taught skilled trades like printing, carpentry, and wagon making, there were not enough places for all who wished to study and not enough money to support them. In addition, African students suffered the further disadvantage of not having English, the language of instruction, as their first language.[238]

Jabavu recommended that the South African government redress the inequities by dividing the school curriculum into two streams, one geared to those seeking a collegiate or professional career, the other for those seeking employment in trade, agriculture, or industry. (Here Jabavu echoed his father's arguments at the 1911 Universal Races Congress, and took the middle ground between Washington's and Du Bois's positions on African-American education.) He charged the government with allocating the necessary resources and ensuring that black and white students had equal access to the educational system, and were judged equally by it.[239]

Deeply impressed by Tuskegee's Agriculture Department, and apparently unaware of the hardships that the recent passage of the Natives Land Act promised to cause (the act allotted 7 percent of the Union's land for Africans, who then comprised 67 percent of the population),[240] he also urged the South African government to support the "introduction and systematization of Native Agricultural Students . . . Native Rural Supervisors . . . [and] Native Farm Demonstrators."[241] As at Washington's Tuskegee—which kept 1,000 acres under cultivation, and maintained 1,200 head of stock—black people would teach black people how to be more efficient farmers.[242] This did not imply any support for segregated education on Jabavu's part; indeed, he explicitly opposed it and argued for uniform standards for black and white students. But faced with the reality of segregated education in South Africa, he linked the expansion of African education to an expansion of job opportunities for black South Africans.[243]

Jabavu's report was well received; the Secretary of Native Affairs considered it "a document of value which should be of real assistance to the Government when considering the question of Native education in the Union," but the department never published it. The report was shelved during World War I; D. D. T. Jabavu included it in abridged form in *The Black Problem*, published in 1920.[244] His inclusion of the report in his first book reflected how deep an impression Tuskegee had made on him. When he left at the end of September 1913, he pledged "to keep in close touch and relation with your institution and to get further advice and suggestions from here when I shall be, as I hope, engaged in educational work in my own country." Though there is no evidence to suggest that he did "keep in touch,"[245] he would continue to invoke Tuskegee as a model throughout much of his career, particularly—in spite of the very limited access Africans had to land—for agricultural education.[246]

BIRMINGHAM AND SOUTH AFRICA

From the southern United States, D. D. T. Jabavu headed back to the United Kingdom, arriving in Birmingham on October 17, 1913. He returned to his lodgings at Kingsmead College and began attending lectures at the Secondary Education Department of the University of Birmingham. As a candidate for the Secondary Teachers' Diploma, he took courses in psychology, teaching methods, educational theory and history, and "Hygiene and Sanitation"— courses somewhat reminiscent of the Tuskegee curriculum. Students attended a minimum of five hours of lectures per week and spent three mornings per week teaching at a local university-approved school.[247]

Jabavu did his practice teaching at Queen Mary's Grammar School in Walsall, a boys' school on the outskirts of Birmingham.[248] He taught English, geometry, algebra, Latin, and history to students in standards three and four (grades five and six).[249] He made a good impression; the headmaster, E. N. Marshall, observed that Jabavu "became most popular with both boys and masters."[250] The classics master, F. A. Morgan, praised Jabavu highly:

> I have known Mr. Jabavu both as a Colleague and as a friend since September, 1913, and early formed a very high opinion of him. He is a keen and quick-witted man of culture who has ideals as well as ideas, and a distinct charm which made him no less noticeable than welcome in any society.
>
> As a teacher he impressed me with his power of discipline, his competence and his influence over boys, an influence which was not only cheerful but inspiring.
>
> In fact he seems eminently fitted for any educational post that requires brains and character.[251]

Jabavu's instructors at the University of Birmingham were even more generous in their praise. Professor R. A. Jones, who lectured in education, described Jabavu as "one of the best students in the subject with whom I have had dealings during the past ten years."[252] It would appear that in teaching, D. D. T. Jabavu had found his niche. He had graduated with a third-class pass from the University of London in 1912; when he graduated from the University of Birmingham with a Secondary Teacher's Diploma in July 1914, he did so with first-class honors.[253]

He also seems to have found Birmingham a fairly congenial place to live, though there is no reason to believe that Birmingham in 1913 was a less racist city than London in 1912. Perhaps the supportive environment of Kingsmead College, the Society of Friends, and the university itself made more bearable the prejudice he would have encountered in the wider community. Certainly he enjoyed his time at the university; Prof. Jones noted that Jabavu was "deservedly popular in the University, and his social qualities have endeared him to everybody." Those skills were much in evidence at a gathering of Asian students in November 1913, reported in the university's student magazine, *The Mermaid*: "Mr. Davidson Jabavu, an African student, put the matter in a nutshell when he said a 'How d'ye do!' and a cigarette do more to promote good feeling between members of different nations than any amount of vague theorizing about the brotherhood of nations."[254] It was a philosophy seductive in its simplicity, but it was also a philosophy out of step with the events shaping the country he was leaving, and the one to which he was returning.

When Jabavu sailed from England on September 17, 1914,[255] six weeks after the beginning of the First World War, the European brotherhood of nations had collapsed. He shared a cabin with Saul Msane (the only other black passenger on board), a member of the South African Native National Congress delegation that had traveled to London in 1914 to protest the passage of the 1913 Natives Land Act.[256] Msane spent his time playing checkers and chess in the smoking room,[257] while the more sociable Jabavu encountered prejudice firsthand when two Capetonians (of the one hundred he and Msane estimated were aboard) objected to him playing the piano for an appreciative audience, and then, with the support of the other South Africans on board, sent "a request to the Captain to the effect that the 'nigger' be removed from the top deck and socially ostracised."[258] The captain of the Australian-registered ship refused, to the delight of Jabavu's supporters.[259] By the time the ship had docked at Cape Town on October 8, 1914, however, D. D. T. Jabavu had learned to his dismay that his "flannels and . . . University College blazer"—the outward markings of his education—could not protect him from "the well-known ill-bred colonial negrophobism of the southern States of America and the Transvaal."[260] The lesson learned revealed a curious flaw of logic, for having identified Capetonians as his primary tormentors, he still laid responsibility for the taunts he endured on the Transvaalers' shoulders, unwilling, it seems, to attribute the specter of illiberality to his beloved Cape.

The South Africa to which D. D. T. Jabavu returned in 1914 was very different from the Cape Colony he had left eleven years earlier—irrevocably changed by the passage of the 1909 South Africa Act and the 1913 Natives Land Act. Nor was the new Union much more stable than the Cape Colony he had left in April 1903, just under a year after the end of the South African War. In 1913 and 1914 white and African miners had struck on the Witwatersrand and in the Orange Free State, and on October 9, 1914, the day after D. D. T. Jabavu landed in Cape Town, Afrikaners opposed to South Africa's entry into the First World War in support of the United Kingdom rebelled.[261] "The stupid rebellion up North," as D. D. T. Jabavu dismissively described it—revealing a shift away from the pro-Afrikaner sympathies he had held as a young boy during the South African War—delayed his departure from Cape Town by three days. He arrived back in King William's Town on October 14, 1914, in time to celebrate his twenty-ninth birthday with the "Old Folks at Home" on the 20th.[262]

What D. D. T. Jabavu brought back to South Africa with him was a literary education from the universities of London and Birmingham, a sense of Christian morality strengthened at the African Training Institute and Kingsmead College, and a solid introduction to industrial and agricultural training garnered at the African Training Institute, the Kensington Business College, and the Tuskegee Institute. Teaching, first at Lovedale and then at the South African Native College at Fort Hare when it opened in February 1916, would become D. D. T. Jabavu's main occupation, and the manner in which he earned his living. But teaching was much more than a job to Jabavu; it took on the aspect of a mission,[263] and that mission was to spread the news of the benefits of education not only to his own students, but to all who would accept the logic of progress through education.

2 The Educating of Africans, 1915–1944

D. D. T. Jabavu's formal education had been Western from start to finish, and so understandably was the message he passed on to his various constituencies inside and outside the South African Native College at Fort Hare. At the core of Jabavu's educational philosophy was the belief in the capacity of Africans for progress through education. What Africans were progressing toward was the civilized society idealized by the Cape liberal tradition—a society that would judge them on their merits and not by the color of their skin. From his base at the South African Native College, this then was the essence of the message D. D. T. Jabavu took to the African teachers and farmers of the eastern Cape.

THE SOUTH AFRICAN NATIVE COLLEGE

The idea of a South African college for the "talented few"[1] of African students dated to the late nineteenth century, and with its emphasis on progress through education,[2] it was intimately linked to the Cape liberal tradition.[3] As early as 1878 Principal James Stewart of the Lovedale Institution had envisioned a "Native University—Christian in its spirit, aims and teaching" evolving from Lovedale,[4] but the idea really gained credence when it was raised as an issue before the South African Native Affairs Commission of 1903–5.[5] A conference held shortly after Stewart's death in December 1905 drew 160 delegates from the Cape Colony, the Transvaal, the Orange River Colony, the Transkeian Territories, and Basutoland,[6] among them Tengo Jabavu, who ironically (or perhaps shrewdly) made the case for an Inter-State Native College by arguing that Africans educated in England or the United States "may come back with ideas that will unfit them for their life here."[7]

Tengo Jabavu could not have known in 1905 that it would be nine years before his eldest son would return home, and there was a real concern—voiced by James Henderson, Stewart's successor at Lovedale—that Africans who had been sent by separatist churches to colleges in the southern United States would "bring back with them the attitude of mind towards Europeans which the former slavery of the States, and the present hostility towards the black race and the lynching, have inculcated."[8] The realization that Africans were actively seeking postsecondary education, and would continue to do so, generated support for a local college to meet their needs, and protracted negotiations over the funding, location, and curriculum of the proposed Inter-State Native College began in 1907.[9]

The college scheme was not without its critics. Henderson, though a strong supporter, acknowledged that the limited educational opportunities available to whites served to strengthen white opposition to providing higher education for blacks, and Dr. Thomas Muir, who had succeeded Sir Langham Dale as Superintendent General of Education for the Cape Colony, was deeply opposed to the project, feeling that the courses offered by Lovedale were sufficient to meet African needs.[10] Opposition also came from African quarters. The South African Native Congress (SANC), established in 1898 by the founders and patrons of *Imvo Zabantsundu*'s chief rival, *Izwi Labantu*, had started collecting funds in 1902 for an African college to be built as a memorial to Queen Victoria.[11] When Fort Hare, a former colonial outpost near the town of Alice and across the Tyumie River from Lovedale, surfaced as the likely site for a college,[12] the SANC feared that the Inter-State Native College would be a white-dominated, Lovedale-controlled, Presbyterian college.[13] The Queen Victoria Memorial Scheme could not, however, compete with the support accorded the Inter-State scheme. In 1908, citing Tengo Jabavu's decision to send D. D. T. Jabavu to the United Kingdom, the South African Native Races Committee—composed of white legislators and educators from the four South African colonies, Basutoland, Bechuanaland, Swaziland, and Southern Rhodesia—endorsed a college for Africans as an idea whose time had come.[14]

Tengo Jabavu traveled extensively and lobbied actively in the pages of *Imvo Zabantsundu* on behalf of the Inter-State Native College project. By 1912 he and other authorized collectors had secured £10,613 in subscriptions for the college, including £8,000 from the Transkei Territories General Council (TTGC) and £1,000 from the DeBeers mining company.[15] Both promoter and critic, Tengo Jabavu shared the concerns of his opponents in the SANC that the new college be nonsectarian. He also proved to be a divisive influence. In his insistence that the Inter-State Native College be more than a mere replica of Lovedale, and that the principal be a non-Lovedalian, Tengo Jabavu managed to alienate most of the Executive Board planning the college,[16] and many prominent Africans—including Isaac Wauchope and the Rev. John Bokwe[17]—who regarded Lovedale as the premier school for Africans, and an admirable model for the proposed college.[18] Bokwe nevertheless voted to elect Tengo Jabavu to a seat on the college's new Governing Council in 1915, observing that he was "the only *Native* candidate mentioned in the [nominating] list [and] . . . having no Native in the Council of a Native College would give colour to unending suspicion at its establishment."[19] College planners were sensitive to this issue; the first offer of appointment to the college staff was made to D. D. T. Jabavu.[20]

The dispute between Tengo Jabavu and other supporters of the college ended in a draw. The United Free Church of Scotland donated the land for the college at the Fort Hare site,[21] and thirty-four-year-old Alexander Kerr, a Scot and a Presbyterian—but a non-Lovedalian—was appointed principal.[22] The college's constitution declared it "a Christian College, and, while no special religious tests may be applied, all the members of the Staff shall be professing Christians and of missionary sympathies."[23] The mission churches of the United Free Church of Scotland, the Anglican Church, and the Wesleyan Methodist Church agreed to build denominational hostels for students at the college.[24] It was in fact this careful attention to sectarian interests that allowed the college's promoters to portray the South African Native College (as it was now called) as a nonsectarian institution.[25]

Ironically, while Tengo Jabavu was ruffling feathers at Lovedale, D. D. T. Jabavu was teaching there. He had taken an unpaid position teaching Latin in the high school while the final preparations for opening the South African Native College were made. The inspector who visited Lovedale in August 1915 reported on the "disappointing condition" of the school, noting that no students were being prepared to take the matriculation certificate in either 1916 or 1917, hardly a good omen for the prospective college next door. The inspector did, however, note D. D. T. Jabavu's presence: "It is interesting to remark that a native is helping temporarily in the higher work. He is well qualified both academically and professionally, and though still young and inexperienced, he made a very favourable impression."[26]

The South African Native College (popularly known as Fort Hare) was formally opened on February 8, 1916 by Prime Minister Louis Botha.[27] The ceremony, recounted by D. D. T. Jabavu for the London-based *South African Ambassador*, was a grand event, attended by thousands of guests and delegates from throughout southern Africa: "All classes and conditions were here—Bishops, Canons, Priests, Revs., Chiefs, Merchants, Government Officials, and so on *ad infinitum* to the meanest and lowliest Gqumahas[h]e pauper."[28] Jabavu added his own touch of theater to the festivities by donning full academic regalia and creating, by his own estimate, "one of the sensations of the day, for some of the hundreds of raw natives sitting on the Fort Hare heath [who] while I passed up and down, vainly wondered whether the hood was some mystical shroud or a sort of bag or 'haversack.'"[29] Jabavu's self-conscious paternalism toward "raw natives" underlined both Fort Hare's mission to educate "civilized men" and Jabavu's own sense of himself as a civilized man. Class consciousness and theatrics aside, his sense of his place in history was secured when he joined Kerr on "the crest of the Fort Hare hillock where the platform and tents were," to shouts from the audience of "look and look and LOOK!"[30] The college itself was less impressive; in February 1916 it consisted of four small, all-purpose houses on the 320-acre site.[31]

Two days after the opening ceremony, Kerr and Jabavu began selecting students for the two-year matriculation course.[32] With only 25 percent of African children attending school (mostly at the primary levels) and an adult literacy rate of 12 percent, the pool of candidates was limited.[33] At its birth, the "baby College"[34] was little more than a glorified high school.[35] Its two instructors accepted twenty-one of twenty-eight students who applied, and in the end welcomed eighteen to the first class on February 22, 1916. Among their number were two African women and two white men, the sons of Lovedale missionaries. Kerr and Jabavu comprised the entire teaching staff.[36] The two men divided the syllabus between them: Kerr taught English, mathematics, and physical science; Jabavu took on Xhosa, Zulu, Sesotho, South African and European history, and Latin.[37] Perhaps under the influence of his colleague, Kerr also introduced a bit of Tuskegeean philosophy to the new college by insisting that students do manual labor, which initially meant building the college (and less tangibly, its reputation), from the ground up.[38]

Jabavu's dedication to the college was extraordinary, though it is worth noting that he had little choice, and must have been conscious that his own reputation would rise or fall with the success or failure of the college. Within the first three years of Fort Hare's existence, he established a weekly study circle for students,[39] advised the Students' Council as a member of the Finance Committee, chaired the Literary Society (established to "foster a taste for the best literature," and to "aid its members in developing a fluency of expression in public speaking"), and served as president of the Sports Club, which arranged rugby, soccer, cricket, and tennis tournaments.[40] He established a college choir, which he took on a successful tour of Cape Town in 1919;[41] for a brief period, he supervised the Methodist hostel[42] and advised the Students' Christian Association.[43] To this seemingly endless list of activities, he would also add an impressive record of service to the community beyond the college's gates.

Outside of Fort Hare, Jabavu served as secretary of the Teachers' Christian Association (TCA), which had been founded in April 1916 and which by the following July boasted a membership of 150.[44] At the second annual meeting of the TCA in July 1917, he identified the organization's goals "to unite teachers in . . . seeking a richer personal spiritual life," and in "prayer for each other and their pupils."[45] Jabavu was a moralist, and his lectures to teachers frequently focused on the necessity of "moralizing leisure time."[46] In a 1918 address to the Natal Native Teachers' Conference, he spoke about teachers' obligations to themselves, their students, and their communities. He recommended that they set an example by abstaining from alcohol (as Jabavu himself did),[47] practicing Christianity sincerely (which he tried to do), engaging in manual labor and agriculture (about which he pontificated), reading widely (as he did), and if necessary forming a reading club, arguing: "If you teachers aspire to real civilization you must first learn to become students all your life."[48] A potential byproduct of this learning process—in Jabavu's opinion—would be the recording of history from an African viewpoint, a counterweight to "present books on the subject . . . from the pens of Europeans who, biased on the side of their own people . . . too often present the Native at a disadvantage."[49] Here was a hint of African nationalism—but that the viewpoint would be from the perspective of educated Africans also went without saying.

Despite the high moral tone Jabavu took in his speeches to teachers, he was aware that most African teachers faced real hardship. As a lecturer at the South African Native College, Jabavu earned £250 in 1916.[50] By contrast, the best-paid African teacher at the lower school levels could expect to earn about £105 a year in 1919,[51] or about one-third the average salary of a white teacher.[52] By 1932, Jabavu observed, many African teachers were still earning as little as £30 a year, "a salary less than a quarter of the wages earned by many illiterate black policemen."[53] From Jabavu's perspective, literacy clearly conferred a social status that demanded a certain standard of living if teachers were to be examples to their communities.

For African teachers, part of the problem was that while white teachers' salaries were paid by the provinces, most African teachers worked for financially overextended missions or churches, which received only limited government funding. There were, in 1919, no government schools specifically for Africans.[54] In a speech to the King Teachers' Association at Emdizeni in November 1919, Jabavu nevertheless insisted that the solution lay in the teachers' hands. The answer, he told his African audience, was to "begin at once in your own district to organise a teachers' meeting for every five mile radius, and multiply your branches."[55] White teachers had successfully lobbied for increased salaries because they were organized,[56] and in 1920, Jabavu took the lead in establishing the Cape Native Teachers' Association (later the Cape African Teachers' Association). In 1921, he founded the South African Native Teachers' Federation (of which the various provincial organizations were members),[57] and remained active in both organizations until 1936, when he resigned to devote more time to his political interests.[58] This professional and fraternal interest in teachers was directly linked to his own career, since it was their students who eventually made it to Fort Hare.

In 1921, however, the South African Native College was still functioning largely as a high school. It had yet to graduate any students, though one student—Z. K. Matthews—had registered for the B.A. degree course.[59] In his memoirs, Matthews recalled the "vital and unquenchable enthusiasm" that Jabavu brought to the teaching of Latin,

> which can be a very dull subject indeed. But Latin was interesting because Jabavu was interesting. . . . His love of language was such that in his classes we discovered both the richness of the ancient tongue and the power of the English into which it might be translated. By his own peculiar alchemy, Jabavu brought the dead to life. Latin became one of the most popular subjects.[60]

The promise Jabavu had shown at Walsall and Lovedale was fulfilled at Fort Hare. Students who had studied Latin with him fifty years previously could still quote Latin phrases almost thirty years after his death, and delighted in mimicking the stutter that plagued him when he got excited.[61] J. M. Mohapeloa jokingly recalled that students always suspected Jabavu of hiding the teacher's guide under the desk while teaching Latin,[62] and Jabavu himself conceded his weakness in Sesotho and Setswana.[63] Still Mohapeloa spoke for many former students when he observed: "You might hold back laughter, but you'd think, ah yes, here's this good old boy who never had ill feelings towards anyone. He was always trying to be as nice as possible to any of the people that he had dealings with."[64]

AFRICAN FARMERS

That reputation proved useful when Jabavu joined the Rev. J. E. East in establishing a Native Farmers' Association (NFA) at Rabula (thirty miles northeast of Alice) in the Keiskammahoek district of the Ciskei Reserve in 1918. James Edward East was an African-American missionary of the National Baptist Convention. Born and raised on a farm in Alabama, he had been posted to Qanda in the nearby Middledrift district in 1906. For years he tried with little success to convince his Mfengu and Xhosa neighbors to adopt new methods of cultivation and new crops (peanuts, watermelon, sweet potatoes, wheat, and millet, in addition to the staples of maize and pumpkins). Part of the difficulty was East's lack of fluency in Xhosa, and a chance meeting on a train with D. D. T. Jabavu, on his way home from England in 1914, solved the problem. After a lengthy discussion of "Booker Washington's agricultural methods," and numerous follow-up conversations, the two men decided to try to organize African farmers. East did the teaching and Jabavu did the interpreting. When East returned to the United States in 1920, Jabavu remained active in the NFA. In 1925, he helped found the South African Native Farmers' Congress (SANFC),[65] and by 1934, more than forty eastern-Cape NFAs were affiliated to it.[66]

East and Jabavu probably chose Rabula, in the Keiskamma River basin at the heart of the Keiskammahoek district, for its good soil and ample rains. It was, however, quite congested. Only 134 of its 220 square miles were available to 15,489 Africans, which translated to a population density of 116 people per square mile.[67] The problems identified by East and Jabavu in the late 1910s — among them land shortages, overstocked commonages, antiquated implements, and lack of water and fencing—bear a striking resemblance to the findings of researchers from the National Council for Social Research who surveyed the district between 1947 and 1951.[68] The 1952 report of the Keiskammahoek Rural Survey described the district "as representative of conditions in the Ciskei as a whole," and suggested that it reflected "many of the major problems . . . common to all Native reserves in Southern Africa."[69] What is particularly noteworthy about East's and Jabavu's efforts in 1918 is that they identified the problems facing this small section of the Ciskei reserve more than a decade before government officials turned their attention in the 1930s from the effects of drought and soil erosion on white farmers[70] to the effect of environmental decline on the viability of African farmers.[71]

In 1918 the Keiskammahoek district was a mixture of communal lands, quitrent tenants, and, despite its location in the Ciskei Reserve, freehold property owners.[72] Sir George Grey (then governor of the Cape Colony)[73] had begun granting freehold tenure to Mfengu along a strip of land extending from King William's Town to Fort Hare in 1856, with the intent of establishing a buffer zone to protect white settlers from the Xhosa to the north. Rabula itself was a freehold village where farms had first been surveyed between 1865 and 1870. Though most of the titleholders were Mfengu, they included a few whites.[74] Indeed, when Jabavu bought his own farm at Rabula in 1920, he purchased it from a white man, Friedrich Wilhelm Schroeder. By the standards of the Glen Grey Act (with its eight-to-ten-acre plots),[75] the farms at Rabula were substantial. Jabavu's own farm (which cost him £660), was slightly over forty-seven acres;[76] a neighbor's was thirty-eight acres.[77]

The farmers whom East and Jabavu organized at Rabula in 1918 were clearly, as the historian Sean Redding has argued in her study of African farmers in the Umtata district of the Transkei Reserve, members of the tiny African middle class.[78] At a time when an African farm laborer might earn as little as £6 a year, perhaps 1 percent of the Cape's African population could afford farms on the scale of Jabavu's.[79] Still, from the mid-1920s, the South African Native Farmers' Congress promoted individual land tenure as the ideal, and sought from the government the same sorts of subsidies on seed, fertilizer, and transportation accorded white farmers.[80] Though not immune to drought, postwar inflation, or disease,[81] these middle-class farmers were, in the language of the NFA, "the more energetic and progressive members of the community."[82]

Writing about farming in *The Black Problem* in 1920, the example of success Jabavu held up was that of Stephen F. Sonjica, treasurer of the first Native Farmers' Association. Sonjica had joined the mounted police during the 1877 Cape Frontier War. He managed to save £80, retired from the police force, bought some cattle, and rented some land at Qanda. Initially he and his wife worked the land, but within five years, they were producing and selling enough grain for Sonjica to purchase his own land and hire laborers to work it. Sonjica acquired his £1,000 bank balance, readers of *The Black Problem* learned, not only because he took East's advice and used horses to deep-plough his fields, but because he adopted "modern methods of profit-making." Rather than sell their produce to the local white traders and watch them get fat,[83] Sonjica contended that "no native farmer is worth calling a farmer who has no agent in a big town through whom he may dispose of his produce at market prices. 'A farmer without an agent in town,'" he insisted, "'was not a farmer but a boy!'"[84]

While farmers like Sonjica were the ideal, NFA membership was not limited to just the more successful farmers, or even to private landowners. By November 1919, 253 African farmers from throughout the eastern Cape had joined the first NFA, many of whom were farming four-to-six-acre quitrent farms (even smaller than the Glen Grey allotment) or communal lands.[85] Those who joined the NFAs and later the SANFC were by definition open to progressive ideas in farming.[86] In their public lectures, East and Jabavu sought to address both the issues beyond the control of African farmers, notably "the insufficiency of their arable land," and those within their control, including the "lack of organisation, . . . the unsuitability of their implements, commonage questions, the need for new methods, the lack of ploughing oxen, their unprotected fields, their unwise disposal of produce, [and] their ignorance of market prices."[87] In monthly meetings throughout 1919 and into 1920,[88] East and Jabavu sought to convince farmers (as Jabavu had argued to teachers in 1918) that they could solve many of their own problems if only they would organize and educate themselves.[89]

These were the ideas introduced in government betterment schemes beginning in the 1930s, and African resistance to them, as the historian William Beinart has argued, was rooted in the desire to retain "control over their land, cattle and settlements."[90] When Jabavu toured the Herschel district in 1922, he encountered a local variant of this later process. The Herschel district was located in the northeastern Cape Province (along the southern borders of Basutoland and the Orange Free State), and it had been settled by a mix of peoples—Hlubi, Tlokoa, and Sotho—who had "scattered on the southern Highveld" during the Mfecane in the 1820s. Later immigrants to the area included Thembu, as well as Mfengu who had originally settled among the Xhosa in the eastern Cape.[91]

The historian Colin Bundy has suggested that the ethnic mix of the Herschel district made it "freer than most from the constraints of tributary authority."[92] Methodist missionaries were also prominent in the district and many Africans were Christians; indeed, Jabavu observed, "we noticed very few people who belonged to the red-ochred folk" (that is, non-Christians), "except among the Thembu."[93] The district also included 800 African voters. It was thus men like himself who hosted Jabavu during his tour of Herschel and who populated the ranks of the local NFA.[94]

Overall, however, Jabavu found the district quite "backward," especially in "the Hlubi region," where people were "tied by the manacles of outdated customs; there is no progress. . . . Education is suspected and feared."[95] The district as a whole was suffering the classic problems of overpopulation, overstocking, and soil erosion.[96] That the Hlubi region was largely Christian—usually a sure guarantee of progressive thinking from Jabavu's perspective—indicated that something else was going on. What people were resisting was the introduction of Transkeian Territories General Council (TTGC) control in the district. As Jabavu reported in his series of articles on Herschel in *Imvo Zabantsundu*, "people refuse to protect their lands from erosion by planting papyrus trees and aloes, saying that this would perhaps herald the introduction of the council, a puppet government which everyone fears."[97] White officials tended to see the TTGC as an efficient and controllable forum for the expression of African opinion,[98] and Jabavu himself favored the introduction of a similar council in the Ciskei in the 1920s.[99] Those who opposed the TTGC in Herschel saw it as the thin edge of an increasing wedge of government control in an essentially independent district, and managed in the early 1920s to block its introduction.[100] In doing so, from Jabavu's perspective, they also effectively blocked the introduction of progressive methods of farming.

This bias in favor of progressive farming and civilized Africans carried over into Jabavu's advocacy of agricultural instruction in schools. Following the Tuskegee model, Jabavu urged that agricultural training be introduced at all levels of the curriculum.[101] That education would be ideally extended not just to African farmers, but also to African farm laborers.[102] In 1919 the NFA took up the issue of farm labor in response to complaints by the white East London Farmers' Association that there were too many "spoilt Kaffirs" who refused to work on white farms. The NFA responded that if white farmers paid decent wages that could compete with those offered on the Witwatersrand mines, there would be no shortage of labor. Revealing their own biases, NFA members argued that it was white farmers who had been spoiled by the "class of people who render such service . . . raw or 'red' in the blanket stage, having no school fees nor church dues to pay, no clothes to buy for their children who move indecently clad about their master's estate, and, not infrequently, the adults being insufficiently clad to be presentable at any civilised home."[103] White farmers needed "to adjust themselves to the new status of the Native rather than to seek to drag the Native back to a primitive life they [had] outgrown once and forever."[104] While Jabavu's tour of Herschel in 1922 would reveal that many Christianized Africans were hardly progressive in their farming methods, his credo remained "equal rights for civilized men." If African workers were paid a decent wage and taught the "necessity of work,"[105] both white and black would benefit.[106]

This tacit acknowledgment of the dominance of white farmers over the economy of the eastern Cape did not lessen the NFA's defense of African farmers. The East London Farmers' Association's proposal in September 1919 that Africans in the eastern Cape be denied the right to purchase land drew an immediate response from the NFA.[107] Essentially, white farmers were advocating the introduction in the Cape Province of the 1913 Natives Land Act, already in effect in the Transvaal, Orange Free State, and Natal provinces. The 1913 Act had segregated Africans on 7 percent of South Africa's land, and effectively blocked them from renting or purchasing additional land.[108] Whatever white farmers might have wished, the Natives Land Act had been declared invalid in the Cape Province in 1917, after a successful legal challenge established that denying Cape Africans access to land would jeopardize their franchise rights.[109] The East London Farmers' Association proposal, the NFA asserted, was "tantamount to a policy either to drive" Africans "forcibly back to the raw condition of the blanket stage or to force them to supply cheap labour as the only escape out of an intolerable existence."[110] Yet what the law could not achieve for white farmers, easier access to capital could. In 1916 Africans owned less than 0.5 percent of the Cape Province's land, and occupied another 8.5 percent in the form of reserves. Increasing Africans' access to affordable, well-watered land was the one problem the Native Farmers' Associations could not easily solve.[111]

While the NFAs searched for solutions, Jabavu responded enthusiastically in 1920 to an editorial in *The Christian Express* that suggested developing the overworked congested lands of the Ciskei and the Transkei for rural industries rather than farming them. Jabavu pointed to the repeated business failures of African traders, carpenters, and bootmakers, but thought the *Express*'s suggestion of a small-scale cloth manufacturing industry based on local wool a good one.[112] In a nod to Washington's Tuskegee Institute, he also added a plea for an overhaul of the education system, arguing that "the insufficiency of the native labour supply, its unreliable character, and the bad workmanship of the available labour" could be explained in part by "the prevailing system of native elementary education which is too bookish and provides no systematic and sensible training in the habit of regular manual work . . . and none in domestic science and agriculture, the most important occupations in native economic existence."[113] Though at one level this was an ironic statement for a college lecturer to make, it reflected Jabavu's essential pragmatism, and recognized the reality of the lives of most Africans living in the eastern Cape. That the majority of Africans would remain laborers or small-scale farmers did not, however, deny their potential for progress through education.

AFRICAN STUDIES, AFRICAN RIGHTS

Fort Hare practiced what Jabavu preached—it hired its first lecturer in agriculture, P. Germond, in 1919 and, in addition to their "bookish education," students were required to cultivate their own garden plots.[114] The college also set up an experimental farm and worked to introduce improved strains of crops and cattle to local African farmers. In 1923 Fort Hare also began sponsoring annual agricultural shows for African farmers.[115] This practical approach to the needs of the surrounding community helped establish the college as a real presence, even as it expanded its curriculum and staff to include the less tangible pursuits of psychology, economics, chemistry, physics, mathematics, and Afrikaans.[116]

Though it catered to an African clientele both inside and outside its gates, at the top levels the South African Native College was hardly "Native" at all. Jabavu was the only African instructor for twenty years, and when Kerr fell ill with typhoid fever in October 1923 and went home to Scotland for treatment, it was W. T. Murdock (the new lecturer in mathematics) who served as acting principal in Kerr's absence. In 1923 the South African Native College was not yet ready for an African principal.[117]

At the end of 1923, however, the college got its first African graduate—Z. K. Matthews, who, because the South African Native College had yet to be officially accredited, received his B.A. as an external student of the University of South Africa. The first graduation ceremony was held on May 3, 1924, for Matthews and Edwin Ncwana, who received the College Diploma in Arts.[118] The "baby College" had grown up, and in mid-1924, the South African Native College was finally recognized officially as an institution of higher education under the 1923 Higher Education Act.[119]

As the college expanded its horizons, so too did D. D. T. Jabavu. He had long been influenced by Booker T. Washington and by the work of Charles T. Loram, who had also studied African-American education and whose 1917 monograph *The Education of the South African Native* was then the seminal work on the subject. Though not uncritical of Loram's text—he rejected Loram's assertion that African languages should be allowed to die out[120] — Loram's educational philosophy served almost as a synopsis of Jabavu's view of his own mission in life:

> The progress of the nation is largely the result of the efforts of the great men of its own and other races. The South African Native Question must, to a large extent, be solved by the Natives themselves through the efforts of their leaders; and if the European section of the community is wise, it will hasten the day of this solution by affording the very best education in its power to the talented few, who will not only be able to transfer to their own people the results of European civilisation, but will, by their example, influence . . . [and] effect a rapid uplift of the Native people.[121]

The role of the educated African was thus that of an interpreter between white and black South Africa.[122] That a bookish education was unsuited to the needs of most Africans was an idea with which Jabavu could agree—it was the line of reasoning he followed in his work with the Native Farmers' Associations and in his advocacy of agricultural education in African schools. Where Loram and Jabavu differed was on the ultimate fate of the "talented few." The historian R. Hunt Davis has argued that Loram's educational philosophy was predicated on the "two basic premises of continued white rule and a rural orientation for Africans,"[123] an essentially segregationist approach that left little room for the incorporation of "civilized" Africans—the talented few in the 1920s, but potentially all Africans—into a greater South African society. Thus while Loram regarded himself as a "friend of the natives," and was concerned with their welfare,[124] he was not advocating "equal rights for all civilized men," which remained the core of Jabavu's educational philosophy.

In addition to Washington and Loram, Jabavu also followed newer trends in education. In the mid-1920s, he introduced a course in Bantu Studies at Fort Hare.[125] To the courses in comparative philology, languages, and literature he was already teaching, he added the new anthropological perspective coming out of Alfred Radcliffe-Brown's department of social anthropology at the University of Cape Town.[126] Radcliffe-Brown argued for the need for a scientific or systematic knowledge of African customs as a prerequisite for establishing the boundaries "of some kind of harmonious relation" between blacks and whites.[127] The message appealed to both white "friends of the natives" and white government officials who appropriated anthropology in an attempt to solve what was then termed the "Native problem,"[128] or less euphemistically, the problem of how to maintain white rule in South Africa when the ratio of blacks to whites was five to one.[129] Government officials, especially after the election of J. B. M. Hertzog's National Party in 1924, tended to use anthropology to justify segregation, dismissing "the culturally assimilated and missionary-educated native . . . [as] somehow fraudulent," or as the government ethnologist G. P. Lestrade would argue in 1931, as "'about as original as a glass of skim milk.'" Lestrade insisted that

> there is a middle way between tying him . . . [the African] . . . down or trying to make of him a black European, between *repressionist* and *assimilationist* schools . . . it is possible to adopt an *adaptationist* attitude which would take out of the Bantu past what was good, and even what was merely neutral, and together with what is good of European culture, build up a Bantu future.[130]

This was a clear rejection of the assimilationist Cape liberal model.

Among the white liberals—that is, those whites who, in the absence of a formal Liberal Party, considered themselves the "friends of the natives"[131]—the attitude toward the uses of anthropology was somewhat more confused. Prominent among the "friends of the natives" were Loram, J. D. Rheinallt Jones (who would become secretary of the South African Institute of Race Relations [SAIRR] in 1929), and Edgar Brookes, who would serve in the Senate as a representative of Africans from 1938 to 1952.[132] All shared a concern for African welfare and favored a pragmatic approach that sought to ease the restrictions faced by blacks in practical ways. In 1926, for example, Loram wrote to Rheinallt Jones to argue that the five-year-old interracial Joint Council system should be "local and non-political. . . . If the Joint Council is bound to a votes for blacks policy . . . it will be harder to get the blacks in

Pretoria a swimming bath. Without *achieving* practical local reforms, the Joint Councils will fade away."[133]

Loram favored segregation, and in the early 1920s Brookes and Rheinallt Jones were also persuaded by its logic. Indeed Brookes's Ph.D. thesis, *The History of Native Policy in South Africa from 1830 to the Present Day*, which advocated a policy of differential development, was published in 1924 with financial assistance from J. B. M. Hertzog. By the late 1920s, Brookes had rejected segregation.[134] Rheinallt Jones, while attracted to the positivist approach of the anthropologists,[135] ultimately rejected its use as a justification for segregation or "retribalization," arguing that "the emergence of the Bantu from the power of animism and the tribal organisation that is based upon it" was "inevitable." As the historian Paul Rich has pointed out, this was in essence a reformulation of "many of the ideas of the nineteenth-century 'civilising mission' fostered by the missions in newer, more secular terms."[136]

Jabavu laid out his own approach to anthropology in a July 1929 speech to the South African Sciences Congress. The speech reflected the influences of Washington, Loram, and Radcliffe-Brown, and also acknowledged the ongoing political debate about segregation. Jabavu informed his audience that

> the ideal situation is that the African aborigines should be led in their development by leaders of their own race. These leaders must possess, as a prerequisite, an understanding of their primitive tradition as well as the highest ideals of European culture, such as can be obtained through knowledge of their own people, a knowledge not of a haphazard nature but such as is collected and studied on scientific lines in accordance with recent research, so they will be able to preserve and develop all that is valuable in the native tradition. While the study of the subject can be efficiently accomplished by Europeans, as it is indeed being excellently done at the present time, it is natural and desirable that the Africans be guided by those of their own blood, with whom they have a bond of identical interests and mutual confidence born of single kinship.[137]

This claim of shared identity with "raw natives" suggested a noteworthy shift in Jabavu's thinking and, on the surface, it seemed to place him among the African scholars who, the philosopher V. Y. Mudimbe has asserted, rediscovered the works of Edward Wilmot Blyden—the father of Pan-Africanism—in the 1920s.[138]

Blyden was born on the West Indian island of St. Thomas in 1832 and died in Sierra Leone in 1912.[139] A strong supporter of black immigration to West Africa, Blyden celebrated the "civilizing" effects of African-Americans and West Indians (both of whom had been exposed to European culture) on "primitive" Africans. According to Mudimbe, however, Blyden ultimately rejected Western ideology as "irrelevant to African authenticity."[140] His most famous work, *Christianity, Islam and the Negro Race*, argued in part that "Christianity had a retarding influence upon the Negro, while that of Islam had been salutary."[141] A lifelong Methodist, Jabavu could reject neither Christianity nor the Cape liberal tradition to which it had contributed. He used anthropology not, as Mudimbe has suggested, "to open a vigorous debate on the limits" of the discipline,[142] but rather to assert Africans' potential for progress. Though Jabavu's 1929 speech indicated that he had clearly come to value "primitive tradition," his respect for it—like that of the white "friends of the natives"—seemed often more theoretical than heartfelt.[143]

This is not to suggest that Jabavu's ambivalence toward African culture somehow made him less African.[144] He clearly defined himself as an African, he taught African languages, and he wrote and published books in Xhosa. In the early 1930s he asserted that the "systematized training in attitudes and behaviour towards all elders and superiors," which all African children received, was "an education well worth copying, even by western civilization, for it indelibly impresses correct manners."[145] He could argue with equal conviction that whites seemed unaware "that the country as a whole . . . [was] being kept economically backward by the presence of large numbers of illiterate aboriginal Africans."[146] Thus the same Africans who had something to contribute to Western civilization were dragging South Africa down because "the masses of the ruling race"[147] did not want Africans to become truly civilized. Jabavu categorized people not according to the color of their skin, but according to their capacity for civilization. That Jabavu believed white men had the same capacity to be uncivilized as black men was clear from his 1913 article in the *Kent Messenger*. In the anthropological debate over adaptation or assimilation, Jabavu remained true to the Cape liberal tradition. What remained significant about Africans from Jabavu's perspective was their capacity for Western civilization, and it was this capacity that would ideally allow for their incorporation into an egalitarian South African state modelled on the Cape liberal tradition.

By the early 1930s, however, the prospect that the Cape liberal model would become the dominant political form in South Africa seemed rather remote. Prime Minister J. B. M. Hertzog's National Party had been in power since 1924 and was advocating a policy of comprehensive segregation, which, if approved by parliament, would severely circumscribe African rights. As an educator, Jabavu's pronouncements in the context of the threat and then the reality of that reduction in rights suggested an almost nationalistic perspective that was not ultimately borne out by his political career.

While Fort Hare became a center of ANC Youth League activism in the late 1940s,[148] in the early 1930s it was hardly a hotbed of political activity.[149]

When white members of the Communist Party of South Africa (CPSA) attempted to speak at the college in August 1933, they were barred from the campus and students were forbidden to attend CPSA meetings held in nearby villages.[150] The Communists responded by pitching a tent on a hill near the college and a few students did sneak out to meet them.[151] In his history of South Africa, former CPSA member Edward Roux observed that the "communists found that anti-religious propaganda in the sense of attacks upon theological beliefs did not meet with any ready welcome among Africans."[152] Though Kerr always gave Jabavu time off to pursue his political interests,[153] even he was granted few opportunities to air his Christian liberal politics at the college. At the height of the battle against Hertzog's proposed segregation bills, Jabavu spoke at Fort Hare only twice, in October 1935 and March 1936.[154] Kerr's own history of the college made no mention of either Jabavu's participation in the All African Convention (founded to coordinate the protest against Hertzog's bills) or Z. K. Matthews's participation (he had joined the staff in 1936 as a lecturer in anthropology and law) in the All African Convention and later in the African National Congress.[155]

Still, politics affected education in very practical ways, from funding for primary and secondary schools[156] to the opportunities open to the graduates of the South African Native College. It was this latter issue that Jabavu addressed when he testified before the Interdepartmental Committee on Native Education when it visited Fort Hare in October 1935.[157] The committee's primary goal was to determine the extent to which the Union government should take over the administration of African education from the missions.[158] The hearings, however, took place against the backdrop of the growing African opposition to Hertzog's proposed land and franchise bills, which had been published in April 1935. Implicit in the committee's approach was the question of whether educated Africans were more inclined to oppose the government than uneducated Africans.[159] Jabavu thought not:

> It is not because of his education, but because of the limitations of his environment that a man is dissatisfied. Trained men find that at the end of their course there is very little to compensate them for the long time they have been in training. . . . The only sphere where we can absorb as many as can be educated is in the teaching profession. . . . In other spheres they are limited by the fact that there are few openings for them.[160]

It was this lack of opportunity for educated Africans which seems to have prompted Jabavu, despite his opposition to segregation, to argue that African schools should be run by Africans.

In 1939 Jabavu and Z. K. Matthews took on G. H. Welsh, the Chief Inspector for Native Education, over the issue of white teachers working in African schools. The central point of contention was whether or not there was a preponderance of white teachers in senior positions.[161] Welsh provided a comprehensive list of the numbers of teachers employed[162] and pointed to the lack of qualified African teachers as justification for the high proportion of white teachers.[163] Jabavu had acknowledged that "there is a great shortage of qualified teachers" in his testimony before the Interdepartmental Committee on Native Education in October 1935, but maintained that this did not explain the dearth of qualified African teachers holding senior posts.[164] This was the core of Matthews's and Jabavu's response to Welsh in 1939. Since the career opportunities for educated Africans were limited, they argued, Africans should be given first consideration for senior positions in African schools.[165] Welsh was unmoved, and though Jabavu's and Matthews's argument suggested elements of a nascent African nationalism,[166] Jabavu remained a gradualist—what he ultimately sought was greater rights for Africans within the existing white state.[167] Ironically, it was only after the introduction of apartheid in 1948 that Z. K. Matthews was appointed acting principal of Fort Hare.[168]

The desire to preserve the "half-loaf" allotted to Africans (especially after their removal from the common voting roll in the Cape Province in 1936, and thus any semblance of direct electoral influence) may have motivated Jabavu's efforts in October 1941 to limit the numbers of non-African students studying at the South African Native College. In an open letter addressed to the principal, the members of the Senate, and the members of the Governing Council, Jabavu argued that the number of non-African students at Fort Hare should be reduced to reflect their proportion in the general population.

In 1941 there were sixteen Coloured students, sixteen Indian students, and 182 African students enrolled at Fort Hare. Thus 7.5 percent of Fort Hare's students were Coloured and 7.5 percent were Indian. By comparison, 8.1 percent of the Union's population was Coloured and 2.4 percent was Indian.[169] Therefore only Indians were truly over-represented at the college. Jabavu nevertheless contended that neither group had contributed anything to the foundation of Fort Hare and both had other options for higher education—Coloureds could attend the University of Cape Town and Indians could register in University of Natal extramural classes. He traced "the present signs of disrespect to constituted authority, exhibited at prayers, at Church services, and in our social relations between student body and staff . . . to the different traditions under which many of the Coloureds and Indians are brought up."[170] Jabavu did not, however, suggest that the college's white lecturers be replaced, and his position thus appears to have had more to do with what he perceived as disrespect for Christian tradition at the college than with either African nationalist leanings or any antipathy toward Indians or Coloureds.

Though Jabavu's proposal may have been influenced by the student strike at Fort Hare in September 1941, when three-quarters of the student body boycotted classes for three days, this connection seems tenuous at best. Students struck to protest the actions of the boarding master of the dining hall, who had slapped an African woman working in the college's kitchen after she broke a plate. In the ensuing investigation, the woman's uncle, who also worked in the college's kitchen, defended the boarding master, who nevertheless resigned. Students were ordered back to classes and the two who refused to return were dismissed. One left to join the army; the other, Nelson Mandela (who would rise to prominence in the ANC Youth League in the late 1940s, and after a lifetime of struggle, become president of South Africa in 1994),[171] applied for readmission but was refused.[172]

How many Coloured and Indian students took part in the strike is unclear. Given the genesis of the strike, it seems unlikely that Coloured and Indian students were at the forefront of the protest; perhaps Jabavu was simply looking for a scapegoat in October 1941. Beyond a desire to protect African students' interests, the reasoning behind his proposal to reduce the number of Indian and Coloured students at the South African Native College remains a mystery, as does the nature of the disturbances he implied they were causing. Though he had helped Kerr choose the entering class in 1916, by 1941 Jabavu appears to have had little influence over Fort Hare's admission policies, and the college continued to admit Coloured and Indian students.[173]

PROFESSOR JABAVU

In 1942 D. D. T. Jabavu (along with W. T. Murdock and the Rev. D. J. Darlow, who was chair of the Department of English) was formally granted the rank of professor, a title by which he had been popularly known since 1916.[174] The college had changed significantly in the twenty-six years since Jabavu had joined Kerr on the then two-member faculty. It had grown in terms of buildings, students, and staff and, most significantly, in terms of reputation. By the 1940s, Fort Hare had become the premier college for Africans in southern Africa, and was drawing students from throughout the region.[175]

That Jabavu's reputation had grown along with the college's was clear from the response to his retirement in October 1944 at age fifty-nine.[176] Perhaps most telling was an editorial in the newspaper *Inkundla ya Bantu* (Bantu Forum), which rarely missed an opportunity to criticize his political missteps.[177] The newspaper ran an editorial so effusive it read like a eulogy: "When posterity seeks to know what Jabavu did for the nation, Fort Hare shall stand out as a monument he set up. . . . Professor Jabavu was a loyal soldier fighting for the freedom of his people and as he retires from Fort Hare, he goes with the deep gratitude of the community in whose service he gave his life so self-sacrificingly."[178] Though the article may well have been a subtle attempt to encourage Jabavu to retire from politics at the same time, he did not take the hint.

What had informed Jabavu's career as a teacher both inside and outside Fort Hare's gates—and what would inform his political career—was a belief in Africans' potential for progress—specifically, their progress toward an idealized European civilization that would reward their accomplishments and ignore their color. This was the lesson Jabavu taught his students at Fort Hare, and the message he took to teachers and farmers in the countryside. All these constituencies were clearly exclusive, and Jabavu's self-conscious distinctions between "raw" and "civilized" Africans only served to underline further the basic exclusivity of the Cape liberal tradition.

What broadened the tradition was its openness to all who accepted the ideals of education and progress, and significantly, as Jabavu's lectures to teachers and farmers revealed, Christianity. Missions dominated the field of education in South Africa well into the 1940s and it was no accident that J. E. East—an innovator in farming education—was also a missionary. If education was the means to progress, Christianity provided its moral center once achieved. Jabavu's Christian faith informed his interpretation of the Cape liberal tradition, and it also, through the South African and international missionary community, afforded him a platform to voice African concerns.

3 "What Methodism Has Done for the Natives," 1903–1957

In South Africa, the histories of Christianity and liberalism are intimately entwined. Both the philosopher Alfred Hoernlé and the historian Edgar Brookes traced South African liberalism back to its nineteenth-century missionary roots,[1] and Jabavu himself considered the Cape liberal tradition "perfectly Christian."[2] Though there is a clear conflict between Christianity as "an affirmation of a transcendent authority over all human institutions" and liberalism as "a celebration of human freedom," the historian Richard Elphick has argued that the two traditions shared a "preoccupation with freedom and with the responsibility of the individual," as well as a "progressive view of history; and a common egalitarian tradition."[3] Thus D. D. T. Jabavu's Christian faith drew him naturally to the liberals, and his liberalism drew him back to the missionaries, who in turn provided him with another forum in which to promote his belief in the potential of Africans for progress.

To write about an individual's spiritual life in the absence of private papers is admittedly problematic. Nevertheless, D. D. T. Jabavu's writings about his Christian faith do offer the biographer both warning and insight. The warning is to resist the temptation to chop the subject's life into tidy thematic blocks:

> [O]ur great difficulty is due to our dividing life into water-tight and separate compartments. We have to learn that life is one for the priest, for the lawyer, for the bookkeeper, and all walks of life. Life is one single whole and therefore religion is not divided from it but is in the common life as well as in all life.[4]

The insight is a sense of Jabavu's own vision of his place in South African society:

> In my case, my profession is that of teacher, but I have always tried to discharge
> my duties with the consciousness that I am also a missionary with remarkable
> opportunities to carry on mission work according to the needs of my environ-
> ment.[5]

Fulfilling the dictates of his faith necessarily carried Jabavu beyond the strict
confines of a teacher's classroom, and into the wider community. To be a
Christian by Jabavu's definition demanded that he also be an activist.

D. D. T. Jabavu moved in social circles whose members were mission educated and in which adherence to a Christian denomination was the accepted
and expected standard for entrance. Published documents issued by political,
farming, and teaching organizations from the 1920s through the 1940s (the
period during which Jabavu was most active) do reflect a certain Christian
veneer.[6] It is possible, as his daughter Noni Jabavu suggested, that D. D. T.
Jabavu's faith was more form than content.[7] Ultimately, however, one must
gauge the depth of his faith from his actions (hundreds of church sermons[8]
and extensive community service) and from his words (numerous speeches
and articles on the subject of Christianity and "What Methodism Has Done
for the Natives").[9] It is Jabavu's words (his public addresses) more than his
deeds (establishing teachers', farmers', and voters' organizations) that are the
subject of this chapter.

THE METHODISTS, THE MISSIONARIES, AND THE JABAVUS

The Wesleyan Methodist Church of South Africa traced its origins to Great
Britain and to the critique of its founder, John Wesley, of the Church of
England (the Anglicans).[10] Ordained a deacon in the Anglican Church in 1725,
Wesley underwent a conversion experience in 1738, and began preaching that
salvation from sin through faith in Christ alone and conscious knowledge of
God were possible.[11] Enough Anglican ministers found Wesley's direct, unen-
cumbered style and simple message threatening that they banned him from
preaching in their churches.[12] Wesley and his brother Charles took to the roads,
covering thousands of miles every year to carry their message to largely work-
ing-class audiences: printers, weavers, grocers, and laborers.[13] The Methodist
Church[14] was thus in its essence a missionary church,[15] an orientation institu-
tionalized with the establishment of the Wesleyan Missionary Society in October 1813.[16]

In the early nineteenth century, southern Africa was one of the most active
mission fields for the Protestant churches,[17] and the first two Wesleyan Meth-

odist missionaries arrived in Cape Town shortly after the end of the Napoleonic wars. They did so at the request of the British soldiers and sailors stationed there, but were denied permission to preach by the officially Anglican colonial government.[18] Methodism gained a firmer footing with the arrival of the 1820 settlers, many of whom were Methodists, and a third missionary, the Rev. William Shaw, who quickly expanded his mission beyond catering to the settlers to evangelizing the peoples of the eastern frontier. In 1823 he established the first mission to the Xhosa near Grahamstown,[19] thus guaranteeing, according to the theologian John De Gruchy, "that the Methodist Church would eventually have the most black African members of any mainline denomination."[20]

By the time Tengo Jabavu was born at Tyatyora in 1859, the Methodist missionary enterprise in the eastern Cape was well established. Methodism enjoyed early success among the Mfengu, who may have been drawn to the missions by the promise of security and the prospect of social mobility;[21] indeed, such motives may have led Tengo Jabavu's Christian convert parents to settle near the Methodist mission at Healdtown.[22] Being a Methodist meant reading the Bible, and it appears that both Ntwanambi Jabavu and Mary Mpinda learned to read, as did their children.[23] The transition from one set of religious beliefs and social practices to another, however, was not always smooth—Ntwanambi Jabavu, for example, protested when Tengo registered for school at Healdtown under the surname Jabavu (according to Christian, or more accurately, European practice), apparently fearing that any missteps by his son would reflect legally on him.[24]

It is also likely that Tengo Jabavu was circumcised at some point in the 1870s, following Mfengu custom, despite the then strong opposition of the Methodist missionaries. Circumcision (*ukwaluka*) and the initiation process surrounding it was the essential rite of passage from boyhood to manhood— the sine qua non for entry into civil society—among Xhosa-speaking peoples.[25] A similar rite of passage for girls (*intonjane* or *ukuthombisa*) did not involve circumcision.[26] The historians Vincent Gitywa and Wallace Mills have also suggested a link to existing religious practices among Xhosa-speaking peoples, arguing that circumcision represented in part a link between the living and the dead; Mills has argued that without circumcision "the young male could never be accepted by the ancestors."[27] Usually several boys (ranging in age from seventeen to twenty-one) from a given area would be initiated at the same time. A ten-day secluded healing period followed the actual operation and was followed in turn by a ritual killing and ceremonial feast, and finally by a two-to-three-month period of seclusion during which the boys covered themselves with white ochre. Once their instruction on their rights and responsibilities was complete, they washed off the clay (and with it their ritual impurity) and entered society as men.[28]

What missionaries focused on were the "immoral," "indecent," and "heathen" dancing and feasts that accompanied initiation,[29] but in general they found themselves in a difficult theological position with respect to male circumcision since the Hebrews of the Old Testament had practiced the rite.[30] Missionaries did succeed in getting the *abakweta* dances accompanying male initiation banned by the Cape Parliament in 1891,[31] and as late as 1911 the Wesleyan Methodists passed a resolution at their annual conference banning circumcised youths from attending Methodist mission schools. Most missionaries, however, moved gradually toward a tolerance of the rite, recognizing that their converts had to be men as well as Christians.[32] Even the Methodists found tolerance prudent; they followed their 1911 dictum by resolving in addition that a student could be readmitted if he showed "signs of repentance," promised to comport himself in a disciplined manner, and had the support of the superintendent of his circuit.[33]

In the mid-1920s, delegates to the General Missionary Conference tried another tactic; they urged the government to investigate "the working of the circumcision schools, with a view to the protection of life, which is . . . sometimes sacrificed by the unhygenic methods of operating."[34] The government duly investigated the schools, and reported in 1926 that their operation warranted "no interference, and only the slightest amount of Government supervision." J. F. Herbst, then Prime Minister J. B. M. Hertzog's Secretary for Native Affairs, went on to observe: "It may also be premised, on account of the nature of the rites which form a part of the deeply-rooted religious *psyche* of the people, that any interference, and almost any supervision on the part of the Government with these schools would cut Native susceptibilities to the quick."[35] The government's response reflected the essential conflict between the missionaries, who favored "detribalization," and the Hertzog government, which favored "retribalization," a process they arguably perceived to be enhanced by the continued existence of the circumcision schools.[36]

Beginning in the 1920s, D. D. T. Jabavu would strenuously oppose the government's attempts at "retribalization" inherent in its segregationist policies. Yet there is little doubt that he was circumcised as a young man. As a devout Methodist, it is likely that D. D. T. Jabavu (as well as Tengo Jabavu, and perhaps Ntwanambi Jabavu) rejected the religious implications of circumcision.[37] He was, however, fully aware of the social implications. Had Tengo Jabavu not been circumcised, he could not have achieved the prominence he did in the eastern Cape in the late nineteenth and early twentieth centuries. The Rev. Tiyo Soga, who was not circumcised, encountered serious prejudice from the people he was meant to serve; parents withdrew their children from his mission school at Emgwali because they did not consider him a man.[38] He was effectively an *inkwenkwe*—a boy—and indeed *inkwenkwe* was D. D. T. Jabavu's favorite taunt when his male students at Fort Hare made a mistake, implying clearly that he himself was circumcised.[39]

D. D. T. Jabavu probably underwent initiation early in 1903 (at age seventeen), after finishing standard six (grade eight) at the (Presbyterian) Lovedale Institution in December 1902 and before sailing for Britain in April 1903. The ceremony took place near the Methodist mission at Healdtown,[40] and though the Wesleyans had moderated their opposition to circumcision somewhat by the early 1900s, it is noteworthy that D. D. T. Jabavu by the time of his own initiation had finished school at a non-Methodist institution. Around the same time—though probably before he was circumcised—D. D. T. Jabavu was accepted as a lay preacher by the Wesleyan Methodist Church,[41] further underlining the Methodists' inability to control all aspects of the lives of even their most Westernized and Christianized parishioners, as well as the Methodists' willingness to turn a blind eye to those parishioners' infractions.[42]

A similar melding of Christian and African traditions was evident in August 1916,[43] when D. D. T. Jabavu (just shy of his thirty-first birthday) married Florence Tandiswa Makiwane,[44] then a twenty-year-old teacher at Lovedale.[45] Like her husband, she was from a Christian Mfengu family, though the Makiwanes were Presbyterians rather than Methodists. Her father, like her new father-in-law, had been a talented student—Elijah Makiwane entered Lovedale in 1865, at age fifteen, and within five years was appointed assistant editor of Lovedale's journal, *Isigidimi Sama Xosa*. In 1876 he was appointed editor of *Isigidimi*, a post he held until he was succeeded by Tengo Jabavu in 1881. From 1877, when he was ordained a minister of the Free Church of Scotland, he also led a congregation at Macfarlan, ten miles northeast of Lovedale.[46] In arranging the marriage of their children, Tengo Jabavu and Elijah Makiwane may have hoped, with the union of two prominent African Christian families,[47] to establish a dynasty.

The marriage did produce four children,[48] but it was a rocky one, in part because the proud and fiercely independent Florence Makiwane—in keeping with the example of her aunt, Daisy Makiwane Majombozi, who had worked for *Imvo Zabantsundu* in the 1880s[49]— aspired to be more than a wife.[50] There is also some evidence that D. D. T. Jabavu had originally planned to marry an Englishwoman in 1913, just before his return to South Africa.[51] Noni Jabavu recorded the musings of friends and relatives that the horse-loving Jabavu "had come safely through his young manhood in England without marrying some English girl since those people too are horse-worshippers."[52] Marriages between whites and Africans were not unknown in the eastern Cape: Tiyo Soga had married Janet Burnside while studying in Edinburgh in the 1850s, but the couple encountered considerable prejudice.[53] Whatever D. D. T. Jabavu may have planned in 1913, at least in his published writings, he voiced the then common opposition to "mixed" marriages,[54] and he did ultimately agree to enter into an arranged marriage.

The young couple had about a year to get to know each other before Florence Makiwane was sent in late 1915 to Kingsmead College in Birmingham, in keeping with the conviction of her father and of Tengo Jabavu that an educated man must have an educated wife.[55] What she studied at Kingsmead is unknown, but music (which she studied when she returned to Kingsmead in the early 1920s) was probably high on the list.[56] She returned to South Africa only two days before the wedding.

The wedding ceremony took place at the Richmond Hill Native Wesleyan Church near Port Elizabeth. The bride wore a white gown and veil; the groom donned a morning suit.[57] Yet *lobola* (bridewealth) was also exchanged between the two families, a custom that D. D. T. Jabavu opposed. Writing in *The Black Problem* in 1920, Jabavu enumerated the positive and negative aspects of the practice. Among the pluses: "The system endows the wife with esteem in the eyes of her husband, inasmuch as he secures her only after an outlay of much trouble"; among the minuses: "Woman becomes a commodity that is purchased by the highest bidder, and since this is a purely business negotiation as between parents, there is no element of esteem; contempt for the woman is the consequence."[58] Early missionaries had frowned on the practice for these very reasons, and the debate over its efficacy continued well into the twentieth century.[59]

The Makiwane family nevertheless appears to have received the standard "ten head of cattle"[60] from the Jabavus, and the *lobola* also included "a first-class saddle,"[61] a gift to Florence Makiwane appropriate to a courtship conducted largely on horseback. Tengo Jabavu took out a mortgage of £230 on his property at Briedbach in July 1916, possibly to help finance the wedding and assist his son with the *lobola* for his bride.[62] The decision of the Jabavus and the Makiwanes to follow the *lobola* custom was more evidence of the ongoing process of accommodation between the Methodists and their African converts. Whatever his own misgivings about the custom, D. D. T. Jabavu did not object in 1916. He was motivated, it seems likely, by respect for his father's wishes.

Respect for his father was a theme that ran throughout D. D. T. Jabavu's published writings. While he did acknowledge that Tengo Jabavu could be temperamental,[63] his eulogistic 1922 biography of his father made it clear that the image of the father that the son wanted to present to the public (and arguably to emulate) was that of a great man:

The Romans have a proverb that runs thus: . . . Nobody has ever been a great man without some inspiration from God. . . . If this is true of any individual, it is true of Tengo Jabavu. His religious devotion, his absolute trust in God in all his mundane affairs and his mystic love of dwelling with the unseen spiritual forces, saturated his whole life and activity. He continually moved enshrouded by an atmosphere of religion, his outlook on life and affairs being first and last a religious one. His craving for prayer and holding converse with God was insatiable. The morning and evening domestic worship at his residence were regularly occasions of church solemnity, his exercises being of the 'good old time religion' type.[64]

By his son's account, Tengo Jabavu led a "perfect moral life"—he neither drank nor smoked—a life that gained him "respect among Europeans." About his "moral integrity," D. D. T. Jabavu added, "there 'were no whisperings.'"[65] If Methodism had had saints, Tengo Jabavu would have been canonized.

Tengo Jabavu's devotion to the Wesleyans was indeed considerable. He joined the Wesleyan Methodist Conference of South Africa at its inception in 1883 and remained a member throughout his life, becoming a fixture on the Committee of Management for the Healdtown Institution. He canvassed for funds for the conference's Twentieth Century Fund, and in 1913 persuaded the conference to support the proposed South African Native College.[66] On the local level, he served as a circuit ward from 1884 to 1916, frequently bailing out the King William's Town Mission Station; at his death, the conference owed his estate £200. Such generosity went largely unacknowledged, raising the ire of his son: "For these sacrifices he received little or no thanks from his people, sacrifices that actually jeopardised his journal and the bread of his children. On the contrary he was ignorantly suspected and openly accused by the more illiterate Church members, of converting Church funds to his own use!" Despite D. D. T. Jabavu's disclaimer in his biography of his father, there clearly was some "whispering" about Tengo Jabavu's "moral integrity." An official investigation by the conference, however, cleared him of any wrongdoing.[67]

Though not uncritical of missionaries, the elder Jabavu saw them, in general, not as "conquerors," but as "servants of God."[68] By his son's account he accepted their message (if not their methods) wholeheartedly, and it was with evident pride that D. D. T. Jabavu recorded his father's own missionary activities: "He was justly proud of belonging to the Methodist Church, a church rightly described as the most aggressive missionary organisation in South Africa. He appreciated at its true value the great work of Salvation it had wrought for Native heathen people in his land."[69] In 1891 Tengo Jabavu converted King William's Town resident Richard Mbiko, described by D. D. T. Jabavu as "a wild heathen renegade . . . pressed by [Tengo] Jabavu to attend school, in the teeth of his father's opposition, until he could read and write."[70] Similarly, D. D. T. Jabavu reminisced about accompanying his father to the Wesleyan Methodist Synod at Tsomo in 1902: "His joy was irrepressible as he surveyed the Transkei villages then almost destitute of all signs of heathendom, where but a decade before every other individual flourished the red blanket and red ochre, the emblems of heathenism."[71] Neither father nor son appear to have put much stock in the observation by Cape Colony Superintendent of Education Langham Dale in his 1892 Education Report, that many Africans saw the missionaries, and especially their schools, as agencies "that weaken[ed] and then efface[d] all tribal b[o]nds and customs."[72]

The father set the example and the standard for the son. Recalling his childhood, D. D. T. Jabavu wrote, "my father, when I was a little boy, used to take me out into the bush and there he went down on his knees with me under a big bush and started to pray. He didn't tell me I should do it, but he made an example for me, again and again."[73] As D. D. T. Jabavu grew into adulthood, his father's expectations became clearer: "He kept telling me, 'My son, I am educating you to go and be a servant to your people.'"[74]

The religious (and attendant cultural) legacy that D. D. T. Jabavu inherited from his father was as powerful as the educational legacy that had compelled him to spend eleven years abroad. As a third-generation Christian, D. D. T. Jabavu was equally compelled to honor his father in the service of the Methodists. He said as much in a 1931 speech titled "After Three Generations." Asked for a critical appraisal of missionary activity in South Africa, Jabavu demurred, observing: "Being a mission product I fear I dare not, because according to my custom, I can't criticize my own father. I stand here only in a position to estimate what my father has done."[75] While D. D. T. Jabavu's assessment of what his father (an African) had done for the Methodists bordered on hagiography, his broader assessment of what Methodism had done for the "Natives," and of the missionary legacy, was more balanced, and often quite critical. His public speeches reflected the ongoing reevaluation of the missionary enterprise in South Africa in the period between the two world wars[76] and moved from a particular assessment of Methodism to a more general analysis of the impact of Christianity and a call for ecumenism, and finally in the 1940s to a plea for the establishment of an African Indigenous Church.

"What Methodism Has Done for the Natives"

Appropriately enough, D. D. T. Jabavu made his first major pronouncement on the impact of Methodism on Africans at a 1919 Wesleyan Conference meeting to plan the commemoration of the arrival of the 1820 settlers in South Africa. He cast his speech in the form of a question: "What share has the humble Native in the celebrations of the arrival of these settlers? What has he to do with them? Have they done anything at all for him? My reply is Yes, very much."[77] The settlers brought "progressive methods in industry" and in agriculture, established towns, and built railways—they revolutionized the economy of the eastern Cape. The religious and social framework underpinning this transformation was provided by the Methodist missionaries who accompanied the settlers, though at least in the early stages of the missionary enterprise there was a clear distinction between the Methodist settlers and their ministers.

While the settlers divided their new economy according to a racial hierarchy, the early Methodist missionaries, in D. D. T. Jabavu's recounting, rejected it, "treating the Native as a brother even in social life."[78] The measure of this Christian behavior was the missionaries' willingness to stay in Africans' huts and eat their food while evangelizing in the eastern Cape. Jabavu made it clear, however, that the ultimate goal of the Methodists was not to lower themselves to the Africans' level, but rather to raise Africans to the European level: "Amidst the spiritual darkness of the Natives, [the missionaries] introduced worship."[79] Thus while Jabavu shared the settlers' and the missionaries' concern with progress, he preferred the missionary version, because it was tempered by egalitarianism.

In the interest of "civilized" standards, African converts were schooled, dressed in Western clothing, and, at least in theory, fully incorporated into the administrative structure of Wesleyan Methodism. Incorporation meant paying dues to support the administrative structure, and these obligations often caused real hardship; "in fact it is notorious among natives that to be a Wesleyan is to be a slave to the task of perpetual money-paying for one's religion."[80] This reality touched home for D. D. T. Jabavu (whose own donations started with 10s. yearly in 1916 and rose to £3 6s. by 1941),[81] when on his way to England in 1903, he gave his impoverished grandfather some money, only to be astonished by his response: "'Thank you my grandson. I shall now be able to pay up my debts in the church.'"[82] The positive side to this monetary hardship, in Jabavu's opinion, was that it made the church financially independent, and unbeholden to overseas benefactors.[83] The downside of the system was that theoretical administrative equality did not preclude the existence of separate black and white Methodist churches, nor did it prevent the Reverend Manyena Mokone from breaking with the church in 1892 (after several black ministers were excluded from a meeting of white Wesleyan ministers) and establishing the separatist Ethiopian Church.[84]

As a third-generation Methodist, D. D. T. Jabavu—though not entirely dismissive of African social customs—was rather dismissive of African religions, including nonmainstream interpretations of Christianity. In his biography of Tengo Jabavu, D. D. T. Jabavu recorded his father's assessment of Enoch Mgijima's millenarian Israelite sect,[85] which in 1921 clashed with authorities over the sect's illegal settlement at Bulhoek, outside Queenstown. Asked by the government to negotiate with the Israelites, Tengo Jabavu came away "full of praise for the thirst of prayer and worship he had observed" in Mgijima's followers, but condemned their "transgression of the law of the land," and offered his opinion that "Native Ministers were not yet sufficiently educated to expect success when divorced from intelligent control."[86] Preaching against the dangers of "an untrained intellect,"[87] D. D. T. Jabavu echoed these sentiments in an address to Fort Hare students in May 1921. By the mid-1920s, however, the South African government was attempting to introduce a comprehensive program of segregation. Though D. D. T. Jabavu remained critical of the "intellectual and . . . religious immaturity of most of the leaders" of the separatist churches, he had by then acquired a greater sympathy for the "movement because it symbolizes the general ambition of the Bantu for liberation—liberation from being underlings to the Europeans in various phases of life, namely: economic, political and religious."[88] The important point was that while church leaders should possess "trained intellects," they need not be white.

D. D. T. Jabavu's Christianity was theologically sound according to Western standards; the ancestor he honored was his Methodist grandfather, Ntwanambi, not anyone from the generation of his "pagan" great-grandfather. The problem, as D. D. T. Jabavu saw it, was that while the early missionaries were Christian in their behavior, it did not necessarily follow that the early settlers were. Settlers built themselves towns, but restricted Africans to locations; they introduced advanced agricultural methods, but exploited Africans as cheap labor and confined them to congested reserves; they built technologically advanced railroads, but restricted African use of them.[89] In lauding Shaw, Stewart, and Moffat for "treating the Native as a brother," Jabavu was directly criticizing white missionaries who by the early 1920s seemed to have abandoned this central Christian tenet both for themselves and their white parishioners.[90]

White missionaries were not unaware of the flaws in the system that they and other whites had created.[91] Writing in *The South African Outlook* in March 1923, the editor D. A. Hunter observed: "The Natives have been detribalized by a 'white standard of civilization' which has sought simply to exploit the Native in its own material interests."[92] Jabavu's solution to the malaise, which he outlined in a speech in April 1923 marking the end of the Wesleyan Centenary celebrations, was a call to activism and to evangelism.[93] Missionaries had to accept that they were no longer dealing with the "race of children" encountered by their pioneering forebear, but with an intellectually advanced, politically conscious, and increasingly ambitious people with very real problems.[94] The church had to recognize that it could not "confine itself to the spiritual interests alone of a people otherwise persecuted by rulers of the same colour as its officials in the Conference."[95] If the church was to remain relevant to these "new Africans,"[96] it had to embrace activism,[97] and tackle "quasi-political problems like Labour Conditions, Wages, Pass Laws, Land [and] Segregation . . . in a direct manner . . . to justify itself as standing for the tutelage of the subject races."[98]

This call to activism nevertheless contained a spiritual component:[99]

> The new century is going to exact more spirituality from all of us who claim to be Christians. We cannot save others when we ourselves are lacking in faith. . . . We must lay great stress on the evangelistic side of our work. The war cry and challenge of the forthcoming century is that we must go forth to win and possess greater lands from the Kingdom of the Evil One. May we be enabled to show our gratitude to God for what Methodism has done for us during the past century by going forth in His strength to win more followers for His banner to the glory of His Heavenly Kingdom and to the salvation of the Bantu Race.[100]

While Jabavu was calling on African evangelists to act—he argued that the time had come for African ministers to replace white ministers in predominantly African circuits[101]—his injunction reflected the concerns of white missionaries as well. For supporters of the United Missionary campaign, launched in 1925 in an attempt to find common ground among the forty-three Protestant mission societies in South Africa,[102] the solution to the deteriorating standard of living of most Africans was a rejection of "measures born of fear or racial self-interest," and an embrace of "a high Christian liberalism."[103] This was the language of the Social Gospel. Implicitly and explicitly, its definition and relevance permeated missionary discourse in South Africa in the interwar period.[104]

"CHRISTIANITY AND THE BANTU"

The Social Gospel had its origins in the response of Protestant clergy to the social ills wrought by the processes of industrialization and urbanization in late-nineteenth-century America.[105] The essence of Social Gospel teaching was that "society, not just individuals, stood under God's judgment and that Christians were obligated to act directly on the social order to effect its reconstruction."[106] Among the more cautious advocates of this often radical ideology (its extreme adherents advocated reconstructing society and its institutions from the ground up)[107] was Booker T. Washington,[108] whose pragmatic approach to the education of African-Americans had greatly influenced D. D. T. Jabavu and many South African missionaries.[109] Among South African advocates of the Social Gospel were Charles T. Loram and Edgar Brookes. According to Elphick, the Social Gospel helped define the link between Mission Christians and Christian liberals between the two world wars, and it also shaded, in an attempt to fulfill its obligations, into the ecumenical movement.[110]

In South Africa the ecumenical movement found its voice in the General Missionary Conference, founded in 1904 as a forum to discuss issues of mutual interest and as a way to foster "a feeling of unity which previously was almost non-exist[e]nt," and to promote "missionary comity founded upon a better acquaintance with, and a sincerer regard for, each other's methods of work."[111] Further inspiration came from the International Missionary Council, established in 1921,[112] and from the 1920 Lambeth Conference of Bishops of the Anglican Communion, which met to discuss the prospect of church reunion, recognizing that "everywhere in the Christian world there is a desire to do away with the present state of disorder and chaos."[113] Cooperation and mutual respect were the watchwords of the South African movement, although there was some interest in church reunion,[114] especially among the branches of the Methodist Church.[115]

The 1925 United Missionary Campaign reflected the contention of many South African missionaries that denominationalism was marring the reception of the Christian message.[116] In "Christianity and the Bantu,"[117] an article written in 1927 for the New York-based Student Volunteer Movement for Foreign Missions, Jabavu pointed to denominationalism as part of the explanation for the declining appeal of Christianity, particularly among young Africans. Denominationalism complicated existing divisions among Africans and undermined the conversion process: "when Africans are visited by rival mission boards they inevitably ask, 'How many Gods are there? Which god are we asked to believe?'"[118] Missionary competitiveness resulted, in Jabavu's opinion, in absurdities like thirty-four different mission churches serving 5,000 Africans living in Nancefield location near Johannesburg.[119] Jabavu himself practiced what he preached; from the 1920s through the 1950s he gave sermons or read lessons at Wesleyan Methodist, Baptist, and Presbyterian churches. He did the same at the indigenous churches—the Order of Ethiopia, the Bantu Presbyterian Church, and the Bantu Baptist Church—whose clergy and administrators were African, though they remained affiliated with the older parent churches.[120]

In the mid-1920s there was also some support within the African National Congress for establishing "'one great African Church under ecclesiastical rule,'"[121] which would unite the separatist churches. The ANC was then losing members to the Industrial and Commercial Workers' Union (ICU), and its president, the Wesleyan Methodist minister Zaccheus R. Mahabane[122] saw the church as a way to bolster the ANC's sagging popularity and appeal to "'the innermost mind of patriotic Africans.'" An "Organising Committee" of "'all leading ministers'" would "appoint and ordain bishops, ministers and evangelists," while delegating "'certain powers' to 'National Leaders, Chief Organisers, and Messengers of the Formation of the Church.'" This unwieldy structure effectively delayed the church's establishment, although the idea persisted into the 1930s.[123]

In 1927 Jabavu identified still more pressing issues than denominationalism that contributed to African disenchantment with the churches. The reality that most white South Africans did not behave in a Christian fashion was a constant affront,[124] but the chief complaint against the missionaries was that while they had attended to their converts' souls, they had neglected their land rights. As Jabavu observed in 1927:

> It is quite common now to hear a native tub-thumper addressing a crowd of his fellow-men and decrying Western missions on the ground that 'they told you to close your eyes and pray, and the other whites came and took away the land from behind your back while you kept your eyes closed.' And this: 'At first we had the land and the white man had the Bible; now we have the Bible and the white man has the land.'[125]

Missionaries in the Cape addressed the charge in the 1927 "Report on the Economic Condition of the Native People," prepared by the Ciskei Missionary Council.[126] Though the 1913 Natives Land Act had never gone into effect in the Cape, population pressure and the limited availability of arable land made the land issue as pertinent as it was in the northern provinces. The report acknowledged chronic land shortages (39 percent of African men were without land in one district, and access to land was scarce throughout the Ciskei), food shortages (only two-thirds of districts surveyed were self-sufficient in food over the course of a given year), and dependence on migrant labor (about one-third of all families relied on wages earned in urban areas).[127] The report concluded that "the Native economic situation as a whole in the Cis-keian area is . . . unsound, unstable and deteriorating," and while some of the problems could be attributed to poor agricultural practices on the part of Africans, the "main causes of the bad economic position of the people, are . . . mostly represented as lying outside themselves."[128] Since the problem was how to obtain "more land outright on a large scale," the council recommended a variety of pragmatic options, including the introduction of tenant farming on leases, cooperative farms run by Africans, and, most significant, persuading white farmers to pay their African laborers a living wage. These were the arguments Jabavu had been making through the Native Farmers' Associations and the South African Native Farmers' Congress. Finally, the report issued a challenge: "We must ask ourselves if our Mission Churches and still more our Mission schools are doing the whole work required of them as agencies of Jesus Christ of whom it is said that He went about doing good."[129] How could missionaries recreate the scriptural Kingdom of God on earth in the increasingly secular twentieth century?[130]

This question was one of concern to missionaries who met at the Jerusalem meeting of the International Missionary Council in March and April 1928. The Rev. Rufus M. Jones, professor of philosophy at Haverford College in Pennsylvania, argued that it was not Islam, Buddhism, Hinduism, or Confucianism that posed the greatest challenge to Christianity, but rather "a world-wide secular way of life and interpretation of the nature of things." By secular, Jones meant the absence of "a realm of spiritual reality" operating in everyday life. Two-thirds of Americans, he contended, had "no definite connection or affiliation with any form of organized Christianity."[131] Two-thirds of black South Africans were also non-Christian,[132] and while the circumstances of their lives were often very different from those of black or white Americans, the issue for South African missionaries was the same: how to make the message of Christianity relevant to the great mass of unconverted Africans.

Jabavu attended the Jerusalem meeting along with the Rev. Max Yergan, an African-American missionary serving as secretary of the YMCA-affiliated Student's Christian Association (Native Section) of South Africa,[133] and the Rev. W. H. Murray, superintendent of the Dutch Reformed Church in Nyasaland.[134] Missionaries had been gathering at international meetings since the 1850s; the Jerusalem meeting was the seventh in an ongoing series and its 240 delegates were drawn from Europe, the Americas, Asia, Africa, and the Middle East.[135] The eight-volume report of the meeting covered a wide range of topics, including the relationship between Christianity and other religions, religious education, the role of indigenous churches, and the application of the Christian message to modern-day industrial and rural problems.[136]

Jabavu, on a six-month sabbatical leave from Fort Hare, attended as a representative of the South African Methodist Conference and the American Board of Commissioners for Foreign Missions.[137] Traveling to Jerusalem through London, Jabavu collected one of his favorite anecdotes when he stopped in at Edinburgh House, headquarters of the International Missionary Council. The doorman misunderstood him and announced: "Please, Sir, Mr. Jehova has come from South Africa and is going to Jerusalem."[138] Inadvertent though the pun was, it nevertheless reflected Jabavu's personal agenda in attending the conference. Though he waited for the sessions to end before he undertook an extensive tour of Palestine and Egypt, to a certain extent the International Missionary Council meeting took a back seat to what became a personal voyage of discovery, a search for the earthly evidence of "the kingdom of heaven" that had entranced him as a child.[139]

In the diary he kept of his travels, published in Xhosa as *E-Jerusalem* on his return, he described his visits to the historical sites of Christianity. Replete with biblical references, it revealed both the breadth of his knowledge of that text and the impact the experience had on him. At Nazareth, he baptized himself with water from the well where "Mary . . . the mother of Jesus used to fetch water."[140] Standing on the banks of the river Jordan, he found himself overcome by emotion:

> When I looked at that river I doubted whether I was in my senses, it was as though I was dreaming, I did not know whether I was still alive. Maybe I had died suddenly at home and now I [was] crossing the Jordan of death and . . . was on my way to heaven. In those doubts I looked carefully at [the] Jordan and felt I would know more about this when I [was] back home. I took a few leaves as a remembrance and filled a bottle of water and baptised my son who was born soon after my return.[141]

More than any of his articles (published largely for English-speaking audiences), this passage suggests the depth of D. D. T. Jabavu's faith. Though possessed of a good sense of humor and a natural sense of melodrama, Jabavu's delivery as a lay preacher was flat and monotonous, as if he felt that emotion should not intrude on the serious matter of religion.[142] On the banks of the river Jordan, however, he was free to experience the "Kingdom of Heaven."

That Jabavu took full advantage of his visit to the Holy Land did not, however, preclude his participation in the meeting he was there to attend. Though he did not contribute any formal papers for discussion at the conference, he did join delegates from Korea and India at the open public meetings held at St. George's Cathedral in Jerusalem,[143] and took part in the council's discussion of "The Christian Mission in Light of Race Conflict." It was this topic—which comprised volume 4 of the published report—that was most noteworthy from a South African perspective. The volume reflected its American and African contributors' concerns that the racist behavior of white Christians was alienating potential converts around the world who were not white.[144] This was certainly the tone of Jabavu's own lament that more and more black South Africans seemed to be turning toward Islam rather than Christianity: "One of the great difficulties in the way of black people in South Africa building up their own Church is the feeling that even under the Christian missions there is no equality in Church or State."[145] The church, he implied, had moved too far away from its egalitarian roots.

The links between race, religion, and politics were explored in the published proceedings by the African-American missionary Max Yergan and by J. Dexter Taylor, a white missionary attached to the American Board in Durban (who unlike Yergan was not present in Jerusalem). Both men identified the crux of the South African problem from the African perspective. In his brief discussion paper on "The Race Problem in Africa," Yergan credited white South African Anglicans, Presbyterians, and Wesleyan Methodists for protesting the 1926 amendment to the 1911 Mines and Works Act (the Colour Bar Act),[146] and the Dutch Reformed Churches for beginning to discuss racial issues,[147] but argued forcefully that the evangelization of Africans had to be viewed in the context of a changing continent-wide economic and political order. In the South African case this demanded that missionaries acknowledge that the greatest problem facing black South Africans was not racism in and of itself, but rather the attendant issue of land hunger.[148] In a much more comprehensive article, discussing the history and contemporary circumstances of the "Relations between the Black and White Races in South Africa,"[149] Taylor argued that "although the problem of race relationships is ultimately a spiritual one—the mutual recognition of each other's rights, the intelligent appreciation of each other's viewpoints, and a reasonable amount of sacrifice in each other's interests . . . the immediate concrete point of difficulty in that relationship is the land."[150] Dispossessed people did not make willing converts.

What, then, did Africans want, and what were the missionaries to do? Jabavu offered one answer in "Christianity and the Bantu":

> Young educated Africa appeals for sympathy with her legitimate aspirations towards religious autonomy; for the dissemination of liberal views in press, pulpit and platform on the right of the Bantu to a happy future in the land of their birth; for protection in the settlement of land questions so inseparably bound up with the principle of religion; for the inculcation of Christian principle on native affairs in white homes, schools, farms, towns or clubs; for the kind of life that Jesus would have led had he lived as a white man today in South Africa.[151]

Here was a clear conflation of liberal and Christian values on Jabavu's part. What educated Africans wanted, if not a complete reconstruction of South African society, was a substantial restructuring of it, in which missionaries (and white liberals) would take a role, but not the leading role.

In 1928 a restructuring of South African society was in process, though it was the antithesis of the one Jabavu argued that Africans desired. Since his election in 1924 heading up a National-Labour pact government, Prime Minister J. B. M. Hertzog had sought passage of a package of legislation designed (among other things) to rationalize the land segregation system introduced in 1913 and to deny the franchise to those Africans who exercised it. Defending the franchise was the not-so-hidden agenda of a series of weekend lectures, ostensibly about the Holy Land, that Jabavu delivered throughout the eastern Cape in the second half of 1928. Typical of these speeches was one Jabavu made in August 1928 to the King William's Town Native Welfare Society (of which his brother Alexander was a leading member), in which he interwove his criticisms of "Hertzogian Segregation" with the resolutions of the Jerusalem Conference stressing interracial harmony and condemning prejudice.[152] It was the protest against Hertzog's un-Christian legislation that would take Jabavu abroad again in late 1931, this time back to England and then to the United States.

E-*Amerika* (In America)

The agenda of the first leg of Jabavu's tour was singularly political. He toured England in mid-December 1931 as the one-man deputation of the Non-European Conference. The conference had been established in 1927 by Dr. Abdullah Abdurahman, the leader of the African People's Organisation, which represented the interests of Coloured South Africans.[153] Abdurahman, along with Tengo Jabavu, had been a member of the 1909 delegation that traveled to London to protest the passage of the South Africa Act; the founding of the Non-European Conference in 1927 marked the first attempt in eighteen years "to bring together all groups of South African non-whites in a united front to present their grievances to white South Africa,"[154] and it enjoyed the enthusiastic support of D. D. T. Jabavu.

In all, Jabavu would deliver sixteen speeches about "Native disabilities" in December 1931. He had come, he informed his British audiences, "to place before the British people a full statement of [the conference's] views on the matter of equal rights and the status of Non-European citizens in the British Empire."[155] He had come to counteract Prime Minister Hertzog's 1930 speech in London, in which he had urged the British government to adopt the Union of South Africa's policy—the denial to blacks of equal treatment in all matters of church and state—in its African possessions. Hertzog's ultimate aim had been to persuade the British government to turn the Swaziland, Bechuanaland, and Basutoland protectorates over to the Union. Jabavu assured his audience that "we Blacks much prefer direct rule under the Imperial Government, for we still look to Great Britain as our fountain of justice and regard her as our paramount protector,"[156] and he outlined thirty-seven reasons— ranging from pass laws to poll taxes and proposed segregation legislation— why the Non-European Conference felt that the British government should retain control over its African possessions outside South Africa. Chief among these was to spare their African citizens the illiberal treatment suffered by black South Africans. Of that suffering Jabavu wrote: "I spoke about our misery in Africa until I cried."[157]

The second leg of Jabavu's 1931 trip took him to the United States, where in rapid succession he attended the convention of the Student Volunteer Movement for Foreign Missions in Buffalo, visited Boston at the invitation of the American Board of Commissioners for Foreign Missions, and attended the Foreign Mission Conference of North America in Atlantic City. Though "Native disabilities" remained a subtheme in Jabavu's various lectures,[158] he downplayed the political angle for his American audience. In Britain, political appeals still potentially carried some weight; the passage of the Statute of Westminster in 1931 had not eliminated the right of appeal to the Judicial Committee of the British Privy Council.[159] Political appeals were wasted on an American audience and were potentially alienating, especially to some white audiences, given the political repression of African-Americans in their own states.

The connections between American and black South African churches were long-standing. The white American Board of Commissioners had established its first mission to the Zulu in 1835.[160] In 1896 the Reverend James Dwane, a former Wesleyan Methodist minister who had joined Mokone in establishing the Ethiopian Church, had traveled to the United States on behalf of the Ethiopian Church to seek affiliation with the African Methodist Episcopal (AME) Church. Founded by a former slave in 1796, the AME Church (like the Ethiopian Church) had broken with the Methodist Episcopal Church in the United States over the issue of color discrimination.[161] In 1898 Bishop Henry Turner of the AME Church visited South Africa and named Dwane Mission Bishop of South Africa. The relationship was short-lived. AME members in the United States did not recognize Dwane's elevation, and Dwane himself was disappointed by the lack of funding forthcoming from the United States.[162] While Mokone and the bulk of the Ethiopian Church members decided to stay with the AME Church,

Dwane broke away in 1899 and joined the Anglican Church as head of the Order of Ethiopia. While the AME Church in South Africa flourished and the Order of Ethiopia declined,[163] it was this latter structuring—a semi-independent, black-led church affiliated with a mainstream, white-dominated church with worldwide connections—that D. D. T. Jabavu favored.[164]

At the end of December 1931 Jabavu arrived in Buffalo to address the Student Volunteer Movement for Foreign Missions, the body for which he had written his 1927 article "Christianity and the Bantu." The movement had been established in 1886 with the goal of spreading the Christian gospel throughout the world. It was integrated into the American YMCA by its then-president Dr. John R. Mott, in 1890. Mott, appointed president of the World YMCA in 1926, had also served as the president of the 1928 Jerusalem Conference, where he had met Jabavu.[165] Mott himself would tour southern Africa in 1934.[166] At Buffalo 2,000 students (white and African-American) from 600 colleges in the United States and Canada gathered for the eleventh quadrennial convention to consider "present world conditions from the Christian point of view."[167]

Jabavu led the roundtable discussion on "White and Black in South Africa"[168] and gave two lectures, published in the convention report as "After Three Generations" and "Christian Service in Rural and Industrial South Africa." The first chronicled the experience of conversion in his own family as an example of a wider process and was notable for Jabavu's own admission of the debt of gratitude he owed the missionaries: "I stand here not as a type of the Africans in my country, because I am really an accident thrown up on top of those multitudes who are standing in the background."[169] Acknowledging the extent to which traditional leaders had been marginalized by this tiny educated elite by the early 1930s, he added: "Every black man who is a leader of any importance is a product of missionary work. Outside of missionary work there is no leadership."[170] Educated Africans had taken on the role of middlemen between white South African society and the "multitudes" of Africans "standing in the background."[171]

At the roundtable, Jabavu explained to his fellow delegates that "the white rulers," driven by their fear of these mission-trained black leaders and of the millions of Africans they claimed to represent, "had evolved a system of legislation that had the notoriety of being the most repressive in civilization" in order to protect themselves.[172] It was the missionaries' duty to study the situation and "explore all possible solutions from a practical Christian angle," using as their guides volume 4 of the Jerusalem Conference report and (in a bit of self-promotion) Jabavu's own forthcoming pamphlet, "Native Disabilities."[173] What the missionaries could actually do, Jabavu outlined in his second lecture, "Christian Service in Rural and Industrial Africa."

Jabavu's second lecture reflected the still ambiguous nature of the relationship between missionaries and their African converts. While acknowledging that he himself was an "accident," he was equally anxious to assert that there were a great many Africans just like him, and that the slides of "backward" peoples shown to the convention delegates presented a skewed picture.[174] While he wanted each missionary to be self-aware, and to know when to leave, in order that he might guard against

> the danger of . . . being absorbed in his own leadership of the people and thus becoming indifferent to the genuine efforts of native Africans or else positively determined to crush out of existence anything like initiative on the part of the black man, because the missionary fears that this might overshadow his or her own work,[175]

he also wanted the missionaries to stay and help Africans.[176] Their assistance, however, needed to be very practical and focused, as indeed missionaries had long striven to be.[177] As models, Jabavu praised the African-American missionary Max Yergan for his work with the Student's Christian Association in South Africa,[178] and the African-American missionary J. E. East, whom Jabavu had helped establish a farmers' association in the eastern Cape in 1918.[179] Jabavu also touted the white American missionary Ray E. Phillips for his work with urban Africans and his establishment of the Bantu Men's Social Centre in Johannesburg.[180]

Jabavu reserved his greatest praise for his wife, Florence Makiwane Jabavu, a nonordained African missionary like himself. In 1927, with a small grant from the New York-based Phelps-Stokes Fund,[181] Florence Jabavu had launched the Zenzele movement in the eastern Cape to teach domestic skills to rural African women. She taught women not to wean their children on coffee and tea (thus helping reduce the high infant mortality rate), how to make soap out of ox fat, and how to cook pumpkin (a staple) in a variety of palatable ways.[182] In essence, she tried to redress the negatives of "western civilization"[183]—the reliance on false necessities (coffee and tea) and the obsession with cleanliness—with homegrown solutions. Quite logically, Florence Jabavu's work also figured prominently in D. D. T. Jabavu's speech in Boston on January 8, 1932, to the Department of Women's Work of the Massachusetts Congregational Conference and Missionary Society.[184]

Virtually ignored in Buffalo, where the one newspaper reference to him (despite his prominence at the conference) chronicled his enjoyment of a hot dog,[185] Jabavu received a hero's welcome in Boston. In addition to his speech to the Massachusetts Congregational Conference, he addressed the Race Relations Committee of the Greater Boston Federation of Churches, was interviewed by the local newspapers, and earned a gushing review from Dorothy Cushing, editor of the American Board journal *The Missionary Herald*.[186] Hard hit by the worldwide economic depression, the American Board had little but words to offer:[187]

> 'Veni, vidi, vici!' said Caesar. 'Veni, vidi, vici!' might echo Jabavu. Caesar was speaking of Pontus. Jabavu . . . indisputably the outstanding Bantu leader of South Africa today . . . might be speaking of the United States. A sane man, well balanced, self-controlled. A jolly man, with a rollicking laugh. . . . a truly lovable man . . . that's Jabavu of South Africa—Christian gentleman. . . . Everybody liked him— because they sensed his friendliness and knew he liked them. 'A vibrant and engaging personality,' said one newspaperman—a white.[188]

The irony that a black man should receive such an ebullient reception in the United States in 1932 was clearly not lost on Cushing. Commenting on Jabavu's observation that "'The United States, with all its faults, is *just* to the Negro,'" Cushing observed: "Professor Jabavu is evidently referring to *legal* not social status. He is not ignorant of the fact that the black man in America cannot always do what he pleases, but he feels that the restrictions imposed are at least not *legal,* and not supported by the majority of people."[189]

Coping with the burden of legalized racism was a theme in Jabavu's last speech, delivered to the Foreign Mission Conference in Atlantic City in mid-January. Founded in 1894, the conference was affiliated with the International Missionary Council. With interests in Asia, Latin America, and Africa, it defined itself in Social Gospel terms as "a fellowship of kindred spirits in the world-embracing crusade for the Kingdom of God."[190] In his speech, "The Meaning of the Cross in the Life of the World Today," Jabavu identified color prejudice as "one of the crosses we have to bear, the cross of continual insult in our lives, insults making us uncomfortable in our own land . . . because we are hated for a reason which we can't control. We can't help our pigment." While Jabavu's own response was to turn the other cheek, he acknowledged that not everyone agreed with him: "They say, 'Oh, you are too soft. You are too compromising. What you want now is direct action and tell the white man what you feel about him.'"[191] These accusations would follow him throughout his political career.

Two other themes dominated Jabavu's final American speech. Both reflected an increasing openness in his thinking about religion, perhaps the result of his embrace of social anthropology in his teaching at the South African Native College. Bemoaning the increasing compartmentalization (or secularization) of "present-day civilization . . . especially the compartment of religion," he praised African religious practices. "In the African mind," he argued, "there is a oneness about things, oneness about religion, together with daily life and wealth and work and discipline."[192] While whites tended to isolate themselves, stressing individuality, blacks, Jabavu argued, were inheritors of a "tradition of sharing," which meant few went hungry, either spiritually or materially. It was this simplicity and sacrifice that was closest to the message of Christ.[193]

Similarly, Jabavu expressed his respect for the separatist churches, despite his earlier questioning of their intellectual and religious maturity. Describing the travails of the members of a small independent church who had walked 600 miles to Pretoria to ask for land for their church, Jabavu observed:

> I don't know whether there is a need for conversion. I sometimes have tried to ask myself. It is so easy for us to criticize them and say, 'oh, they are religious cranks,' but it may be harder to criticize ourselves.
>
> Perhaps the time has come to criticize ourselves. Perhaps it is for me to ask myself, 'Have I not missed the right way of serving God? Am I making sufficient sacrifices such as are indicated by this group whom I regard as a spurious church?'[194]

Perhaps these "religious cranks" were as Christian as Africans who belonged to mainstream denominations. It was this theme of autonomy for African Christians that Jabavu would take up when he returned to South Africa early in 1932.

AN AFRICAN INDIGENOUS CHURCH

In 1932 Jabavu published *E-Amerika* (In America), which collected the twenty articles he had written in Xhosa for *Imvo Zabantsundu* about his travels in the United States,[195] where he had spent the bulk of his time talking to and about missionaries. For his Xhosa-speaking audience, he praised "the work of the early missionaries in promoting schooling," but then observed that "there are enough missionaries, evangelists and black preachers to do missionary work among my people." What was "hurtful" was that they often did not "have any measure of autonomy in their work."[196] In *E-Amerika*, Jabavu argued that only the Order of Ethiopia (affiliated with the Anglican Church), the Bantu Presbyterian Church (affiliated with the United Free Church of Scotland), and the avowedly separatist African Presbyterian Church offered a black minister freedom from being a servant to a white minister. Without completely cutting themselves off from whites, Jabavu suggested, blacks should be ministered to by blacks. White or foreign missionaries should limit themselves to organizing youths, as Ray Phillips did in Johannesburg and Max Yergan did at Fort Hare. The real focus of white missionaries should be the white community: "The vast majority of whites among us," Jabavu contended, "are heathens and non-believers."[197] The evidence was in their un-Christian treatment of black South Africans.

For many members of the African National Congress, the idea of one united African church, first proposed in the mid-1920s, retained its appeal. Only when the Anglican minister James Calata was elected secretary-general of the ANC in 1936 did he convince his colleagues to abandon the idea of a racial church as the foundation for national unity.[198] Calata nevertheless contributed to keeping the idea alive when he appeared to support the idea of an indigenous African Church in a 1938 article in *The South African Outlook*: "I appeal to history and see the methods of evangelization and church organization of the barbarian English people when the Roman Bishops took great pains to see that not the Roman Church but the 'Ecclesia Anglicana' was established in England. Should not the same ideas inspire the founding and organization of the Church of Africa?"[199] In 1939 the idea was proposed again by a small group of Orange Free State intellectuals, including James Moroka (a doctor), Jacob Nhlapo (a teacher), and Paul Mosaka (a businessman).[200] They traced the growth of the independent church movement in the 1930s to the segregationist policies pursued by the government, and hoped to restore a sense of African community by uniting the various separatist churches into one African church.[201] They were unable to secure the support of the separatist churches, and the idea of a United African Church was again abandoned.

Jabavu included a synopsis of Moroka's, Nhlapo's, and Mosaka's argument in his pamphlet *An African Indigenous Church (A Plea for Its Establishment in South Africa)* when he revived the plan yet again in February 1942. That the idea had already failed twice appeared not to dissuade him. By 1942 the All African Convention (a broadly based federation of political organizations Jabavu had helped found in 1935 to fight government legislation intended to restrict further Africans' already limited voting and land rights) had been eclipsed by a resurgent ANC. A successful indigenous church might well have restored Jabavu's political stock.[202] In addition, South Africans had been fighting in the Second World War for two and a half years, and "schemes for post-war reconstruction"[203] were much under discussion, following on the American and British joint declaration of the Atlantic Charter in August 1941. The charter promised, among other things, "support for the right of peoples to choose their own form of government."[204] Jabavu extended this argument to the religious sphere.

Jabavu's proposal was slightly different from the 1939 version. Whereas the earlier proposal had argued for a union of separatist churches, Jabavu would build his church around the indigenous churches—the Order of Ethiopia, the Bantu Presbyterian Church, and the Bantu Baptist Church—self-governing churches "launched by the good offices of the existing missionising bodies."[205] His definition derived from the findings of the 1928 Jerusalem Conference, which attempted to define an indigenous church institutionally as a "church as it has been developed through the work of missions recognized by its members as an institution in which they are at home, which they are able to love, and in which they feel a sense of proprietorship. . . . without losing the fellowship of the older churches and suffering the loss of financial aid," and spiritually as a "natural fellowship of believers, whose outward form and inward growth are alike to be determined by the indwelling Spirit of Christ."[206] The essence of Jabavu's indigenous African church was that it was self-ruling, and based on the model of the black churches he had encountered in the United States in 1913, "the hub around which all . . . social and business enterprise centred."[207] He was less forthcoming than earlier advocates about the practical details of setting up the church, suggesting little beyond a conference in Bloemfontein.[208]

Moroka, Nhlapo, and Mosaka had argued that a United African Church would encourage "greater inter-denominational and inter-racial cooperation."[209] It was Jabavu, however, who made the clearer argument for how a racially based church would allow for greater "inter-racial cooperation." Independence, he argued, did not equal separation, nor did it suggest any ingratitude on the part of African converts. African Christians were not rejecting their white benefactors, but rather asking them to accept that their job was done and that their African charges were capable of running their own affairs. In other words, it was time to grant civilized Africans their equal rights. It was in the process of working together as equal partners that interracial relations would improve. Further opportunities for cooperation would come through membership in the International Missionary Council. The creation of an indigenous church was not then an acceptance of the government's policy of segregation, but an assertion of African pride and autonomy.[210]

This was a potentially radical assertion, though it appeared much less so when Jabavu extended his analysis to include asserting African control over the mission stations and schools. While the American Board had appointed African principals at some of its schools, the Methodists had not.[211] In criticizing the Methodists' reluctance to do so, Jabavu's language evoked a bygone age: "African Governors or Principals of educational or missionary institutions in South Africa are no longer miracles or monstrosities. I am not asking for the moon. I am humbly pleading for a whole-hearted and Christianly adoption of a policy already accepted and functioning."[212] If white Christians would continue to be a disappointment, so too would black Christians, at least on the issue of a united African church. Like each proposal before it, Jabavu's "plea" for an African Indigenous Church in South Africa failed.

"Except the Lord build the house, they labour in vain that build it"

What, then, may one conclude, based on what he wrote, about Jabavu's Christian faith?[213] He honored his father both in words and by remaining a loyal member of the Methodist Church. Echoing the missionaries' own process of self-examination in the interwar period, he urged the churches to embrace even greater activism. While he acknowledged the debt of gratitude he owed to the missionaries, he wished to see them replaced by Africans at all levels. His presence at a variety of international missionary conferences suggests that he was regarded as a spokesman for black South African Christians. Most important, he was a religious man; he believed the closing line to his 1942 article proposing an African indigenous church: "Except the Lord build the house, they labour in vain that build it."[214] He believed, as he had stated ten years earlier, that "life is one single whole and therefore religion is not divided from it but is in the common life as well as in all life."[215]

He continued, in the absence of an African church, to practice ecumenism, preaching in a wide variety of African churches throughout the 1940s and into the 1950s. He read his last lesson in 1957, two years before his death.[216] Significantly, a consistent favorite was the parable of the good Samaritan, about a man who rescued his neighbor when he found him lying by the side of the road, beaten and robbed.[217] The moral of the story, "Love the Lord your God with all your heart and with all your strength and with all your mind," and "Love your neighbor as yourself," was a fitting description of the manner in which D. D. T. Jabavu tried to conduct his own life, and goes far to explain his activism in the realms of teaching, farming, and politics. What was clear from all Jabavu's "missionary" work, and especially from his political career, however, was that he saw himself not as the victim beaten and robbed, but as the good Samaritan, working to secure "equal rights for all civilized men."

Fig 1. John Tengo Jabavu and his family, 1898. Left to right: Richard Rose Innes, Sol Mvambo (a family friend), Davidson Don Tengo, Elda Sakuba Jabavu holding Yates (who died in infancy), Alexander Macaulay, John Tengo, Wilson Weir (courtesy of Harrison Wright).

Fig 2. John Tengo Jabavu and D. D. T. Jabavu, around 1903 (UNISA).

Fig 3. D. T. Jabavu while a student at the African Training Institute in Colwyn Bay, Wales. William Hughes, the institute's founder, is in the middle of the back row. Jabavu is seated second from left in the first row (Jabavu Crosfield Collection).

Fig 4. D. D. T. Jabavu in 1911, while a student at the University of
London (UNISA).

Fig 5. D. D. T. Jabavu in 1914, while a student at Birmingham
University (UNISA).

Fig 6. D. D. T. Jabavu, probably on board ship returning to South Africa in
1914 (UCT).

Fig 7. D. D. T. Jabavu in October 1914, on his return to South Africa (UNISA).

Fig 8. Lovedale Missionary Institution Staff, 1913. Florence Makiwane is on the far right of the first row (UCT).

Fig 9. D. D. T. Jabavu and Florence Makiwane after their wedding, August 1916 (UNISA).

Fig 10. Students at the South African Native College at Fort Hare, 1918. D. D. T. Jabavu is in the center of the front row, Alexander Kerr is sitting to his immediate left (UNISA).

Fig 11. Helen Nontando (Noni) Jabavu in 1921 (UNISA).

Fig 12. Florence Makiwane Jabavu while a student at Kingsmead College in 1922 (UNISA).

Fig 13. Staff of the South African Native College at Fort Hare in 1926. D. D. T. Jabavu is third from the right in the front row; Alexander Kerr is fourth from the left (UNISA).

Fig 14. All African Convention deputation, February 1936. Left to right: A. W. G. Champion, A. S. Mtimkulu, H. S. Kekane, J. M. Dippa, D. D. T. Jabavu, H. Selby Msimang, S. J. Mvambo, Z. R. Mahabane, R. H. Godlo (courtesy of Harrison Wright).

Fig 15. D. D. T. Jabavu with his son Tengo Max in the early 1950s (UNISA).

4 The Rise of an African Politician, 1920–1936

When D. D. T. Jabavu signaled his formal entry into the political arena with the publication of *The Black Problem* in 1920, he was in his mid-thirties.[1] His seemingly late embrace of politics was at least in part more evidence of his respect for his father. Tengo Jabavu had mapped out his eldest son's education, helped build the South African Native College where he would spend his professional career, and set an example for religious activism. Tengo Jabavu had also been one of the most prominent African politicians in the Cape Colony in the late nineteenth and early twentieth centuries. His reputation had been seriously damaged when he questioned British motives and expressed pro-Afrikaner sympathies during the South African War, somewhat rejuvenated by his protest against the color bar included in the 1909 South Africa Act, and all but eliminated by his initial support of the new Union's Natives Land Act in 1913.

The Natives Land Act had been introduced into parliament by Tengo Jabavu's old friend Jacobus W. Sauer, a long-standing supporter of the Cape liberal tradition and the African franchise. After Union in 1910, Sauer had served first as Minister of Railways and Harbors and then as Minister of Native Affairs for the ruling South African Party.[2] In his 1922 biography of his father, D. D. T. Jabavu attributed his father's support of the Natives Land Act—his "one great mistake"—to his blind faith in Sauer. Tengo Jabavu, his son asserted, believed "that no evil could befall his people at Sauer's hands . . . that Sauer would as usual, be resourceful enough to manipulate this admittedly wicked law for the ultimate good of Natives, trusting that, by a series of diplomatic exceptions and exemptions, its disastrous effects would be avoided."[3] This was Sauer's hope too, but he died shortly after introducing the legislation in parliament—a death brought on, many believed, by the anguish of betraying his principles.[4]

Less partisan critics, most notably the Tswana journalist Sol Plaatje, were not so generous in their assessment of Tengo Jabavu's motives. Plaatje had edited *Imvo Zabantsundu* for Tengo Jabavu while he was in London in 1911 attending the Universal Races Congress, and the two men were friends.[5] In 1912 Plaatje had been a founding member of the South African Native National Congress (SANNC, later the African National Congress), established to lobby for African rights in light of the passage of the 1909 South Africa Act. Tengo Jabavu had not joined the SANNC (which included among its ranks Tswana, Zulu, and Xhosa members); instead he founded his own South African Races Congress, whose supporters were mainly Mfengu.[6] This political rivalry, however, paled beside Tengo Jabavu's support of the Natives Land Act.

In the Cape Province in 1913, the impact the act would have was unclear because of the connection between land and franchise rights. If Cape Africans lost access to their land, many also would lose their right to vote, which had been explicitly protected under the 1909 South Africa Act. (When the Natives Land Act was challenged in court in 1917 by a Cape African voter, it was declared ultra vires in the Cape Province on these grounds.)[7] In the Transvaal and in Natal, Africans squatting on white farms were allowed to remain where they were until provision was made for the addition of more land to the existing reserves. In the Orange Free State, however, white farmers evicted their black squatters; the resulting migration of starving Africans into the Transvaal was documented by Plaatje in *Native Life in South Africa*, published in 1916.[8] Plaatje's book also included a scathing critique of Tengo Jabavu, whom Plaatje accused of dishonestly manufacturing support for the Natives Land Act to please his masters in the ruling South African Party.[9]

Thus in a very real way, D. D. T. Jabavu had to deal with the ghost of his father's "one great mistake," and with the assumption, as Henry Tyamzashe would observe in 1923, that he was like his father—that is, that he was loyal to the government above the "race." D. D. T. Jabavu confronted the issue by addressing his father's critics in 1922 in *The Life of John Tengo Jabavu*.

In attributing Tengo Jabavu's support of the 1913 Natives Land Act to his "blind faith" in Sauer, D. D. T. Jabavu was attempting to downplay his father's guilt (an interpretation that had echoes in his rejection of the Mfengu slavery myth in 1935).[10] Yet the biography was not completely uncritical. In his son's opinion, the senior Jabavu had further compounded the mistake of supporting the Natives Land Act in two ways. First, by his own arrogance: he "lacked the power to reconcile himself with his opponents in frank discussion. Instead he ignored them as small fry, [and] . . . refused to recognise them, except to condemn them and ridicule their methods in his newspaper."[11] Second, Tengo Jabavu guaranteed the end of his political career by deciding to run against Walter Rubusana in the 1914 election for the Cape Provincial Council. Though blacks were excluded from the Union parliament, the nonracial franchise still existed in the Cape Province, and Rubusana had held the seat since 1910. Tengo Jabavu's candidacy in 1914 split the black vote along ethnic lines, with Mfengu voting for Jabavu and Xhosa for Rubusana, who was also a founding member of the SANNC. The white contender for the seat, A. B. Payne, won.[12] By 1917 Tengo Jabavu had withdrawn his support for the 1913 Natives Land Act, and he supported Rubusana's run for the Cape Provincial Council in the same year.[13] He failed, however, to resuscitate his political reputation and remained marginalized until his death in 1921.[14]

D. D. T. Jabavu wrote the above assessment of his father in 1922, after Tengo Jabavu's death, and after he himself had become active in politics. To acknowledge his father's errors publicly made good sense for his own political future, and asserted his legitimacy as a spokesman for African interests. The cause he took up was the defense of the Cape nonracial franchise, which came under attack from the South African government in the mid-1920s and 1930s. D. D. T. Jabavu led the battle to retain the rights of African voters in the Cape Province, and, it was hoped, to extend those rights throughout the Union. When the confrontation reached its climax in late 1935 and early 1936, he was at its center as president of the All African Convention. The fight itself was defined by an endless round of conferences that brought together government officials, concerned blacks, and sympathetic whites. Jabavu attended them all, and what he said made it clear that in his defense of the Cape nonracial franchise, he drew his inspiration from the nineteenth-century Cape liberal tradition.

THE BLACK PROBLEM

In the tumultuous period following the end of the First World War in 1918, the Cape liberal tradition, with its emphasis on "equal rights for all civilized men," was out of step with the aspirations and concerns of most Africans. Rural Africans were hit particularly hard by inflation, drought, unstable grain prices, and the Spanish influenza epidemic of 1918 and 1919.[15] In urban areas, African workers responded to the increased pressures with boycotts and strikes, and occasionally with riots.[16] In Cape Town, Clements Kadalie began organizing Coloured and African dockworkers, and in 1919 he established the Industrial and Commercial Workers' Union (ICU).[17] On the Witwatersrand the International Socialist League (the forerunner of the Communist Party of South Africa) was attempting to organize African miners and laborers.[18]

It was against this backdrop that Jabavu observed in 1920 in the preface to *The Black Problem* that "the Bantu People are in a state of positive discontent."[19] While sympathetic to the economic plight of the majority of Africans, Jabavu was critical of the organizations that attempted to help them, particularly the Socialists. "Bolshevism and its nihilistic doctrines are enlisting many Natives upcountry," and "socialism of the worst calibre is claiming our people," was the warning he issued in *The Black Problem*. For Jabavu, the most "alarming feature" of this trend was the argument that "Christianity must be opposed and rooted out, for it is a white man's religion which the white man himself does not act upon," a perspective distinctly at odds with his own.[20]

Jabavu's alternative liberal cure for African angst entailed first, "the appointment of officials with tested sympathy towards Natives in all departments of Government," and second, "our being able to produce well-educated Native leaders trained in a favourable atmosphere, who will be endowed with commonsense, cool heads, with a sense of responsibility, endurance, and correct perspective on things."[21] Thus, acceptance of the legitimacy of the white government, and an understanding of how it worked, remained the best way for Africans to secure greater rights.

In essence, then, there existed two streams of African political activism in the 1920s. One consisted of popular movements that attempted to organize African workers; the other reflected the interests of the tiny elite of educated Africans, who nevertheless considered themselves to be representatives of the wider African population.[22]

This is not to suggest that the members of the educated African elite who conferred with the government throughout the 1920s and 1930s were satisfied with its policies. African anger, Jabavu asserted, was fueled by the government's failure to consult them about legislation that directly affected their lives—most notably the 1913 Natives Land Act—but also including the 1920 Native Affairs Act.[23] Introduced by Prime Minister J. C. Smuts, the 1920 act created a Native Affairs Commission (all of whose members were white) to advise the government on issues relating to Africans, and extended the local council system first set up in the Cape Colony's Glen Grey district under the 1894 Glen Grey Act.[24] Councils would oversee local government and recommend policy to the national government, but would operate only in the African areas recognized under the 1913 Natives Land Act.[25] The 1920 Native Affairs Act also introduced annual Native Conferences designed to "gauge . . . native opinion." White liberals and prominent Africans responded favorably to the act; John Dube of the Natal SANNC[26] considered it "the best attempt yet made to meet the requirements of the bulk of the Native people."[27]

The historian Saul Dubow has argued that Smuts's 1920 Native Affairs Act represented "the highpoint of liberal segregation in both its ideological and administrative forms."[28] Smuts was a Cambridge-educated Afrikaner from the Cape Province. As leader of the centrist South African Party from 1919 through 1950, he served as prime minister from 1919 to 1924, and again from 1939 to 1948.[29] In Smuts's approach—despite his failure to consult Africans initially about the 1920 Native Affairs Act—D. D. T. Jabavu found much that reminded him of the Cape liberal tradition. At a meeting of the Native Farmers' Association called to discuss the then-Native Affairs Bill in June 1920 (the proceedings of which he included in *The Black Problem*), Jabavu praised the "great and statesmanlike speech of General Smuts wherewith he introduced the second reading of the Bill in Parliament,"[30] and suggested that "in the electing of the Commissioners and Councillors the Government would have a splendid opportunity of giving the Native people the first step in the use of the franchise."[31]

Jabavu's respect for Smuts was not one-sided; according to the historian Kenneth Ingham, Jabavu was the only African politician whom Smuts took seriously, a compliment that could as easily be a curse. Yet as Ingham has also argued, with Smuts, "logic went overboard when the native question was under discussion. Human considerations pushed him in one direction, instinct in another."[32] Smuts supported the Cape African franchise;[33] indeed, by the late 1920s he was arguing privately for the introduction of a Union-wide Cape-style franchise based on property and income qualifications high enough to exclude most Africans, and a civilization test from which all whites would be exempt.[34] At the same time, Smuts also favored territorial segregation and separate development for most Africans.[35] (The African farmers who met with Jabavu in 1920 did in fact question Smuts's continued support for the 1913 Natives Land Act.)[36] Thus, like many white liberals in the 1920s, Smuts's understanding of segregation was often contradictory, perhaps unavoidably so. As the historian John Cell has observed, "Confusion has been one of segregation's greatest strengths and achievements."[37]

African farmers in the Cape in 1920 were less concerned with Smuts's muddled interpretation of segregation, however, than by what might happen to African political rights in the province if "Hertzog's party got hold of the reins of Government."[38] Like Smuts, J. B. M. Hertzog was an Afrikaner, and a lawyer, though from the Orange Free State. A strict segregationist, he had helped found the conservative Afrikaner-based National Party in 1914. As prime minister from 1924 to 1939,[39] Hertzog would introduce the two key pieces of segregation legislation—the Representation of Natives in Parliament

Bill and the Natives Land (1913) Amendment Bill (later the Native Trust and Land Bill)—that would define black political opposition in the 1920s and 1930s.

Jabavu was inclined throughout much of his own political career to see Smuts as an ally of the liberals and Hertzog as an enemy. Dubow has suggested, however, that the difference between Hertzog and Smuts was more one of style than substance: while Hertzog emphasized color as the point of distinction, and sought to disfranchise black voters in the Cape Province, Smuts's approach focused more on class, and did not reject the gradual inclusion of rural and urban African elites into the white power structure.[40] It was this aspect of Smuts's reasoning—despite his support of territorial segregation—that led D. D. T. Jabavu to view Smuts generally as a sympathetic voice in government.[41]

Jabavu's own political style meanwhile was further shaped by his 1921 meeting with the West African educator James E. K. Aggrey, then touring South Africa as a member of the Phelps-Stokes African Education Commission.[42] Aggrey was pursuing his Ph.D. in education at Columbia University when he was recruited in 1920 by Thomas Jesse Jones, the Director of Education for the Phelps-Stokes Fund and widely considered an expert on issues concerning African-Americans.[43] In addition to his impressive educational achievements, Aggrey was a dynamic public speaker, and in him Jones discovered the "good African" he sought.[44] According to the historian Kenneth King, Jones's "good African" supported racial cooperation, willingly took advice on his education, avoided politics, took pride in being African, and planned to return to Africa to serve his people—a definition that fit D. D. T. Jabavu almost as well as it did Aggrey. Aggrey's long tenure in the United States and D. D. T. Jabavu's political activism made them less than perfect models, but their shared message of "moderation, gradual reform, political compromise and Christian moral uplift"[45] more than compensated.

It was this message that was at the core of the Joint Council movement, launched as a result of Aggrey's and Jones's visit. Patterned on the interracial councils set up in the southern United States in the late 1910s,[46] the first Joint Council of Europeans and Africans was established in Johannesburg in 1921, in a conscious attempt to address the divisions in South African society that had led to the wave of postwar strikes.[47] Within a decade there were more than two dozen Joint Councils throughout South Africa.[48] Prominent among the members of the Joint Council movement were Charles T. Loram and J. D. Rheinallt Jones, and they convinced Howard Pim, a Quaker lawyer who was the president of the Johannesburg Native Welfare Society, to establish the Johannesburg Joint Council.[49] With its emphasis on consultation, it complemented the structures set up by the 1920 Native Affairs Act.

Aggrey lectured throughout South Africa, and his message of racial cooperation was generally well-received by white audiences.[50] Black audiences tended to be somewhat more critical of his Tuskegee-style message,[51] which substituted the metaphor of the piano for Washington's "fingers and hand": "you can play a tune of sorts on the white keys, and you can play a tune of sorts on the black keys, but for harmony you must use both the black and white."[52] This approach ran counter to the growing popularity of the New York–based black nationalist leader Marcus Garvey. Garvey's call of "Africa for the Africans"[53] enjoyed wide popular appeal in South Africa in the 1920s; among its prominent supporters were Clements Kadalie of the ICU, James Thaele, the leader of the African National Congress (previously the SANNC)[54] in the western Cape, and, by the end of 1925, the Rev. Z. R. Mahabane, then president of the national ANC.[55] Thus, though the overt purpose of the Phelps-Stokes commission and of Aggrey's lecture tour was educational, the historians Robert Hill and Gregory Pirio have argued that its message was covertly political,[56] as D. D. T. Jabavu's assessment of Aggrey's visit revealed:

> His African origin was a real advantage to him for it gave him the ear of the whites who otherwise, on account of their dread of Ethiopian doctrines, are always suspicious of American Negroes; whilst it secured him the attention of the indigenous Africans who, ever since the reports of Marcus Garvey's Black Star Fleet, have had their eyes turned to overseas Negroes for succour from the prevailing economic depression as well as for liberation from the injustice of the white man in whom they are tending to lose faith. He convinced the former in a single address more effectually than any amount of argument has done in a generation, that in the British colonies and America there are Negro intellectuals who have assimilated European culture in its refined form with rational mentality; while he disillusioned the latter of the African Republic mirage, giving them instead an edifying message of self-help based on Booker Washington's principles and on Christian ethics.[57]

For Jabavu, Aggrey had effectively politicized Washington's message. Rejecting Bolshevism, Garveyism,[58] and Ethiopian separatism, Jabavu held up Aggrey as the model for Africans to emulate.

Late in 1922, Jabavu tried his hand at playing only the white keys on Aggrey's piano. In an unattributed piece in the December issue of *The South African Outlook* titled "Black Peril and Colour Bar,"[59] he wrote about white fears of blacks from the perspective of a white man. In publishing the article anonymously, he clearly wanted to ensure that name recognition would not color his readers' responses to it. *The South African Outlook*'s audience, however, was composed largely of missionaries and mission-educated Africans, who would have agreed with much of what Jabavu said.[60]

Jabavu acknowledged that the "Black Peril"—defined as "the ever present danger to which a small settler community, surrounded by savage neighbours . . . lay exposed"—had historical legitimacy. Yet he argued that by 1922 the term applied, by a twisted logic, "not as of old to barbarism . . . but to the progress of the Black Races along the lines of industrial development! Having feared the Natives because of their lack of civilisation, we are now shewn the greater danger of their repairing this deficiency; having dreaded their savagery, we are now asked to dread equally their lack of savagery."[61] The real "black peril," he argued, was created by the lethargy inspired in whites by the existence of an industrial color bar.[62] Removing it, from the perspective of economic liberalism, would not—as some feared—spell disaster. Rather, "it would mean greater competition. . . . For the superior White Race," which had no cause to fear competition.[63]

Keeping the color bar in place, denying Africans progress in industry, and in addition holding their land in "trust," Jabavu argued, only ensured future conflict. "Our hatred of the black," he asserted, "has its deepest root in the consciousness of the injury done to him."[64] Whites could only ensure their future by abandoning the notion of "'A White South Africa,'" and instead being "content with a part we might retain . . . [and] make . . . 'really White.'"[65] This was in fact a call for "some sane and workable system of segregation," but not one that allotted one-fifteenth of the Union's land to four-fifths of its people. Many white liberals in the early to mid-1920s would have agreed with him.[66]

Missionaries and liberals recognized, as Jabavu wrote in 1922–23, that "while we are talking of and drinking to the future 'White South Africa,' fingers are already writing upon the walls of our house. A White South Africa! The thing, under the existing circumstances, is a sheer and utter impossibility."[67] In September 1923 they convened the first European-Bantu conference in Johannesburg, sponsored by the Federal Council of the Dutch Reformed Churches (DRC).[68] While historically more notable for its disdain of Africans as inferior peoples,[69] the DRC had established a missionary society dedicated to evangelizing black South Africans in 1857.[70] Though never officially the state church, South Africa's prime ministers since Union in 1910 had been Afrikaners, and the DRC had long represented Afrikaner aspirations and nationalism.[71]

Reflecting the goals of the 1920 Native Affairs Act, the Federal Council convened the 1923 meeting to allow missionaries and liberals to "get better acquainted with each other, and to confer together concerning the interests of Europeans, coloureds and natives, who have been brought together by the hand of God in this country, from the viewpoint of Christian civilization."[72] The conference brought together representatives of missionary societies, welfare societies, the nascent Joint Council movement, the members of the Native Affairs Commission, and such prominent Africans as D. D. T. Jabavu and the Rev. Z. R. Mahabane, then president of the Cape branch of the African National Congress.

In 1923 Hertzog's National Party was still in opposition, and his comprehensive segregation scheme as yet only a rough outline.[73] Mahabane nevertheless expressed his concern about the persistence of an extreme school of segregationists who advocated complete geographical segregation, "i.e., the removal of the entire Bantu population from its present places of domicilium and its final settlement somewhere in the Kalahari Desert," an approach Mahabane deemed completely unacceptable.[74]

But Mahabane—and by extension the ANC—was not completely opposed to segregation. The territorial segregation outlined by the 1913 Natives Land Act was acceptable, Mahabane allowed, provided the act was amended "to provide for the allocation of at least 50 per cent of the land within South Africa for native occupation."[75] This was of course a substantial revision of the 1913 Land Act, and Mahabane added a further qualifier: the acceptance of an equitable division of territory did not eliminate "the claim for direct representation in the legislative bodies of the land—the Union Parliament and the Provincial Council."[76] Though D. D. T. Jabavu agreed adamantly with Mahabane's stance on the franchise, he would remain skeptical about the prospects for "an equitable division" of South Africa's land between blacks and whites.

DEFENDING THE CAPE FRANCHISE, 1925–1927

At the end of June 1924, J. B. M. Hertzog's National–Labour Party Pact government took office, replacing Smuts's South African Party, which had been the ruling government party since 1910.[77] At Smithfield in the Orange Free State in November 1925, Hertzog outlined his proposed solution to the "Native problem," a problem that embodied white South Africa's need to control African labor and its desire to protect "white civilisation."[78] Hertzog's approach was hardly unique. A political color bar had been enshrined in the 1909 South Africa Act, and the South African Party itself had passed a lengthy list of segregative legislation, including the 1911 Mines and Works Act (which had introduced an industrial color bar), the 1913 Natives Land Act (which had delimited areas for African occupation), and the 1923 Native (Urban Areas) Act (which restricted African residence in cities and towns).[79]

What was different in 1925 was Hertzog's goal of replacing the existing piecemeal system of segregation with a uniform, Union-wide Native Policy. Central to that goal was his desire to disfranchise Cape African voters.[80] Along with the color bar, the Cape's nonracial franchise had been entrenched in the 1909 South Africa Act and required a two-thirds majority of a Joint Sitting of the House of Assembly and the Senate to remove it.[81] For Hertzog, it was *the* obstacle to a uniform Native Policy.

Hertzog proposed four bills. The first, the Coloured Persons' Rights Bill, sought in part to differentiate between Coloureds and Africans by removing Africans from the common voting roll in the Cape, and proposed to extend the franchise for Coloureds throughout the Union. Under the second bill, the Representation of Natives in Parliament Bill, Africans throughout the Union would then be represented by seven white members of parliament (MPs), elected by a council of Africans nominated by the governor-general. Further representation would be provided by the third bill, the Union Native Council Bill, which proposed—in an adaptation of the Native Conferences convened under the 1920 Native Affairs Act—an additional Union-wide council for the expression of African opinion. Fifteen African councillors would be appointed by the governor-general; another thirty-five would be elected by the same voters who elected the seven white MPs. Further compensation for the loss of the common franchise was offered in the form of the final bill, the Natives Land (1913) Amendment Bill, which promised to release more land for purchase or hire by Africans.[82]

When the Native Conference met during the first week of December 1925, neither Jabavu nor his colleagues who listened to Prime Minister Hertzog reiterate his plans thought the scheme sane or workable. Hertzog's real goal was, in Jabavu's words, to trap "the black man . . . between the agricultural serfdom of landlessness and the industrial serfdom of a colour bar—a veritable case of the devil and the deep sea."[83]

In response to the threat to the franchise, Jabavu (with his brother Alexander as secretary) established the Cape Native Voters' Convention (CNVC). The CNVC met for the first time on December 17, 1925, in King William's Town, where the members set up a national fund and established a permanent committee representing all the parliamentary divisions in the Cape "for the purpose of carrying out . . . propaganda in defence of the Cape Native franchise rights." Among the convention's first resolutions was to declare "its categorical and most emphatic opposition to the Government's segregation policy."[84]

D. D. T. Jabavu systematically dismantled Hertzog's proposals in an article published in the *International Review of Missions* in mid-1926. His assessment of the prime minister's preoccupation with the "Native question" reflected a clear undercurrent of hostility:

> Out of this welter of contradictory views as regards the correct methods of governing the subject races emerges what is popularly called 'The Native Question.' The expression has been so much used in South Africa that the Bantu have begun to be bored at being called a 'Question.' For why should they be a Native Question to the white man any more than they regard him as a White Question? Is it the Bantu or the European, they ask who squeezed by economic congestion and land hunger in his Native habitat, migrated to find a haven of rest in hospitable and spacious Africa? Which of the two is really the problem?

Yet the article also reflected a basic pragmatism:

> We must, however, admit that these queries are belated and futile because the white man to-day claims Africa by the simple reason of his conquest and that not only by arms but by virtue of superior resources of capital, business enterprise and intelligent organisation.[85]

Hertzog's segregation scheme, Jabavu informed his readers, was just the latest proposal to address the so-called "Native question." Of the existing policies, he advocated the general adoption of the Cape liberal tradition, which through the nonracial franchise that constituted its essence, promoted equality and progress. He rejected the practices of the "Repressionists" of the other three provinces, who denied blacks political rights and severely restricted their economic opportunities "as impracticable and fraught with supreme danger for the future of South Africa."[86]

He was equally dismissive of the notion of comprehensive segregation. Of its five elements—territorial, industrial, political, social, and educational—he put aside the last three, "because social and educational segregation are already in being, as the result of evolution dictated by local convention," and "political segregation . . . will automatically follow once territorial segregation is possible."[87] With a keen eye to the economic realities of South Africa, he noted that industrial segregation

> presupposes two things: first that the black man is able to conduct his commerce and pursue his present vocations alone and divorced from the white man; secondly that the white man is able to carry on all forms of unskilled work on the roads, on the farms, in the stores, in the kitchens and underground at the mines, independently of the black man.

"Both hypotheses," he contended, were "equally impossible in South Africa."[88] The same was true of territorial segregation—whites were simply unwilling to give up the necessary land, and if true territorial segregation was unattainable, then segregation was a fallacy.

Conscious of his international missionary audience, Jabavu cast his rejection of Hertzog's segregation proposals in religious terms: "If the white people of South Africa were Christian enough to do the Bantu justice in a thoroughgoing scheme of territorial segregation then the future would be promising. But unfortunately Christianity has not yet been practised to that extent."[89] "The black man," Jabavu asserted, "does not ask for much, only for justice, justice in land distribution, justice in economic opportunity and justice in political representation. This is no excessive demand."[90]

Hertzog's bills were published in the *Government Gazette* at the end of July 1926.[91] When the delegates to the government Native Conference met again in Pretoria at the beginning of November 1926, it was justice they sought. Charles K. Sakwe, a member of the Transkei Territories General Council, set the tone for the conference by moving that each bill be considered separately on its own merits.[92] The interdependence of the package of bills—particularly of the franchise and land bills—made them impossible to accept. Jabavu seconded Sakwe's motion, and appealed to the government to look to the future:

> If the Natives were driven to believe that injustice was being meted out to them then they might be a real danger to the whites, and the grandsons of all those present might have to face that position. . . . The stopping of the franchise would be purely transient—it could not last. Their future generations would be in a position to insist upon getting fair play.[93]

The theme was taken up by Transvaal delegate Selope Thema, who rejected the Representation of Natives in Parliament Bill and argued in addition that the Cape franchise be extended to the northern provinces.[94]

Delegates also rejected the land bill, which restricted Africans to buying land communally in prescribed "tribal" areas. Jabavu (revealing in his remarks some prejudice against the "illiterate chiefs" who comprised the "great majority of the fifty" delegates to the conference) confessed that "he was anxious that the door be left open for individual tenure. Communal occupation was all right for the masses."[95] Private land ownership was of course intimately linked to the voting rights of "civilized" Africans in the Cape Province. Ironically, it was Jabavu's friend, the literate chief Shadrack Zibi, who had left the congested eastern Cape in 1923 and settled on rented land in the Transvaal,[96] who took Jabavu to task for his exclusivism. No less an elitist himself, he nevertheless wanted the government to improve conditions in the reserves to prevent educated Africans from leaving, for the exodus meant that none were "left to uplift the masses." "A people," he argued, "were not judged by the few but by the masses."[97]

In January 1927, Jabavu published his defense of the rights of "the few" Africans who exercised the franchise in the Cape. By the end of 1926, there were 14,182 African voters in the Cape, up from 6,663 in 1910.[98] The implicit theme of Jabavu's two-part article in *The Cape Times*[99] was that whites had no cause to feel threatened by the increase in the number of African voters. The article embodied the concepts that defined Jabavu's worldview—civilization, Christianity, and British justice—and outlined the arguments that formed the core of his case for the retention of the Cape franchise.

The history of the franchise debate, Jabavu informed his readers, "enables us to judge that the motives inspiring the officials of the then British parliament were born of the essential Christian ethic, namely: 'Do unto others as you would have them do unto you.' They were founded on a system of unimpeachable equity to all human beings regardless of colour, race or creed." Cecil Rhodes had crystallized those motives in his dictum "equal rights to all civilised men south of the Zambesi," which, Jabavu argued, clearly left "the door open for all to qualify for true citizenship and a voice in the councils of state in which civilised men were bound for the same destiny."[100]

Jabavu also rejected the policy of "retribalization" implicit in the Hertzog bills. "Our tribal system," he noted, "is being gradually dislodged by the European democratic system and will ultimately be eliminated . . . as education spreads. It is useless to urge tribal communism as our ultimate goal in the face of the Union Act based on British individualism which is the enemy of communism." Whites had nothing to fear and everything to gain by granting full citizenship to educated black South Africans, who were by definition civilized. The Cape franchise, he asserted, was "nothing less than the noblest monument of the white man's rule, emblematic of his genuineness in practising the precepts of Holy Scripture towards the subject races."[101]

It is tempting to read a bit of cynicism into Jabavu's defense of the franchise in *The Cape Times* in 1927, especially since in stressing the Christian heritage of the Cape liberal tradition as a counterpoint to the spread of communism, he was ignoring the essential pragmatism of a tradition rooted in the attempt to stabilize the Cape Colony's frontier in the mid-nineteenth century. Certainly there was some bitterness in his testimony before the government's Select Committee on the Native Bills in May 1927.

Perhaps as a result of his very public stance on the franchise issue, however, Jabavu was initially excluded from the list of witnesses called to testify before the committee. He wrote to complain to Dr. Abdullah Abdurahman, the prominent Cape Coloured leader and founder of the African People's Organisation (APO). Jabavu lamented his apparent exclusion from the committee and sought Abdurahman's assistance:

> I met Dr. Rubusana today and learnt that he has been notified to give evidence before the Select Committee on the Native Bills. Apparently I am being passed by. If you could use your influence with some of the Committee members like Mr. Krige, Sir Thomas Smartt and General Smuts and advise them to ensure my being officially summoned as, of all the Natives, I have paid most attention by writing and organisation to the Franchise Question and my evidence should, by right, be heard.[102]

The statement was true enough, though it revealed both Jabavu's arrogance and his fear of being overlooked. While Jabavu may have been the only African politician whom Smuts took seriously, Hertzog was prime minister in 1927, and it appeared that he was less enamored of Jabavu. Abdurahman expressed his sympathy, noted that "the A.P.O. has also been ignored," and promised to contact "some of the committee to ensure your being called to give evidence."[103]

Whether through Abdurahman's influence or not, Jabavu did testify before the Select Committee on the Native Bills on May 30, 1927.[104] Perhaps smarting from his initial exclusion from the list of witnesses, his tone was less gracious than usual:

> You ask whether I have ever tried to place myself in the position of the white man and view these Bills from his standpoint. Yes, I have done that, and I feel if I were a White man I would take the view which the liberal minority of White men in the country take, and would be more generous than the average White man is today.[105]

Aside from this one jab, he said virtually nothing new. Almost word for word, his testimony followed the text of his 1926 article in the *International Review of Missions* and his 1927 articles in *The Cape Times*.[106]

THE NON-EUROPEAN CONFERENCE, 1927

If Jabavu's ego had been bruised in 1927, Abdurahman—with whom Jabavu had been planning a Non-European Conference for two years[107]—was smarting over ICU National Secretary Clements Kadalie's response to his invitation to the conference:

That while the I.C.U. welcomes the suggestion for a Non-European Conference arranged to be held at Kimberley in June next; in view of the fact that the conveners of this Conference have been recognised as agents of certain European political parties and as the I.C.U. is essentially a Trade Union Organisation, decides to send an unofficial delegation to Kimberley with a specific purpose to watch that those well known political agents do not use that Conference for their self interest.[108]

"You will now appreciate," Abdurahman wrote to Jabavu, "my reluctance in taking the initiative to summon a conference of non-European organisations. It makes one feel disgusted and inclined to drop the whole business. However, I do not intend to use this letter to wreck the movement."[109] It was Jabavu's turn to sympathize with Abdurahman, and he advised him: "Please do not take the I.C.U. too seriously. Their meetings are always overdone by a number of senseless and tactless extremists even when they mean well." Discretion was the best approach, Jabavu counseled, since "the bulk of public opinion will be behind the movement without your going down on your knees to this party. Only, take care not to remark on their attitude and simply ignore it."[110]

Jabavu's criticism of Kadalie actually ran counter to the line followed by his brother Alexander as editor of *Imvo Zabantsundu*. A vice president of the ICU in the 1920s, Alexander Jabavu insisted that the ICU was the only truly representative mass organization,[111] described Kadalie's speeches as "strong, brave and outspoken but never seditious or calculated to arouse anarchy,"[112] and urged the government to invite Kadalie as a delegate to the annual Native Conference. He did not hesitate, however (perhaps in deference to his older brother), to criticize Kadalie's more "provocative" and "intemperate" remarks.[113]

The conference opened as planned in Kimberley on June 23, 1927.[114] Its goal was simple—to gather together representative Non-European organizations to discuss topics of mutual interest, focusing mainly on economic and social rather than political issues.[115] Organizations represented at the conference included the APO, the ICU, the ANC, "the Bantu Union, several Indian Associations, and several bodies of Bantu Chiefs, Farmers and Teachers."[116]

At the opening session, Jabavu counseled unity and moderation and expressed his anxiety "not to be misunderstood by the world outside."[117] Possibly in response to concerns voiced by Native Affairs Commission member Charles T. Loram—who apparently feared that "the proposed conference was a clandestine conspiracy of anarchists bent on plotting some sinister revolution against the Government"[118]—and seeming to confirm Kadalie's accusations, Jabavu stated "that he had been enjoined from Government circles not to attend [the] Conference, that if he came he would be associating with extremists."[119]

One of those "extremists" was Kadalie's lieutenant A. W. G. Champion,[120] who, ignoring Jabavu's caution to avoid disunifying political statements, asserted that since the ICU had helped put Hertzog's government into power, it had every right to criticize it. Though the ICU rejected Hertzog's bills outright in 1927, Kadalie had in fact supported Hertzog in the 1924 election, asserting then that "segregation was natural." What Kadalie had hoped to gain in 1924 was "a more equitable division of the country."[121] Champion's hostility at the 1927 Non-European Conference reflected the ICU's disenchantment with Hertzog's government—Champion, for example, demanded to know why whites were permitted to sit on the stage at a black conference. Abdurahman informed him that they sat there at the discretion of the chairman.[122]

Such minor disagreements aside, delegates did agree on the importance of economic development. Alexander Jabavu asserted that "the I.C.U. stood for the economic development of non-Europeans"[123] and Abdurahman extended the hand of friendship to the ICU, moving "that this Conference urges all the associations to take steps towards mutual economic improvement by starting businesses controlled by non-Europeans to provide labour for their people and to support existing business concerns organised by non-Europeans," and noting that "the moving of this resolution ought to have been entrusted to one of the members of the I.C.U., who were more familiar with industrial and commercial enterprises."[124] In the spirit of the moment, D. D. T. Jabavu asserted rather irreligiously that "the first Gospel he commended was 'seek first the kingdom of money and of ownership of soil and many other things shall be added on to you.'"[125] Lest the conference delegates give the impression of ignoring the Native Bills entirely, Jabavu moved the following resolution:

> That this Conference deeply deplores the unsympathetic attitude of the Legislature towards non-Europeans as expressed in some of the contemplated legislation, which has a tendency also to divide, and urges the respective organisations to take whatever steps they deem necessary to prevent the continuance of such a policy.[126]

WHITE LIBERALS AND THE AFRICAN FRANCHISE

While retaining the Cape African franchise was D. D. T. Jabavu's passion in the mid-1920s, the same could not be said of his white allies, many of whom were decidedly more ambivalent. The Joint Council movement in the 1920s was largely concerned with social welfare issues, and in 1927 it still "retained a considerable sympathy towards some form of equitable territorial separation,"[127] as a quid pro quo for the loss of the Cape African franchise. In part, this could be traced to the prominence of Brookes, Pim, and Rheinallt Jones—all of whom had more than a passing familiarity with liberal segregationism—in the Joint Council movement. What they did do, however, was publicly support the retention of the Cape African franchise, echoing Jabavu's arguments that Africans had never abused it, and posed no threat to whites.[128]

The extent to which pragmatism had come to dominate the white liberal discussion of the African franchise was evident in the debate on the issue in the June 1928 edition of *The South African Outlook*. The journal's editor, D. A. Hunter, observed that while he personally supported the retention and extension of the franchise, "in the seventy years of its existence the Native voters on the register have risen to only 14,900 out of a Cape Native population of 1,640,162 as compared with a roll of European voters of 395,000 out of a population of 1,679,900." It could not, therefore, he concluded, "have exercised any very great influence upon events."[129] Hunter suggested two adaptations of the separate roll proposed in Hertzog's Representation of Natives in Parliament Bill. First, Africans would send "a College of representatives to Parliament who would speak authentically for [them]." Second, Africans could choose to be represented by Africans.[130]

Though Jabavu could agree with the second suggestion, he vehemently disagreed with any compromise on the franchise in his reply to Hunter, which appeared in the July issue of *The South African Outlook*:

> Bitter experience has taught us that in these affairs it is wiser to stick to what we have than to take chances and throw our valuable privileges into the melting pot of Parliamentary amendment whence things emerge quite different from copious promise. However much the virtues of the present franchise be decried we greatly prize what we have and would not like to see our hard-won constitutional position dug out of its present entrenchment.[131]

Jabavu's position on the franchise and a host of related issues was formalized with the publication of *The Segregation Fallacy* by the Lovedale Press in October 1928. The book was a collection of articles, touching on politics, education, and religion, that Jabavu had written between 1922 and 1928. Included in the volume were "Hertzogian Segregation versus the Cape Native Policy," "The Disfranchisement of the Cape Native," and "The Segregation Fallacy." In the preface he wrote: "We trust this effort will arouse all loyal citizens of South Africa to do something to save the country from further mistakes committed under the policy of Segregation."[132]

Jabavu himself took this charge seriously, and early in February 1929 he was back in Cape Town, this time as a delegate to the second National European-Bantu Conference. As in 1923, the conference gathered together representatives from the Joint Council movement and from a variety of church, welfare, and trade organizations. The papers delivered reflected the concerns of these groups with agricultural development, industrial organization, and health issues. Though Jabavu did not deliver a paper, he did serve on committees appointed to study the "Administration of Justice" and the "Franchise."[133] At the opening session, which dealt with the "Agricultural Development of Native Areas," he emphasized the connections between the franchise and land ownership in the Cape. Though some delegates, notably Charles T. Loram, objected to the franchise issue being discussed at the conference, confrontation, at least on the first day, was avoided.

Jabavu and Loram met again that evening at the Conference of Joint Councils and Native Welfare Societies called to establish the Inter-Racial Council of South Africa, the forerunner of the South African Institute of Race Relations (SAIRR). Howard Pim was elected president; Jabavu and J. W. Mushet became the new organization's vice presidents. Rheinallt Jones was elected secretary, and J. Dexter Taylor became the treasurer. Officers included Edgar Brookes, the Rev. W. Y. St. George Stead of Grahamstown, a Professor Burchell of Pietermaritzburg, and, in addition to Jabavu, four prominent Africans—Selope Thema, John Dube, the Rev. Abner Mtimkulu, and Dr. James S. Moroka.[134]

Loram was not elected to the executive of the interim council in February 1929, although he exerted considerable influence over the organization's finances, courtesy of his American connections. The Carnegie Corporation of New York funded the venture with an initial grant of £750 per annum for five years, and the Phelps-Stokes Fund contributed an unspecified amount. Building on the work of the existing Joint Councils, Loram hoped to establish the Inter-Racial Council as a nonpolitical body; its tentative agenda was to research the social and economic aspects of the "Native question."[135] Jabavu's objections to the concept of a "Native question" aside, it was clear from the outset that he thought the distinction between social, economic, and political concerns a false one.

The issue of the African franchise came up again on the third and final day of the European-Bantu Conference, on a motion by Sir Clarkson Tredgold of the Cape Town Joint Council. Loram countered by proposing that the franchise not be discussed at all, since "a vote on the Native Franchise would divide the Conference which was otherwise in agreement. It was urgently necessary," he added, "to carry all sections together on the economic and social questions." Pulling out his trump card, he "quoted the late Dr. Aggrey as saying 'It is better to take all the people a little way than to take a few a long way.'" Jabavu, though he respected Aggrey's approach,[136] rejected Loram's proposal, observing

> that it was merely chance that the issue was political. An abstract principle was involved and it could not be just ignored because it happened to rub shoulders with politicians. Franchise rights were being attacked, rights which had not only never been abused, but had been so prized that those whom the natives had sent to Parliament had adorned it. Members of the Conference could not allow these rights to disappear without a struggle.[137]

Conference delegates agreed with Jabavu, resolving that there should "be no infringement of existing rights," and expressing their regret at "the Native Franchise being made an election issue."[138]

In response to the threat to the Cape franchise and to the ambivalence of the Joint Council "friends of the natives," Tredgold and James Rose Innes (a veteran of nineteenth-century Cape politics), along with Henry Burton and J. W. Jagger—all Cape liberals—founded the Non-Racial Franchise Association (NRFA) in May 1929,[139] the same month that the theoretically apolitical South African Institute of Race Relations was formally launched.[140] Rejecting the essential pragmatism of most white liberals in the 1920s, these men defended the Cape franchise on constitutional grounds, and argued that the fairest solution was an across-the-board civilization test for all citizens, black and white. While they were arguing from principle rather than pragmatism, they were doing so very much in the nineteenth-century tradition of Cape liberalism. If black voters ever became a real threat to whites, the government could simply raise the voting qualifications as had been done repeatedly in the nineteenth century.[141] Nevertheless, the NRFA upheld the Cape liberal tradition's promise of a future South African society in which all civilized men would be equal partners.

A reprieve in the battle for the retention of the Cape nonracial franchise came on February 12, 1929, when the Representation of Natives in Parliament Bill and the Coloured Persons' Rights Bill were introduced in parliament. The required two-thirds majority to remove the entrenched Cape nonracial franchise from the South Africa Act was not met, and the bills failed to pass. The division over the bills followed party lines: Smuts's South African Party opposed Hertzog's National-Labour Party pact and the bills were defeated on the third reading.[142] Smuts had real objections, particularly to Hertzog's franchise proposals, but he also had practical concerns—it was widely believed that at least six (and perhaps as many as seventeen) South African Party MPs in the eastern Cape depended on African voters for their reelection.[143]

But Smuts's victory, whatever his motive, was short-lived. During the 1929 election campaign, Smuts expressed his support for one "great African dominion stretching unbroken throughout Africa,"[144] an allusion to Cecil Rhodes's Cape-to-Cairo vision, with whites in charge. Hertzog skillfully manipulated Smuts's speech to make it appear that Smuts was in favor of a black-led South Africa.[145] In doing so, Hertzog won the "Black Peril" election, and the National Party took office in June 1929, with seventy-eight seats to the South African Party's sixty-one.[146] Hertzog was one step closer to his goal of a uniform, Union-wide Native Policy.

THE HERTZOG BILLS, 1929–1935

Jabavu meanwhile continued his battle to retain the franchise. An assessment of his success, and a revealing commentary on the nature of his relationship with the South African Native College's principal, Alexander Kerr, was offered by Margery Perham when she visited Fort Hare in November 1929. Perham, a lecturer at Oxford University, described herself as "a young and obscure female don" who had received a Rhodes Trust Travelling Fellowship with the vague charge to study "colour problems" in Africa.[147] She traveled widely throughout southern Africa, and kept a diary of her experiences.[148] In Alice she encountered "D. D. T. Jabavu, perhaps the most famous living South African native." She had been impressed by *The Segregation Fallacy* and told him so, but found her interview with him "was marred . . . by Mr. Ker[r] staying with us the whole time." Still, she "got the impression of a highly educated man, clearheaded and lively, with an important part to play as an intellectual pioneer of the Bantu, but not perhaps a man of great wisdom or force." Though she left the door open "to revise [her] hasty judgement," Kerr "confirmed it, saying that the father was the bigger man."[149] D. D. T. Jabavu's reaction to Margery Perham has not survived.

D. D. T. Jabavu did not lack detractors, but he counted among his supporters poets and composers who celebrated his accomplishments and enhanced his public image. M. M. Sihele's November 1929 poem, coinciding with Perham's visit, praised Jabavu as "you who is respected by whites."[150] That theme was echoed in "Hayi abant'Abamnyama" (Ho! the black people), a song by the composer Benjamin Tyamzashe (Henry's brother) that praised Jabavu with the line "khanda lomlungu Jili," translated as Jili (Jabavu's clan name), "the head [or brains] of a white man."[151] Meant as a compliment, it could just as easily be construed as an insult. Still, it was "Education and Brains"—a clear evocation of Wauchope's "paper and ink"—that Jabavu argued should be the weapons of choice when he spoke to the Cape Native Voters' Convention in Queenstown in December 1929. The battle, he told his audience, was over the right to vote and access to land; in Jabavu's words: "I have the right to vote by the ground I own. If we lose our lands we lose our vote."[152]

Access to land was the subject of Jabavu's speech in Sophiatown near Johannesburg a few days later. Perham was in the audience and her reaction to the speech made her an unwitting apologist for Hertzog's policies and underlined Jabavu's skills as an interpreter of complex legislation: "He worked through some of the laws, especially with regard to land. I am sure that most of what he said was true. But some was exaggerated. It was all a subtle piece of suggestion. 'The white man has taken 80 percent of your land and is now going to defraud you of the rest.'" Perham thought this a needless distortion of the well-deserved "counts against the white man," since the percentage was "based on the whole Union and the Bantu never advanced into a large proportion of its present area. And it must be said," Perham added, "that much of the land, especially the Transkei, is very good land, whereas his figures embrace huge areas of karoo or desert of little good to anyone, except for the most extensive farming."[153] Better informed commentators, Jabavu among them, were more familiar with the history of African land claims, and with the long-standing worries over soil erosion in the Transkei, which made it less than the best land.[154]

On the whole, Perham was "disgusted" by Jabavu's speech: "The natives, who worship academic qualifications, seem to regard him almost as a god. . . . But the longer he spoke the more I felt that it was a positive danger to have a man of his character exalted as a leader. Like Smuts on the other side, he is almost too clever at manipulating his own liberalism."[155] Perham did not explain precisely the danger Jabavu posed; after all, he possessed no real political power. The course he advocated, as recorded by Perham, was hardly a radical one: "He urged them to resist oppression, to collect money, to unite, to fight. But to fight with the pen and the brain, not the spear." In Perham's opinion, however, "a Professor's job is to teach and write and not direct political agitation," and Jabavu's audience, in any event "had, many of them, no pen and little political knowledge with which to fight."[156]

In contrast, Jabavu's own perception of his job as a professor included educating Africans about their political rights. This much was evident in his impassioned article on "Native Voting Rights," which appeared in *The Cape Times* on April 8, 1930.[157] Jabavu was responding to suggestions by "some of the best friends of the natives"—whom he did not identify—"that we should change our attitude towards the Prime Minister's franchise proposals and should offer to meet him halfway in regard to alterations in the Cape Native vote." Jabavu rejected any possibility of compromise on the franchise, and quoting Sol Plaatje of the ANC, wondered: "What sort of South Africa is to be expected if the Premier's native franchise proposals are rammed down the unwilling throats of the intelligent natives who are the united vanguard of Bantu progress?"[158] What the government was trying to do, from Jabavu's perspective, was force civilized and educated Africans back into an uncivilized state. For his part, Jabavu found it "hard to believe that the majority of Europeans in South Africa will for all time remain impervious to right dealing as they are in our day." While professing that "our fate is inevitable, our cause doomed," he still found room for optimism, noting that "the cause of Christianity itself was apparently doomed at one time."[159]

The following week Jabavu was back in the pages of *The Cape Times*, this time responding to a reporter's query about his opinion of the government's proposal to abolish the Native Conferences established under the Native Affairs Act of 1920, and held yearly between 1922 and 1926. Jabavu's response might be interpreted as a veiled threat or, in Perham's language, a manipulation of his own liberalism. If the government abandoned consultation with Africans, he asserted, it "would be putting back the clock of progress at least a decade." The abolition of the Native Conferences

> would supply ammunition for the guns of Communists, Anarchists and others who are constantly preaching disrespect of European authority. It will also discourage us, who have always been on the side of obedience to the Government and order in all our affairs, for we have become accustomed to act as the connecting link between the Government and our people on different legislation.

Ignoring the civilized African middlemen would be a disservice not only to Africans, but to all South Africans. Such a decision on the government's part, Jabavu contended, would "force us all into one camp as an opposition to the Government and European authority."[160]

Whether Jabavu's words had any effect or not, the Native Conference convened in Pretoria in December 1930 (for the first time in four years), despite the government's insistence that it did not feel it was "their duty to call together a Native Conference."[161] For Jabavu, the conference was unsettling, as he reported to Howard Pim: "Re the Native Bills, Marwick and Nicholls tackled me at Pretoria urging me to take Pelem's line and making all sorts of meretricious financial offers if I surrendered the present vote. I stood my ground all the more firmly as a result of the Women's enfranchisement and beat them."[162] "Pelem's line," at least in Marwick's and Nicholls's interpretation, was a willingness to relinquish the vote in the Cape Province for more land for Africans throughout the Union.

J. S. Marwick and Heaton Nicholls were South African Party MPs from Natal who were also members of the Joint Select Committee on the Native Bills, which had begun redrafting Hertzog's bills in 1930. Though the enfranchisement of white women in 1930[163] had further undermined the influence of black male voters in the Cape Province, it was not enough to satisfy Marwick and Nicholls. To the right even of Hertzog in their desire to abolish all African representation in parliament,[164] and on the outs with Smuts and most of the South African Party as a result,[165] they promised Jabavu that parliament would vote £30 million for the purchase of land in return for African support for the abolition of the franchise. Nicholls and Marwick then reported to Rheinallt Jones (the secretary of the SAIRR, of which Jabavu was a vice president) that Jabavu had agreed to the scheme. Rheinallt Jones suggested that Jabavu write to J. H. Hofmeyr, one of Smuts's chief advisers (and considered an ally by the liberal forces)[166] to deny the rumor.[167] Jabavu duly wrote to Hofmeyr denying all association with Nicholls's and Marwick's plan, and vowing "to die holding the fort of non-discrimination between citizens on grounds of race alone until the forces of Christianity, justice and civilisation become strong enough to overpower mutual suspicion."[168]

Having failed with Jabavu, Nicholls next approached fellow Natalian John Dube (who had been the SANNC's first president in 1912), where he met with more success. Dube toured throughout South Africa collecting signatures from prominent Africans allegedly favoring a compromise that would trade the vote for more land. Those who signed Dube's document included Jabavu's ally in the Ciskei, Meshach Pelem, as well as Selope Thema and H. Selby Msimang. Dube even went so far as to suggest that "Jabavu himself would be willing" to sign if he did not fear that he would "lose his influence."[169] An enraged Jabavu wrote to Rheinallt Jones: "I am totally opposed to signing this or any such document," adding, "Mr Dube had no authority to cadge for Cape signatures, as I have found out he has already done . . . in the Transkei; behind my back, as I am the recognised *President* of the Cape Native Voters' Convention and head of the Cape."[170] In 1930, on the issue of the franchise, Jabavu found himself at odds with Dube, and, seemingly, with many members of the African National Congress, including Pelem, Thema, and Msimang.

At the beginning of January 1931, Jabavu traveled to Bloemfontein to chair the third Non-European Conference. He did not contribute much to the discussions (which were dominated by the three rival branches of the now fractured ICU which had sent representatives to the conference),[171] though he did support a resolution to send a delegation to the United Kingdom to present the Non-European Conference's concerns to officials of the British government. To that end, the conference moved a "unity resolution,"[172] stressing the "urgent necessity of establishing a central body to be known as the *All Non-European Federal Council of South Africa*."

Pixley Seme, the newly elected conservative president of the ANC, dissented from the unity resolution, stating that "the non-European congress was endeavouring to throw dust in [our] eyes with its unification project. The whole thing . . . struck him as a conspiracy against the Europeans, and the A.N.C. was not going to be a party to it."[173] The charge was hotly denied by Alexander Jabavu in an editorial in *Imvo Zabantsundu* which, echoing his brother's sentiments, he titled "Disunity a Curse." "Dr. Seme or anyone else," he argued, "need not fear obliteration if his congress joins the Non-European Congress. It is the duty of every non-European to join forces in combating the laws of this country which discriminate against us by reason of being non-white." That particular admonition applied equally to the Industrial and Commercial Workers' Union, which Alexander Jabavu condemned for using the conference "as a court of appeal to settle differences among the I.C.U."[174]

The third Non-European Conference revealed that the popular movements (or at least those organizations that aspired to be mass movements)—in particular the ICU and the ANC—had fallen on hard times by 1931.[175] This was partly the result of internal disputes, but also the result of increased state repression, especially after the passage of the Riotous Assemblies (Amendment) Act in 1930.[176]

In the end, the Non-European Conference did send a delegation to the United Kingdom in 1931. Its sole representative was D. D. T. Jabavu, who stopped briefly in England on his way to the Student Volunteer Movement conference in New York, which was paying his way to the United States.[177] Jabavu hoped to persuade the British government to use its influence to get the South African government to rethink its Native Policy.[178] He met Malcolm MacDonald (the son of the British prime minister, Ramsay MacDonald) at the Colonial Office, and spoke before gatherings of the Royal Institute of International Affairs, the Society of London Interdenominational Ministers, the London Group for the Study of African Affairs, and the Society of Friends.[179] Sixteen speeches on "Native disabilities" to a variety of audiences garnered him sympathy but no action.

Back home, the debate over Hertzog's bills had settled into a holding pattern, as had the extraparliamentary opposition. At the 1933 European-Bantu Conference, Jabavu again railed against segregation and argued for the retention of the Cape African franchise.[180] Even his language was tired, recalling his 1926 article in the *International Review of Missions*: "The Black man does not ask for much—only for justice, justice in land distribution, justice in economic opportunity and justice in political representation."[181]

The turning point came in 1933, when Hertzog's National Party and Smuts's South African Party formed a coalition. There were a number of reasons for this decision. Both parties had been shaken by the impact of the worldwide depression of 1929 to 1932 on the South African economy.[182] The splintering of the Labour Party in 1928 and 1929 had reduced the National Party's parliamentary majority; within the South African Party, MPs from Natal were pushing for greater regional powers, and its Transvaal wing was seeking a rapprochement with the National Party. The coalition was a response to these problems, and in the May 1933 election, the combined party won 144 of 158 parliamentary seats.[183]

In December 1934 the two parties agreed to fuse into a single United Party, with Hertzog as prime minister and Smuts as deputy prime minister.[184] After nine years in opposition, Smuts was probably looking forward to exercising real power again.[185] Though one of the seven points on which Hertzog and Smuts had agreed to form a coalition in 1933 was a vaguely defined "solution of the 'native question' through the maintenance of 'white civilisation' and political separation,"[186] Smuts refused to agree to the abolition of the Cape African franchise, which he had long publicly supported. Thus the creation of the United Party did not result in a cohesive Native Policy, though fusion ultimately did make the passage of the Native Bills easier, opening the way for Hertzog to secure the two-thirds majority of a Joint Sitting of both houses of parliament necessary to abolish the Cape African franchise.[187]

After five years of deliberation, the Joint Select Committee on the Native Bills presented the bills to parliament in April 1935. Of the original four bills, only the Representation of Natives in Parliament Bill and the renamed Native Trust and Land Bill remained, and both had been modified. Under the terms of the 1935 Representation of Natives in Parliament Bill, no additional African voters would be placed on the Cape common roll, although those already on it would be allowed to remain. The Cape African vote would thus die out naturally with those who had exercised it. Africans throughout the Union would be represented by four elected senators,[188] in addition to the four nominated senators provided under the 1909 South Africa Act. A Natives' Representative Council (NRC) would supplement the Senate representation. The council would consist of the Secretary of Native Affairs, the five members of the Native Affairs Commission, four nominated African members, and twelve elected African members, for a total of twenty-two. Although its reports would be presented to both houses of parliament, the NRC would operate in a purely advisory capacity—it would not have any legislative authority.[189]

One important change had been made to the Native Trust and Land Bill. Rather than simply making more land available for purchase by Africans, parliament would purchase the land for them. The total amount of land to be purchased remained 15,225,000 acres (7.25 million morgen). Africans would ultimately have access to just over 13 percent of the Union's land, up from the 7 percent allotted under the 1913 Natives Land Act.[190] Together with the Representation of Natives in Parliament Bill, the Native Trust and Land Bill represented Hertzog's solution to South Africa's "Native problem."

The publication of the bills elicited an immediate response from black activists. Jabavu's first response to the tabling of the bills was forthright and pragmatic. In May 1935 he wrote to Rheinallt Jones: "I see no hope of saving the franchise, now that it has been abolished by agreement in the fusion party. Nevertheless I am prepared to give the government a full run for their money by dying hard so that we may go down fighting."[191] By August 1935 he had written a pamphlet, *Criticisms of the Native Bills*. After identifying the Cape African franchise as the central target of the bills and outlining his standard defense for its retention, Jabavu noted:

> We Black people generally divide the white race in this country, insofar as governing policy is concerned, into Dutch and English, or north and south, or repressive and liberal people. But this division has proved to be erroneous, because there are many important cross-currents that make such an artificial division doubtful.[192]

Heaton Nicholls, one of "the Englishmen of Natal, a province that boasts of its British traditions,"[193] with whom Jabavu had crossed swords in 1930, personified just how artificial the division was. A staunch segregationist, Nicholls pushed for an end to the nonracial franchise, and to prevent disfranchised Africans from posing a still greater threat, proposed a policy of trusteeship. Essentially, this was another word for "retribalization"; Nicholls hoped to "redirect the political development of Africans away from 'communism' by the revival of . . . 'communalism.'"[194] Nicholls's plan ran counter to everything Jabavu held dear and had fought for over the past decade. After the government was persuaded by the South African Institute of Race Relations to sponsor a series of regional Native Conferences in September 1935 to give Africans a chance to voice their objections to the bills,[195] Jabavu published a second pamphlet, titled *Native Views on the Native Bills*, in which he summarized the proceedings of the regional conferences, and took Nicholls to task.[196]

As if confronting white enemies was not struggle enough, in October 1935 Jabavu found himself questioning the loyalty of a white ally. Responding to a letter from E. J. Evans, the editor of the East London *Daily Dispatch*, Rheinallt Jones wrote, "the Cape African franchise as it is today will have to go." Evans then passed the information on to the East London Joint Council and "to a special meeting of local Europeans." Jabavu learned of the exchange of information during a trip to East London, and promptly wrote to Evans, informing him that he had "the authority of Mr. J. D. Rheinallt Jones to say that his views on the Native bills are absolutely identical with mine . . . namely, no compromise whatever nor weakening in the Cape Native vote."

Jabavu then wrote to Rheinallt Jones asking for a clarification of his position:

> As this situation seems to make you face both ways, and much importance is being attached to your apparent weakness on the franchise matter I write to ask you to give me what is the real position, so that I may know where exactly I stand, for I fear your name is going to be used by Mr Evans as against me and the multitudes of East London whites and blacks who are identified with me on this matter.

Rheinallt Jones immediately wrote to Evans, stressing that the SAIRR had taken no official position on the bills "beyond publishing a purely scientific and objective description and analysis," thus inadvertently acknowledging that the SAIRR's fact-finding, if not intentionally a political act, was clearly open to political interpretation. Stressing that he was expressing his personal opinion only, Rheinallt Jones informed Evans: "I am opposed to any system of political representation which does not recognise the right of qualified Natives to citizenship. In the consideration of any alternatives to the present Cape Native Franchise the safeguarding of the central principle of common citizenship is essential."[197] Though Rheinallt Jones's personal support was undoubtedly reassuring to Jabavu, his reluctance to take a public stance on the bills as secretary of the SAIRR sent an undeniably mixed message, which called into question the reliability of the "friends of the natives."[198]

THE ALL AFRICAN CONVENTION

In December 1935 Africans turned to each other, convening the first All African Convention (AAC) at Bloemfontein. The idea of holding a convention had originated with Alfred B. Xuma, a prominent Johannesburg physician who had not previously been active in politics, and with two members of the ANC—Z. R. Mahabane and Selope Thema (who five years earlier had supported the idea of trading the Cape African franchise for more land).[199] Keen to present a united front in opposition to Hertzog's bills, they proposed that Jabavu and Pixley Seme, then president of the ANC, serve as the co-conveners of the All African Convention.

Seme, however, proved a reluctant participant; the historian Peter Walshe has described his support for the AAC as "less than fulsome." Under Seme's tutelage, the ANC itself had lost its way, declining by 1935 into little more than a private political club.[200] Ultimately it was Xuma who would become the AAC's first vice president.[201] Jabavu for his part had never joined the ANC. Though party membership was less significant in the 1930s than it would later become (by 1940, for example, the ANC had only 1,000 members),[202] Jabavu did enjoy being the dominant presence in a given organization, as a 1964 interview with the Rev. James Calata suggested. A Xhosa clergyman who would serve as secretary-general of the ANC from 1936 to 1949, Calata observed of Jabavu: "When he came, he was the only man, graduate, who was outstanding and we spoilt him because we felt that nobody could compete with him, and he got into that habit and that mentality and he wouldn't join other bodies led by other people."[203]

The charge of arrogance was the very criticism that D. D. T. Jabavu had leveled against his father in his 1922 biography. Rather than join the SANNC in 1912, Tengo Jabavu had established the rival South African Races Congress. That its members were predominantly Mfengu had helped undermine Tengo Jabavu's influence as a spokesman for all Africans.

In the mid-1930s, however, African politics were relatively free of ethnic considerations; among the initiators of the All African Convention, Mahabane was Sotho, Thema was Pedi, and Xuma was Mpondo.[204] The proposed AAC was thus truly African, and for D. D. T. Jabavu this was part of its appeal. In May 1935 he had participated in the celebrations commemorating the centenary of the Mfengu pledge to the British in 1835, and had used the occasion as an opportunity to argue against the Xhosa-Mfengu divide and for greater African unity. Insisting that one of the "dangers which face us" is "hating other black people," Jabavu had asserted, "It is the whites who benefit by divide and rule. We do not benefit by it."[205] A month later, in June 1935, he responded enthusiastically to Xuma's invitation to chair the All African Convention.[206] Any boost to Jabavu's ego aside, it was fitting that after ten years of public agitation against any diminution of African rights, D. D. T. Jabavu should be offered the presidency of the AAC.[207]

The All African Convention held in Bloemfontein in mid-December 1935 gathered together over 400 delegates representing a wide variety of political, religious, and social organizations. The message sent to white South Africa was clear: "It is now due to the powers that be to pay regard to this united spontaneous expression of Black Africa on these Bills."[208]

The convention issued a long series of resolutions opposing both the Representation of Natives in Parliament Bill and the Native Trust and Land

Bill. Xuma was particularly critical of Chapter IV of the land bill, which permitted the eviction of African squatters from land not expressly legislated for their use. Echoing Jabavu's response to the Natives Land (1913) Amendment Bill first proposed by Hertzog in 1925, Xuma observed that the intent of the bill was clearly to create a permanent labor supply for white farmers near African areas, thereby condemning Africans to "everlasting economic slavery."[209] Xuma's resolution that the offending section be dropped from the bill passed unanimously. With respect to the representation bill, AAC delegates warned that denying Africans participation in the governing of their country "would inflame passions and fertilize soil on which propagandists will sow the seeds of discontent and unrest."[210] This was not the fate the AAC delegates wished for South Africa. The wiser path was to extend the franchise Union-wide, rather than eliminate it in the Cape.

In his address to the convention, Jabavu asserted: "There are Black men today fully capable of sitting and representing their people in the House of Assembly. Why are they not there?"[211] For D. D. T. Jabavu, these were the civilized men worthy of the equal rights enshrined in the old Cape liberal tradition. The convention delegates ratified Jabavu's implicit assumption, unanimously acknowledging the fairness of a civilization test in a supposedly democratic society. What they opposed in a democratic society was a civilization test based on color.[212]

The delegates further resolved to make no compromise in their opposition to the abolition of the Cape African franchise, to make a direct appeal to senators, MPs, and the governor-general to reject the bill, to make an appeal to King George V and the British parliament, and to send a deputation to the next session of the South African parliament to present the AAC's resolutions. Above all, the convention asked the government for more time to consider the bills.[213]

Neither the substance of the AAC's resolutions nor its plan for opposing the bills were without their critics. Writing in *Ilanga lase Natal* (The Natal sun) after the convention was over, John Dube expressed disappointment that the "proceedings of the Convention were throughout dominated by the one object of retaining the Cape franchise at all costs." The convention, he contended, "appeared to overlook the interests of the great mass of Bantu people and their urgent need for more land, in their desire to maintain for the privileged few, the right of franchise."[214] Clements Kadalie meanwhile argued against the AAC's approach, observing that past experience had proven the futility of deputations. Communist Party member John Gomas's critique took a different form; he urged the AAC to establish local committees to organize protest meetings and make the convention a truly activist mass organization.[215]

Despite these criticisms, Jabavu could observe in December 1935 that the "harmony of the Convention was remarkable, when one considers its conflicting elements of extremists, die-hards, moderates and those who actually favoured the Bills."[216] Walshe has described the convention as perhaps the most representative ever held,[217] but Edward Roux, in his study of black politics, dismissed the notion that the federally organized AAC, given the disarray of the ANC and the ICU—its largest member organizations—was representative of anyone but its 400 delegates.[218] There is little doubt, however, that the December 1935 meeting marked the high point of D. D. T. Jabavu's prominence as a spokesman for African rights.

The harmony extended to the public meeting called by the AAC and sponsored by the Joint Councils in Cape Town on January 19, 1936. For the AAC it was a day of prayer, during which Africans asked "for the Almighty's guidance and intervention in the dark cloud of the pending disfranchisement of the Cape Natives by the Parliament of South Africa."[219] The Almighty ultimately failed to intervene, and D. D. T. Jabavu's long fall from political grace began.

5 The Fall of an African Politician, 1936–1948

D. D. T. Jabavu's fall from political grace began with a meeting between the All African Convention and Prime Minister Hertzog during the first week of February 1936.[1] Led by Jabavu, the AAC delegation included A. W. G. Champion, H. Selby Msimang, Z. R. Mahabane, A. S. Mtimkulu, and R. H. Godlo.[2] The meeting had been arranged (but was not attended) by Smuts, who considered the Senate representation and the Natives' Representative Council proposed under the Representation of Natives in Parliament Bill inadequate compensation for Africans who would lose the common franchise in the Cape Province.

Though Hertzog had resisted any concessions concerning the representation bill before his meeting with the AAC, after the meeting he proposed extensive changes. Rather than gradually eliminating the African franchise by adding no new African voters to the common roll in the Cape, as proposed under the 1935 version (no. 1) of the bill, the new version (no. 2) would place African voters in the Cape on a separate roll. Further voters could be added to the roll, and African voters would continue to exercise an individual vote, electing three European members to the House of Assembly, and two Cape provincial councillors. The Senate representation and the Natives' Representative Council, which had been outlined in version no. 1 of the bill, were retained in version no. 2 and, according to the historian W. K. Hancock, Smuts considered these changes, together with the additional land allocated under the Native Trust and Land Bill, sufficient compensation for the loss of the nonracial franchise in the Cape.[3]

The origins of what D. D. T. Jabavu would later call the "notorious compromise" bill (or version no. 2) remain murky. Both Hertzog and Smuts maintained that the compromise bill had been proposed by the AAC delegation.[4] Yet Smuts had written of Jabavu to friends in September 1935: "from repeated conversations his views are well known to me. He approves our whole

121

scheme—with the single and vital exception of the Cape Native Franchise. Here he will never budge, and I certainly don't blame him."[5] Smuts was perhaps a trifle optimistic in his assessment of Jabavu's position, since protecting the franchise demanded that he reject any land deal that threatened African voting rights, as the AAC had done at its conference in December 1935. Hertzog's collected papers also fail to shed any light on his February 1936 meeting with the AAC delegation;[6] thus what transpired at the meeting to change Hertzog's mind remains a bit of a mystery.

According to Walshe, however, the "compromise originated with a group of Eastern Province MPs who took the initiative in contacting Jabavu and later Godlo . . . and Mahabane." In those discussions, Jabavu and his colleagues stressed their opposition to any change to the Cape African franchise, but they muddied the waters by suggesting that they would privately support any efforts to retain the common franchise if their own public efforts failed. The eastern Cape MPs apparently misinterpreted this as unqualified AAC support for the compromise of a separate roll for Cape African voters.[7]

While waiting to speak with Hertzog again, the AAC delegation recalled its executive to Cape Town. On the evening of February 14, they held a public meeting to "clear the air," where they decided they could not accept any compromise in contravention of the mandate from the December 1935 Bloemfontein convention. They rejected Hertzog's revised Representation of Natives in Parliament Bill. Although they planned to issue a unity resolution outlining the AAC position,[8] Umteteli wa Bantu (The mouthpiece of the African peoples)[9] beat them to the presses. On February 15 Umteteli reported, probably in reference to the private support but public rejection of compromise distinction made by Jabavu and his colleagues, "Bantu Divided on Native Bills," adding: "It is thought that much will depend on the ultimate decision of Professor Jabavu."[10]

When Hertzog introduced the Representation of Natives in Parliament Bill (J.S. 2-'36) on February 17, 1936, it contained—despite the objections of the AAC delegation—the proposed separate roll for African voters in the Cape Province.[11] The blame for accepting the separate roll and betraying the resolutions of the All African Convention fell on the shoulders of D. D. T. Jabavu. Family history seemed to be repeating itself. Tengo Jabavu had lost his political reputation when he supported the 1913 Natives Land Act; now, in an ironic twist, D. D. T. Jabavu's political reputation came under attack at another turning point in South African history.

Prominent Africans, including A. B. Xuma, then vice president of the AAC, suspected that Jabavu had agreed to the separate roll for Cape African voters.[12] I. B. Tabata, in his history of the AAC, expressed no doubt that Jabavu and the AAC deputation had accepted the compromise, and he depicted the educated African elite of the AAC as naive pawns of opportunistic white liberals.[13] Certainly Jabavu's ties to white liberals were close, as a letter from Maurice Webb of the South African Institute of Race Relations to Edgar Brookes in late February 1936 indicated:

> For your own information Grant tells me that Jabavu is privately inclined to accept the compromise, albeit with reluctance. He will not publicly do so as he feels that he is tied to the findings of the Bloemfontein Conference. I asked Grant if I might pass this on to you knowing that you are anxious to know where D. D. T. J. stands. He said, Yes, with the obvious reservations that he was conveying his impression, and must not commit Jabavu.[14]

White liberals were a favorite target of Tabata, an AAC stalwart in the 1930s who would go on to establish the Trotskyist-influenced Non-European Unity Movement (NEUM) in 1943, though more recently the historian Paul Rich has also questioned the sincerity of white liberals.[15] Still, it is worth acknowledging that the orientation of most of the "friends of the natives" remained fundamentally pragmatic in 1936. If in the heyday of liberal segregationism in the mid-1920s they had seen the African franchise as a "potential menace," by the 1930s they "dismissed it as a useless institution"[16] which they defended with ambivalence.

Yet not everyone believed that Jabavu was to blame. In a letter to the editor of *Umteteli wa Bantu* which suggested that not all white liberals were pragmatists in the 1930s, R. F. A. Hoernlé, O. D. Schreiner, and W. H. Ramsbottom of the Johannesburg Joint Council questioned the principles of the "so-called" liberal MPs from the Cape, and suggested that the compromise had allowed them to vote, with clearer consciences, for a bill they wanted to support. Ramsbottom also wrote directly to Hertzog, proposing—in an adaptation of the Cape liberal tradition similar to that Smuts had privately suggested in the late 1920s—that the franchise be extended Union-wide, but include an education qualification high enough to limit the number of African voters.[17] In their letter to *Umteteli*, Hoernlé, Schreiner, and Ramsbottom questioned Hertzog's motives in accepting the compromise, noting that it spared Hertzog from relying on D. F. Malan, who had broken away from the National Party in 1934 to form the Purified National Party in opposition to the new United Party.[18] Malan's defection had threatened Hertzog's prospects for getting his two-thirds majority. Accepting the compromise bill brought the eastern Cape MPs on board and saved Hertzog from having to rely on Malan,[19] who opposed the United Party in general, and any representation (including Senate representation) for Africans in particular.[20] In this interpretation of the compromise process, whether Jabavu or any of his colleagues willingly accepted the changes to the Representation of Natives in Parliament Bill was of little relevance.

Similarly, in a 1988 interview, Wycliffe Tsosti, who succeeded Jabavu as president of the AAC in 1948, stated that while Jabavu "was not the villain, he was surrounded by villains."[21] Though Tsotsi did not name names, Msimang was a member of the AAC deputation, and Dube and Thema were among the members of the AAC executive called to Cape Town in mid-February 1936. All three had expressed their willingness in 1931 to trade the vote for more land.[22] For his part, D. D. T. Jabavu's statements over the period from 1925 to 1936 establish that he was neither politically naive nor above criticizing his white allies. Nevertheless, before the dust had cleared in March 1936, Jabavu felt compelled to issue—through the SAIRR—an official denial that the AAC had accepted the compromise bill.[23]

THE ALL AFRICAN CONVENTION, 1936–1937

The Representation of Natives in Parliament Bill passed by a vote of 168 to 11 in April 1936. The dissenting MPs (five of whom were from the Cape) were led by Smuts's close ally J. H. Hofmeyr, who opposed the "qualified, inferior citizenship" the act granted Africans.[24] Jabavu wrote to thank Hofmeyr; he did not contact Smuts.[25] Smuts had voted in favor of the bill, though the historian Jeremy Krikler has argued that the "odd and unconvincing argument . . . Smuts used to justify his support of Hertzog" revealed that "he had not rationally accepted the abolition of the Cape franchise: 'I have always consistently maintained the position, and I do still take the position that if the Cape native franchise has to be taken away, it must only be for the very gravest of reasons." Yet Smuts did not identify those grave reasons, other than to argue illogically that he was voting to abolish the old Cape nonracial franchise because the Cape African franchise "was in danger of being taken away by Parliament."[26] The Native Trust and Land Bill passed in June 1936,[27] and Hertzog had achieved his goal of a coherent Union-wide Native Policy.

At the end of June 1936 the AAC met for a second time, in an emergency session to discuss the recent enactment of the Hertzog bills. Only 206 delegates attended, down from 400 the previous December. The AAC's reason for existence had been to protest against the bills, and *Umteteli wa Bantu* argued that their passage had "sealed the fate" of the organization. Similarly, the Communist Party newspaper *Umsebenzi* (The worker)—on the opposite end of the political spectrum from the Chamber of Mines–backed *Umteteli wa Bantu*—was losing patience with the AAC, and criticized its leaders for "Wasting Time and Energy on Trivialities." The Communist Party saw the AAC (as I. B. Tabata later would), as a parliament for Africans, and what they wanted from the AAC was action and unity and leadership. In 1936, however, the AAC's potential for action was limited by its shoestring budget of £100, the bulk of which went to printing the conference minutes.[28]

That the All African Convention in defeat did not cease to exist owed a great deal to D. D. T. Jabavu. Depending on the perspective of the critic, he was motivated by either altruism or egoism. In his June 1936 presidential address, he urged delegates to develop a "world outlook" on the incidence of repression and to realize that "the supreme task of this Convention is to protect the interest of Africans not only in the Union but in all Africa."[29] It was Italy's invasion of Abyssinia in October 1935 that inspired Jabavu's embrace of Pan-Africanism:[30]

> All Africans, as well as all other non-White races of the world have been staggered by the cynical rape by Italy of the last Independent State belonging to indigenous Africans. After hearing a great deal for twenty years about the rights of small nations, self-determination, Christian ideals, the inviolability of treaties, humane warfare, the sacredness of one's plighted word, the glory of European civilisation, and so forth, the brief history of the last eight months have scratched this European veneer and revealed the White savage hidden beneath.[31]

The parallel Jabavu was attempting to draw was clear: South Africa had figuratively raped its black citizens as effectively as Italy had Abyssinia. The white savage had revealed himself to his black ward. Civilization, Christian morality, and the prospect of common citizenship crumbled in the face of the onslaught. It was the most radical public stance D. D. T. Jabavu ever took, and it seems to have been quite calculated.

While the white press engaged in yellow journalism—the *Natal Advertiser* reported the speech under the headline "Civilisation Denounced . . . Speech by Professor Jabavu," and *The Cape Mercury* titled its article "Professor Jabavu's Assault on White Civilisation"[32]—whites were not Jabavu's target audience. Jabavu's concern was the emergence of H. Selby Msimang (who had signed Dube's 1931 petition supporting the abolition of the African franchise in return for more land), as a prominent—and divisive—voice within the AAC. In March 1936 Msimang published *The Crisis*, in which he argued that the passage of the Native Bills meant that Africans "are not part of the South African community . . . between the European and ourselves there is no longer any community of interests." He then proposed the solution Mahabane had suggested in 1923: "it behoves us to demand a complete segregation on a fifty-fifty basis to enable us to establish our own State and government wherein to exercise our political, economic and social independence without the inconvenience of islands dotted all over the country."[33] In April 1936 Msimang sent Jabavu a copy of his "Programme of Action," in which he advocated that the AAC completely reject the legitimacy of the white South African government and demand the division of South Africa into two exclusive states—one white and one African.[34] Jabavu's response was not favorable, as he wrote to Rheinallt Jones in mid-June: "I have nothing to do with the document in question. . . . I have not approved it, because I am waiting for its consideration together with the others" at the AAC conference.[35]

At the June 1936 conference of the AAC, Jabavu's condemnation of Italy was thus a skillful diversion in an essentially moderate speech.[36] The AAC felt compelled to respond publicly to the new acts, and Jabavu proposed three options. The first was to boycott the new acts, which would "startle White South Africa, attract the notice of the rest of the world and win our rights by using the fear of bloody revolution as a weapon of propaganda." The problem with engaging in revolution, Jabavu contended, was that it required complete unity of action among Africans—which did not exist—and even if it did, one could not be sure of what the outcome would be. The second option was unconditional acceptance of the acts, which offered no advantages since it required that Africans recognize the laws as just. Jabavu favored the third option: "To evolve an intermediary policy of using what can be used and fighting against all that we do not want."[37] This was in essence the path of least resistance and, in Jabavu's opinion, of greatest potential advantage. It was also the path favored by Jabavu's white allies in the South African Institute of Race Relations, and at the end of the conference, Jabavu could report to Rheinallt Jones: "All went O.K. at [Bloemfontein] and we rejected that insidious propaganda of illegal action and concentrated on constructive work throughout."[38]

The "Programme of Action" ultimately adopted by the AAC in June 1936 was far removed from Msimang's, and he eventually left the AAC and joined the ANC.[39] There were resolutions of protest directed against the Representation of Natives in Parliament Act and the Native Trust and Land Act, and a special resolution condemning the Italian invasion of Abyssinia,[40] but protest continued to take place largely through meetings, petitions, and deputations. The AAC executive did set itself two tangible goals. The first was to draft a constitution for the AAC, to be ratified at the next conference scheduled for December 1937. The second was to establish a National Shilling Fund for Food, Land and Freedom, the goal of which was to help people to help themselves. "There is much to be done," Jabavu concluded in June 1936. In another nod to Pan-Africanism, and indeed to internationalism, he added: "The work is great but the laborers are few. We appeal also to the rest of Africa and overseas to all peoples of African descent and other non-White races, as well as white races who are in sympathy with our universal cause."[41]

D. D. T. Jabavu went overseas for a third time in September 1937 to attend the Friends World Conference in Philadelphia. While the conference report makes no mention of his participation beyond his presence, several of the commissions convened by delegates—including "The Individual Christian and the State," "Methods of Achieving Economic Justice," and "Methods of Achieving Racial Justice"—would have been of interest to him.[42] Though Jabavu had joined the Society of Friends while at school in England in 1914, he was a Quaker in spirit only and an ecumenist in practice. Nevertheless for Jabavu, as an individual Christian facing the state, much of what the delegates had to say could easily have described recent events in South Africa: "Two great obstacles to the development of the world-wide community of life are the conception that national sovereignty absolves a state from ordinary moral judgments and that its natural end is power over other people and in opposition to them." The Quakers' charge "to struggle against inertia in political life," and their assertion that "our loyalty is not only to the state as it is, but as it may become,"[43] in a sense embodied Jabavu's own agenda in the United States—to spread the message of the All African Convention.

He did this in New York on September 7, 1937,[44] at the invitation of Max Yergan, who had been elected the AAC's Secretary for External Affairs after he left South Africa in 1936.[45] What Jabavu said was not recorded, though part of his agenda was to feel out support and possible funding for the idea of his retiring from teaching to become the full-time paid president of the AAC.[46] Yergan's plans for the AAC as outlined in his 1937 report were equally grand. To encourage interest in South Africa, he had established the International Committee on African Affairs, whose goals were research, education, and facilitating cooperation among African peoples both on the continent and of the diaspora. He hoped to persuade England and France (with their colonial interests in Africa) and the United States (with its large African-American population) both to fund his programs and to rethink their policies toward black people.[47] To promote the interests of the AAC further, Yergan had also joined the National Negro Congress, which shared Yergan's (and the AAC's) focus on "improved working conditions, increased wages, more political rights, better housing and health conditions, and improved educational facilities" for blacks.[48]

Jabavu addressed these issues himself when he stopped in England on his way back to South Africa. At a meeting at Friends House in London, he outlined the terms of the Representation of Natives in Parliament Act, the

Native Trust and Land Act, and the Native Laws Amendment Act. This last act had passed in 1937. As Jabavu related, "It laid down, among other things, that no black man may own a house or land in any urban area: that each town is to be asked how many natives it thinks necessary for its labour supply, and the town clerk is to make a sort of Domesday book of the 'surplus' population to be evicted." He also argued, as he had done in London in December 1931, against the transfer of the Protectorates to South Africa, still very much an issue in 1937. At least part of the solution to combatting the increasing oppression of black South Africans was "wider publicity for African affairs and . . . an awakening of public opinion."[49]

Jabavu himself had just such an opportunity when he was interviewed on television by the British Broadcasting Corporation on September 15, 1937. The interviewer, Hubert W. Peet, tried to keep the conversation light, asking Jabavu about teaching at Fort Hare and about the pronunciation of Xhosa, but Jabavu still managed to promote the AAC: "I've the honour of being president of the All African Convention. This is a federation of all kinds of Bantu organisations—farmers, teachers, and so on, which consult together to promote the advancement and to protect the interests of the Native Race in South Africa."[50]

The third AAC conference "to protect the interests of the Native Race" was convened at Bloemfontein in December 1937. Only 130 delegates attended,[51] a reflection perhaps of Jabavu's still bruised reputation. Among the delegates was the African-American political scientist Ralph J. Bunche,[52] who attended the AAC conference at the invitation of Z. K. Matthews, whom Bunche had met while Matthews was studying in the United States.[53] According to Bunche:

> Matthews says Jabavu is becoming a mistrusted leader—feeling is growing that he will sell out to the whites or compromise too greatly. They say he was tickled pink when some white M.P. protested against the extension of the native curfew laws 'to educate[d] natives like Jabavu'—and flattered that his name was mentioned in Parliament; gloated that he had been thus able to save the educated native from this humiliation.

Matthews apparently favored disfranchising all Africans to encourage unity.[54] Yet whatever misgivings Matthews had, he did not express them publicly and though he joined the ANC in 1940, he remained a member of the AAC until 1943.[55] Bunche himself found Jabavu quite engaging: "Jabavu is a really comical old fellow. He had my sides splitting with the travelogue, graphically illustrated by grotesque gestures, of his recent trip to America to attend the Quaker meeting,"[56] but the negative image was reinforced when Bunche met Rheinallt Jones. Rheinallt Jones, Bunche recorded, "is skeptical about

Jabavu—he thinks the old man is untrustworthy and far behind the caliber of Matthews."[57]

Jabavu's public radicalism at the June 1936 conference of the AAC had clearly contradicted his private assurances to Rheinallt Jones, and Matthews's intellectual gifts did indeed exceed Jabavu's. Matthews earned his degree from the South African Native College in the proscribed four years, and held a master's degree from Yale University.[58] While Rheinallt Jones found Matthews more trustworthy than Jabavu in 1937, by the late 1940s and early 1950s, Matthews would far eclipse Jabavu as a spokesman for African nationalism.[59] For their part, many prominent black politicians—Matthews and later Tabata among them—became increasingly uneasy about Jabavu's close ties to white liberals. Thus it was Jabavu's tragedy after the passage of the Native Bills in 1936 to be thought too radical by some of his white liberal allies and too conservative by many of his African colleagues.

Nevertheless, in December 1937 D. D. T. Jabavu remained president of the All African Convention, in part because of the continuing power vacuum in African politics (though an increasingly revitalized ANC had sponsored a conference on African unity in the Transvaal in August 1937),[60] and in part, as A. P. Mda recalled, because Jabavu remained "a respected national figure who could draw delegates to a conference where they could then be politicized."[61] Mda, then twenty-one years old, attended the 1937 AAC conference, only to dismiss the AAC as "devoid of substance and inspiration."[62] Yet delegates to the conference were hardly morose. Xuma as vice president asserted: "Anyone who will endeavour to wreck the principle of unity that gave birth to the All African Convention will be doing so for personal reasons and will be a traitor to Africa."[63]

Unity, and an understandable pragmatism, were also central to the AAC constitution passed at the conference, the preamble of which stated:

> Whereas it is expedient in view of the situation created by the 'Native' Policy of segregation, discrimination and other repressive measures definitely adopted by the Government and Parliament of the Union of South Africa . . . the African races of South Africa as a national entity and unit should henceforth speak with one voice, meet and act in unity in all matters of national concern.[64]

Xuma's puffing aside, the AAC was not even united within. While many AAC members thought that the Natives' Representative Council should be "given a try," neither Jabavu nor Xuma, despite their prominence, ever ran for it.[65] Xuma, cynical after the passage of the Native Bills, did not consider the "government-controlled body . . . promising."[66] Jabavu's reluctance to run for the NRC[67] may have been rooted in a similar desire to distance himself from a government with which he had so recently been suspected of collaborating (including by his vice president, Xuma). Or, he may have still been hoping in December 1937 to become the full-time paid president of the AAC. Though Jabavu's own opinion of the NRC alternated between criticism and praise, his younger brother Alexander did run for election as an AAC candidate and sat as a member of the NRC from 1937 to 1942.[68] Despite these internal contradictions, the AAC in 1937 proclaimed itself the voice of the African people, devoted to "act in unity in developing political and economic power."[69]

THE ALL AFRICAN CONVENTION, 1940–1943

Under its new constitution the AAC met every three years, and when it did so in December 1940 the world had changed dramatically. The United Party government had split in September 1939 over the issue of South African participation in the Second World War. Hertzog as prime minister argued for neutrality, Smuts as his deputy favored joining Britain against Germany. The House of Assembly voted eighty to sixty-seven to enter the war, and Smuts again became prime minister, with J. H. Hofmeyr as his deputy.[70] Though many African leaders hoped that the combination of Smuts and Hofmeyr might lead to a lessening of segregation, they would be disappointed.[71]

When the executive committees of the AAC and the ANC met in July 1940, they passed a Resolution on the War. The resolution expressed "their loyal sympathy with the British Commonwealth of Nations in the difficult task that has been thrust upon it," and urged the government to "consider the expediency of admitting the Africans of this country into full citizenship in the Union with all the rights and duties appertaining to that citizenship," including the right to bear arms.[72] When Jabavu was criticized at the December 1940 meeting of the AAC for "not giving a lead on the war problem" as president, he defended himself by referring delegates back to the July resolution,[73] though he did remain largely silent on the issue of the war. By March 1942 Smuts, faced with the prospect of protecting 1,500 miles of coastline, was seriously considering arming black South Africans. When he proposed the idea to parliament, the Nationalist opposition "seized greedily at this opening to inflame passions and exploit prejudices. Fancy arming the Natives, who are likely to use their weapons against the Whites!" Ultimately nothing came of the proposal.[74]

When the AAC and the ANC met in December 1940, at the top of their agenda was a recognition of the need to clarify the relationship between the two organizations. A considerable overlap in membership remained, although Xuma had replaced Mahabane as president of the ANC and Mahabane had replaced Xuma as vice president of the AAC.[75] Writing to Jabavu, the ANC's secretary-general, James Calata, proposed that the All African Convention appoint "a committee of three representatives to meet in joint committee [with] three representatives from the African National Congress to consider how the two bodies could co-operate to bring about a united effort in the political struggle of the race."[76] In December 1940 the joint committee—composed of the presidents, chairmen, and secretaries of the AAC and the ANC—were able to reach an agreement, vague though it was. The ANC, they decided, "shall confine itself to the political aspirations and constitutional rights of the Africans and to other cognate matters," while the AAC "shall be the co-ordinating and consultative committee of African National organisations dealing with social, educational, economic, political and industrial matters."[77]

This was more of a recipe for disagreement than cooperation, as a February 1941 article in *Inkundla ya Bantu* suggested. *Inkundla*, though sympathetic to the ANC, was notable for its even-handedness in dealing with African politics. The article referred to the AAC as a "dying ember," and offered a cutting assessment of D. D. T. Jabavu: "It was when he failed to venture on a boycott of the Bills that his influence waved [*sic*] . . . this was the climax of his almost life-time struggle . . . for the African cause. Men in high public places err once and surely thereafter their way is downwards."[78]

In fact at the December 1940 conference of the AAC, only sixty delegates showed up, making moot the question of how representative the AAC actually was. The delegates included Rheinallt Jones, who had been elected to the Senate representing Africans in the Transvaal in 1937. Forsaking the apolitical stance he had previously insisted on as secretary of the South African Institute of Race Relations, Rheinallt Jones "urged closer co-operation between organised bodies and Parliamentary representatives."[79] Rheinallt Jones's decision, along with other white liberals, to enter parliamentary politics (Edgar Brookes was also a senator)[80] was less inconsistent with the approach of the SAIRR than it appeared on the surface. While the SAIRR concerned itself with collecting statistics on African welfare, liberals in parliament, Rheinallt Jones assured the AAC, took this process one step further and pushed for more land, better wages, "the removal of the colour bar, and the granting of pensions to Africans."[81] Jabavu for his part questioned the whole structure that Rheinallt Jones had embraced, observing: "Three years have gone by and one wonders whether the Government makes proper use of our Members of the Representative Council as we anticipated. . . . it appears to act in a merely advisory capacity to the Native Affairs Department."[82]

At the special session of the AAC called in December 1941, I. B. Tabata, who was emerging as the organization's dominant voice, criticized both the Natives'

Representative Council, which he dismissed as "a complete dud. . . . neither Native nor Representative nor Council,"[83] and the white representatives of Africans in parliament, who pled for Africans in "the same way that any White liberal, churchman or Joint Council man pleads. The African is your greatest asset, so it is not wise to waste it so recklessly and kill the hen that lays the golden eggs." He had nothing personally against these white representatives, Tabata hastened to add, for "they are only members of their class. They are liberals and as such they are unable to see the African really as an equal."[84]

In Tabata's opinion, Msimang had been right to call for a boycott of the Native Bills in 1936, but the real problem for Africans was not the farcical unrepresentative structure—which Tabata rejected outright—but rather the lack of leadership. In the six years of its existence, he argued, the AAC had "failed to achieve any positive results in the struggle for the liberation of our people."[85] Part of the blame lay with the ANC, which from "the outset . . . was lukewarm towards the Convention and reluctantly joined it."[86] Indeed, only a few days before Tabata's speech, A. B. Xuma had declared in his presidential address to the 1941 ANC conference that "the African National Congress is the mouthpiece of the African people of the Union of South Africa."[87] The ANC, however, bore only part of the blame for the weakness of the AAC. The AAC had burdened itself with a cumbersome "Federal constitution, meetings every three years," and had made no attempt to establish any branches of the main organization.[88] Add the dictatorial and bureaucratic nature of the AAC leadership to the mix, Tabata asserted, and "you will understand why there are not 400 delegates as in the first session, why the people don't talk Convention, and why they have lost faith in it."[89] There were in fact only forty-seven delegates at the 1941 meeting, and the official minutes acknowledged only the "somewhat warm debate" in which Tabata had participated.[90]

Tabata was a Trotskyist,[91] but the growing division within the AAC was arguably as much generational as ideological. Jabavu was fifty-six in 1941, and Mahabane, his vice president, was sixty, while Tabata was thirty-three.[92] Though Tabata had lost faith in the AAC's old guard, he had not lost faith in the AAC's potential to become the legitimate parliament of the African people—more legitimate than the ANC, which in its twenty-nine-year history, Tabata asserted, had proved to be "no threat . . . at all"[93] to a succession of white governments. To his colleagues in 1941 who pointed to the powerlessness of the AAC, Tabata answered, "That may be so. But there is still one thing the Convention can do. Tell our people the truth about the N.R.C. Tell them what it is and what it stands for. In exposing deception it can do the greatest service to our people."[94]

What D. D. T. Jabavu thought of Tabata's outburst in 1941 is not a matter of record. In 1942, however, he did offer some of his own criticisms of African political representation, published—significantly enough—in a SAIRR pamphlet. "Some Criticisms of the Act and Its Results" reflected just how far apart he and Tabata had grown. While acknowledging that the "method of election is extremely unsatisfactory," Jabavu insisted that the "work of the representatives, all round, cannot be too highly praised. We are satisfied with their work under really trying circumstances. We owe them a big debt of gratitude."[95]

This theme carried over into Jabavu's rather more critical analysis of the Atlantic Charter, in which he again praised the NRC, whose representatives had "rightly pressed the government for a clear interpretation" of the charter in November 1942.[96] The Atlantic Charter had been jointly issued in August 1941 by the American president, Franklin Roosevelt, and the British prime minister, Winston Churchill, who envisioned a world free from "war, want, tyranny, and fear." [97] The charter outlined the principles on which a democratic world order would be built after the defeat of Nazi Germany.[98]

Smuts had embraced the charter, and for a brief period in the early 1940s it did appear that his government was moving toward a dismantling of the system of segregation it had inherited from Hertzog. Under Smuts's direction, the government appointed a Social and Economic Planning Council to consider postwar reforms, and an Inter-Departmental Committee to study how to improve living conditions for Africans in urban areas. In a speech to the South African Institute of Race Relations in January 1942, Smuts declared segregation a failure, and the government approved increased pensions, workmen's compensation, unemployment insurance, health benefits, and secondary education opportunities for Africans. "The liberal reforms adumbrated in 1942," Davenport has maintained, "unleashed a predictable reaction" both from the more conservative members of the governing United Party and from the Nationalist opposition,[99] and reform fell victim to the United Party's need to win the next election.

Jabavu's June 1943 assessment of the Atlantic Charter reflected his disenchantment with Smuts's government:

> The original terms of the Charter are couched in grandiose language that easily satisfies complacent communities that find this world a fairly comfortable place to live in. But in the case of the Black races that inhabit South Africa, this charter can mean something great and epochal if given a close and conscientious interpretation by the rulers that be. On the other hand, it may amount to nothing more than empty words.

Only if the application of the charter in South Africa fulfilled its promise and let Africans choose the form of their government and participate in it, accorded Africans land rights, and ended racial discrimination, could it have any real impact. If the charter did not achieve these goals, then it was, in Jabavu's opinion, "an empty shell so far as Africans are concerned."[100] Jabavu's implicit criticisms of the Smuts government's response to the charter gave him some common ground with Tabata, even as his support for the Natives' Representative Council put him at odds with the younger man. Still, at heart Jabavu remained a liberal in the old Cape tradition, a philosophy Tabata found barely tolerable.

Coinciding with Jabavu's statement on the Atlantic Charter in June 1943, Tabata's Western Province Committee of the AAC (WP) issued "Calling All Africans," a four-page history of the AAC that invited Coloureds and Indians to join Africans at the December 1943 convention of the AAC, in unity against the oppressive white government.[101] In July 1943 the AAC (WP) drafted a "Manifesto of the All African Convention," which was subsequently redrafted as "A Call to Unity" in August 1943.[102] On July 6, 1943, Tabata sent a curt letter to Jabavu requesting that he attend a meeting of the AAC (WP) in Cape Town, apparently to discuss the manifesto. Jabavu had written to Tabata at the end of June to inquire where Tabata thought they might find funding for delegates to attend the AAC conference in December, and suggesting that he himself might not attend in the absence of such funding. Though the government had often approved discounted rail tickets for African conference delegates,[103] Tabata responded that delegates could turn to their own organizations for assistance, and that many of them were in any event "men of means," and that even for those who were not, the time had come for them "as leaders of their people . . . to make some sacrifices for their race." Tabata admitted to finding Jabavu's suggestion that he might not attend "very disturbing. . . . It would not do to hold such an important meeting in the absence of its President." He then proposed moving the AAC convention from Bloemfontein to Queenstown to make it cheaper for Jabavu to attend, but revealed his disdain for the older man's penny-pinching by insisting that he travel to Cape Town immediately to attend the AAC (WP) meeting on July 11th.[104]

Whether Jabavu attended the meeting is unclear. What is certain is that in September 1943 he sent a copy of the AAC (WP) "Manifesto" to Rheinallt Jones.[105] Neither the July 1943 version nor the updated version adopted by the AAC executive committee on August 26, 1943[106] was particularly radical. Indeed, the August 1943 "Call to Unity," while it reiterated many of the points Tabata had made in his 1941 speech to the AAC, was notably gentler in tone: "Now is not the time to start with recriminations as to who was responsible, whether it was the failure of the leadership or the apathy of the masses. It is of far greater importance for us to realise our mistakes, to learn from them and to find a way out."[107] Africans, Tabata argued, had to accept that they would achieve nothing by humbly pleading with a government intent on keeping them slaves.[108] There was only one option left: "to fight for our rights as citizens of our country." The way to go about it was to forge a united front with Coloureds, who had established the Anti-CAD in February 1943 to protest the government's establishment of the segregationist Coloured Affairs Department (CAD), and with Indians whose South African Indian Congress (SAIC)—established in 1923—was enjoying a renaissance as Indians' rights also came under government attack.[109]

To that end, the AAC and the Anti-CAD drafted a "declaration of unity" that included a ten-point program of demands. The declaration condemned segregation and demanded equal citizenship for all non-whites. In its assertion "that the continuation of the present system in South Africa, so similar to the Nazi system of Herrenvolk, although it may lead to . . . temporary prosperity for the ruling class and race, must inevitably be at the expense of the Non-Europeans and lead to their ruination," the program was not far removed from the position of many liberal critics of the government's policies.[110] The rather minimalist ten-point program (almost literally ten declarative sentences) was, as the political scientist Thomas Karis has pointed out, "notably lacking in Marxist formulations."[111] It demanded the introduction of universal adult suffrage, compulsory free education, freedom of speech, press, and assembly, and "full equality of rights for all citizens without distinction of race, colour and sex." Perhaps its most radical formulation was a demand for the "*revision of the land question in accordance with the above.*"[112]

Publication of the "Call to Unity" was delayed until December 1943, largely because, as Tabata wrote to his friend and colleague A. C. Jordan, "Jili grab[bed] the manifesto and hand[ed] it to the govt via Rheinallt Jones."[113] Despite Tabata's increasing invective against white liberals, Jabavu had remained a member of the South African Institute of Race Relations.[114] His stated motive for sending the proclamation to Rheinallt Jones (the secretary of the SAIRR) was to secure funding for its printing,[115] and more than likely Jabavu felt he was simply sharing information with a trusted colleague.[116] Ultimately, however, the proclamation ended up in the hands of the Criminal Investigation Department, which released it within a week,[117] after Jabavu had written to Rheinallt Jones: "Personally I think this manifesto is no stronger tha[n] that of the 'African Democratic Party,' which has been allowed wide advertisement, with its 'fight' and 'militant action' proposals, and I cannot see what harm will result to the State if all its sections of population receive better wages, etc."[118]

Though Jabavu may have been guilty of nothing more than poor judgment, Tabata was enraged:

The act that Jili committed is worse than murder. He is guilty of mass murder. He has sabotaged the movement of the people at the most crucial moment. The whole country is grasping for a lead. The manifesto gives it. . . . If we miss the opportunity the race is doomed to a life [of] misery and destitution in the near future. From now on, every death of a Black child, due to starvation, malnutrition, T.B.[,] the rise of infantile mortality, unemployment, all miseries suffered by the Blacks, shall be heaped on Jili's head. He is responsible for nipping in the bud a movement that would have safe-guarded the people in the coming difficult times. He does not know what oppression is. He does not feel it. In fact he is in the same position as the liberals who thrive on the Blackmans [sic] sufferings. All these mealie-mouthed white liberals, these Moltenos, are in lucrative positions today because there is an oppresse[d] Blackman. Do you think that the Moltenos, the Margaret Ballingers . . . would have smelt parliament if there were not the oppressed Blacks. Do you think there would have ever been the Institute of Race Relations to enable . . . R Jones to earn more than £1000 per annum if there were not the fear [of] downtrodden Blacks. Do you think a grotesque mediocrity like Jabavu would have filled an exclusive position with all the honour attached to it if the Black man wasn't a chattel slave?[119]

Donald Molteno was a liberal in the old Cape tradition—indeed, he would advocate the reintroduction of a qualified black franchise in the 1950s. Molteno had been elected to parliament representing Africans in the Cape Western Electoral Circle (Tabata's district) in 1937.[120] Margaret Ballinger was also a representative of Africans in the House of Assembly. With Hyman Basner, a former Communist Party member who represented African interests in the Senate, she supported Paul Mosaka's African Democratic Party (ADP), which called for "both mass action and the enlistment of white supporters."[121] Ballinger supported the reforms proposed by Smuts's government in the early 1940s, and Gerhart has described her as "conscientious in her efforts to advance African interests," though she did not "work very closely with African leaders."[122]

All this was irrelevant to Tabata, who was unconcerned with whether white liberals were good or bad, left or pragmatic;[123] he dismissed them all because they participated willingly in a bankrupt system. Tabata's wrath in late 1943 was softened only slightly by the closing lines of his invective, which suggested that even he might have found his own anger a bit excessive: "No I must stop. I didn't intend to write."[124] Although it is unclear whether Jabavu was aware of Tabata's letter, by November 1943 he was ready to quit the AAC. Writing to Xuma (with whom he still hoped to establish an AAC-ANC coalition), he informed his former vice president of his decision to step down from the presidency of the AAC, "for the position needs a much younger man than myself in the present state of African mentality."[125]

THE NON-EUROPEAN UNITY MOVEMENT

Despite this resolve, Jabavu ultimately chaired the meeting of the AAC and the first meeting of the Non-European Unity Movement, both held in Bloemfontein in mid-December 1943. Seventy-two delegates, up slightly from 1940, but including Indians and Coloureds, attended the AAC conference.[126] Among the issues discussed was the possibility of union with the ANC. It was Jabavu who reported the results of the sitting of the Joint Committee of the ANC and the AAC on December 16, 1943—that the "A.A.C. shall be the recognised political mouthpiece of the African people." Tabata, backed by AAC secretary T. I. N. Sondlo and Anti-CAD member Janub Gool,[127] protested that the AAC should be recognized instead as "the official mouthpiece of the Non-European community." Delegates to the convention approved the narrower African definition and urged "the A.N.C. in the name of unity to come back to the A.A.C. so that the unity that was demonstrated in 1935 and continued to 1941 should be recovered and improved upon."[128]

Writing in *Inkundla ya Bantu* Jordan Ngubane (who would shortly help found the ANC Youth League),[129] responded to this lack of progress with another scathing commentary that struck out at both Jabavu and Xuma:

> Professor Jabavu is an old man, and if he wants to go to his grave still at the head of some organisation—motley assembly that it may be . . . Dr. Xuma is still young and still with a political future to build, and if he thinks he is building that future by following Professor Jabavu around every corner he will one day wake up alone in that desert of oblivion which now is the Professor's exclusive domain.

Jabavu came in for even more criticism (and some praise) for his alliance with the NEUM. While Ngubane conceded that Jabavu was "an African liberal—if there can be anything of the sort,"[130] who genuinely believed in Non-European unity, as did "all progressive thinkers," he insisted that "naked realism demands that at present this ideal must be regarded as still a 'consummation, devoutly to be desired.'" Africans first had to put their own house in order, and Xuma was thus obliged to direct his attention to the ANC.[131]

The first conference of the Non-European Unity Movement in December 1943 drew nine representatives of the Anti-CAD and seven delegates from the AAC. The South African Indian Congress sent its regrets, explaining that its members were busy fighting the Pegging Act, but were nevertheless fully behind the NEUM.[132] The meeting was very brief; indeed, Tabata described it as "preliminary," and urged delegates not to "delude themselves with the idea that because they had held this conference therefore the unity of the Non-European was an accomplished fact." A good six to twelve months of planning, Tabata added, were required before the NEUM got off the ground.[133] Remarkably, despite Tabata's animosity, Jabavu was elected chairman of the new organization, a grudging recognition, apparently, of his continued usefulness as a figurehead.[134]

Tabata himself admitted just how useful Jabavu remained in his letter to him of February 23, 1944.[135] The official launching of the Non-European Unity Movement was being delayed by the South African Indian Congress, whose representatives, A. I. Kajee and A. Ismail,[136] were reluctant to join the NEUM "in view of the existing disunity among the Africans themselves." While Tabata dismissed the friction between the AAC and the ANC as "a domestic matter that falls outside the scope of Non-European Unity at the present moment," and professed no objection to Kajee and Ismail consulting with Xuma, he was concerned about Kajee's plan to visit Jabavu. Kajee had told Tabata that he intended to consult Jabavu before making his recommendation to the SAIC about joining the NEUM. To Jabavu, Tabata stressed: "It is important that you state the case clearly to him. If we are to launch the campaign the Indians must be in it. . . . I am just afraid that the delay on the part of the Indians might throw the whole movement of the Non-Europeans back for decades."[137] Whatever Jabavu said, he convinced the South African Indian Congress to join the NEUM, and their delegates were present when the Second Unity Conference opened in Johannesburg on July 8, 1944.

Though intimate, the relationship between the AAC and the NEUM remained vaguely defined. As Tabata wrote to Jabavu, "The point I should like to make clear—I do not know if you agree with me—is this: that while the A.A.C. initiated the Unity Movement, yet the A.A.C. still retains its identity and still lives on its own rights as the mouthpiece of the African people."[138] It was the AAC, not the NEUM, that issued the proclamation "Along the New Road" on July 7, 1944, the day before the Second Unity Conference.[139] Yet the tone of the proclamation was very much that of the NEUM:

> Just over six months have passed since we met in Bloemfontein. It was there that we took several important decisions. We decided to turn away from the old road of passivity to the new road of leadership. We totally rejected the policy of segregation and we agreed upon the road of Unity with other Non-European groups. Without doubt these were very important and very good decisions. But when we

turn to look at the practical steps taken to apply these decisions and translate them into action, we have no cause to be satisfied with ourselves. . . . Our attitude has . . . been one of waiting, and the people's enthusiasm and hope after the last Convention, has begun to sag. While the people everywhere are on the move, while the militancy of the masses is rising everywhere, *we* wait; *we* hesitate to give the lead.[140]

"Along the New Road" was an attempt to respond to the militancy evident in such events as the Pretoria riots of December 1942 and the Alexandra bus boycott of August 1943.[141] It outlined a policy of noncollaboration, beginning with the rejection of the Natives' Representative Council and the parliamentary representation of Africans, neither of which had achieved anything tangible. "We cannot," the proclamation's authors asserted, "even begin to fight for our political rights as long as we maintain this sham representation."[142] Beginning in mid-1944, the AAC and the NEUM embarked on a propaganda campaign and "called for a boycott of segregated institutions."[143]

Thus, nine years after leading the battle to retain the nonracial franchise in the Cape Province, D. D. T. Jabavu found himself a member of an organization that dismissed the limited African franchise remaining in the Cape as a "sham." When the NEUM conference opened on July 8, 1944, Jabavu as chairman played mediator between the AAC and the Anti-CAD—both of which had accepted the ten-point program—and the South African Indian Congress, whose representatives would not endorse it.[144] The role of mediator—of peacemaker—seems to have been Jabavu's motive for remaining a member of the AAC and the NEUM, and he would spend the next four years trying to find a middle ground acceptable to the NEUM, the AAC, and the ANC.

To that end, Jabavu had also invited Xuma to attend the NEUM meeting, but the ANC president had declined. In a sense this was a case of turnabout being fair play—Jabavu had declined Xuma's invitation to attend a meeting of "leaders of African thought" to discuss the Atlantic Charter in December 1943, which had culminated in the publication of Xuma's pamphlet, *Africans' Claims*.[145] Like the AAC's ten-point program, Xuma's pamphlet called for "full citizenship rights" and the "redistribution of land."[146] Xuma's main concern, however, was rebuilding the ANC, and he was ambivalent toward the AAC and the NEUM. He had also remained supportive of those ANC members (including Matthews) who continued to sit on the Natives' Representative Council.[147] In 1944, in any event, Xuma was more interested in the nascent ANC Youth League than in the AAC or the NEUM.[148]

The young, mostly professional men who founded the ANC Youth League (with Xuma's blessing),[149] while attracted to the pro-boycott position of the

AAC and the NEUM, were still more drawn to "the historic strand of exclusivism in African political thought and the desire to promote African self-reliance and national pride" than they were to the idea of Non-European unity.[150] Prominent among this group were its theorists, Anton Lembede and A. P. Mda, as well as Walter Sisulu,[151] Oliver Tambo, and Nelson Mandela, the latter two of whom were former students of Jabavu's at Fort Hare.[152] Hoping to rejuvenate the ANC by broadening its appeal to young Africans, they established the ANC Youth League in April 1944. It was not until December 1949, however, that the ANC and the ANC Youth League adopted their own "Programme of Action,"[153] long after the AAC issued its 1943 "Call to Unity" and the NEUM had endorsed the AAC's "Along the New Road" in 1944.

At the NEUM conference in July 1944, delegates from the South African Indian Congress stumbled over the very first point of the AAC's program, the demand for universal adult suffrage. As Kajee explained, Indians "in Natal . . . did not wish to disturb the franchise position because if they did so they would create the impression that they were out to establish political supremacy," and it was the strategy of the SAIC "not to frighten the Europeans."[154] While Kajee acknowledged the ten-point program as an activist "Charter of the Rights of Man," the SAIC favored compromise and a more gradual approach.[155] Jabavu did his best to find the middle ground, noting that "as he saw the position . . . they were divided on the question of method, rather than aims," and that he felt that delegates "should try and reconcile the different viewpoints and . . . work out general principles. He did not think [the delegates] should embarrass the Indians in their policy of gradualness and compromise."[156] Gradualness and compromise were of course the hallmarks of the Cape liberal tradition, but B. M. Kies, a founding member of the Anti-CAD and an ally of Tabata, rejected Jabavu's defense of the South African Indian Congress, arguing: "it meant that if and when the S.A.I.C. think it fit and proper to co-operate then they are at liberty to do so, which in effect means that they need to co-operate only when it suits them,"[157] a position irreconcilable with the ten-point program.

The Second Unity Conference thus ended in a stalemate, although delegates did resolve to meet again in Cape Town in January 1945.[158] Jabavu was ill and did not attend this Third Unity Conference. In his absence, Z. R. Mahabane served as chairman.[159] Indian representatives did attend, but this time they were from the radical Anti-Segregation Council of Durban. After they ousted Kajee from the SAIC in October 1945, they ultimately aligned themselves not with the NEUM but with the ANC.[160]

Jabavu was again in the chair at the Fourth Unity Conference in Kimberley in December 1945, but Mahabane had been elected president. Neither the South African Indian Congress nor the ANC sent representatives, but

Mahabane's position as the ANC's chaplain made him an appropriate symbol of unity despite his sixty-five years.[161] Slowly but surely, Jabavu was being pushed to the periphery of the NEUM. Jabavu extended the greetings of the AAC (which had met in Bloemfontein a few days before) and, in an embrace of NEUM language, expressed the AAC's "urgent hope that the Unity Conference will impress upon the delegates the urgency of the formation of Co-ordinating Committees throughout the Union." Tabata had accused the AAC of inaction in 1941; in 1945 Jabavu argued that "these local Committees will serve as defence Committees against the concerted onslaught on the remaining rights of the Non-Europeans."[162]

Jabavu also praised the NEUM's "Declaration to the Nations of the World," issued in July 1945 by Mahabane and two Anti-CAD stalwarts, G. H. Gool and E. C. Roberts.[163] "If the foundation of the peaceful world is to be secure," the declaration's authors argued, "then the scourge of Hitlerite tyranny must be uprooted not only in Europe but also in South Africa."[164] Jabavu's endorsement was significant because the declaration openly attacked Smuts for his embrace of freedom abroad and white supremacy at home.[165] Jabavu, despite the misgivings he had expressed in mid-1943 about the willingness of the Smuts government to apply the principles of the Atlantic Charter in South Africa, still retained considerable respect for Smuts.

Jabavu was only slightly more voluble at the December 1946 conference of the NEUM. Mahabane's presidential address chronicled the government's continued pattern of repression—the segregationist Asiatic Land Tenure and Indian Representation Bill was introduced in 1946, and a strike by African mineworkers on the Rand in August 1946 had been brutally suppressed. While Mahabane praised the Natives' Representative Council's decision to adjourn in protest of the government's policies, other delegates were less generous.[166] S. A. Jayiya, joint secretary of the NEUM, observed acidly that the AAC had called on members of the NRC "to resign en bloc from the sham Council" in 1943, and that it was "only now, after more than 10 years that they have decided to adjourn as a 'supposed' protest against the Government."[167] Jayiya's outburst and his depiction of NRC members as "quislings" prompted Jabavu to enter the discussion and counsel moderation since, he argued, many of those NRC members might still be won over to the NEUM.[168]

The other issue Jabavu addressed at the 1946 conference was that of the expropriation of property. Though of immediate significance to Indians in 1946, it was, in the opinion of delegates, "a national issue; there was no difference between the Natives Land Act, the Indian Land Tenure Act and Expropriation for the Coloured. Expropriation meant residential segregation, and it was necessary for the people to take immediate action."[169] Jabavu agreed, observing that "the policy of the Government is that no Non-European should own land,"[170] a policy that ran counter to the Cape liberal tradition, in which property ownership had been the agency of civilization.

Though he had learned to speak the NEUM's language, privately Jabavu remained uncomfortable with the AAC-NEUM strategy of boycotting the Natives' Representative Council and the parliamentary elections. In September 1947 Donald Molteno, the representative for Africans in the western Cape, wrote to Jabavu asking for a clarification of the AAC's boycott policy, of which he had just learned. Molteno professed to being confused, since the AAC had asked him to run for parliament in 1937.[171] In reply, Jabavu sent a "strictly confidential" letter confirming that the AAC had indeed adopted a boycott policy in 1944, and adding that Cape African voters meeting in Queenstown in December 1946 had agreed "to boycott all the next elections, as a protest against the ineffectiveness of the 1936 Hertzog Acts." He admitted that when he had tried to intrude into the discussion, he found himself "overwhelmed by the youthful majority who were strong in their views and who forced me to refrain from exerting any influence on the discussion by reason of my being Chairman." That his own frame of reference remained the Cape liberal tradition was clear:

> My conviction is that the African public is at present suffering from confused thinking, complicating the 1936 Hertzog legislation with the original 1854 Native franchise. My people do not understand that the present vote was not granted by Hertzog but was merely reduced in scope and segregated from the European franchise. Hertzog merely changed its operation by creating separate rolls and restricting Native members down to three. The present vote is therefore a remnant of the 1854 original vote, and to boycott it is tantamount to seeking its absolute abrogation regardless of the privileges of citizenship that it [co]ntinues to carry despite its truncated form. It is for that [rea]son that I personally wish to continue exercising my vote for the [National] Assembly and Provincial Council.[172]

He added that he saw nothing to be gained by boycotting the Natives' Representative Council "beyond embarrassing and exacerbating the Government," and felt equally confused about the boycott of the 1936 Native Trust and Land Act, disinclined as he was "to advise my people to leave the Trust lands, in order to boycott the 1936 Acts." Ultimately, Jabavu confessed to Molteno, "It will be my duty next December to come out into the open and make a stand one way or the other." Until then, he would follow his conscience and leave "the boycott matter . . . to the Africans themselves as expressed by their organisations."[173]

Jabavu did not get the opportunity to air his views publicly in December 1947. As Tabata wrote to Mahabane in October 1947, "I have to ask myself the question: If we call a unity conf. in Dec. what would be its tasks? . . . If we look back to the last Conf. & examine all the speeches made & the resolutions passed, we find that nothing new can be added. It would be a case of repeating ourselves." Tabata wanted to wait and see what impact the United Nations negotiations between the United States and the Soviet Union—which Smuts was attending—would have on South Africa. Nevertheless, he asked Mahabane to contact Jabavu and arrange a December conference for the AAC. Tabata's intent seems to have been to underline the distinction between the NEUM and the AAC and to stress the AAC's role as an African parliament.[174] Mahabane for his part invited Xuma and the ANC, but the conference does not appear to have taken place.[175] When the NEUM did meet again in March 1948, Jabavu was unable to attend and thus missed the opportunity to "make a stand."[176]

TURNING POINT: 1948

In February 1948 Smuts's government had released the Fagan Report *(Report of the Native Laws Commission, 1946–48)*.[177] It contained, according to Davenport, "much that was acceptable to moderate black opinion."[178] The report proposed the establishment of a system of labor bureaus to control the flow of workers from the countryside to the urban areas, and suggested (as members of the NRC had long done) that workers be allowed to bring their families to the cities. The proposal that villages be built in the reserves to accommodate landless Africans was more problematic because of the long-standing overcrowding of the reserves. On the issue of the pass laws, the report was ambiguous, recommending that passes should be retained in the form of identity cards, but that workers could apply for them on a voluntary basis. The report, issued only a few months before the election, "with none of its recommendations yet tested in practice or in public debate, offered the electorate," Davenport has contended, "a liberal aspiration rather than a policy." In opposition to Smuts's United Party stood Malan's National Party, whose rival Sauer Report offered a clear-cut policy of apartheid—segregation writ large.[179] When the election was over in May 1948, the National Party had won, and the "liberal aspirations" of "moderate blacks" were dashed yet again.[180]

Just how well D. D. T. Jabavu still fit into this category, despite his long association with the NEUM and the post–Hertzog bills AAC, was apparent in the letter he wrote to Smuts the month before the election:

Although I cannot wield any influence to get you back to Parliament with your noble team of fellow-Ministers I may possibly possess enough 'soul-force' (satyagraha) to help you back to power by wishing and praying for your party to enjoy all the good luck there is about.

Hoping the South African European electorate will be inspired by sanity and wisdom to do the right thing by you and the United Party, I am your humble but zealous well-wisher.[181]

Jabavu's prayers (and his allusion to Mahatma Gandhi's success in achieving independence for India) did Smuts no good, and they would have incensed Tabata had he known about them. When Malan arrived in Pretoria on June 1, 1948, he proclaimed that "today South Africa belongs to us once more." In claiming South Africa for the Afrikaners, he inaugurated a process that would make Africans "strangers in their own country" to an extent that Hertzog could only have imagined.[182]

Also in June 1948, Tabata wrote to Nelson Mandela of the ANC Youth League in an attempt to draw him into the AAC, which Tabata depicted again as the spontaneous creation and legitimate representative of the African people. Drawing a clear distinction between the ANC and ANC Youth League, Tabata insisted that the older organization—with its long history of collaboration with the government, most recently in the Natives' Representative Council—was morally bankrupt.[183] Mandela's response was not recorded, and though he had considerable respect for Tabata, he would later dismiss the AAC-affiliated Cape African Teachers' Association as "a group of intellectual snobs who derive their inspiration from the All-African Convention."[184]

Significantly, Tabata was not among the signatories to "A Call for African Unity," issued on October 3, 1948. Among the dozen prominent African politicians who did sign the statement were Xuma (who had called them together), Jabavu (who signed second to Xuma), Z. R. Mahabane, R. V. Selope Thema, J. S. Moroka, Z. K. Matthews, A. W. G. Champion, Paul R. Mosaka, R. H. Godlo, R. G. Baloyi, R. T. Bokwe, and L. K. Ntlabati.[185] They were protesting the threat—represented by apartheid—to African education, freedom of movement, land and residential rights, and employment opportunities. The solution they proposed, "the Unification of the main African political organisations—the African National Congress and the All African Convention into 'THE ALL AFRICAN NATIONAL CONGRESS,' united and inspired by common principles and a common programme of action for the achievement of the liberation of the African people,"[186] was more than a decade old and it had failed repeatedly. The hope it embodied belonged to an older generation, and it was not insignificant that of the group of twelve, only Matthews, Bokwe, and Godlo were under fifty, and only Mosaka was under forty. It also represented an ideological position at odds with the AAC-NEUM embrace of a broader Non-European, rather than a narrower African unity. Half the members who signed the statement had served or were serving on the Natives' Representative Council;[187] thus in essence Jabavu, Mahabane, Moroka, and Thema—the only active members of the AAC who signed "A Call for African Unity"—were, given the official boycott policy of the AAC and the NEUM, consorting with the enemy.[188]

This tension was much in evidence at the joint conference of the ANC and the AAC called in December 1948 by Xuma and Jabavu. Jabavu's support for Xuma in October and December 1948 seems to have been rooted in a sincere desire to forge an African union in response to the National Party victory in May, and a determination finally "to come out into the open and make a stand," as he had written to Molteno in September 1947. Delegates to the joint conference—including 116 from the ANC and 40 from the AAC—could not, however, find common ground.[189] Tabata laid out the AAC conditions for unity: acceptance of the AAC's ten-point program, retention of the federal structure of the AAC, acceptance of the principle of Non-European unity and of the policy of noncollaboration. He also informed the conference "that the A.A.C. had decided to give Congress [the ANC] a given percentage of the seats on the Executive of the proposed Convention of the two bodies." The ANC delegates could not swallow Tabata's arrogance.[190] Matthews observed that to "the average Congress person the proposal of the A.A.C. seems to mean that one mouthpiece of the African people (the A.A.C.) is wanting to swallow up the other mouthpiece (the A.N.C.)," and suggested that they spend a bit more time discussing the unification process.[191] Moses Kotane (who was also general secretary of the Communist Party of South Africa) questioned the efficiency of the AAC's federal structure. Jiyaya, responding on behalf of the AAC, "accused the ANC of insincerity."[192]

Deeply saddened by the exchange, Jabavu announced, "I am desperate. Let us at least go away having said something." He then read the October "Call for African Unity" he had signed jointly with Xuma, only to have his own AAC reject it. Mahabane then stepped in and suggested that a committee composed of Xuma and Matthews from the ANC and Jabavu and Tabata from the AAC issue its own statement based on the "Call for African Unity." Again the AAC rejected the motion. Finally—according to the conference notes—Jabavu, "ignoring the members of the A.A.C. delegation, who were sitting on one side of the House . . . put his suggestion to adopt the statement of . . . 3/10/48 to [the] Conference for the third time. When the House agreed to it, he shouted 'It is carried.'"[193] Of course, it had not carried at all and though a second joint conference was held in 1949, the AAC and the ANC never did form a union.[194]

For Jabavu, it was a sad end to a career of political activism that had spanned three decades. His reward for his disloyalty to the pro-boycott principles of the AAC and the NEUM was the election of Wycliffe Tsotsi to the presidency of the AAC.[195] A few months later, Jabavu would corner Leo Sihahli's mother at a funeral to express his dismay at the behavior of the younger members of the AAC (including her son) at the conference.[196] For the most part, however, he withdrew gracefully from the political stage in December 1948 to make room—as he had written to Xuma five years before—for the "much younger man" that the position demanded "in the present state of African mentality."[197]

6 Final Years, 1948–1959

Early in 1948, D. D. T. Jabavu wrote to his daughters, Noni and Lexie, then both living in London. The South African general election had not yet occurred, Jabavu's own ouster from the AAC was eight months in the future, and he was in a reflective mood:

> It is odd to me to think I am in my 63rd year of age, for sometimes I feel as light-hearted as 20, then alternatively 30 to 40 when I was in the lime light of public life, then 40 to 50 when I was going great guns in Government controversies, then 50 to 60 when I deliberately simmered down to be quiet and to watch the activities of those I had trained, while now over 60 I am busy recollecting and writing down the records of things likely to be forgotten if I do not rescue them from oblivion.[1]

D. D. T. Jabavu had been fifty years old when the Representation of Natives in Parliament Act and the Native Trust and Land Act passed in 1936, and the fight against the two bills had marked the high point of his political prominence. Whether he "simmered down" deliberately after 1936 or did so because he had no choice, is impossible to gauge but writing to his daughters in April 1948, that was how he wished to remember it.

By May 1948 it became clear that one thing Jabavu could not rescue was the Cape liberal tradition. D. F. Malan's National Party won the general election on an apartheid platform. In December 1948 the liberal forces in parliament lost their foremost spokesman when J. H. Hofmeyr died. Hofmeyr had stood in 1936 as one of the eleven Members of Parliament opposed to the Representation of Natives in Parliament Bill, and he had condemned apartheid in 1948 as a "cloak for repression and nothing else."[2] An advocate of "equality of opportunity," though not of "social equality and race-mixture," Hofmeyr was in many ways Jabavu's counterpart among white liberal politicians.[3] Of

Hofmeyr, Jabavu wrote, "In our day Hofmeyr has been severely denounced for being a liberal, and an election has been fought and won on that ticket. If his liberalism is a political sin then . . . we are living in degenerate days of political delinquency where justice is by popular acclamation classified as wrong, for vote-catching purposes, and where repression is called decency."[4] Published in January 1949, after he himself had been edged out of the political arena by activists who rejected the notion that only civilized men were qualified to represent black interests, Jabavu's article was as much a commentary on his own fall from political grace as it was a eulogy of Hofmeyr's liberalism.

While Jabavu had been marginalized politically by the late 1940s, his record of activism continued to garner him the respect of members of the international community. In December 1949 he traveled to India as a delegate to the World Pacifist Meeting. The attraction of India for pacifists had been Mahatma Gandhi, who had encouraged "non-violence on an extensive scale as a means for attaining the freedom of India, and India had become free."[5] After Gandhi's assassination in January 1948, the World Pacifist Meeting became a memorial to him.

With its faith "in the essential unity of mankind above all barriers of race, creed or culture," and its belief "that no human being or group has any right to dominate or exploit other human beings or groups,"[6] pacifism had much in common with liberalism.[7] Jabavu's presence at the 1949 meeting was particularly appropriate, since Gandhi—who had practiced law in South Africa from 1893 to 1914—had acknowledged that the "history of the Satyagraha struggle is for all practical purposes a history of my life in South Africa, and especially of my experiments with truth in that sub-continent."[8] *Satyagraha* literally meant "soul-force" or "truth-force," and it embodied as its central principle a love of the oppressor coupled with a hatred of oppression.[9] Jabavu himself had percipiently invoked satyagraha when he had written to extend his best wishes to Smuts (an often indifferent liberal, but a liberal nevertheless), on the eve of the 1948 election.[10]

The concerns of the World Pacifist Meeting reflected the state of the world in 1949. The Cold War and the implications for world peace of the ideological conflict between the Soviet Union and the United States dominated the debates, but delegates also discussed the 1947–48 war between India and Pakistan, the fate of the Palestinians in the year-old state of Israel, and the impact of the National Party's policy of apartheid in South Africa.[11] By the time D. D. T. Jabavu arrived in India in December 1949, the first major piece of apartheid legislation—the Prohibition of Mixed Marriages Act—had already passed. The act, which prohibited all interracial marriages, would be followed the next year by the Population Registration Act, which assigned every South African to a racial category, and by the Group Areas Act, which segregated South Africans residentially by race.[12]

Jabavu's participation in the World Pacifist Meeting was limited. He took part in the discussion on nationalism, and the conference notes recorded his observation that "his people had so little land left to them by the white man, that 'independence' would be meaningless and 'nationalism' seemed to him a false slogan."[13] While Jabavu may have been offering a criticism of the Afrikaner nationalism that had given birth to apartheid,[14] at least one delegate interpreted Jabavu's comments as a criticism of African nationalism only. Manilal Gandhi (one of Gandhi's sons still living in South Africa) observed that he "could not agree with Prof. Jabavu's attitude to the nationalism of South African Negroes, which he welcomed."[15] In 1949 Jabavu remained a gradualist, more comfortable with advocating "equal rights for all civilized men" than with demanding—as the African nationalists did—"equal rights for all citizens."[16] Like the nationalists, however, he became increasingly critical of the apartheid state.

On his way back to South Africa early in 1950, Jabavu stopped in Kenya and Uganda, then respectively a British colony and a British protectorate. In Kenya, where the best land was controlled by a white settler population of less than 30,000, and where the government was run by "imperialists . . . who do not accept the wishes of the British parliament," Jabavu saw much that reminded him of South Africa.[17] In Uganda, where there were fewer than 8,000 white settlers, and where the Ugandans themselves owned land, Jabavu thought he had found a bit of heaven: "People do not know [the] colour bar here. The people are civilized. People talked about education and general affairs and I felt as though I was in Queen Victoria's England."[18] For Jabavu, Uganda in 1950 evoked the late-nineteenth-century Cape Colony of his youth, and it was telling that the model of civilization Uganda represented—even as Jabavu celebrated the relative absence of whites—was British. Yet the British colonial administration in Uganda had seized much of the best land and given it to white settlers in Kenya, and, in addition, had undermined the potential for unity in Uganda by treating the old "'kingdom' of Buganda as though it were a distinct separate unit within the Protectorate of Uganda."[19] If Jabavu was aware of these policies in 1950, he did not acknowledge them in *E-Indiya nase East Africa* (In India and East Africa), the travelogue he wrote on his return to South Africa. What his travels in Kenya and Uganda did was convince him that the greater the number of whites in a given country, the more its African population suffered.

Jabavu had made a similar observation more than twenty years earlier when he noted, "Is it the Bantu or the European . . . who squeezed by economic congestion and land hunger in his Native habitat, migrated to find a haven of rest in hospitable and spacious Africa? Which of the two is really the problem?"[20] In 1926, even with Hertzog newly in power and his segregative representation and land bills under discussion, liberalism had still seemed a valid approach to addressing the issues that divided white and black South Africans. By 1950 the situation had changed dramatically, as Jabavu acknowledged in the graduation address he delivered at the South African Native College at Fort Hare in 1951. The speech brought him full circle at Fort Hare, from the first African lecturer in 1916 to the first African graduation speaker thirty-five years later. The speech also revealed his disenchantment with apartheid South Africa and his increasing doubts that the definition of South Africa would ever be extended to include its black subjects, civilized or not. Full of hope in 1916, he was resigned in 1951.

The South African Native College, Jabavu observed, had been an ideal: "a microcosmic cross-section of educational South Africa, and also of the great world of modern Civilisation. . . . a centre around which all the colour groups of the South African population meet at a high level of education." Yet even Fort Hare had failed to discover "a way of living together on terms of mutual respect."[21] Graduates would enter an inhospitable world that, Jabavu warned, "for a great part opposes all that Fort Hare stands for," and was possessed of "an amazing tendency for misrepresenting people." South Africa in 1951 was "a world neither idealist nor realist, a world often wrong or hesitant in doing the sensible thing in politics, religion and economic life, a world particularly hostile to what it calls the 'Fort Hare product.'"[22]

Nevertheless, in 1951 Jabavu could still find room for hope, advising graduates to study "the life of Mahatma Gandhi, the greatest non-White leader thrown up by the last 100 years,"[23] and urging them (in the language of the Cape liberal tradition) to serve their community, and use their "higher education for [the] uplift . . . [of] less privileged groups." That, he concluded, was "the quintessence of Goodwill in Action, in Gandhian philosophy, and in true Christian faith." It was the manner in which Jabavu had tried to live his own life, and it was a road that was neither downhill nor easy—for Christ it had ended in crucifixion, for Gandhi in assassination.[24] For D. D. T. Jabavu, the end would be far less dramatic, though no less difficult, as he watched his vision of a South Africa that would accord "equal rights to all civilized men" fade into obscurity.

In defeat Jabavu did not retreat into silence. In 1952 he privately published *Imbumba yamaNyama* (Unity is strength). At the heart of the book were the lengthy lists of Xhosa clan names he had collected during a lifetime of traveling throughout the eastern Cape. He gave particular emphasis to his own clan—

the Ntlangwini—leading the anthropologist Cecil Manona to question the accuracy of Jabavu's text.[25] Yet *Imbumba* was far more than an exercise in ego, or a simple rescue effort "of things likely to be forgotten." *Imbumba* also operated on several additional levels: it recalled Jabavu's 1929 assertion that African history should be written by Africans; it included a forceful plea for Xhosa-Mfengu unity reminiscent of his 1935 dismissal of the "Fingo Slavery Myth"; and it suggested a marked decline in his lifelong respect for the British.

Jabavu's inspiration for *Imbumba yamaNyama* had been Tiyo Soga's 1917 record of Xhosa oral history, *Intlalo kaXhosa* (Life and customs of the Xhosa). Soga, Jabavu argued:

> did a good thing by setting an example for us by writing his book for the following reasons: the educated people in the past were not interested in their history. What was in fashion was the reading of books on black history which were written by whites and those books were written for use at school, and their aim was to pass examinations and that was all. The history of the nation was kept in the heads of praise poets, the wise men and the old men.[26]

In 1954 Jabavu published (again privately) *Izithuko*, or "Praise poems" about himself.[27] Unlike *Imbumba*, with its much broader focus, *Izithuko* may be seen as an act of egoism, or perhaps more generously—given its emphasis on Jabavu's political activism in the 1920s and 1930s—as an autobiography of sorts.

The second theme in *Imbumba*—the plea for Xhosa-Mfengu unity—was also a familiar one in Jabavu's writing. Despite Jabavu's insistence in 1935 that the rivalry between the groups was a divide-and-rule tactic concocted by whites, the friction persisted in the rural eastern Cape. In 1942 the Xhosa clergyman and ANC secretary-general James Calata, then chairman of the Ntsikana celebrations, together with Solomon Tontsi, chairman of the Mfengu festivities, issued a joint declaration calling for unity.[28] Yet a decade later, Jabavu still felt compelled to address the issue and even to a title his book, in a direct reference to the Xhosa-Mfengu divide, "Unity is strength."

Jabavu had argued in favor of Xhosa-Mfengu unity throughout his career. In the praise poems in *Izithuko* he was described variously as an Mfengu and as a "man of Ngqika," a reference to the Xhosa chief Ngqika, whose lands once included Jabavu's birthplace, King William's Town.[29] Significantly, the author of two of the praise poems was the Xhosa poet S. E. K. Mqhayi, who had been the subeditor of *Izwi Labantu*, the newspaper established in opposition to Tengo Jabavu's *Imvo Zabantsundu* in 1897.[30] In two poems dating from the late 1920s (when D. D. T. Jabavu was busy defending the Cape franchise) Mqhayi described him as "the man of the Ngqika," suggesting that D. D. T. Jabavu's insistence on a broader African identity in the 1920s was accepted even by those who had once opposed Tengo Jabavu, and indeed had encouraged African voters in the late nineteenth century to "abandon Jabavu, for he is only a Fingo [Mfengu] and is taking you to the Boers [Afrikaners]."[31]

Writing in *Imbumba* in 1952, D. D. T. Jabavu seemed to take his argument for Xhosa-Mfengu unity one step further when he identified himself not simply as a Xhosa speaker, but as a "Xhosa proper . . . born in Xhosaland."[32] The historian J. D. Omer-Cooper has suggested that Jabavu was reacting to the extreme "pattern of colour discrimination" introduced after 1948, which led "the more highly educated" among the Mfengu "to identify themselves with the language and traditions of the Xhosa."[33] For Jabavu, however, aligning himself with the Xhosa was not a new position, though his language in 1952 was more forceful than it had been when he dismissed the "Fingo Slavery Myth" in 1935.

In 1952 (as in 1935) Jabavu explicitly rejected what he considered the artificial divide between the Xhosa and the Mfengu introduced by the British in 1835. The Mfengu celebration, Jabavu argued in *Imbumba*, should become an opportunity "to commemorate the acceptance of the Mfengu among the Xhosa" rather than an occasion to remember the Mfengu pledge to the British in 1835.[34] A lifelong Anglophile, in 1952 he declined "to comment on the vows which were made by Sir Benjamin D'Urban on behalf of Queen Victoria because the white people did not honour their side of the bargain."[35] D'Urban's pledge in 1835, "To protect the Mfengu from their enemies . . . To provide them with education and the Word of God . . . To give them land," had seemed, even by the time of the 1935 Mfengu centenary celebration, as barren as the Peddie district where many of the Mfengu had settled.[36] Against apartheid, the Mfengu pledge to embrace Christianity, to remain loyal to the government, and to educate their children, offered no protection.

By identifying himself as a "Xhosa proper" in 1952, D. D. T. Jabavu was not, however, dismissing the Mfengu or rejecting his own Mfengu heritage. At the heart of *Imbumba* after all was a discussion of Jabavu's own clan, the Ntlangwini—who were Mfengu. In Jabavu's opinion, the white state had always been the major beneficiary of the Xhosa-Mfengu feud; with the introduction of apartheid, the stakes became much higher for black South Africans. By including the Mfengu among the Xhosa clans in *Imbumba*, Jabavu was arguing that unity was indeed strength, and was challenging both Xhosa and Mfengu to recognize that, as Africans, they were natural allies whose common enemies were those whites who attempted to divide them.

Yet neither his disenchantment with apartheid nor his invigorated sense of African identity led the sixty-six-year-old Jabavu to return to political activism. He did not participate in the Defiance Campaign,[37] which began in April 1952 and which adopted Gandhi's methods of passive resistance.[38] Launched by the ANC in cooperation with the South African Indian Congress, the Defiance Campaign effectively paralyzed large sections of the eastern Cape. Protesters peacefully, but pointedly, broke "curfew laws, and defied 'Europeans only' notices at railway stations and in post offices." Port Elizabeth and East London were epicenters of the demonstrations, and of the 8,326 people arrested, 70 percent were from the eastern Cape.[39]

D. D. T. Jabavu, the documentary evidence suggests, remained aloof from this grassroots campaign. In August 1952, Alexander Kerr nominated Jabavu for an honorary Ph.D. from Rhodes University, but the university declined to honor Jabavu, explaining to Kerr "that while it was sympathetic to . . . [his] proposal, it felt that having regard to the present state of the country politically it would not be wise to proceed with such a nomination at the present moment."[40] In his reply to the committee, Kerr observed:

> unless there has been some public statement, of which I am unaware, by Prof. Jabavu in the present crisis in race relations, out of line with his known usual moderation, I should myself have thought that the opportunity of signalizing approval of the . . . liberal viewpoint, provided by the conferment of such a mark of distinction as contemplated upon a recognized Bantu leader, would have been highly expedient politically at this present moment.

Kerr added that granting Jabavu the degree would enhance Rhodes University's international standing, since conversations with colleagues in the United Kingdom had convinced him "that some such gesture by S. Africa is much needed to help to dissipate some present misconceptions about our attitudes to our non-European groups."[41] Only in mid-1953, after the Defiance Campaign had ended,[42] did Rhodes University confer an honorary Ph.D. on D. D. T. Jabavu. The ceremony took place at the University College of Fort Hare (as it was now called) in April 1954.[43]

Jabavu for his part had no doubts that the attitude of the white South African government toward its "non-European groups" had hardened considerably since 1948. Under the 1953 Bantu Education Act, all African schools— including those run by missionaries—fell under the control of the Department of Native Affairs. Students at the lower levels were taught in the vernacular; for upper-level students, Afrikaans (in addition to English) became compulsory. The act introduced a "differential syllabus . . . geared to what the Government considered African educational needs to be."[44] In apartheid South Africa, Africans were to be laborers.[45] The passage of the Bantu Education Act effectively eliminated education as a route of African progress. For D. D. T. Jabavu, who had dedicated his life to training an African elite that now seemed to have no hope of ever achieving equality, it was a considerable blow.

In mid-1954 he left South Africa and took a six-month position as the acting principal of Bamangwato College at Moeng, fifty miles north of Palapye in the Bechuanaland Protectorate, then a British possession. The college had been founded in 1948 by the Ngwato chiefdom, and offered its students academic, business, and agricultural training.[46] In 1954 the college's white principal had just resigned, and board members hoped that "if a black man could hold the position temporarily this would make it easy for the committee to appoint a black person" permanently.[47] For Jabavu it was a delightful experience: "I must not hide the fact that you feel good when you have authority. You must remember that I am tasting authority for the first time. I was taken up when people addressed me as 'Principal.'"[48] As in Uganda, Africans in the Bechuanaland Protectorate owned land, and there were few white settlers: "I can spend a whole month without seeing a white face until I go to Palapye . . . to fetch the post."[49] Bamangwato College renewed Jabavu's faith in British fair play, but deepened his despair about South Africa, "a place where our education is being made inferior." Of Bechuanaland, he wrote, "If I was still young, I would emigrate to this country together with my family."[50] For D. D. T. Jabavu, the South Africa of his youth, and of his dreams, no longer existed.

As if this were not heartbreak enough, shortly after Jabavu returned to South Africa at the beginning of 1955, personal tragedy struck. His only son, Tengo Max—then in his final year of medical school at the University of the Witwatersrand—was killed in a shooting accident near Johannesburg.[51] It was, as the magazine Drum observed, the "End of a Great Line."[52] Tengo Max Jabavu's assailant, Solomon Lefty Mafuko, was apparently a close friend with whom the younger Jabavu had been socializing that evening. Mafuko—who had been drinking heavily—was sitting in the back seat of Tengo Max Jabavu's car playing with a revolver, which he claimed discharged accidentally. In an ironic twist, Mafuko was defended by Nelson Mandela, then a young lawyer and perhaps the most visible of the younger generation of African politicians who had risen to prominence in the late 1940s. Thus Mandela, who had symbolically—if not actually—helped end Jabavu's political career, now also helped free the man who ended Jabavu's line. Mafuko received a sentence of two years imprisonment with hard labor, suspended for three years, and a £50 fine.[53] D. D. T. Jabavu took his son's death stoically, telling friends "that God had taken what he had given. . . . if he showed sorrow it would be questioning the work of the Lord."[54]

Despite his fortitude, Jabavu's friends worried about his well-being. Florence Jabavu had died four years previously at the age of fifty-five.[55] Concerned that Jabavu would be alone in his grief (Noni was still living in London, Lexie was in Uganda), Alexander Kerr encouraged Godfrey Mzamane—the lecturer in African languages at Fort Hare—and his wife Ethel to buy a house near Jabavu's.[56] Two weeks after his son's death, Jabavu married Betty Marambana, who had spent most of her working life as a domestic servant in East London. Unlike Florence Jabavu, who had been well educated for her time, Betty Marambana did not speak fluent English and had had little formal education. The marriage surprised many; Healdtown resident Benjamin Mbete recalled that he had difficulty understanding why a man who had dedicated his life to teaching would marry a woman who could barely read. D. D. T. Jabavu nevertheless chose Betty Marambana as the companion of his old age, and she did help ease his grief.[57]

His son's death, however, marked a turning point in D. D. T. Jabavu's life. In the four years between Tengo Max's death in March 1955 and his own death in August 1959, he made only three public appearances. He delivered two sermons, both in February 1957, and in October 1957 he visited Lovedale to accept the Medal of the Royal African Society[58] in recognition of his long record of community service.[59]

He continued to write—*IziDungulwana* (Tidbits) about his sojourn in the Bechuanaland Protectorate was published in 1958—and he remained an interested observer of South African politics. In June 1955, while D. D. T. Jabavu mourned for his son, members of the ANC, the South African Indian Congress, the South African Coloured People's Organisation, and the white Congress of Democrats gathered as the Congress of the People at Kliptown near Johannesburg and issued the Freedom Charter. Multiracial in tone, the charter asserted that "South Africa belongs to all who live in it, black and white," and demanded equal rights and redistribution of the land.[60]

If unity is strength, as Jabavu had argued in 1952, the Congress of the People seemed to have little prospect for success. Within the ANC itself—which constituted the largest of the four member groups of the Congress Alliance—the Africanists objected to the multiracial tone of the Freedom Charter. From the Africanist perspective (as Marcus Garvey had proclaimed in 1920), "Africa was for the Africans."[61] Africanists accused the Congress Alliance (with its separate African, Indian, Coloured, and white organizations) of duplicating the divisions of apartheid, and they resented that the Congress of Democrats, the South African Indian Congress, and the South African Coloured People's Organisation participated on "an equal basis . . . in a Congress Alliance in which they saw themselves as the rightful core organisation in virtue of both their stand on behalf of the indigenous dispossessed, and their enormous numerical ascendancy."[62]

From the Africanist perspective, the equality promised to South Africa's non-African minority groups by the Freedom Charter seemed patently unfair.[63] Africanists feared that the Marxist-leaning Congress of Democrats,[64] whose members had been among the main authors of the Freedom Charter, planned a "Communist takeover" of the Congress Alliance, which would then "be used to further the interests of the Soviet Union." Africanists also suspected that the white Congress of Democrats was positioning itself to protect white rights in a postapartheid South Africa.[65] When the ANC finally ratified the Freedom Charter in April 1956, the Africanists again objected, finally breaking away in April 1959 to found the Pan Africanist Congress under the leadership of Robert Sobukwe.[66]

Individual liberals had also attended the Congress of the People in June 1955, but the multiracial Liberal Party had declined to take part officially, to avoid having to share a platform with the Congress of Democrats, which was running against the Liberal Party in the parliamentary elections for the three seats representing Africans in the House of Assembly. D. D. T. Jabavu had not joined the Liberal Party when it was founded in 1953, but their endorsement in 1955 of a qualified nonracial franchise—even as it put them at odds with the broader egalitarian goals of the Congress Alliance[67]—was closest to Jabavu's own position.

That Jabavu remained a critical observer of black protest politics in the 1950s was evident in his last book, *IziDungulwana*. He professed himself generally unimpressed by the younger generation of African politicians, toward whom he harbored some lingering bitterness. Buried among the descriptions of Bamangwato College and of his travels in the Bechuanaland Protectorate was the following passage:

About ten years ago there were comments from various sources saying this is the time for the young people. The old people who are used to leading black affairs must step down because their time is over. . . . The government does not listen to them. It is the youth who must lead the way. . . . Yet these people become confused when there is a need to define this new approach. People talk about this new strategy when they do not know what it is. Then people start despising each other . . . and those who do not support this new move are forsaken. . . . The old people did not have any difficulty in this regard because they knew that whether you are old or young it is experience which says the most. . . . The youth is only interested in inheriting things it has not worked for. A person who says the youth must lead reminds me of the fable which says the tail of the snake once said it does not like being led by the head. The tail was given a chance to lead . . . [but] it had no eyes. The tail led until the snake got into a fire and burnt [up]. Our courts and our government and we must know that the youth is the tail. The bible says a nation with no vision perishes. I am now old and I have no faith in young people. I do not say they must not be present in our meetings. I only say I do not have faith in them.[68]

The raw emotion of this passage—written ten years after the introduction of apartheid—was almost palpable. Perhaps its most curious aspect was the line: "Our courts and our government and we must know that the youth is the tail." In *E-Indiya nase East Africa, Imbumba yamaNyama,* and even elsewhere in *IziDungulwana,* Jabavu had expressed his disillusionment with the white South African government in the 1950s. That he would blame the younger generation of African politicians for the divisions of the 1950s suggests that, at some level, he still believed that white racism — even in its extreme apartheid form — could be cured by moral suasion rather than by confrontation. His bitterness was misplaced, for ultimately it would be "those he had trained" who would free South Africa and gain equality for all its citizens.

On May 4, 1959, Jabavu was hospitalized in East London to treat an infected ulcer on his right leg. In his last letter to his daughter Noni, written in a very shaky hand, he told her that he was "likely to remain here two or three weeks."[69] He would never leave; he died three months later on August 3, 1959, at the age of seventy-four.[70] Benson Dyantyi, the *Drum* journalist who visited him in the hospital during his illness, noted with dismay that "on Jili's table, on my last visit, I saw only a few messages wishing him a speedy recovery." Dyantyi recalled how "as a youngster, growing up in a period when I doubted whether perhaps black people might not be inferior after all, Jili's memoirs and his tours inspired me and dispelled my fears." Was it now the case, Dyantyi wondered, "that the women and men of Africa had forgotten" — as Jabavu himself had seemed to fear in 1958 — that he had "provided light when it was dark?"[71]

They had not forgotten—2,000 mourners attended his funeral on August 10, 1959, at Middledrift;[72] 250 people showed up at the service to erect a memorial headstone to him on July 8, 1963. At the second service Alexander Kerr, who had shared D. D. T. Jabavu's belief in education and progress and with him had built Fort Hare, delivered the eulogy:

From many of the regions of this wide country we are gathered to commemorate his life and work because he was a true pioneer in the uphill task of building a civilized community.

He was one of the first to cross the line that divides one stage of culture from the next higher, and to this advantage he added the distinction of leading others along the route he had himself followed. . . . He was under no illusion about the slowness with which changes among the masses of the people can be brought about. By his churchmanship . . . and his family tradition, he was committed to constitutional, non-violent methods of advocacy, and was convinced that sound public opinion would in time have its result in real progress along the whole social and political front.[73]

In July 1963 Kerr was speaking as much to the leaders of apartheid South Africa, and to the black activists opposing them, as he was praising his old friend. In 1959 the Promotion of Bantu Self-Government Act—which laid the groundwork for the founding of the independent African homelands and removed the last white representatives of Africans from parliament—had passed, as had the Extension of University Education Act, which introduced apartheid into the universities. Fort Hare, once "a microcosmic cross-section of educational South Africa," would become a university for Xhosa speakers only. In March 1960 police opened fire on members of the Pan Africanist Congress peacefully protesting against the pass laws at Sharpeville, killing sixty-seven people. In April 1960 the government banned both the Pan Africanist Congress and the African National Congress. A year later, in May 1961, South Africa declared itself a republic, severed its remaining ties with Britain,[74] and withdrew into isolationism. In November 1961 the ANC responded by establishing a military wing; in December 1961 Umkhonto we Sizwe (The spear of the nation) undertook its first acts of sabotage against the apartheid state. Five months after Kerr spoke at Middledrift, in December 1963, the apartheid regime granted the Transkei limited self-government, the first step on the road to an independence that would be recognized by no other nation but South Africa itself.[75]

In praising D. D. T. Jabavu's dedication to progress, and education, and nonviolence, Kerr was delivering an ode to a South Africa that in 1963 no longer existed, if indeed it ever had. Kerr's eulogy evoked the South Africa envisioned by the Cape liberal tradition, a South Africa that theoretically welcomed educated Christian black men with open arms, promising to ignore the color of their skin if they promised in turn to embrace European traditions. In the Cape Colony of D. D. T. Jabavu's youth, there had seemed—in accepting this model—a real hope of attaining "equal rights for all civilized men." In the South Africa of his adult years, such dreams had been quashed, though the retention of the African franchise in the Cape Province, and the continuance of liberal discourse, had allowed a tantalizing illusion of influence—a "ghost of equality"—to persist at least until the passage of the Representation of Natives in Parliament Act in 1936.

In the apartheid state of his old age, a disillusioned Jabavu criticized the oppressive white government and argued for African unity, as he had done for much of his career. Though he condemned "the white people" who "did not honour their side of the bargain," he stopped far short of a complete rejection of Western civilization, and he was equally critical of the often fractious younger generation of black activists who had dismissed him for his own liberalism. Yet to remember Jabavu as a bitter old man who failed politically is to do him a great disservice. Jabavu's emphasis on elite politics rather than grassroots organization did limit his chances for success, but then the cards were always stacked on the side of a succession of white governments. It would take another thirty-five (often bloody) years after Jabavu's death in 1959 for black South Africans to win their freedom.

D. D. T. Jabavu accomplished a great deal in his long life. When the Royal African Society awarded him its Medal in 1957, the accompanying description praised him as "a distinguished African educationist who has dedicated his life to the advancement of his people."[76] Jabavu had helped train several generations of young men and women at Fort Hare, and beyond the college's gates he had organized African teachers, farmers, and voters. As a lecturer on religious and political issues, he had helped keep the concerns of black South Africans before an international audience. When he accepted the Medal of the Royal African Society in 1957, what he said summed up succinctly his motivation for a lifetime of public service. D. D. T. Jabavu told his audience that as a young man, he had been advised "to do something for his people, not to get something out of them."[77]

Note on Method

Very few of D. D. T. Jabavu's private papers have survived. The main sources for this book were Jabavu's published writings in Xhosa and in English, supplemented by contemporary newspaper, journal, and magazine articles, and the collected papers of notable South Africans, black and white. My deepest scholarly debt is to Cecil Wele Manona of the Institute for Social and Economic Research at Rhodes University, who translated Jabavu's works in Xhosa into English, and who shared his insights about their significance and their accuracy.

A small number of Jabavu's private letters from the late 1940s and early 1950s do survive in the papers collected by his daughter, Helen Nontando Jabavu Crosfield (the author Noni Jabavu).[1] Written in English to Noni Jabavu and her English husband, Denis Preston, then living in London, they paint the picture of a generally contented retiree. The collection also contains an assortment of newspaper clippings from the mid to the late 1950s, some photographs, a copy of the 300-page report on the Tuskegee Institute that D. D. T. Jabavu prepared for the South African government in 1913, and a copy of Jabavu's curriculum vitae.

There is in addition a small collection of D. D. T. Jabavu's papers held by the University of South Africa. The collection includes a number of Jabavu's publications in Xhosa and in English, some letters and photographs, a selection of calendars from the South African Native College, and, buried in the list of "Miscellany," item 6.3, "Exercise books with lists of names."[2] Along with the copy of his vita from the Jabavu Crosfield collection, this last item proved to be the key to tracing much of Jabavu's public career, for in one of the books he had listed every speech he had made, conference he had attended, and sermon he had given between 1923 and 1957. Using this list as a guide, I was able to undertake a systematic search of newspapers, journals, and magazines for articles by or about Jabavu, as well as a search of the various archival collections.

The calendars of the South African Native College, a complete set of which was available at the University of Fort Hare (as the college is now called), also

---

1. Jabavu Crosfield Collection. Approximately three-quarters of the material in this collection concerns Noni Jabavu's career as a journalist in England, Uganda, and South Africa.
2. Jabavu Collection, UNISA, Preliminary Inventory, 5.

proved helpful. Through the 1940s, each yearly calendar listed the graduates of the college to date, their major course of study, and their hometown or village. I cross-checked these names against the telephone listings, and then wrote to inquire if the individual had graduated from the college, had studied under Jabavu, and whether he or she would be willing to speak with me. In a few instances, I made an initial visit to an address, and then one or two follow-up visits before I was finally granted an interview. Overall, the response was positive, and people were extremely generous with their time.

It is these interviews that provide the personal glimpses of Jabavu that appear in the book. Since many of the individuals interviewed had graduated from the South African Native College, and most had had some (usually missionary) education in English, the interviews were conducted in English. While a few informants were in their sixties, most were in their seventies and eighties, since they would have had to have attended the South African Native College in the early 1940s at the latest to have studied with Jabavu before he retired in 1944. Between October 1987 and October 1988, I interviewed more than fifty individuals, and copies of these tapes have been deposited at the Institute for Advanced Social Research (IASR) at the University of the Witwatersrand. Following the advice of IASR fellow Tim Couzens, who interviewed extensively for his biography of H. I. E. Dhlomo, I kept my interviews loosely structured. I asked broad questions about topics that interested me—teaching, politics, religion, family life—and more specific questions depending on how the informant responded.

One notable exception to this pattern was my interview with A. P. Mda, which took place by candlelight in Mafeteng, Lesotho, in August 1988, shortly before I left Africa. Mda, a noted political theorist, had helped frame the ANC Youth League's platform in the late 1940s. So intimidated was I by Gail Gerhart's description of Mda's towering intellect that I designed extremely specific questions to prove to him that I was well prepared.[3] Towering intellect he proved to be, but he was also one of the most engaging and kindest people I have ever met; I do not doubt that our three-hour discussion ultimately led me toward a much more sympathetic assessment of Jabavu's politics, especially in his later years.

In general, those interviewed painted a portrait of D. D. T. Jabavu consistent with that suggested by the public record of his life. The interviews also occasionally posed a dilemma for me as a biographer, since mixed in with the political commentary and the social history was a fair bit of gossip. Jabavu's relationship with his first wife was often strained; they lived apart for many

---

3. Gerhart, *Black Power*, 124–35.

years, though they had reconciled by the time of her death in 1951. If he wore any "mask," it was perhaps one that hid this private turmoil. It is the use and misuse of this sort of evidence that opens the biographer to charges of gossip mongering and voyeurism, and to the assertion that the phrase "scholarly biography" is an oxymoron.[4] Ultimately I decided that in this study of Jabavu's public lives, I would simply acknowledge that his first marriage was a rocky one, and leave it at that.

No biographer, and indeed no historian, can claim to have written a definitive work. There is little question, for example, that this book would be very different if it had been written by a Xhosa-speaker. It is also very much the case that in the course of writing about someone else's life, all biographers (and perhaps especially first-time biographers), learn as much about themselves as they do about their subject. I have often wondered how I would feel if someone knew as much about my life as I have learned about D. D. T. Jabavu. I would hope that even with their subject safely dead, they would try to be fair, and generous, and to tell—as much as it is possible to do in the cynical age in which we live—the truth.

---

4. Robert Skidelsky, "Only Connect: Biography and Truth," 1; Janet Malcolm, "Annals of Biography: The Silent Women," *New Yorker*, August 23 and 30, 1993, 86; Karen J. Winkler, "'Seductions of Biography': Scholars Delve into New Questions about Race, Class, and Sexuality," *Chronicle of Higher Education* 40, no. 10 (October 27, 1993): A6.

Abbreviations in Notes and Bibliography

ABC	American Board of Commissioners for Foreign Missions Archives
CA	Cape Archives Depot, Cape Town
CAD	Central Archives Depot, Pretoria
CMT	Chief Magistrate Transkei
DSAB	*Dictionary of South African Biography*
GNLB	Government Native Labour Bureau
HU	Harvard University
KHK	Keiskammahoek
LC	Library of Congress
MOOC	Master of the Supreme Court
NTS	Native Affairs
TAD	Transvaal Archives Depot
UCT	University of Cape Town
UFH	University of Fort Hare
UNISA	University of South Africa
UWL	University of the Witwatersrand Library
YDSL	Yale Divinity School Library
YUL	Yale University Library

NOTE ON TRANSLATIONS

D. D. T. Jabavu's works in Xhosa (listed in the bibliography under the subheading "Selected Writings of D. D. T. Jabavu") were translated into English by Cecil Wele Manona. The translations themselves have not been published and are designated in both the notes and bibliography by the term *[unpub.]*. All page references in the notes are to these unpublished translations, which are in the author's possession. In a few instances, the punctuation and spelling in the translations have been changed to correspond with American rather than South African style.

NOTES

Introduction

1. D. D. T. Jabavu, [Curriculum Vitae], Helen Nontando Jabavu Crosfield Collection, in the care of Harrison M. Wright, Professor Emeritus, Swarthmore College, Swarthmore, Pennsylvania (hereafter Jabavu Crosfield Collection); "Death Notice. Davidson Don Tengo Jabavu," Master of the Supreme Court, Grahamstown, no. 1080/59.

2. W. M. Tsotsi used the phrase the "ghost of equality" in a 1941 article about Jabavu. W. M. Tsotsi, "Gallery of African Heroes Past and Present: Davidson Don Tengo Jabavu," *Inkundla ya Bantu* (The Bantu Forum), June 1941. (I am grateful to Robert Edgar for this reference.) D. D. T. Jabavu, *The Segregation Fallacy and Other Papers: A Native View of Some South African Inter-Racial Problems* (Lovedale, 1928), 29. T. R. H. Davenport, *South Africa: A Modern History*, 3d ed. (Toronto, 1987), 570.

3. A phrase inspired in part by William Zinsser, *Extraordinary Lives: The Art and Craft of American Biography* (New York, 1986).

4. Saul Dubow, *Racial Segregation and the Origins of Apartheid in South Africa* (Houndmills, England, 1989), 150–51.

5. Zinsser, *Extraordinary Lives*, 17–18.

6. Shula Marks, *The Ambiguities of Dependence in South Africa: Class, Nationalism, and the State in Twentieth-Century Natal* (Johannesburg, 1986), 2. See also Frantz Fanon, *Black Skin, White Masks*, trans. Charles Lam Markmann (New York, 1967).

7. D. D. T. Jabavu, "Christian Service in Rural and Industrial South Africa," *The Christian Mission in the World Today*, Report of the Eleventh Quadrennial Convention of the Student Volunteer Movement for Foreign Missions, Buffalo, New York, December 30, 1931, to January 3, 1932, ed. Raymond P. Currier (New York, 1932), 65.

8. A phrase borrowed from Jane Starfield, "'Not Quite History': The Autobiographies of H. Selby Msimang and R.V. Selope Thema and the Writing of South African History," *Social Dynamics* 14, no. 2 (1988): 24.

9. Frieda Matthews described her husband, the scholar and ANC leader Z. K. Matthews, in this manner. Frieda Matthews, *Remembrances* (Bellville, South Africa, 1995), 37.

10. D. D. T. Jabavu, *Imbumba yamaNyama* (Unity is strength), trans. Cecil Wele Manona [unpub.] (Lovedale, 1952).

11. Tim Couzens, *The New African: A Study of the Life and Work of H. I. E. Dhlomo* (Johannesburg, 1985), 1–39. See also Leonard Ngcongco, "*Imvo Zabantsundu* and Cape 'Native' Policy, 1884–1902" (M.A. thesis, University of South Africa, 1974), 39; and André Odendaal, "African Political Mobilisation in the Eastern Cape, 1880–1910" (Ph.D. diss., Cambridge University, 1983), 106.

12. See below, "A Note on Method."

13. Michael Holroyd, "How I Fell into Biography," *The Troubled Face of Biography*, ed. Eric Homberger and John Charmley (New York, 1988), 98–99; Robert Skidelsky, "Only

Connect: Biography and Truth," *Troubled Face of Biography*, 2; Zinsser, *Extraordinary Lives*, 18–19.

14. Among white South Africans, former prime ministers J. B. M. Hertzog and Jan Christian Smuts along with former Cape Colony premier and mining magnate Cecil Rhodes have been the subject of several biographies, including: J. H. le Roux, P. W. Coetzer and A. H. Marais, eds., *Generaal J. B. M. Hertzog: Sy strewe en stryd* (General J. B. M. Hertzog: His triumphs and struggles) (Johannesburg, 1987); Christiann Maruitus van den Heever, *Generaal J. B. M. Hertzog* (Johannesburg, 1943); William Keith Hancock, *Smuts*, vol. 1, *The Sanguine Years, 1870–1919* (Cambridge, 1962), vol. 2, *The Fields of Force, 1919–1950* (Cambridge, 1968); Kenneth Ingham, *Jan Christian Smuts: The Conscience of a South African* (Johannesburg, 1986); Brian Roberts, *Cecil Rhodes: Flawed Colossus* (New York, 1988); Robert I. Rotberg, *The Founder: Cecil Rhodes and the Pursuit of Power* (New York, 1988). While no attempt is made here to provide a comprehensive list of biographies of white South Africans, Phyllis Lewsen's study of the Cape politician John X. Merriman (*John X. Merriman: Paradoxical South African Statesman* [New Haven, 1982]) is noteworthy for both its careful attention to detail and immense readability. In what some might consider an appropriate swing of the academic pendulum, the rather negative scholarly response to Basil Hone's recent book *The First Son of South Africa to Be Premier: Thomas Charles Scanlen, 1834–1912* (Oldwick, N.J., 1993) suggests that it may soon be white South Africans who are hidden from historical view. See, for example, *Historian* 57 (1995): 370; *International Journal of African Historical Studies* 28 (1994): 139.

15. T. D. Mweli Skota, *The African Yearly Register: Being an Illustrated National Biographical Dictionary (Who's Who) of Black Folks in Africa* (Johannesburg, 1930). For a discussion of Skota's work, see Couzens, *New African*, 1–19.

16. E. M. Ramaila, *Tsa bophelo bya moruti Abraham Serote* (The life of Abraham Serote). D. D. T. Jabavu, *The Influence of English on Bantu Literature* (Lovedale, 1943), 5.

17. S. E. K. Mqhayi's *uJohn Knox Bokwe: Ibali ngobomi bakhe* (John Knox Bokwe: The story of his life) (Lovedale, 1925) was reissued as *U-bomi bom-fundisi u John Knox Bokwe* (The life of Reverend John Knox Bokwe) in 1972. In *Ibhibliyografi yolwimi olusisixhosa ukuya kutsho kunyaka we-1990* (Bibliography of the Xhosa language to the year 1990), comp. M. A. Peters and C. P. Bothma, Xhosa text ed. G. T. Sirayi (Pretoria, 1992), only the English language second edition of John Knox Bokwe's *Ntsikana: The Story of an African Convert*, 2d ed. (Lovedale, 1914) is listed. D. D. T. Jabavu's 1943 list also included: A. Lavisa, *Amanqaku bo-ufi Capt. Veldtman* (The life of Captain Veldtman Bikitsa) (Umtata, 1917), issued by the Transkei Gazette; L. N. Mzimba, *Umfundisi Pambani Jeremiah Mzimba: Ibali lobomi nomsebenzi womfi* (The life and work of Rev. Pambani Jeremiah Mzimba) (Lovedale, 1923); and S. E. K. Mqhayi, *U So-Gqumahashe (N. C. UMhala)* (Chief N. C. Mhala of Gqumahashe) (Lovedale, 1921). R. R. R. Dhlomo's *uShaka* (Pietermaritzburg, 1937), a "descriptive dialogue" of Shaka Zulu's life, in Zulu, might also be added to this list. D. D. T. Jabavu, *Influence of English on Bantu Literature*, 9, 22.

18. Jeffrey Peires, "The Lovedale Press: Literature for the Bantu Revisited," *History in Africa* 6 (1979): 157. Peires noted that D. D. T. Jabavu was not a completely disinterested

reader of Xhosa manuscripts for the Lovedale Press; he tended to oppose any mention of ethnic conflict (166).

19. D. D. T. Jabavu, *Influence of English on Bantu Literature*, 22. Jabavu described his own travel books in Xhosa, *E-Amerika* (Lovedale, 1932) and *E-Jerusalem* (Lovedale, 1928), in similar terms.

20. The Lovedale press published S. E. K. Mqhayi's autobiography, *U-Mqhayi wase-Ntab'ozuko* (Mqhayi of the Mount of Glory), in 1939.

21. Nelson Mandela, *Long Walk to Freedom: The Autobiography of Nelson Mandela* (Boston, 1994).

22. Albert Luthuli, *Let My People Go* (n.p., 1962); Z. K. Matthews, *Freedom for My People: The Autobiography of Z. K. Matthews, Southern Africa, 1901–1968*, memoir by Monica Wilson (Cape Town, 1981). See also Thomas Karis, *Hope and Challenge, 1935–1952*, vol. 2 of *From Protest to Challenge: A Documentary History of African Politics 1882–1964*, ed. Thomas Karis and Gwendolen M. Carter (Stanford, Calif., 1972–73, 1987); Thomas Karis and Gail Gerhart, *Challenge and Violence, 1953–1964*, vol. 3 of *From Protest to Challenge*; Fatima Meer, *Higher than Hope: The Authorized Biography of Nelson Mandela* (Johannesburg, 1988; New York, 1990); Francis Meli, *South Africa Belongs to Us: A History of the ANC* (Harare, 1988); Peter Walshe, *The Rise of African Nationalism in South Africa: The African National Congress 1912–1952* (London, 1970).

23. Ellen Kuzwayo, *Call Me Woman* (Johannesburg, 1985); Mark Mathabane, *Kaffir Boy: The True Story of a Black Youth's Coming of Age in Apartheid South Africa* (New York, 1986); Emma Mashinini, *Strikes Have Followed Me All My Life: A South African Autobiography* (New York, 1991); Phyllis Ntantala, *A Life's Mosaic: The Autobiography of Phyllis Ntantala* (Berkeley, 1992); Frieda Matthews, *Remembrances*. Again, no attempt is made here to offer a comprehensive list of autobiographies by black South Africans. Two autobiographical works by Jabavu's daughter Noni, which were particularly relevant to the writing of this biography, should be noted: Noni Jabavu, *Drawn in Colour: African Contrasts* (London, 1960), and *The Ochre People: Scenes from a South African Life* (London, 1963).

24. Shula Marks, *Not Either an Experimental Doll: The Separate Worlds of Three South African Women* (Bloomington, Ind., 1987), 1. Both Frieda Matthews (*Remembrances*, 10, 29–30) and Phyllis Ntantala (*Life's Mosaic*, 230) acknowledge this reality in their respective autobiographies.

25. Starfield, "'Not Quite History,'" 1. Frieda Matthews might disagree with this assessment; she explained in her introduction that she wrote the book for her grandchildren (*Remembrances*, x.) In her concern that they know the truth, however, she shares much with other autobiographers.

26. Starfield, "'Not Quite History,'" 1.

27. This is not to deny that historians select evidence to support a particular argument. Skidelsky, "Only Connect," 2. See below, "A Note on Method."

28. Brian Willan, *Sol Plaatje: South African Nationalist, 1876–1932* (Berkeley, 1984), vii.

29. This was the case with Leonard Thompson's *Survival in Two Worlds: Moshoeshoe of Lesotho* (Oxford, 1975), which revived historical biography in its modern form in

South Africa. The same may be said of Doreen Musson's popular biography of the trade unionist John Gomas (*Johnny Gomas, Voice of the Working Class: A Political Biography* [Cape Town, 1989]).

30. Interview with A. P. Mda, Mafeteng, Lesotho, August 22, 1988. Ashby Peter Solomzi A. P. Mda was born in the Herschel district of the eastern Cape in 1916. He earned a B.A. by correspondence from the University of South Africa in 1946, and worked as a teacher in Johannesburg before qualifying as a lawyer in 1960. With Nelson Mandela, he was a founder of the ANC Youth League in 1944, and served as its president from 1947 to 1949. Gail Gerhart and Thomas Karis, *Political Profiles 1882–1964*, vol. 4 of *From Protest to Challenge: A Documentary History of African Politics 1882–1964*, ed. Thomas Karis and Gwendolen Carter (Stanford, Calif., 1972–73, 1987), 85.

1 Southern Africa and the Wider World, 1885–1914

1. The colony was originally established in 1652 by the Dutch East India Company as a station to reprovision its ships en route to Asia. The colony was seized by the British in 1795, during the French Revolutionary Wars (to prevent it falling to the French), returned to the Dutch in 1803 by the Treaty of Amiens, and claimed by the British again in 1806. Leonard Thompson, *A History of South Africa* (New Haven, 1990), 33, 52. In 1689, 180 French Huguenots who had fled France for the Netherlands after the revocation of the Edict of Nantes in 1685, settled at the Cape. German settlers were added to the mix in the eighteenth century. The dominant culture, however, remained Dutch. As the historian Rodney Davenport has noted, "An originally diverse European settler population was . . . coaxed into cultural uniformity, with the language of the Netherlands and the religion of the Reformed Church for cement." Davenport, *South Africa*, 3d ed., 22–23.

2. The Mpondo remained independent until 1894, when they signed a treaty with the Cape Colony. The Venda were conquered in 1896. Sir Walter Stanford, *The Reminiscences of Sir Walter Stanford*, ed. J. W. Macquarrie, 2 vols. (Cape Town, 1962), 2:1 47–67. Thompson, *History of South Africa*, 89, 123.

3. Approximately 5,000 British settlers arrived in 1820. Thompson, *History of South Africa*, 55.

4. Ibid., 56.

5. Ibid., 88.

6. Ibid., 93.

7. Ibid., 89, 95–96.

8. Ibid., 102.

9. Ibid., 98.

10. Stanley Trapido, "Liberalism in the Cape in the Nineteenth and Twentieth Centuries," *Collected Seminar Papers on the Societies of Southern Africa in the Nineteenth and Twentieth Centuries*, University of London, Institute of Commonwealth Studies (October 1972–June 1973), 55; T. R. H. Davenport, "The Cape Liberal Tradition to 1910,"

Democratic Liberalism in South Africa: Its History and Prospect, ed. Jeffrey Butler, David Welsh, and Richard Elphick (Middletown, Conn., 1987), 31.

11. Thompson, *History of South Africa*, 64.

12. Trapido, "Liberalism in the Cape," 55. See also Stanley Trapido, "The Origins of the Cape Franchise Qualifications of 1853," *Journal of African History* 5, no. 1 (1964): 37–54.

13. Phyllis Lewsen, "The Cape Liberal Tradition: Myth or Reality?" *Race: Journal of the Institute of Race Relations* 12, no. 1 (July 1971): 79.

14. Davenport, "Cape Liberal Tradition," 32; Trapido, "Liberalism in the Cape," 57; see also Trapido, "Cape Franchise Qualifications." White women were granted the right to vote in 1930. Davenport, *South Africa*, 3d ed., 101, 304.

15. D. D. T. Jabavu, *Segregation Fallacy*, 29.

16. Thompson, *History of South Africa*, 114–20; Davenport, *The Afrikaner Bond: The History of a South African Political Party, 1880–1911* (Cape Town, 1966), 147–48.

17. Davenport, *Afrikaner Bond*, 184. The phrase had originally been "equal rights for all white men in southern Africa." Rhodes changed it to "civilized men" in order to court the African and Coloured vote during the 1898 election. George M. Frederickson, *Black Liberation: A Comparative History of Black Ideologies in the United States and South Africa* (New York, 1995), 43.

18. D. D. T. Jabavu, *Segregation Fallacy*, 29, 45.

19. Trapido, "Liberalism in the Cape," 57; Lewsen, *John X. Merriman*, 17.

20. Davenport, "Cape Liberal Tradition," 32.

21. Mandela, *Long Walk to Freedom*, 11.

22. D. D. T. Jabavu, *John Tengo Jabavu*, 8, 16.

23. Though both father and son shared the name Tengo, only the senior Jabavu was generally known as Tengo Jabavu. D. D. T. Jabavu, *John Tengo Jabavu*, 9, 26.

24. Ibid., 7.

25. The anthropologist Monica Wilson has identified individuals with the clan name Jele (Jili) as far north as Tanzania, a testament to the disruptive effects of the Mfecane. Monica Wilson, "The Nguni Peoples," *A History of South Africa to 1870*, ed. Monica Wilson and Leonard Thompson, 2d ed. (Beckenham, England, 1982), 100. See also John Ayliff and Joseph Whiteside, *History of the Abambo Generally Known as Fingos* (1912; reprint, Cape Town, 1962), 2, 91–92, 96.

26. The historian Julian Cobbing has questioned this standard interpretation of the origins of the Mfengu, positing instead that they were refugees from a missionary-supported slave trade off the eastern coast of South Africa. See Julian Cobbing, "The Mfecane as Alibi: Thoughts on Dithakong and Mbolompo," *Journal of African History* 29 (1988): 487–519. Cobbing's interpretation has in turn been questioned by the historians Richard Bouch ("The Mfengu Revisited: The Nineteenth Century Experience of One Mfengu Community through the Eyes of Historians and Contemporaries," *Collected Seminar Papers on the Societies of Southern Africa in the Nineteenth and Twentieth Centuries*, vol. 17, University of London, Institute of Commonwealth Studies [October 1989–June 1990], 81–89), and Elizabeth Eldredge ("Sources of Conflict in Southern

Africa, c. 1800–1830: The 'Mfecane' Reconsidered," *Journal of African History* 33 [1992]: 1–35). For the traditional interpretation of the impact of the Mfecane on the Mfengu, see, J. D. Omer-Cooper, *The Zulu Aftermath: A Nineteenth-Century Revolution in Bantu Africa* (London, 1966), 5n, 164–67.

27. By the late eighteenth century, the Xhosa lineage had split into three major sections: "the Gcaleka centered east of the Kei River; the Ngqika between the Kei and the Fish; and the Ndlambe in the area known as the Zuurveld, west of the Fish." Thompson, *History of South Africa*, 73; J. B. Peires, *The House of Phalo: A History of the Xhosa People in the Days of Their Independence* (Berkeley, 1982), 31, 58–61.

28. The Transkei was bordered on the north by the Umzimkulu River, on the south by the Kei River, and extended west to the Drakensberg Mountain range.

29. D. D. T. Jabavu, *John Tengo Jabavu*, 7; D. D. T. Jabavu, comp., *I-Nkulungwane yama Mfengu 1835–1935 ne si-vivane: Fingo Centenary 1835–1935 and Centenary Fund*, trans. Cecil Wele Manona [unpub.] (Lovedale, [1935]), 4. See also Ayliff and Whiteside, *History of the Abambo*; and Peires, *House of Phalo*, 88.

30. Colin Bundy, *The Rise and Fall of the South African Peasantry* (Berkeley, 1979), 33.

31. The Ciskei region (later the Ciskei Reserve) was bordered on the north by the Kei River, on the south by the Fish River, and extended west to the Drakensberg Mountain range. Les Switzer, *Power and Resistance in an African Society: The Ciskei Xhosa and the Making of South Africa* (Madison, Wis., 1993), 194.

32. The war of 1834–35 was the sixth in a series of nine Frontier Wars beginning in 1779 between Dutch settlers and their Xhosa allies and rival Xhosa chiefdoms, and, continuing after 1806, between the British colonial authorities and the Xhosa. Peires, *House of Phalo*, 75, 110–11; Bundy, *Rise and Fall*, 32–33; Thompson, *History of South Africa*, 73–80. See also Noël Mostert, *Frontiers: The Epic of South Africa's Creation and the Tragedy of the Xhosa People* (New York, 1992), 714–23.

33. D. D. T. Jabavu, *I-Nkulungwane yama Mfengu*, 4.

34. Richard A. Moyer, "The Mfengu, Self-Defence and the Cape Frontier Wars," *Beyond the Cape Frontier: Studies in the History of the Transkei and Ciskei*, ed. C. Saunders and R. Derricourt (London, 1974), 101–26; Richard A. Moyer, "A History of the Mfengu of the Eastern Cape 1815–1865" (Ph.D. diss., University of London, 1976), 422–74; Bundy, *Rise and Fall*, 32–35.

35. Bundy, *Rise and Fall*, 34; Peires, *House of Phalo*, 75; J. B. Peires, *The Dead Will Arise: Nongqawuse and the Great Xhosa Cattle-Killing Movement of 1856–7* (Bloomington, Ind., 1989), 85; Omer-Cooper, *Zulu Aftermath*, 167; Thompson, *History of South Africa*, 52–53.

36. Many of the peoples of Natal, to whom most Mfengu traced their origins, did not practice circumcision. John Henderson Soga, *The Ama-Xosa: Life and Customs* (Lovedale, [1931]), 247–48. For a discussion of initiation, see Wallace George Mills, "The Role of the African Clergy in the Reorientation of Xhosa Society to the Plural Society in the Cape Colony, 1850–1915" (Ph.D. diss., University of California at Los Angeles, 1975), 84; and Vincent Zanoxolo Gitywa, "Male initiation in the Ciskei: Formal Incorporation into Bantu Society" (Ph.D. diss., University of Fort Hare, 1976).

37. Peires, *House of Phalo*, 88; Bundy, *Rise and Fall*, 33; Cecil Manona, "Ethnic Relations in the Ciskei," *Ciskei: Economics and Politics of Dependence in a South African Homeland*, ed. Nancy Charton (London, 1980), 103.

38. Mostert, *Frontiers*, 722.

39. D. D. T. Jabavu, *I-Nkulungwane yama Mfengu*, 1. This interpretation is supported by Peires, who traces the name Mfengu to the Xhosa verb "*ukumfenguza*, 'to wander about seeking service.'" Peires, *House of Phalo*, 88.

40. Ayliff and Whiteside, *History of the Abambo*, 1.

41. D. D. T. Jabavu, "The 'Fingo Slavery' Myth," *South African Outlook*, June 1, 1935, 123–24. See also J. B. Ross, "The Fingo Slavery Myth," *South African Outlook*, July 1, 1935, 134–35; T. M. Makiwane, "The Fingo Slavery Myth," *South African Outlook*, September 2, 1935, 194–95.

42. D. D. T. Jabavu, "'Fingo Slavery' Myth," 123.

43. Ibid., 124.

44. Ibid.

45. The anthropologist Cecil Manona did identify Ayliff as the source of the slavery myth. Manona, "Ethnic Relations in the Ciskei," 101.

46. Peires, *House of Phalo*, 88–89, 110.

47. As the historian Leroy Vail has pointed out, this was hardly a charitable interpretation of Mfengu actions, for it effectively robbed them of agency. Leroy Vail, ed., *The Creation of Tribalism in Southern Africa* (Berkeley, 1989), 3–4.

48. D. D. T. Jabavu, "'Fingo Slavery' Myth," 123. Manona has suggested a similar interpretation. Manona, "Ethnic Relations in the Ciskei," 98.

49. Mandela, *Long Walk to Freedom*, 10–11; Omer-Cooper, *Zulu Aftermath*, 167; Manona, "Ethnic Relations in the Ciskei," 97; Conversation with Nombuyiselo Luphiwana, August 14, 1995. Luphiwana grew up in Idutywa in the Transkei in the 1970s and 1980s. For a discussion of the manipulation of this ethnic divide by the homeland government of Lennox Sebe in the 1980s, see [J. B. Peires], "Ethnicity and Pseudo-Ethnicity in the Ciskei," *The Creation of Tribalism in Southern Africa*, ed. Leroy Vail (Berkeley, 1989), 395–413, and Manona, 106–19.

50. D. D. T. Jabavu, *Imbumba yamaNyama*, 1; D. D. T. Jabavu, "Social Reform," *The Black Problem: Papers and Addresses on Various Native Problems* (Lovedale, 1920), 153; Peires, "Lovedale Press," 166; D. D. T. Jabavu to R. H. W. Shepherd, February 8, 1933, Cory Library for Historical Research, Rhodes University, MS16,321 (hereafter Cory Library). "Fingo Emancipation Day," or AbaMbo Day (after the region in Natal from which many Mfengu came), as Jabavu himself preferred to call it, was first celebrated in 1908; the rival Ntsikana Day celebration began in 1909. Switzer, *Power and Resistance*, 158. The historian John Henderson Soga insisted that "the Fingos are not Aba-Mbo. The majority of the tribes called Fingo are of Lala or Kalanga origin." J. Henderson Soga, *The South-Eastern Bantu (Abe-Nguni, Aba-Mbo, Ama-Lala)* (Johannesburg, 1930), 65.

51. Thirty years later Jabavu was still writing about the issue; he addressed it again in *Imbumba yamaNyama*, which he published privately in 1952.

52. D. D. T. Jabavu, *Imbumba yamaNyama*, 1.

53. Jabavu's efforts at redefinition were hardly unique; as the philosopher Kwame Anthony Appiah has observed: "Every human identity is constructed, historical; every one has its share of false presuppositions, of the errors and inaccuracies that courtesy calls 'myth,' religion 'heresy,' and science 'magic.'" Kwame Anthony Appiah, *In My Father's House: Africa in the Philosophy of Culture* (New York, 1992), 174.

54. D. D. T. Jabavu, "'Fingo Slavery' Myth," 124.

55. D. D. T. Jabavu, "Social Reform," *Black Problem*, 155.

56. André Odendaal, *Vukani Bantu!: The Beginnings of Black Protest Politics in South Africa to 1912* (Cape Town, 1984), 64–91, and "African Political Mobilisation," 171–90, 189; William Beinart, *Twentieth-Century South Africa* (Oxford, 1994), 92–93.

57. In 1895, as premier of the Cape Colony, Cecil Rhodes had financed an attempt to overthrow the Transvaal government and seize control of the gold fields discovered in 1886. Disgust at the failed Jameson Raid led several prominent liberal politicians—including James Rose Innes, John X. Merriman, and Jacobus Sauer, all longtime allies of Tengo Jabavu's—gradually to realign themselves with the Afrikaner Bond, an ethnic political party established in the Cape Colony in 1880. The historian Leonard Ngcongco has argued that it was Tengo Jabavu's alliance with Rose Innes and other "friends of the natives" that led him to support the Afrikaner Bond in 1898. Thompson, *History of South Africa*, 114–15; Leonard Ngcongco, "John Tengo Jabavu, 1859–1921," *Black Leaders in Southern African History*, ed. Christopher Saunders (London, 1979), 151; Davenport, *Afrikaner Bond*, ix, 169, 184–86.

58. D. D. T. Jabavu, *John Tengo Jabavu*, 125–26. While Odendaal deleted the "Fingo" reference in his analysis of the incident, stressing instead the ideological differences between Tengo Jabavu and his opponents, Peires has stressed that Tengo Jabavu's opponents—particularly his longtime nemesis Walter Rubusana—were frequently Xhosa. Odendaal, "African Political Mobilisation," 177; Peires, "Lovedale Press," 161–62.

59. Richard Victor Selope Thema (1886–1955) was born near Pietersburg in the Transvaal into a non-Christian family. He nevertheless attended mission schools, including Lovedale, and passed the School Higher Examination in 1907. He worked as a clerk and became active in the SANNC (ANC) in 1912. He was part of the SANNC deputation to Versailles and the United Kingdom in 1919, and while in London, he took a journalism course. On his return to South Africa, he edited the SANNC newspaper *Abantu-Batho* (The people), and in 1932 he became the editor of the newly founded *Bantu World*. He joined D. D. T. Jabavu in the All African Convention in 1935, and was a member of the government Natives' Representative Council from 1937 to 1951. Gerhart and Karis, *Political Profiles*, 155–57.

60. Davenport, *South Africa*, 3d ed., 554.

61. Henry Daniel Tyamzashe was born in Kimberley in 1880. He graduated from Lovedale, where he studied printing, and became a journalist. In 1925 he was a founding member of the Industrial and Commercial Workers' Union (ICU). Gerhart and Karis, *Political Profiles* 161–62.

62. *Cape Mercury*, November 7, 1923.

63. Ibid.

64. Manona, "Ethnic Relations in the Ciskei," 105.

65. Tengo Jabavu was born in 1859. D. D. T. Jabavu, *John Tengo Jabavu*, 8.

66. An industrial school (named after its benefactor, James Heald) was established at Healdtown in 1857, but closed in 1859 when the colonial government withdrew its funding. It reopened in 1867 to train Africans as teachers and Methodist ministers. Ayliff and Whiteside, *History of the Abambo*, 53–54; Clifford Holden, *A Brief History of Methodism and of Methodist Missions in South Africa* (London, 1877), 336–37; J. Whiteside, *History of the Wesleyan Methodist Church of South Africa* (London, 1906), 236–37, 284; R. Hunt Davis, "School vs. Blanket and Settler: Elijah Makiwane and the Leadership of the Cape School Community," *African Affairs* 78, no. 310 (January 1979): 15–16.

67. *Oxford English Dictionary*, 2d ed., s.v. "matriculation"; "Testimonials in Favour of Mr. John Tengo-Jabavu," D. D. T. Jabavu Collection, Documentation Centre for African Studies, University of South Africa, Pretoria, AAS 47, fol. 6.1 (hereafter Jabavu Collection, UNISA). The newspaper would have been either the *Somerset and Bedford Courant* (1863–1880) or the *Somerset East Advertiser* (1877–1886). *A List of South African Newspapers 1800–1902* (Pretoria, 1983). In 1883 Tengo Jabavu was the second African to earn a matriculation certificate in the Cape Colony; Simon P. Sihlali had been the first in 1881. D. D. T. Jabavu, *John Tengo Jabavu*, 14.

68. The (Presbyterian) Glasgow Missionary Society's school at Lovedale on the Tyumie River opened in 1841. It was named after one of its early promoters, Dr. John Love. R. H. W. Shepherd, *Lovedale South Africa, 1824–1955* (Alice, 1971), 4–5, 13.

69. D. D. T. Jabavu, *John Tengo Jabavu*, 12–13. *Isigidimi Sama Xosa* began as a supplement to Lovedale's *Kaffir Express* (see below, n124) but was published as an independent newspaper between 1876 and 1888. Les Switzer and Donna Switzer, *The Black Press in South Africa and Lesotho: A Descriptive Bibliographic Guide to African, Coloured and Indian Newspapers, Newsletters and Magazines 1836–1976* (Boston, 1979), 45.

70. He briefly considered studying law. D. D. T. Jabavu, *John Tengo Jabavu*, 20.

71. Odendaal, "African Political Mobilisation," 105.

72. Sir James Rose Innes, *Sir James Rose Innes: Selected Correspondence (1884–1902)*, ed. Harrison M. Wright, Second Series, no. 3 (Cape Town, 1972), 3.

73. Both Rose Innes and Weir had substantial African clienteles. Neville Hogan, "The Posthumous Vindication of Zachariah Gqishela: Reflections on the Politics of Dependence at the Cape in the Nineteenth Century," *Economy and Society in Pre-Industrial Africa*, ed. Shula Marks and Anthony Atmore (Burnt Mill, England, 1980), 278, n18. See also Stanley Trapido, "'The Friends of the Natives': Merchants, Peasants and the Political and Ideological Structure of Liberalism in the Cape, 1854-1910," *Economy and Society in Pre-Industrial Africa*, 247–76.

74. In the ensuing battle for readers, Lovedale's *Isigidimi Sama Xosa* lost, closing in 1888. Switzer and Switzer, *Black Press*, 46; D. D. T. Jabavu, *John Tengo Jabavu*, 21–22; Odendaal, "African Political Mobilisation," 106; Leonard Ngcongco, "*Imvo Zabantsundu*," 35.

75. Odendaal, "African Political Mobilisation," 106. See also, Ngcongco, "*Imvo Zabantsundu*," 39; Couzens, *New African*, 1–39.

76. Meshach Pelem was born at Mxumbu near King William's Town in 1859 and worked as a teacher after graduating from Healdtown. In addition to the SANNC, he also established the Bantu Union (in 1919) to promote unity between the Xhosa and the Mfengu. Walter Rubusana was born at Mnandi in the Somerset East district of the Cape in 1858. He graduated from Lovedale in 1882 and was ordained a minister of the Congregational Church in 1884. He would clash with Tengo Jabavu as a journalist for *Izwi Labantu*, and as a candidate for the Cape Provincial Council. Pambini Jeremiah Mzimba attended Lovedale and was ordained the first African minister in the Free Church of Scotland in 1875, before breaking with the church in 1898. Richard Kawa graduated from Healdtown, and wrote an enduring history of the Mfengu, *I-bali lamaMfengu* (The history of the Mfengu) (Lovedale, 1930). Isaac Wauchope graduated from Healdtown and was active in eastern Cape politics. Odendaal, *Vukani Bantu!*, 5–6, 384, 391; Gerhart and Karis, *Political Profiles*, 126, 134–35; Davis, "School vs. Blanket," 16; Z. K. Matthews, "Our Heritage," Z.K. Matthews Papers, Documentation Centre for African Studies, University of South Africa, Pretoria, Acc.101, F.1.15 (hereafter Matthews Papers, UNISA).

77. Odendaal, "African Political Mobilisation," 33.

78. Odendaal, *Vukani Bantu!*, 6.

79. Of 1,127 students who graduated from Lovedale between 1841 and 1886, 369 (33%) became teachers, 58 (5%) became interpreters, 27 (2%) became ministers, and 299 (27%) became farmers. Of Tengo Jabavu's contemporaries, Walter Rubusana, Simon Sihlali, John Knox Bokwe, and Elijah Makiwane were ministers. Robert H. W. Shepherd, *Lovedale South Africa: The Story of A Century, 1841–1941* (Lovedale, 1940), 484. Odendaal, "African Political Mobilisation," 106; Davis, "School vs. Blanket," 16.

80. Odendaal, *Vukani Bantu!*, 7, 385.

81. Ibid., 8. "Imbumba yamaNyama" translated literally as "hard, solid sinew," and was inspired by Ntsikana, an early Xhosa convert to Christianity and a prophet of the faith, who admonished his followers to be unified.

82. Odendaal, "African Political Mobilisation," 105. See also Marks, *Ambiguities of Dependence*, 1.

83. Citing letters Tengo Jabavu wrote to *Isigidimi* in 1879 and 1880, Odendaal has contended that Tengo Jabavu "declared that the time had come for blacks to elect their own spokesmen to parliament. For the 'nation' to rise it was important that they had a say in government" ("African Political Mobilisation," 49). In his biography of his father, however, D. D. T. Jabavu recorded that Tengo Jabavu had turned down an offer to stand for parliament (he did not give the year), on the grounds that "a Native could exert but little influence in a Parliament composed of whites, and . . . their votes would be effectively utilised if given to some suitable European with satisfactory views and sympathy" (*John Tengo Jabavu*, 18).

84. Odendaal, "African Political Mobilisation," 106.

85. D. D. T. Jabavu, *John Tengo Jabavu*, 23–26; Hogan, "Vindication of Zachariah Gquishela," 275–92.

86. D. D. T. Jabavu, *John Tengo Jabavu*, 25–26.

87. Hogan, "Vindication of Zachariah Gquishela," 287.

88. Trapido, "'Friends of the Natives'"; Ngcongco "John Tengo Jabavu," 151.

89. Tsotsi, "Davidson Don Tengo Jabavu."

90. Noni Jabavu, *Ochre People*, 246.

91. Among the African peoples of southern Africa, primogeniture was a rather more fluid notion. Among the Xhosa, for example, the eldest son of a particular house within a polygynous family would inherit the property of that house, but his status within the broader family was a complex matter dependent on whether his affiliation was to the great house, to the right-hand house, or to a minor house supporting one or the other. Soga, *Ama-Xosa*, 54–56; Peires, *House of Phalo*, 21, 27–29, 46.

92. Peires, *House of Phalo*, 104, 244. Richard (1888-early 1950s) was named after the King William's Town lawyer Richard Rose Innes; Alexander Macaulay (1889–1946) may have been named after a local Methodist minister of the same name. In *The Ochre People* (p. 104), Noni Jabavu suggests that Alexander was named after an African-American singer who visited King William's Town with a touring choir, but the choir in question did not pass through town until October 1890, the year after his birth. W. Sampson, *Rev. Alexander McAulay (President of the Conference [1876], as I Knew Him* [London, 1893]), cited in *History of the Church in Southern Africa: A Select Bibliography of Published Material to 1980*, ed. J. W. Hofmeyr and K. E. Cross, vol. 1 (Pretoria, 1980), 292; Z. K. Matthews, "Our Heritage," Matthews Papers, UNISA, F1.9; Veit Erlmann, "A Feeling of Prejudice: Orpheus M. McAdoo and the Virginia Jubilee Singers in South Africa 1890–1898," *Journal of Southern African Studies* 4, no. 13 (April 1989): 343–44. A third son, Wilson (1892–1952), was named after Wilson Weir, who had also helped finance *Imvo Zabantsundu*. Interview with Violet Jabavu (widow of Wilson's son Matthew) and G. Soya Mama (a poet and artist), New Brighton (Port Elizabeth), Cape, August 12, 1988.

93. R. L. Peteni, *Towards Tomorrow: The Story of the African Teachers' Associations of South Africa* (Morges, Switzerland, 1978), 25; "Particulars. Davidson Don Tengo Jabavu," Cory Library for Historical Research, Rhodes University, Grahamstown, PR4159.

94. Monica Wilson, "Cooperation and Conflict: The Eastern Cape Frontier," *History of South Africa to 1870*, 2d ed., ed. Monica Wilson and Leonard Thompson (Beckenham, England, 1982), 265. Wilson did not indicate how many of this 20 percent were Xhosa and how many were Mfengu. The 1891 census of the King William's Town district reported a population of 86,983, including 8,605 whites, and 77,259 Africans, of whom 21,153 (24%) were Mfengu. "King William's Town: Its Rise and Progress," *King William's Town Directory, Visitor's Guide and Resident's Handbook* (n.p., 1902), 15.

95. Davis, "School vs. Blanket," 13.

96. Wilson, "Cooperation and Conflict," 265.

97. Ibid. This was not an absolute division; two prominent exceptions to the general Xhosa opposition to Christianity were Ntsikana and Tiyo Soga, who in 1856 became the first African ordained a minister of the Wesleyan Methodist Church. Peires, *House of Phalo*, 67–74; Janet Hodgson, *Ntsikana's Great Hymn: A Xhosa Expression of Christianity in the Early Nineteenth Century Eastern Cape*, Communications no. 4 (Cape Town, 1980); Davis, "School vs. Blanket," 15–16; Donovan Williams, *Umfundisi: A Biography of*

Tiyo Soga 1829–1871 (Lovedale, 1978), 25. In 1857 many Xhosa embraced the vision of Nongqawuse, a young girl who claimed that if the Xhosa killed their cattle and burned their crops, the whites (and all the havoc they had wrought) would disappear. An estimated 40,000 Xhosa died of starvation; of the survivors, more than 30,000 crossed the border into the Cape Colony seeking work. With Tiyo Soga as chief evangelist, many also converted to Christianity and began attending school. Peires, *House of Phalo,* 75; Thompson, *History of South Africa,* 79–80; see also Peires, *Dead Will Arise.*

98. Quoted in Frank Molteno, "The Historical Foundations of the Schooling of Black South Africans," *Apartheid and Education: The Education of Black South Africans,* ed. Peter Kallaway (Johannesburg, 1984), 73; John David Shingler, "Education and Political Order in South Africa, 1902–1961" (Ph.D. diss., Yale University, 1973), 55. School attendance for white children did not become compulsory in the Cape until 1905.

99. Molteno, "Historical Foundations," 73. This echoed the sentiments Dale had expressed in his first report as Commissioner of Education in 1868. With the exception of teaching, he observed: "To the educated Kaffir there is no opening" (Molteno, 56). Dale used the term "Kaffirs" inclusively to refer to both "Fingoes" (Mfengu) and "Kaffirs" (Xhosa), and exclusively to refer specifically to the Xhosa. The Xhosa language was also referred to as "Kaffir." The term "Kaffir" at the time was not universally considered a pejorative; Walter Rubusana, testifying before the Cape parliament in the 1890s, apparently said: "We are Kaffirs and do not want to be called black." Personal communication, John Shingler, October 27, 1990.

100. John Tengo Jabavu to [Jacobus] Sauer, August 5, 1913. "Davidson Jabavu. Visit to US 1913–1920," NTS 268 2941/1913/F639, CAD.

101. Noni Jabavu, *Ochre People,* 246–48.

102. "A Brief History of the Lesotho Training College," *Basutoland Witness* (Lesotho Evangelical Church; P.E.M.S.), no. 71 (November 1969): 1 (emphasis in original).

103. Ibid., 1, 4; Hans M. Zell, ed., *The African Book World and Press: A Directory,* 4th ed. (London, 1989), 79.

104. Noni Jabavu, *Ochre People,* 249.

105. For a detailed discussion of the origins and repercussions of the South African War, see Thompson, *History of South Africa,* 110–53; Peter Warwick, ed., *The South African War: The Anglo-Boer War, 1899–1902* (London, 1980); Peter Warwick, *Black People and the South African War, 1899–1902* (Johannesburg, 1983); and Andrew Porter, *The Origins of the South African War: Joseph Chamberlain and the Diplomacy of Imperialism, 1895–1899* (Manchester, 1980).

106. L. D. Ngcongco, "Jabavu and the Anglo-Boer War," *Kleio Bulletin,* no. 2 (October 1970): 8, 16. John X. Merriman (1841–1926) was born in England and immigrated to the Cape Colony with his parents in 1848. He worked as a land surveyor before being elected to the Cape parliament in 1869, and served as the last prime minister of the colony (1908–10) before Union. Lewsen, *John X. Merriman,* 19, 305–29, 371. A supporter of the Cape African franchise, Jacobus Sauer (1850–1913) was born in Burghersdorp, became a lawyer in 1871, and was elected to the Cape parliament in 1874. Davenport, *South Africa,* 3d ed., 257, 262; Trapido, "'Friends of the Natives,'" 252–53.

107. Ngcongco, "Jabavu and the Anglo-Boer War," 16.

108. Noni Jabavu, *Ochre People*, 249.

109. Ibid., 249–50.

110. Of the ten children born to Tengo Jabavu and Elda Sakuba Jabavu, only Davidson, Richard, Alexander, and Wilson survived to adulthood. Noni Jabavu, *Ochre People*, 239; Elda Tengo Jabavu, Death Notice 2913/00, vol. 115, fol. 702, MOOC 6.9.408, CA. Tengo Jabavu had four daughters with his second wife—Dorothea Ntombile, Lydia Leila, Priscilla Hannah, and Mary Nomatamsanqa—three of whom survived to adulthood. I was unsuccessful in tracing any of these women when I was in South Africa in 1987 and 1988. "Estate of the Late John Tengo Jabavu," Death Notice 2899/21, vol. 177, fol. 327, MOOC 6/9/1–6/9/3455, CA.

111. The term appears to have begun in August. Lovedale Missionary Institution, *Report for 1902* (Lovedale, 1903), 70–71. Department of Public Education, *Report No. 2319*, Lovedale, Boys' (F.C.) Standard V (School Elementary), November 5–12, 1900; Department of Public Education, Report no. 2029, Lovedale Training School (U.F.C.), October 2, 1901, Lovedale Missionary Institution Papers (uncatalogued collection), Howard Pim Library of Rare Books, University of Fort Hare (hereafter Lovedale Papers, UFH).

112. Interview with James Taylor Davidson and Sipo Makalima, Alice, Ciskei, October 27, 1987; interview with Sipo Makalima, November 23, 1987; interview with Ethel Mzamane, February 12, 1988. James Davidson graduated from Rhodes University with a B.A. in 1927 and taught physics and mathematics, first at Lovedale and then at the South African Native College at Fort Hare from 1934 to 1971. He died on November 7, 1987. Alexander Kerr, *Fort Hare 1915–48: The Evolution of an African College* (Pietermaritzburg, 1968), 275; *Rhodes Newsletter*, June 1988, 12. Sipo Makalima graduated from the South African Native College with a B.A. in 1938 and taught history at Lovedale and at Fort Hare. Ethel N. Mzamane graduated from Lovedale and was closely associated with Fort Hare through her husband Godfrey I. M. Mzamane, who earned a B.A. and an M.A. from the college and joined its staff as a lecturer in African languages in 1947. Gerhart and Karis, *Political Profiles*, 107; Kerr, *Fort Hare*, 276.

113. Dale College was founded in 1877. "Dale College King William's Town," *Eastern Province Herald* (Port Elizabeth), advertisement in *Educational Review* [Supplement], October 12, 1932.

114. D. D. T. Jabavu, *John Tengo Jabavu*, 14; Z. K. Matthews, "Our Heritage," Matthews Papers, UNISA, F1.7, F1.9.

115. *Cape Mercury*, September 3, 1901.

116. Ibid.

117. *Cape Mercury*, September 2, 1901. As Tengo Jabavu noted, a precedent of sorts existed at Stellenbosch College, thirty-five miles northeast of Cape Town. Then also a government high school (it became the University of Stellenbosch in 1918), it counted among its graduates the Rev. N. Goezar of the Coloured Congregational Church and the Rev. D. Gezani of the United Presbyterian Church, Kaffraria. *Cape Mercury*, September 3, 1901; E. G. Malherbe, *Education in South Africa*, vol. 1, *1652–1922* (Cape Town, 1925, 1975–77), 107.

118. This was a relatively new development, at least with respect to mission schools. White students—usually the children of missionaries—regularly attended Lovedale until 1886. Tengo Jabavu studied for his matriculation certificate with Percy Frames, who became a director of the De Beers diamond-mining company in Kimberley. Other white graduates of Lovedale included James Wilson Weir, who backed *Imvo Zabantsundu*, and Saul Solomon, the editor of the *Cape Argus*. An occasional white student studied at Lovedale after 1886; Monica Hunter Wilson (whose father, David Hunter, was then editor of *The Christian Express*) attended as a day student in the 1920s. Shepherd, *Lovedale South Africa: The Story of a Century*, 484, 486; Z.K. Matthews, *Freedom for My People*, viii.

119. "Dale College King William's Town," *Eastern Province Herald*, October 12, 1932.

120. Shingler, "Education and Political Order," 55–56. Muir succeeded Dale as Commissioner of Education in 1892.

121. Lewsen, "Cape Liberal Tradition," 67.

122. *Izwi Labantu* was founded in East London in 1897 by prominent Africans who opposed Tengo Jabavu's decision to support the Afrikaner Bond. Early staff members included the Xhosa poet S. E. K. Mqhayi, who served as subeditor, and Walter Rubusana (also a Xhosa), who provided political commentary. The newspaper ceased publication in 1909. Switzer and Switzer, *Black Press*, 47; Davenport, *Afrikaner Bond*, 184–85.

123. *Cape Mercury*, September 13, 1901.

124. David Alexander Hunter served as secretary and treasurer of Lovedale's Victoria Hospital from 1898 to 1935, and as editor of *The Christian Express* from 1901 to 1932. Shepherd, *Lovedale South Africa: The Story of a Century*, 433, 519; "Mr. D. A. Hunter's Editorship of the 'Outlook,'" *South African Outlook*, April 1, 1932, 73–74. The journal had been founded as *The Kaffir Express* in 1870, renamed *The Christian Express* in 1876, and *The South African Outlook* in 1922 (see above, n69). Switzer and Switzer, *Black Press*, 270.

125. *Christian Express*, October 1, 1901, 145–46. Students at Lovedale could study Latin, but the subject was not widely taught. D. E. Burchell, "African Higher Education and the Establishment of the South African Native College, Fort Hare," *South African Historical Journal*, no. 8 (November 1976): 63.

126. Burchell, "African Higher Education," 67. For a further discussion of African separatist churches, see below, chap. 3.

127. Burchell, "African Higher Education," 61.

128. J. D. Don, "Native Education," *Christian Express*, October 1, 1901, 147.

129. Ibid., 146.

130. Originally named the Congo Training Institute, it was funded largely through donations, and counted among its benefactors King Leopold II, who claimed the Congo for himself in the late 1870s and governed it indirectly through the companies he had granted concessions to to exploit the area's rich rubber resources. Hughes served in the Congo in 1882 and 1883. The institute's name appears to have been changed to the African Training Institute in 1902. Philip Curtin, Steven Feierman, Leonard Thompson, and Jan Vansina, *African History* (Boston, 1978), 457, 476–77; W. Hughes, *Dark Africa and the Way Out; or, A Scheme for Civilizing and Evangelizing the Dark Continent* (London,

1892), 83; K. L. Little, *Negroes in Britain: A Study of Racial Relations in English Society* (London, 1947), 192n.

131. Hughes, *Dark Africa*, 1.

132. Ibid., 83.

133. Ibid., 140–41.

134. Ibid., 127.

135. Little, *Negroes in Britain*, 56. The community increased in size during World War I when 200 black soldiers were stationed in Cardiff.

136. Letter from Noni Jabavu to the author, August 20, 1987. Eileen Southern has traced the origin of the cakewalk to the plantations in the southern United States, where "slave couples . . . competed for a prize, generally a cake, awarded to the pair that pranced around with the proudest, high-kicking steps." *The Music of Black Americans: A History*, 2d ed. (New York, 1983), 253. Londoners apparently first saw the cakewalk on stage in 1898. *Oxford English Dictionary*, 2d ed. (1989), s.v. "cake-walk."

137. Interview with Noni Jabavu, Harare, Zimbabwe, August 2, 1987; Noni Jabavu, *Ochre People*, 162. Fees at the institute were £25 per year, and D. D. T. Jabavu was often short of cash. Tengo Jabavu faced financial difficulties even after *Imvo Zabantsundu* reopened in October 1902; his claim for losses before the War Compensations Commission was turned down, and his manager sued him for back wages. D. D. T. Jabavu, *John Tengo Jabavu*, 49.

138. Jeffrey P. Green, "*In Dahomey* in London in 1903," *Black Perspective in Music* 11, no. 1 (Spring 1983): 23, 40.

139. Quoted in Little, *Negroes in Britain*, 231n.

140. Ibid., 207–8.

141. Ibid., 212, 216; V. Y. Mudimbe, *The Invention of Africa: Gnosis, Philosophy, and the Order of Knowledge* (Bloomington, Ind., 1988), 108.

142. Edward Scobie, *Black Britannia: A History of Blacks in Britain* (Chicago, 1972), 142; Douglas A. Lorimer, *Colour, Class and the Victorians: English Attitudes to the Negro in the Mid-Nineteenth Century* (New York, 1978), 37–38.

143. L. M. Jones and Ivor Wynne Jones, *H. M. Stanley and Wales* (St. Asaph, Wales, 1972), 31.

144. The College of Preceptors was established in 1846 with the aim of "testing . . . the qualifications of teachers with a view to the protection of both the scholastic profession and . . . the public." Additional subjects offered by the College included the theory and practice of education, as well as the more traditional mathematics, Latin, and Greek. J. Vincent Chapman, *Professional Roots: The College of Preceptors in British Society* (Essex, 1985), 28–29. The college archives are uncatalogued, and no information about D. D. T. Jabavu was located during a search in August 1990. Letter to the author from N. C. Matthews, August 17, 1990.

145. "Testimonials in Favour of Davidson Don Tengo-Jabavu" (1914), J. Lennox Papers, Howard Pim Library of Rare Books, University of Fort Hare, Alice, Ciskei, 1 (hereafter Lennox Papers, UFH); University of London, University College Records Office, Records of Davidson Don Tengo Jabavu, 1906–1912.

146. Hans Werner Debrunner, *Presence and Prestige: Africans in Europe: A History of Africans in Europe before 1918* (Basel, 1979), 75. Most blacks in London in the eighteenth century were domestic slaves, many of whom had been brought to London by retired West Indian planters. In the late 1780s, after the abolition of slavery in England, 411 former slaves settled in Sierra Leone with assistance from the English government; a number also returned to the West Indies as free laborers. Little, *Negroes in Britain*, 170, 182–85.

147. Gerhart and Karis, *Political Profiles*, 73–74, 106, 137–38. George D. Montsioa also studied law in the United Kingdom in the early 1900s (p. 96). All four men were founding members of the South African Native National Congress (SANNC) in 1912.

148. D. D. T. Jabavu, "My Tuskegee Pilgrimage 1913" (typescript), Jabavu Collection, UNISA, box 1, 31.

149. Peter Fryer, *Staying Power: The History of Black People in Britain* (London, 1984), 439. The Aborigines' and Anti-Slavery Protection Society was established in 1838 after a royal commission revealed the often brutal treatment suffered by the indigenous peoples of Britain's colonies. *Encyclopaedia Britannica*, 11th ed. (1910), s.v. "Aborigines' Protection Society."

150. D. D. T. Jabavu, "Tuskegee Pilgrimage," 44; Tsotsi, "Davidson Don Tengo Jabavu"; interview with James Taylor Davidson and Sipo Makalima, Alice, Ciskei, October 27, 1987. A November 1913 article in the *A.P.O.* (the newspaper of the African Political Organisation) identified Jabavu as the "principal violinist in the Hampstead Brotherhood Orchestra." *A.P.O.*, November 8, 1913. (I am grateful to Robert Edgar for this reference.) The orchestra may have been part of the Brotherhood Movement, an interdenominational religious organization founded by the Nottingham printer John Blackham in 1875 and dedicated to helping the downtrodden. Willan, *Sol Plaatje*, 201–2.

151. Attempts to identify J. A. North have failed. Letter to the author from G. Ridgley, the British Library, May 16, 1991.

152. The course of study D. D. T. Jabavu followed at the University Tutorial College, also known as the University Correspondence College, is unclear. Chapman, *Professional Roots*, 103.

153. University of London, University College, Records of D. D. T. Jabavu (629). As guardian, North accepted responsibility for ensuring that D. D. T. Jabavu's fees were paid. The total B.A. course cost £32 11s., payable over three sessions.

154. University of London, University College, Records of Davidson Don Tengo Jabavu; letter to the author from P. C. Kennedy, Central Registry, Academic Division, University of London, January 22, 1986; letter to the author from Chris Budden, Records Officer, University College, University of London, March 11, 1986; University of London, University College, *Calendar*, Session MDCCCCXI-MDCCCCXII (1911), 94.

155. Letter to the author from P. C. Kennedy, January 22, 1986; letter to the author from Chris Budden, March 11, 1986.

156. Interview with J. M. Mohapeloa, Maseru, Lesotho, March 30, 1988. Josias Makibinyane Mohapeloa graduated from the South African Native College in 1939 with a B.A. in English, and spent his career teaching in Lesotho. South African Native College, *Calendar for 1942*, 74.

157. Defeated in the South African War, the Afrikaner republics became British possessions as the Transvaal Colony and the Orange River Colony. At Union in 1910 they were renamed the Transvaal Province and the Orange Free State Province. T. R. H. Davenport, *South Africa: A Modern History*, 2d ed. (Toronto, 1978), 140, 174.

158. Pixley Seme earned a law degree from Oxford University, but would have had to have done articles before being admitted to the bar at the Middle Temple in London in 1910, and thus would have earned his degree before the declaration of Union. Alfred Mangena had been called to the bar in 1909, and Richard Msimang was called to the bar in 1910, although it is unclear whether they had earned university degrees. Seme was more the exception than the rule in 1910; British lawyers were not required to be university graduates until 1975, and in the late nineteenth century only 50 percent of the students enrolled at the Middle Temple had graduated from university. Gerhart and Karis, *Political Profiles*, 74, 106, 137; Richard L. Abel, *The Legal Profession in England and Wales* (Oxford, 1988), 47–48.

159. Davenport, *South Africa*, 3d ed., 249–52; Odendaal, *Vukani Bantu!*, 197; L. M. Thompson, *The Unification of South Africa, 1902–1910* (Oxford, 1960), 406.

160. Thompson, *Unification of South Africa*, 406; Lewsen, "Cape Liberal Tradition," 72.

161. Davenport, *South Africa*, 3d ed., 82, 118–19, 242–43. Adult white males in Natal were subject to property and salary qualifications; under Law no. 11 of 1865, however, all men "subject to Native law" were disqualified from voting. An African man could apply for exemption from this law. He then had to meet either the property or salary qualification, and wait for seven years before he could vote. In 1907 there were just six African voters in Natal. Thompson, *Unification of South Africa*, 110–11.

162. Thompson, *History of South Africa*, 150–51.

163. In 1909 white voters made up 85.2 percent of the Cape electorate, African voters represented 4.7 percent, and Coloured voters (of whom there were 14,388) made up 10.1 percent. Thompson, *Unification of South Africa*, 110.

164. Cape African voters represented less than 1 percent of the total African population of the Union. In 1910, the African population of the Union was 4,019,006. The 6,669 African voters (including the six in Natal) thus comprised 0.17 percent of the African population as a whole, and 0.11 percent of the total South African population of 5,973,394. D. D. T. Jabavu, *Segregation Fallacy*, 39; D. Hobart Houghton and Jenifer Dagut, eds., *Source Material on the South African Economy: 1860–1970*, vol. 2, *1899–1919* (Cape Town, 1972), 146; Houghton and Dagut, *South African Economy*, vol. 3, *1920–1970* (Cape Town, 1973), 80; Thompson, *Unification of South Africa*, 110.

165. J. M. Krikler, "The South African Party and the Cape African Franchise, 1926–1936" (B.A. hons. thesis, University of Cape Town, 1980), ii–iii.

166. Trapido, "Liberalism in the Cape," 57.

167. Davenport, *South Africa*, 3d ed., 249–52; Thompson, *Unification of South Africa*, 406; Odendaal, *Vukani Bantu!*, 197.

168. Thompson, *History of South Africa*, 188. The British Commonwealth was a loose association of nations that had formerly been part of the British Empire. Though India

had remained a member of the commonwealth after it declared itself a republic, India, along with Canada, and the African member nations objected to apartheid South Africa remaining a member.

169. "Testimonials in Favour of Davidson Don Tengo Jabavu," Lennox Papers, UFH, 1.

170. A survey of the *Kent Messenger* and the *Kensington Express* revealed no advertisements for the college. The present Kensington College of Business was established in 1982. No office records of Jabavu's time at the *Kent Messenger* have survived. Letter from John Evans (editor of the *Kent Messenger*) to the author, October 21, 1988.

171. D. D. T. Jabavu, "Christmas in South Africa and Other Topics," *Kent Messenger*, December 28, 1912. No further bylined articles by Jabavu appeared in the paper before he left for South Africa in September 1914.

172. See André Odendaal, "South Africa's Black Victorians: Sport, Race and Class in South Africa Before Union," *Collected Seminar Papers on the Societies of Southern Africa in the Nineteenth and Twentieth Centuries*, University of London, Institute of Commonwealth Studies, vol. 15 (October 1986–June 1988), 13–28.

173. The "Congo atrocities"—including flogging, imprisonment and execution, and forced labor—were used by the concession companies to force Africans to collect rubber in King Leopold's private Congo Independent State. Reports of abuses eventually led to the official takeover of the Congo by the Belgian government in 1908. Robert Harms, "The End of Red Rubber: A Reassessment," *Journal of African History* 16, no. 1 (1975): 76–77, 79, 83.

174. D. D. T. Jabavu, "Christmas in South Africa."

175. Lewsen, "Cape Liberal Tradition," 70.

176. D. D. T. Jabavu, "Christmas in South Africa"; *The Concise Columbia Encyclopedia* (1983), s.v., "Hakluyt, Richard," "Milton, John," "Trevelayn, George Otto," "MacDonald, Ramsay," and "Johnston, Sir Harry."

177. The idea of a Universal Races Congress originated with Felix Adler (the founder of the Society for Ethical Culture), at a meeting of the International Union of Ethical Studies held in Eisenach, Germany, in July 1906. Universal Races Congress, *Report of the Proceedings of the First Universal Races Congress* (London, 1911), 6.

178. Universal Races Congress, *Papers on Inter-Racial Problems Communicated to the First Universal Races Congress*, ed. G. Spiller (London, 1911), v.

179. J. Tengo Jabavu, "Native Races of South Africa," *Papers on Inter-Racial Problems Communicated to the First Universal Races Congress*, 336–40.

180. J. Tengo Jabavu, "Native Races of South Africa," 340.

181. Friends Service Council, *Kingsmead, Selly Oak, Birmingham: What It Offers to Friends To-day* (London, 1928), 1. Kingsmead was a member of "The Selly Oak Colleges," an associated group of denominational colleges, offering courses to all members of the community. *Selly Oak Colleges Birmingham* (n.p., 1934), 5.

182. Friends Service Council, *Kingsmead, Selly Oak, Birmingham*, 3.

183. "Testimonials in Favour of Davidson Don Tengo Jabavu," Lennox Papers, UFH, 1.

184. D. D. T. Jabavu, "Christmas in South Africa."

185. Catherine Impey to Booker T. Washington, June 11, 1913, Booker T. Washington Papers, Library of Congress, Washington, D.C., microfilm reel 353 (hereafter Washington Papers, LC).

186. D. D. T. Jabavu, *John Tengo Jabavu*, 7.

187. Hope Hay Hewison, *Hedge of Wild Almonds: South Africa, the Pro-Boers and the Quaker Conscience, 1890–1910* (Portsmouth, N.H., 1989), 163–65, 179.

188. D. D. T. Jabavu, *John Tengo Jabavu*, 42.

189. "Application Jabavu," Society of Friends, Westminster and Longford Meeting, *Minutes*, vol. 28 (1911–1914), minutes 14 (14.12.1911), 12 (18.1.1912), 12 (14.3.1912). His application was approved in March 1912.

190. D. D. T. Jabavu, *John Tengo Jabavu*, 112–13.

191. Society of Friends, Warwickshire North Monthly Meeting, *Minute Book no. 28* (1912–1917), minutes 279, 292, 308.

192. In general, Quakers were more skeptical of tradition, ritual, biblical texts, and the clergy than were Methodists. For a discussion of Quaker beliefs, see Howard Brinton, *Friends for 300 Years: The History and Beliefs of the Society of Friends since George Fox Started the Quaker Movement* (New York, 1952), 32–34, 134, 144–45, 160–62. On Methodism, see Frederick A. Norwood, *The Story of American Methodism* (Nashville, 1974), 16–17, and below, chap. 3.

193. Between August 1902 and July 1916, Tengo Jabavu took out mortgages totaling £1,100 on properties in King William's Town, Peddie, and Briedbach. It is likely that most of the money was used to settle business debts, although some probably went to support D. D. T. Jabavu's education. King William's Town Deeds Office, Deed of Transfer #208/1902 and Deed of Transfer #174/1900; "Estate of the Late Tengo Jabavu," MOOC 6/9/1–6/9/3455, CA.

194. John Tengo Jabavu to [Jacobus] Sauer, August 5, 1913. "Davidson Jabavu. Visit to US 1913–1920," NTS 268 2941/1913/F639, CAD. Alexander Jabavu (1889–1946) trained as a primary school teacher at Lovedale, worked briefly as a teacher in Kimberley, and had joined the staff of *Imvo Zabantsundu* by 1913. He edited the newspaper after his father's death in 1921 until it was sold in 1940. Gerhart and Karis, *Political Profiles*, 39; Matthews, "Our Heritage," Matthews Papers, UNISA, F1.9.

195. Washington had been born into slavery in 1856; after emancipation he attended the Hampton Normal and Agricultural Institute in Virginia, and later taught there, before becoming Tuskegee's first principal. Louis R. Harlan, *Booker T. Washington*, vol. 1, *The Making of a Black Leader 1856–1901* (New York, 1972), 52–57, 100–110.

196. Catherine Impey to Washington, June 11, 1913, Washington Papers, LC. Impey wrote to Washington: "The father . . . and his son are hopeful of opening a door (of education) for their countrymen. They have read of your work at Tuskegee and are greatly impressed with the methods adopted, etc."

197. James D. Anderson, *The Education of Blacks in the South, 1860–1935* (Chapel Hill, 1988), 34; Harlan, *Booker T. Washington*, 1:140; David Levering Lewis, *W. E. B. Du Bois: Biography of a Race, 1868–1919* (New York, 1993), 261–62.

198. Louis R. Harlan, *Booker T. Washington in Perspective: Essays of Louis R. Harlan*, ed. Raymond W. Smock (Jackson, Miss., 1988), 82. According to Hewison, Tengo Jabavu read a copy of *Up from Slavery* sent to him by John X. Merriman. (*Hedge of Wild Almonds*, 288). Phyllis Lewsen, in reproducing Jabavu's letter of thanks to Merriman, dated September 17, 1902, identified the book in question as *The Future of the American Negro*, an outline of the principles of industrial education, published in 1899. John X. Merriman, *Selections from the Correspondence of John X. Merriman 1899–1905*, ed. Phyllis Lewsen (Cape Town, 1966), 359. Whichever book it was, Tengo Jabavu was clearly familiar with Washington's work.

199. Joel Williamson, *The Crucible of Race: Black-White Relations in the American South since Emancipation* (New York, 1984), 57.

200. Ibid., 71.

201. Ibid., 73, 75–76. In 1905 Du Bois organized the Niagara Falls Conference as a forum for African-American leaders—the majority of whom were from the northern states—and did not invite Booker T. Washington. In 1909 the Niagara Movement became a founding member organization of the National Association for the Advancement of Colored People (NAACP), which by 1914 had made inroads into southern cities.

202. Anderson, *Education of Blacks*, 102.

203. William Edward Burghardt Du Bois was born in Massachusetts in 1868. He earned an A.B. from Fisk University in 1888, a second A.B. from Harvard University in 1890, and M.A. and Ph.D. degrees from Harvard in 1891 and 1895. Williamson, *Crucible of Race*, 399–413; Lewis, *Du Bois*, 146; W. August Low and Virgil A. Clift, eds., *Encyclopedia of Black America* (New York, 1981), 326–28.

204. Lewis, *Du Bois*, 261.

205. The phrase "talented tenth" was used to describe "the small number of mostly northern, urban, and college-educated" African-American men and women in the late nineteenth and early twentieth centuries. Lewis, *Du Bois*, 261.

206. D. D. T. Jabavu, "Tuskegee Pilgrimage," 56; D. D. T. Jabavu, "Booker T. Washington's Methods Applied to S. Africa," *Black Problem*, 66. A survey of Du Bois's journal, *The Crisis: A Record of the Darker Races*, from November 1913 through October 1914 revealed several references to South Africa: vol. 6, no. 7 (November 1913): 322; vol. 7, no. 3 (January 1914): 115–16; vol. 7, no. 4 (February 1914): 169; vol. 8, no. 2 (June 1914): 63; vol. 8, no. 3 (July 1914): 123–24, but none to D. D. T. Jabavu. *The Crisis: A Record of the Darker Races*, vols. 7–8 (1913–1914) (reprint, New York, 1969).

207. D. D. T. Jabavu, "Tuskegee Pilgrimage." The UNISA copy is incomplete and in poor condition. I found a complete copy of the manuscript in perfect condition in a broom closet at Kingsmead College in Birmingham (now a Methodist missionary training college) in November 1988. It was deposited at the MCOD/MMS (Methodist Church Overseas Division/Methodist Missionary Society) Archives in London.

208. For an analysis of Bunyan's work, published in two parts in 1678 and 1684, see Lynn Veach Sadler, *John Bunyan* (Boston, 1979), 9–10, 15, 29.

209. Williams, *Umfundisi*, 106–7; Monica Wilson recalled that when she was "growing up in Lovedale . . . the book was constantly read aloud and sometimes acted," and had,

in her opinion, "a great influence on missionaries and converts alike." Monica Wilson, *The Interpreters*, Third Dugmore Memorial Lecture (Grahamstown, 1972), 1. Soga, *South-Eastern Bantu*, xv.

210. D. D. T. Jabavu, "Tuskegee Pilgrimage," 2.

211. Ibid, 2, 7–8.

212. Ibid., 4.

213. Ibid., 6.

214. Ibid., 16–17.

215. Ibid., 18.

216. Ibid., 23–24.

217. Ibid., 25. Jabavu used the term "Jim Crow" in reference to the segregated second-class carriage in which he was forced to ride. The term was used as early as 1832, but its origins remain obscure. C. Van Woodward, *The Strange Career of Jim Crow*, 2d rev. ed. (New York, 1966), 7.

218. D. D. T. Jabavu, "Tuskegee Pilgrimage," 25.

219. Ibid.

220. Ibid., 29. Washington made a two-month tour of Europe in 1910, to gather material for a book comparing poor Europeans and African-Americans. The book, *The Man Farthest Down*, was published in 1912. Harlan, *Washington*, 2:290, 293.

221. D. D. T. Jabavu, "Tuskegee Pilgrimage," 35–37, 39, 44–45, 47–48, 54. Between 1900 and 1909, an average of sixty-nine people per year, 90 percent of whom were African-American, were lynched in the fourteen southern states. Williamson, *Crucible of Race*, 185.

222. Harlan, *Washington*, vol. 2.

223. Harlan, *Washington in Perspective*, 19–21.

224. D. D. T. Jabavu, "Washington's Methods," 66. See also Laverne Brandon, "Booker T. Washington and D. D. T. Jabavu: Interaction between an Afro-American and a Black South African," *A Current Bibliography on African Affairs*, vol. 5, series 2 (1972), 509–15.

225. Harlan, *Washington in Perspective*, 1, 110.

226. D. D. T. Jabavu, "Tuskegee Pilgrimage," 31.

227. He also read Washington's autobiography, *Up from Slavery* (1901) (though he was apparently unable to get a copy of its predecessor, *The Story Of My Life* [1900]), and plowed through *Character Building* (1902), *Tuskegee and Its People* (1905), *The Negro in Business* (1907), *The Life of Frederick Douglass* (1907), *The Story of the Negro* (1910), *My Larger Education* (1911), and *The Man Farthest Down* (1912), unaware that virtually all of Washington's published writings were ghost-written. Davidson Jabavu, "A Report on the Tuskegee Institute, Alabama, U.S.A.," appendix 2, 47–50 (typescript), Jabavu Crosfield Collection, Swarthmore College; D. D. T. Jabavu, "Tuskegee Pilgrimage," 52; Harlan, *Washington*, 1:243–46, 2:193, 291.

228. D. D. T. Jabavu, "Tuskegee Pilgrimage," 32–34.

229. Ibid., 39–44.

230. Ibid., 42.

231. Ibid., 39.

232. Minister of Native Affairs, Pretoria, to B. T. Washington, September 2, 1913, Washington Papers, LC. The cable arrived on September 11, 1913. D. D. T. Jabavu, "Tuskegee Pilgrimage," 54.

233. Tengo Jabavu to [Jacobus] Sauer, August 5, 1913, NTS 268 2941/1913/F63, CAD. Sauer had died on July 24, 1913, but the letter was passed on to the Native Affairs Department. *Dictionary of South African Biography* ([Pretoria], 1968–87), 2:618 (hereafter *DSAB*).

234. Secretary for Native Affairs to D. D. T. Jabavu, September 10, 1913, NTS 268 2941/1913/F639, CAD. How much of the cost of Jabavu's trip to Tuskegee the Society of Friends covered is unclear. Jabavu held another concert at Tuskegee just before he left, intending to use the admission receipts to offset the cost of typing and binding the report; again the amount he raised is unclear. He ultimately submitted a bill for £72 to the NAD in November 1913, for which he was reimbursed in July 1914. D. D. T. Jabavu to Emmett Scott, September 4, 1913, Washington Papers, LC. (Scott was Washington's personal secretary. Harlan, *Washington*, 2:xi-xii.) D. D. T. Jabavu to Minister of Native Affairs, October 30, 1913, and Secretary for Native Affairs to the Acting High Commissioner, London, July 4, 1914, NTS 268 2941/1913/F639, CAD.

235. B. T. Washington to Minister of Native Affairs, September 5, 1913, Washington Papers, LC.

236. Davidson Jabavu, "Report on the Tuskegee Institute," 74.

237. Ibid. For a discussion of W. E. B. Du Bois's experiences as an African-American at Harvard in the 1890s, see Lewis, *Du Bois*, 81, 84.

238. Davidson Jabavu, "Report on the Tuskegee Institute," 74–78.

239. Ibid., 75, 77, 236–37.

240. Davenport, *South Africa*, 3d ed., 259.

241. Davidson Jabavu, "Report on the Tuskegee Institute," 237.

242. D. D. T. Jabavu, "Washington's Methods," *Black Problem*, 46; Davidson Jabavu, "Report on the Tuskegee Institute," 169.

243. D. D. T. Jabavu, "Self-Culture for the Native Teacher: An Address Delivered to the 'King Teachers' Association' at Emdizeni, Debe Nek, C.P., November 1919," *Black Problem*, 88; Shingler, "Education and Political Order," 56.

244. [Secretary for Native Affairs] to J. R. Leisk, Secretary for Finance, July 2, 1914, NTS 268/2941/1913/F639, CAD. D. D. T. Jabavu, "Washington's Methods," *Black Problem*, 27–70.

245. D. D. T. Jabavu to [Emmet] Scott, September 29, 1913, Washington Papers, LC. A search of the Robert R. Moton Papers (Washington's successor as principal of Tuskegee in 1915) and of the Tuskegee University Archives revealed no further correspondence with D. D. T. Jabavu after April 1914. Communication from Cynthia Wilson, Archivist, Tuskegee University Library, Tuskegee, Alabama, July 20, 1993.

246. On Jabavu's support for Tuskegee as a model for African agricultural education, see "S.A. Native Farmer's Congress," Chief Magistrate Transkei (CMT), ref. 43/c, vol. 3/1485, CAD; *Imvo Zabantsundu*, June 18, 1938; *Cape Mercury*, March 26, 1944; and below, chap. 2.

247. "Testimonials in Favour of Davidson Don Tengo Jabavu," Lennox Papers, UFH, 1; University of Birmingham, *Calendar for the Session 1913–1914* (1913), 200–203.

248. Queen Mary's Grammar School was established by Queen Mary in 1554. Encyclopaedia Britannica, 11th ed. (1911), s.v. "Queen Mary's Grammar School."

249. "Staff Register. Walsall Grammar School for Boys. 1879–1924: dates of appointment," Archives of Queen Mary's Grammar School, Walsall, United Kingdom.

250. "Testimonials in Favour of Davidson Don Tengo Jabavu," Lennox Papers, UFH, 2.

251. Ibid., 3.

252. Ibid., 4.

253. Ibid., 1.

254. Ibid., 4; *Mermaid* 10, no. 2 (December 1913): 27.

255. "Copy of South African Newspaper Account of Mr. Don Jabavu's voyage from England to the Cape" (received April 1915), Jabavu Crosfield Collection, Swarthmore College, 1. I was unable to locate a published version of this article.

256. Ibid., 3–4. Saul Msane was born in Natal, educated at the Edendale mission station and at Healdtown, and worked for many years as a compound manager for the Jubilee and Salisbury gold-mining company in Johannesburg. He was a founding member of the Natal Native Congress, and he edited the ANC's newspaper *Abantu-Batho*. He died in the early 1930s. Gerhart and Karis, *Political Profiles*, 104; Willan, *Sol Plaatje*, 174–204.

257. "Copy of South African Newspaper Account," 6.

258. Ibid., 5.

259. Ibid., 6.

260. Ibid., 5.

261. Davenport, *South Africa*, 3d ed., 263, 268–69, 271–72. The rebellion was put down by the end of October.

262. "Copy of South African Newspaper Account," 11.

263. See D. D. T. Jabavu, "Christian Service in Rural and Industrial South Africa," 65.

2 The Educating of Africans, 1915–1944

1. Charles T. Loram, *The Education of the South African Native* (London, 1917; reprint, New York, 1969), 306.

2. Burchell, "African Higher Education," 65–69. For a discussion of the connections between mission Christians and liberals in the twentieth century, see Richard Elphick, "Mission Christianity and Interwar Liberalism," *Democratic Liberalism in South Africa: Its History and Prospect*, ed. Jeffrey Butler, Richard Elphick, and David Welsh (Middletown, Conn., 1987), 65–68.

3. "Extracts from some of the letters sent by former students on the occasion of the retiral of Professor Jabavu, Professor Murdock, and Professor Darlow, 1944," Cory Library, PR4160.

4. James Wells, *Stewart of Lovedale: The Life of James Stewart* (London, 1909), 200.

5. South Africa, *South African Native Affairs Commission 1903–5. Minutes of Evidence* (Cape Town, 1904–[1906]), 2:743; 4:902; Shepherd, *Lovedale South Africa: The Story of a Century*, 261.

6. King William's Town Chamber of Commerce, *Minutes of a Conference of Representatives of the Money Guaranteed towards the Founding of the Inter-State Native College* (n.p., 1907), 6; Burchell, "African Higher Education," 67.

7. Quoted in Burchell, "African Higher Education", 67.

8. Ibid.

9. King William's Town Chamber of Commerce, *Minutes of a Conference.*

10. Burchell, "African Higher Education," 77; Kerr, *Fort Hare*, 6.

11. Odendaal, *Vukani Bantu!*, 16.

12. King William's Town Chamber of Commerce, *Minutes of a Conference*, 29.

13. Odendaal, *Vukani Bantu!*, 66–67.

14. South African Native Races Committee, *The South African Natives: Their Progress and Present Condition* (1908; reprint, New York, 1969), 148. (Bechuanaland is modern-day Botswana; Southern Rhodesia is modern-day Zimbabwe.)

15. "Inter-State Native College. Statement of Receipts and Expenditure to 17th August, 1912," uncatalogued collection, Howard Pim Library of Rare Books, University of Fort Hare, Alice, Ciskei, 1.

16. Other members of the Executive Board in 1912 included Lovedale's principal, the Rev. James Henderson; the Rev. John Lennox, a teacher and theological tutor at Lovedale; Dr. Neil MacVicar, the Medical Superintendent at Lovedale's Victoria Hospital; a Rev. Marais, a theology professor at the University of Cape Town; parliamentarians Col. W. E. M. Stanford, J. W. Sauer, and Col. C. P. Crewe; King William's Town businessman John G. Weir; and Newton O. Thompson and S. P. Gasa. "Inter-State Native College, Statement of Receipts," 2. *DSAB*, 1:766–68 (W. E. M. Stanford); *DSAB*, 2:618–23 (J. W. Sauer); *DSAB*, 3:181 (C. P. Crewe).

17. John Knox Bokwe was born near Lovedale in 1855 and worked for the institution as a bookkeeper for twenty years. He resigned in 1898 to become an editing partner of *Imvo Zabantsundu*, but left in 1900, unable to deal any longer with Tengo Jabavu's dictatorial style. Bokwe was ordained a minister of the United Free Church of Scotland in 1906. D. D. T. Jabavu, *John Tengo Jabavu*, 98, 123; Noni Jabavu, *Ochre People*, 255–56; interview with Frieda Bokwe Matthews, Gaborone, Botswana, August 30, 1988.

18. D. D. T. Jabavu, *John Tengo Jabavu*, 108; Isaac Wauchope to J. Lennox, March 20, 1915, file marked "SANC 1915," Lennox Papers, UFH.

19. J. K. Bokwe to J. Lennox, March 31, 1915, Lennox Papers, UFH (emphasis in original). Bokwe volunteered to Lennox, "You may not be aware that I am one of those who have for long lost confidence in the Editor [Tengo Jabavu], so stopped subscribing to his paper," adding: "I suppose *Imvo* is trying to wreck the College . . . now because some of his plans are not being favoured? An 'axe-grinding' at the back of those plans you will find!" Wauchope initially voted for Tengo Jabavu, but then withdrew his support and recast his vote for Newton Thompson. Isaac Wauchope to J. Lennox, March 1, 1915, and March 20, 1915, Lennox Papers, UFH.

20. Davidson Jabavu to J. Lennox, March 22, 1915, Lennox Papers, UFH.

21. South African Native College, *Report of the Opening of the College 8th-9th February 1916* (Lovedale, [1916]), 5.

22. Kerr, *Fort Hare*, 3.

23. "The South African Native College. Draft Constitution," uncatalogued collection, UFH; South African Native College, *Calendar For 1919*, 8.

24. King William's Town Chamber of Commerce, *Minutes of a Conference*, 7–8; Kerr, *Fort Hare*, 55.

25. Missionary societies would continue to serve as an important source of funding for the college, as would the Transkeian Territories General Council and the government of Basutoland. After its recognition under the 1923 Higher Education Act, the College received government grants linked to the number of registered students. Kerr, *Fort Hare*, 125–26.

26. Cape of Good Hope, Dept. of Public Education, *Report of Public Education. Rept No. 4200. Victoria East. Lovedale A.1. Annual Inspection. 28th–30th August 1915*, Inspection by Mr. Russell, Inspector of High Schools, Lovedale Papers, UFH, 2, 8.

27. South African Native College, *Report of the Opening of the College*, 9.

28. "South African Native College. Extract from Letter from Don Davidson Tengo-Jabavu (with author's permission to reprint)," *South African Ambassador*, July 1916, 6.

29. Ibid.

30. Ibid.

31. H. R. Burrows, *A Short Pictorial History of the University College of Fort Hare 1916–1959* (Lovedale, 1961), 3.

32. D. D. T. Jabavu, "South African Native College," 7.

33. R. Hunt Davis, "Charles T. Loram and the American Model for African Education in South Africa," *Apartheid and Education: The Education of Black South Africans*, ed. Peter Kallaway (Johannesburg, 1984), 108. By 1928 there were still only 7,107 African students studying at secondary schools. In contrast, 377,640 African children were enrolled in mission-run primary schools. They represented, Elphick has contended, "the vast majority of African pupils in southern Africa." Elphick, "Mission Christianity," 69.

34. D. D. T. Jabavu, "South African Native College," 6.

35. Matthews, "Our Heritage," Matthews Papers, UNISA, F1.19.

36. Kerr, *Fort Hare*, 33, 36–37, 275–79. The full-time teaching staff began expanding in 1918.

37. Ibid., 41; Z. K. Matthews, *Freedom for My People*, 51.

38. Z. K. Matthews, *Freedom for My People*, 51; see also Paul B. Rich, "The Appeals of Tuskegee: James Henderson, Lovedale, and the Fortunes of South African Liberalism, 1906–1930," *International Journal of African Historical Studies* 20, no. 2 (1987): 271–92.

39. South African Native College, *Calendar for 1919*, 33.

40. South African Native College, *Calendar for 1918*, 57–59; South African Native College, *Calendar for 1919*, 66–68. He also served three terms on the college's Governing Council as a representative of the College Senate in 1924, 1929–30, and 1937–38. Kerr, *Fort Hare*, 272–74.

41. Z. K. Matthews, *Freedom for My People*, 53; interview with David Van der Ross, Wynberg, Cape, July 9, 1988. David Van der Ross was born in Cape Town and spent his career as a teacher. He attended the Non-European Conferences in the 1920s and 1930s

and was a member of the government's Coloured Advisory Council in the 1940s. Davenport, *South Africa*, 3d ed., 349–50.

42. South African College. *Calendar for 1919*, 33. The Methodist hostel was completed in 1922. Kerr, *Fort Hare*, 75.

43. Alexander Kerr took initial responsibility for the Students' Christian Association in 1916, and Jabavu appears to have formally advised the SCA only once, in 1922. Kerr, *Fort Hare*, 43; South African Native College, *Calendar for 1922*, 64; D. D. T. Jabavu, "Exercise Books with List of Names" [Addresses, 1923–1957], Jabavu Collection, UNISA, fol. 6.3 (hereafter, Addresses [1923–1957], Jabavu Collection, UNISA.). The booklet lists addresses (numbered from 207 through 1158) that Jabavu gave between 1923 and 1957.

44. "Students' and Teachers' Christian Association of South Africa," *South African Ambassador*, October 1917, 6.

45. Ibid.

46. See Couzens, *New African*, 82–124.

47. Jabavu joined the Independent Order of True Templars (a temperance organization) at the age of thirteen in 1898, and remained a teetotaller throughout his life. Noni Jabavu, *Ochre People*, 248–49. In 1923, however, he criticized the proposed prohibition of "Kafir" beer (in favor of municipal beer halls) under the Natives (Urban Areas) Bill, noting that "Kafir beer is the national drink of the natives. It possesses a slight tonic and a distinct food value (a gallon of two and a half per cent Kafir beer contains the food equivalent of 19 ounces of bread), and if used in moderation is not harmful." [D. D. T. Jabavu], "At the 'Bar' of Public Opinion. The Case for Kafir Beer. Failure of Prohibition," *Cape Argus*, March 7, 1923. See also Willan, *Sol Plaatje*, 318–19, 374–75, 379–80.

48. D. D. T. Jabavu, "The Native Teacher out of School," *Black Problem*, 75.

49. Ibid., 76.

50. Draft of advertisement, August 24, 1914, Kerr Papers, Cory Library, PR4088. In July 1920 a draft scale of salaries proposed a salary of £250 for a "full time male lecturer with degree and teaching qualifications." "Draft Scale of Salaries," uncatalogued collection, UFH.

51. Cape officials also recognized the problem. The 1919 *Report of Commission on Native Education* conceded that African teachers' salaries were low, ranging between £18 and £105, and noted that an "illiterate Native post cart driver may get £120 a year." While the commission rejected the recommendation of the King William's Town African teachers' deputation that salaries be raised to £300 a year, it did recommend that base salaries for lower-grade teachers be raised to a range of £44 to £122 10s., and that salaries for teachers with higher qualifications range from £60 to £144 a year. Cape of Good Hope, *Report of Commission on Native Education, 1919* (Cape Town, 1920), 8. Salaries for women teachers were even lower. In general, women teachers (black and white) earned about three-quarters of the salary of an equally qualified male teacher. In 1924 the best-paid female African teacher could expect to earn £74 a year. Florence Makiwane Jabavu earned £45 a year at Lovedale in 1913. "Native Affairs Commission. Proposed Scales of Salaries for Teachers in Training, Secondary, Practising and (Natal) Higher Primary Schools," [ca. 1926], 4, Cory Library, PR4117; W. C. Atkins, "The Cash Value of

Native Education," *South African Outlook*, September 1, 1924, 202; "Department of Public Education, Teachers' Inspection Schedule, Lovedale, November 24, 1913," Lovedale Papers, UFH.

52. Salaries for white teachers throughout the Union were standardized in 1920 according to the Transvaal salary scale. In 1920 the average salary of all certified teachers was £320 per year. Malherbe does not distinguish between salaries paid to male and female teachers. Malherbe, *Education in South Africa*, 1:406.

53. D. D. T. Jabavu, "The Claims of the Bantu," *Eastern Province Herald* (Port Elizabeth), *Educational Review* [supplement], October 12, 1932.

54. Malherbe, *Education in South Africa*, 1:408, 458–61; Elphick, "Mission Christianity," 68–69. This was true also of the South African Native College. Of the £48 tuition in 1922, the government contributed £27, church denominations £16, and the student £5 (Malherbe, 424).

55. D. D. T. Jabavu, "Self-Culture for the Native Teacher," *Black Problem*, 87.

56. Ibid., 85–86; Malherbe, *Education in South Africa*, 1:406.

57. Peteni, *Towards Tomorrow*, 20–22, 25.

58. *Imvo Zabantsundu*, July 4, 1936.

59. Matthews, *Freedom for My People*, 63.

60. Ibid., 53.

61. Interviews with Villiers Bam (Class of 1941) and Edna Khomo Bam (Class of 1943), Maseru, Lesotho, March 30, 1988; Nozipo Ntshona Lebentlele (Class of 1933) and Caroline N. Ramolahloane Khaketla (Class of 1940), Maseru, Lesotho, March 30, 1988; Randall L. Peteni (Class of 1938), Soweto, Transvaal, March 2, 1988. South African Native College, *Calendar for 1944*, 47–48. All of the above informants spent their careers as teachers.

62. Interview with J. M. Mohapeloa, Maseru, Lesotho, March 30, 1988.

63. Ibid. See also D. D. T. Jabavu to Z. K. Matthews, September 28, 1935, Matthews Papers, UNISA, C2.2.

64. Interview with J. M. Mohapeloa, Maseru, Lesotho, March 30, 1988.

65. "S.A. Native Farmers' Congress," CMT, vol. 3/1485, ref. 43/c, CA. Jabavu served as secretary of the SANFC into the 1940s.

66. D. D. T. Jabavu, "A Negro Missionary. The Late Rev. J. E. East, D.D.," *South African Outlook*, November 1, 1934, 251–52; Robert Edgar, "Interview with Miss Gladys East, Friday, July 9, 1982, Philadelphia, Pennsylvania." (I am grateful to Robert Edgar for this reference.)

67. The 1921 census of the district revealed a population of 898 whites, 375 Coloureds, and 15,489 Africans, for a total population of 16,762. D. Hobart Houghton, *Life in the Ciskei: A Summary of the Findings of the Keiskammahoek Rural Survey, 1947–1951* (Johannesburg, 1955), 1–3, 5.

68. Houghton, *Life in the Ciskei*, v; *Keiskammahoek Rural Survey*, 4 vols. (Pietermaritzburg, 1952). See especially Jabavu's December 1919 speech to the Rand Native Welfare Association, which he subsequently published in *The Black Problem*, 106–7.

69. Houghton, *Life in the Ciskei*, v.

70. As early as 1846, Cape Colony officials passed legislation to limit logging in the forests on the southern coast. In 1862 a severe drought prompted the colonial botanist, John Croumbie Brown, to launch an extensive lecture series directed at white farmers, addressing "the dangers of veldt burning, forest destruction and the consequences which it might have for soil erosion and flooding." Concern with conservation at the Cape declined with the passing of the immediate threat of drought, and especially after Brown left the colony in 1866. British imperial officials, however, remained interested in the issue of forest conservation in the Cape and Natal colonies. Even African concerns were acknowledged: the 1880 Natal Forest Commission Report recommended not imposing conservation regulations on Zulu farmers who were at risk of being evicted. Ultimately, however, African interests were ignored to avoid offending the white settler community. Richard Grove, "Early Themes in African Conservation: The Cape in the Nineteenth Century," *Conservation in Africa: People, Policies and Practice*, ed. David Anderson and Richard Grove (Cambridge, 1987), 23, 29, 31–35.

71. William Beinart, "Soil Erosion, Conservationism and Ideas about Development: A Southern African Exploration, 1900–1960," *Journal of Southern African Studies* 11, no. 1 (October 1984): 56, 63, 65.

72. After the passage of the Native Trust and Land Act in 1936, trust lands were also added to the mix. M. E. Elton Mills and Monica Wilson, eds., *Land Tenure*, vol. 4 of *Keiskammahoek Rural Survey* (Pietermaritzburg, 1952), 4.

73. Davenport, *South Africa*, 3d ed., 101.

74. Mills and Wilson, eds., *Land Tenure*, vol. 4 of *Keiskammahoek Rural Survey*, 1–4; Bundy, *Rise and Fall*, 35.

75. Theoretically, the Glen Grey Act was intended to introduce a system of local representation linked to individual land tenure in the Glen Grey district of the eastern Cape. The local council system introduced in the district—which was eventually absorbed into the Transkei Reserve—did evolve into the Transkeian Territories General Council (TTGC), or Bunga. Both Bundy and Davenport have contended, however, that the real point of the act was to draw out workers from the overpopulated Glen Grey District, which abutted a coal-mining area. Quitrent replaced communal tenure, and African men were limited to the ownership of one lot of between four and five morgen (approximately eight to ten and a half acres; one morgen equals two and one-ninth acres). The act thus effectively put small African commercial farmers in the area out of business. Bundy, *Rise and Fall*, 128, 132–33, 135–36; Davenport, *South Africa*, 3d ed., 106, 181. See also Rich, "Segregation and the Cape Liberal Tradition," *Collected Seminar Papers on the Societies of Southern Africa in the nineteenth and twentieth Centuries*, University of London, Institute of Commonwealth Studies, vol. 10 (October 1978-June 1979), 31–41.

76. King William's Town Deeds Office, Deed of Transfer 773/1920.

77. "Closing of Road. Lower Rabula. Jabavu, D.," Keiskammahoek (KHK), 1/KHK, ref. 2/12/3/2, vol. 2, CA. The average farm in Rabula was between thirty and forty acres. *Imvo Zabantsundu*, November 25, 1919.

78. Redding has estimated that the African middle class comprised only 7 percent of Umtata's population, and only 1 percent of the Umtata district as a whole. (Umtata is

the capital of the Transkei.) Sean Redding, "Peasants and the Creation of an African Middle Class in Umtata, 1880–1950," *International Journal of African Historical Studies* 26, no. 3 (1993): 535.

79. D. D. T. Jabavu, *Black Problem*, 123. Redding cites a figure of fifteen shillings a month (£9 a year) for an unskilled male laborer in Umtata in 1920. Redding, "African Middle Class," 534.

80. See, for example, "Minutes of the Tenth Conference of the South African Native Farmers' Congress" (1936), in "S.A. Native Farmers' Congress," CMT, ref. 43/c, vol. 3/1485, CA.

81. Switzer, *Power and Resistance*, 243.

82. *Imvo Zabantsundu*, March 18, 1919.

83. D. D. T. Jabavu, *Black Problem*, 113–16; William Beinart quoted Jabavu on this point in "*Amafelandawonye* (The Die-hards): Popular Protest and Women's Movements in Herschel District in the 1920s," *Hidden Struggles in Rural South Africa: Politics and Popular Movements in the Transkei and Eastern Cape 1890–1930*, ed. William Beinart and Colin Bundy (London, 1987), 235.

84. D. D. T. Jabavu, *Black Problem*, 114–15.

85. *Imvo Zabantsundu*, November 25, 1919.

86. It did not necessarily follow, however, that they all got along with each other. In his summary of the 1947 to 1951 Keiskammahoek Rural Survey report, Houghton noted the tensions between the various types of landholders:

> Although people in communal villages regard themselves as superior to people of the Trust because they have long had land rights, they are referred to derogatorily by freeholders and quitrenters. On the other hand, the people in communal villages have a strongly developed sense of community and neighbourliness, and in their turn tend to regard landowners as rude and anti-social in their individualism. Much of the superior attitude of landowners derives, however, not only from their sense of freedom from authority, but also from their rather better standard of living. [Houghton, *Life in the Ciskei*, 11]

87. *Imvo Zabantsundu*, November 25, 1919.

88. NFA meetings appear to have been annual after 1920. *Imvo Zabantsundu*, December 6, 1921.

89. Ibid.; idem, May 13, 1919; idem, July 22, 1919; idem, July 29, 1919. See also D. D. T. Jabavu, "Native Farmers' Unions," in *Black Problem*, 110–16.

90. Beinart, "Soil Erosion," 83; see also Sean Redding "A South African Town in Black and White: Umtata 1870–1955" (typescript, 1991), 60.

91. Beinart, "*Amafelandawonye*," 222, 224–25. The argument that the people of the Herschel district "were not . . . 'Mfengu' in the sense that the term was usually understood in the Cape," underscores the fluidity of the term (p. 225).

92. Quoted in Beinart, "*Amafelandawonye*," 225.

93. Ibid., 225, 227. In the language of the day, *red* was used to refer to non-Christian Africans in the eastern Cape, who often adorned their clothing and bodies with red ochre. Davis, "School vs. Blanket," 13.

94. Beinart, "*Amafelandawonye*," 226.

95. Ibid., 227.

96. Ibid., 222.

97. Ibid., 231; D. D. T. Jabavu, "Uhambelo Herschel," *Imvo Zabantsundu*, January 16, 1923; January 23, 1923; January 30, 1923; February 6, 1923. (I am grateful to William Beinart for these references.)

98. Beinart, "*Amafelandawonye*," 231.

99. Union of South Africa, *Report of the Native Affairs Commission for the Years 1925–26*, U.G. 17-'27 (Cape Town, 1927), 21.

100. Beinart, "*Amafelandawonye*," 231. Such resistance was not unique to the Herschel District. In Beinart and Bundy's *Hidden Struggles in Rural South Africa*, see: Colin Bundy, "Mr Rhodes and the Poisoned Goods: Popular Opposition to the Glen Grey System, 1894–1906," 138–65; and "'We don't want your rain, we won't dip': Popular Opposition, Collaboration and Social Control in the Anti-Dipping Movement, 1908–16," 191–221.

101. D. D. T. Jabavu, *Black Problem*, 102–3, 105–6, 108.

102. Ibid., 132.

103. Ibid., 123.

104. Ibid., 124.

105. Ibid., 104. Trapido has argued that the "dignity of labour" replaced the dignity of property at the center of the Cape liberal tradition after 1910 ("Liberalism in the Cape," 57), but Jabavu himself dismissed the "dignity of labour" as a "hackneyed phrase empty of content and never acted upon by any sane and sober person." One worked, in Jabavu's opinion, because it paid "economically and physically: there is money in it" (p. 104).

106. D. D. T. Jabavu, *Black Problem*, 130–31.

107. *Imvo Zabantsundu*, September 9, 1919.

108. Davenport, *South Africa*, 3d ed., 259. Africans could appeal for exemption from the act, and that is probably what Chief Shadrack Zibi did. He left the village of Ngcwazi in the Keiskammahoek district for Rustenberg in the Transvaal in 1923. The Native Affairs Department report for 1913–18 lists 137 approved sales to Africans and 219 leases granted to Africans in the Transvaal between 1913 and 1918. Union of South Africa, *Report of the Department of Native Affairs for the Years 1913 to 1918*, U.G. 7-'19 (Cape Town, 1919) , 82–83. Jabavu documented Zibi's success in *U-Kayakulu: Umhlaba otengwa e Rustenberg ngu Nkosi Shadrack F. Zibi* (Great home: The land bought in Rustenberg by Chief Shadrack F. Zibi), trans. Cecil Wele Manona [unpub.] (Lovedale, 1930). See also "The Zibi Rustenberg Farm Scheme," GNLB 154, 224/14/216, Transvaal Archives Depot (TAD). (I am grateful to Harvey Feinberg for this reference.)

109. Davenport, *South Africa*, 3d ed., 259–60.

110. *Imvo Zabantsundu*, September 9, 1919. Davenport has argued that this was precisely the intent of the Natives Land Act, which "aimed specifically to get rid of those features of African land ownership and share-cropping which white farmers found undesirable, and at the same time to increase the size of the African reserves for the more convenient recruiting of labour for the mines." Davenport, *South Africa*, 3d ed., 259.

111. In 1916 Africans owned 0.47 percent (835,743 acres or 397,973 morgen) of the land in the Cape Province, while whites owned 78.1 percent. Union of South Africa, *Report of the Natives Land Commission*, U.G. 19-'16 (Cape Town, 1916), 3-4. (I am grateful to Harvey Feinberg for this reference.) Thompson, *Unification of South Africa*, 410.

112. D. D. T. Jabavu, *Black Problem*, 138, 141–42.

113. Ibid., 141.

114. Kerr, *Fort Hare*, 265; D. D. T. Jabavu, *Black Problem*, 128.

115. Kerr, *Fort Hare*, 265–67.

116. Ibid., 275–76.

117. Ibid., 111–12.

118. Ibid, 112. Edwin Ncwana was a teacher from the Orange Free State who had enrolled at Fort Hare in 1917.

119. Ibid., 125; Malherbe, *Education in South Africa*, 1:424. Under the Higher Education Act (no. 30 of 1923), the South African Native College became eligible for the annual government subsidies allotted university colleges, as well as government loans and grants, and staff came under standard regulations governing leave, engagement, dismissal, and retirement.

120. "The Ultimate Supremacy of the European Language," *South African Outlook*, letter to the editor from D. D. T. Jabavu, March 1, 1918, 41–42.

121. Loram, *Education of the South African Native*, 306.

122. See Wilson, *The Interpreters*.

123. Davis, "Charles T. Loram," 115.

124. Ibid., 109.

125. South African Native College, *Calendar for 1924*, 45, 102–3. Henri A. Junod's *Life of a South African Tribe* (London, 1912–13) was Jabavu's main text; E. B. Tylor's *Anthropology: An Introduction to the Study of Man and Civilization* (London, 1881) and *Primitive Culture: Researches into the Development of Mythology, Philosophy, Religion, Art, and Custom* (London, 1871), Robert H. Lowie's *Primitive Society* (New York, 1920), and Alfred Radcliffe-Brown's *Andaman Islanders: A Study in Social Anthropology* (Cambridge, 1922) were recommended for consultation, as was the Report of the 1883 Commission on Native Laws and Customs.

126. The department had been established in 1920. See A. R. Radcliffe-Brown, "Science and Native Problems: How to Understand the Bantu," *Cape Times*, January 9, 1924, reprinted, with an introduction by Adam Kuper, in *Anthropology Today* 2, no. 4 (1986): 17–21; and D. D. T. Jabavu, "Science and the Native. Study of African Life and Languages. Professor Radcliffe Brown's Lectures. Impressions of the Cape Town Vacation School," *Cape Times*, March 24, 1924. (I am grateful to Rob Gordon for these references.) Alfred Reginald Radcliffe-Brown (1881–1955) was born in England and earned a B.A. from Cambridge University in 1905. His groundbreaking study, *The Andaman Islanders* (1922), turned "social anthropology from its preoccupation with historical development and psychological extrapolation to the comparative study of persistent and changing social structures." He was chairman of the department of social anthropology at the

University of Cape Town from 1920 to 1925. David L. Sills, ed., *International Encyclopedia of the Social Sciences*, vol. 13 (New York, 1968), 285.

127. Quoted in Martin Legassick, "The Rise of Modern South African Liberalism: Its Assumptions and Social Base," paper presented to the postgraduate seminar on Ideology and Social Structure in Twentieth Century South Africa, Institute of Commonwealth Studies, University of London, March 1972, 14.

128. Ibid., 13–15; Paul Rich, *White Power and the Liberal Conscience: Racial Segregation and South African Liberalism* (Manchester, 1984), 54–63; Dubow, *Racial Segregation*, 34–38.

129. D. D. T. Jabavu, "Higher Education and the Professional Training of the Bantu," *South African Journal of Science* 26 (December 1929): 935.

130. Quoted in Dubow, *Racial Segregation*, 36 (emphasis in original); see also Z. K. Matthews, *Freedom for My People*, 117.

131. Legassick, "Modern South African Liberalism," 11. This definition excluded white communists, who, while they considered themselves "friends of the natives," were not liberals. Elphick, "Mission Christianity," 66. See also Trapido, "'Friends of the Natives.'"

132. Gerhart and Karis, *Political Profiles*, 11, 43–44.

133. Quoted in Legassick, "Modern South African Liberalism," 21 (emphasis in original).

134. Edgar H. Brookes, *The History of Native Policy in South Africa from 1830 to the Present Day* (Cape Town, 1924), 320; Dubow, *Racial Segregation*, 28–29; Catherine Higgs, "The Political Thought and Career of Edgar H. Brookes" (B.A. hons. thesis, Queen's University at Kingston, 1984), 3–19. Brookes insisted that a clear distinction be made between segregation, which he defined as geographical or territorial separation, and separate racial and cultural development of blacks and whites, for which he coined the term differential development. For Brookes's rejection of segregation, see Edgar H. Brookes, *The Colour Problems of South Africa: Being the Phelps-Stokes Lectures, 1933, Delivered at the University of Cape Town* (Lovedale, 1934), vii–viii, 1; idem, *White Rule in South Africa 1830–1910* (Pietermaritzburg, 1974), 7; idem, *A South African Pilgrimage* (Johannesburg, 1977).

135. Indeed this approach would be reflected in the fact-finding mission of the South African Institute of Race Relations.

136. Rich, *White Power*, 56–57.

137. D. D. T. Jabavu, "Professional Training of the Bantu," 934.

138. Mudimbe, *Invention of Africa*, 133–34.

139. Hollis R. Lynch, *Edward Wilmot Blyden: Pan-Negro Patriot 1832–1912* (London, 1967), xiii–xiv.

140. Mudimbe, *Invention of Africa*, 104, 114.

141. Lynch, *Edward Wilmot Blyden*, 55.

142. Mudimbe, *Invention of Africa*, 134.

143. Jabavu's support of "primitive tradition" was selective. In his 1924 critique of Radcliffe-Brown's summer lecture series at the University of Cape Town, Jabavu praised the "Bantu family unit" and aspects of *lobola* (bridewealth), noted that polyg-

amy was "fast dying out," and dismissed witchcraft as absurd. D. D. T. Jabavu, "Science and the Native."

144. For a discussion of the definition of African, see Appiah, *In My Father's House,* chap. 4.

145. D. D. T. Jabavu, "The African Child and What the School Makes of Him," *Educational Adaptations in a Changing Society.* Report of the South African Education Conference Held in Cape Town and Johannesburg in July, 1934, under the Auspices of the New Education Fellowship, ed. E. G. Malherbe (Cape Town, 1937), 433.

146. D. D. T. Jabavu, "Claims of the Bantu."

147. Ibid.

148. Gail M. Gerhart, *Black Power in South Africa: The Evolution of an Ideology* (Berkeley, 1978), 110–11, 127.

149. Kerr, *Fort Hare,* 241.

150. Edward Roux, *Time Longer than Rope: A History of the Black Man's Struggle for Freedom in South Africa,* 2d ed. (Madison, Wis., 1964), 276.

151. Interview with James Taylor Davidson and Sipo Makalima, Alice, Ciskei, October 27, 1987.

152. Roux, *Time Longer than Rope,* 2d ed., 276.

153. Interview with James Taylor Davidson and Sipo Makalima, Alice, Ciskei, October 27, 1987; Z. K. Matthews, *Freedom for My People,* 56–57.

154. D. D. T. Jabavu, Addresses [1923–1957], Jabavu Collection, UNISA.

155. Kerr, *Fort Hare.*

156. R. Hunt Davis, "The Administration and Financing of African Education in South Africa 1910–1953," *Apartheid and Education: The Education of Black South Africans,* ed. Peter Kallaway (Johannesburg, 1984), 127–38.

157. *South African Outlook,* September 2, 1935, 196.

158. Union of South Africa, *Report of the Interdepartmental Committee on Native Education,* U.G. 29-'36, 5. Ultimately the Union government did not take full control of African education until 1953. Davis, "Administration and Financing of African Education," 127.

159. Union of South Africa, *Report of the Interdepartmental Committee on Native Education,* U.G. 29-'36, 86–89.

160. Ibid., 88.

161. "European Teachers in Bantu Schools: An Important Statement by the Chief Inspector of Native Education," *South African Outlook,* November 1, 1939, 237.

162. Ibid. Only in the Practising Schools (primary schools attached to teacher-training institutions), where there were 4,087 African teachers and thirty-three white teachers, did the number of African teachers exceed the number of white teachers. In secondary and high schools by comparison, eleven of thirty-five white teachers were principals; there were only two African principals.

163. Ibid., 238.

164. Union of South Africa, *Report of the Interdepartmental Committee on Native Education,* U.G. 29-'36, 88.

165. "European Teachers in Bantu Schools," letter to the editor from D. D. T. Jabavu and Z. K. Matthews, *South African Outlook*, December 1, 1939, 267.

166. Jabavu made a similar argument in 1942, insisting that agricultural demonstrators in African areas be African. D. D. T. Jabavu to M. V. L. Ballinger, March 3, 1942, Margaret Ballinger Papers, Historical and Literary Papers, University of the Witwatersrand Library, Johannesburg, A410, B2.14.13. Margaret Ballinger taught history at Rhodes University and at the University of the Witwatersrand before being elected to parliament as a representative of African voters in the Cape Eastern district in 1938. She remained an MP until the last vestiges of African representation were abolished in 1960. Gerhart and Karis, *Political Profiles*, 4–5.

167. As the political scientist Gail Gerhart has noted, the definition of nationalism is problematic: "most historians and political scientists are forced to conclude, rather tautologically, that people comprise a nation if they think of themselves as comprising a nation." Jabavu's speech to the 1929 South African Sciences Congress suggested that he was moving toward the idea that Africans comprised one nation. By the definition that "nationalism inevitably seeks expression through the creation of a nation-state," however, Jabavu's acceptance of the legitimacy of the existing white-controlled state made him a nationalist of the gradualist persuasion. Gerhart, *Black Power*, 11.

168. Z. K. Matthews, *Freedom for My People*, 189. Matthews served as acting principal of the college in 1956 at the invitation of the College Council, which hoped, in appointing an African, to quell student unrest. Matthews was aware that in accepting the post he might appear to be supporting—as a black man heading a black college—the logic of apartheid. As he noted in his memoir, this would be true whether he succeeded or failed: "Some people suggested that I was unwise in taking this job. It was the usual trick of Europeans to put an African into an impossible position in order that he should fail" (p. 190). For a further discussion of apartheid, see below, chap. 6.

169. South African Native College, *Calendar for 1944*, 74; Stuart Jones and André Müller, *The South African Economy, 1910–1990* (Houndmills, England, 1992), 128.

170. [Open letter from D. D. T. Jabavu], October 13, 1941, Cory Library, PR4201.

171. Mandela was arrested in 1963, charged with treason in 1964, and released in 1990. He became president of the ANC in July 1991, and president of South Africa in May 1994. Gerhart and Karis, *Political Profiles*, 72; *Facts on File: World News Digest with Index* 51, no. 2643 (July 18, 1991): 546E3; Mandela, *Long Walk to Freedom*, 538–39.

172. Kerr, *Fort Hare*, 241–42. Mandela remembered the incident slightly differently, noting that Kerr had given him the summer to think over his apology. Mandela did not return to Fort Hare, but went instead to Johannesburg to avoid an arranged marriage. Mandela, *Long Walk to Freedom*, 44–45, 48. Mandela subsequently finished his degree at the University of South Africa and opened a law practice in Johannesburg. Gerhart and Karis, *Political Profiles*, 72.

173. By 1942 the percentage of Coloured students had dropped to 7.3 (16 of 219), and the percentage of Indian students had risen to 16.9 (37 of 219). How many of these students were non-Christians is unclear—the records list students as Methodist, Presbyterian, Anglican, and Others. In 1941 there were thirty-seven students in this category;

the following year Others had increased to fifty-six. South African Native College, *Calendar for 1944*, 74–75.

174. "Professorships at Fort Hare," Cory Library, PR3106; "Early Days at Fort Hare. Farewell to Pioneer Professors," *Alice Times*, October 26, 1944.

175. Matthews, *Freedom for My People*, 121–22, 127.

176. "Extracts from some of the letters sent by former students on the occasion of the retiral of Professor Jabavu, Professor Murdock and Professor Darlow, 1944," Cory Library, PR4160.

177. Switzer has described *Inkundla ya Bantu* (subtitled *The Bantu Forum*) as "the last, and most important, African owned and controlled newspaper before the Nationalists gained power in 1948." It was founded in Natal in 1938 as *The Territorial Magazine*, changed its name in 1940, and published its last edition in 1951. Though sympathetic to the ANC, *Inkundla* was not above criticizing it, and was evenhanded in its treatment of other African political organizations, including Jabavu's own AAC. Switzer and Switzer, *Black Press*, 43–44.

178. *Inkundla ya Bantu*, November 17, 1944.

3 "What Methodism Has Done for the Natives," 1903–1957

1. R. F. Alfred Hoernlé, *South African Native Policy and the Liberal Spirit: Being the Phelps-Stokes Lectures, Delivered before the University of Cape Town, May, 1939* (Cape Town, 1939), viii; Brookes, *Colour Problems of South Africa*, 81. Both Lewsen and Davenport have traced Cape liberalism back to its British roots and stressed the influence of the "Christian humanitarianism" of the early-nineteenth-century British missionaries in the shaping of the Cape liberal tradition. Lewsen, "Cape Liberal Tradition," 69–70; Davenport, "Cape Liberal Tradition," 21, 30.

2. D. D. T. Jabavu, *Segregation Fallacy*, 29–30.

3. Elphick, "Mission Christianity," 65.

4. D. D. T. Jabavu paraphrasing the Rev. T. Z. Koo (from China) in D. D. T. Jabavu, "After Three Generations," *The Christian Mission in the World Today*, Report of the Eleventh Quadrennial Convention of the Student Volunteer Movement for Foreign Missions, Buffalo, New York, December 30, 1931, to January 3, 1932, ed. Raymond P. Currier (New York, 1932), 44–45.

5. D. D. T. Jabavu, "Christian Service," 65.

6. See for example, S. Johns, *Protest and Hope, 1882–1934*, vol.1 of *From Protest to Challenge*, ed. Thomas Karis and Gwendolen Carter, doc. 41b, 214–16; docs. 41d–44, 218–57; doc. 50a, 337–38; Karis, *Hope and Challenge*, doc. 21, 162–66; "S.A. Native Farmers' Congress," CMT, ref. 43/c, vol. 3/1485, CA; D. D. T. Jabavu, *Black Problem*, 70–98.

7. Interviews with Noni Jabavu, Harare, Zimbabwe, August 2 and August 3, 1987. Though raised in the Methodist Church, Noni Jabavu is not a practicing Christian. See Noni Jabavu, *Ochre People*, 257–58 and *Drawn in Colour*, 130. J. M. Mohapeloa described

Jabavu as more of a "churchman" than a religious man. Interview with J. M. Mohapeloa, Maseru, Lesotho, March 30, 1988. Other informants had few doubts that D. D. T. Jabavu's faith was sincere. Interview with J. T. Davidson and Sipo Makalima, Alice, Ciskei, October 27, 1987; interview with Sipo Makalima, Alice, Ciskei, November 23, 1987. The sociologist Leo Kuper, in his study of Christian Africans in Natal, concluded: "For many Africans conversion to Christianity was seemingly a serious commitment, and not merely a matter of expedience," begging the question of for how many Africans conversion was expedient. Leo Kuper, *An African Bourgeoisie: Race, Class and Politics in South Africa* (New Haven, 1965), 191. The anthropologists Jean Comaroff and John Comaroff make a similar argument in *Of Revelation and Revolution: Christianity, Colonialism, and Consciousness in South Africa* (Chicago, 1991), 1:248–49. See also Norman Etherington, *Preachers, Peasants and Politics in Southeast Africa, 1835–1880: African Christian Communities in Natal, Pondoland and Zululand* (London, 1978), chaps. 3, 4.

8. D. D. T. Jabavu, Addresses [1923–1957], Jabavu Collection, UNISA.

9. D. D. T. Jabavu, *What Methodism Has Done for the Natives* (Lovedale, [1923]). Published in Xhosa as *Umsebenzi wama Wesile ku Bantsundu* (The work of the Methodists among blacks), trans. Cecil Wele Manona [unpub.] (n.p., [1923]). (The publication date was identified as 1923 in D. D. T. Jabavu, *An African Indigenous Church: A Plea for Its Establishment in South Africa* (Lovedale, 1942), 12.)

10. Whiteside, *Wesleyan Methodist Church*, 5–6. A devout Christian, Wesley and his fellow believers were disparagingly nicknamed Methodists by their fellow students at Oxford in the 1720s, who mocked Wesley's regular church attendance and "methodical" visits to those ill or imprisoned (p. 3).

11. These were not new ideas; Wesley shared them with others who sought to reform the Church of England—including Puritans (Calvinists)—although he rejected the Calvinist doctrine of predestination. The historian Richard Elphick has identified the Protestant Reformers, including the Wesleyans, as broadly "Calvinist," in the sense that "these groups regarded the Bible as their sole authority for belief and practice, emphasized the fallen nature of man, preached salvation solely by grace through faith, practiced an austere and comparatively non-sacramental form of worship, insisted on an iron discipline in moral matters and were heirs to an activist tradition of 'cleansing church and nation' in the name of God." Richard Elphick, "Africans and the Christian Campaign in Southern Africa," *The Frontier in History: North America and Southern Africa Compared*, ed. Howard Lamar and Leonard Thompson (New Haven, 1981), 281.

12. Whiteside, *Wesleyan Methodist Church*, 5–6.

13. John W. De Gruchy, *The Church Struggle in South Africa*, 2d ed. (London, 1986), 10, 14. Many Protestant missionaries to South Africa had similar class origins—among prominent members of the London Missionary Society, John Philip had started out as a weaver; Robert Moffat was a gardener. Elphick, "Africans and the Christian Campaign," 279.

14. The first Methodist chapel was built in 1739; by 1767 there were over 100 scattered throughout England. The Methodist Church nevertheless remained affiliated with the Church of England until 1791, when a formal break was made. Whiteside, *Wesleyan*

Methodist Church, 14; Isser Woloch, *Eighteenth-Century Europe: Tradition and Progress, 1715–1789* (New York, 1982), 300.

15. Whiteside, *Wesleyan Methodist Church*, 23–33.

16. Allen Lea, "The Wesleyan Methodist Church of South Africa," *Christianity and the Natives of South Africa: A Year Book of South African Missions*, ed. J. Dexter Taylor (Lovedale, [1928]), 211.

17. Elphick, "Africans and the Christian Campaign," 279; Etherington, *Preachers, Peasants and Politics*, 24. The London Missionary Society (LMS), a nonsectarian body founded in 1795, had "as its sole object the spread of the knowledge of Christ among the heathen." Later affiliated with the Congregational Churches of "England and the Colonies," the LMS sent its first missionary, J. T. van der Kemp, to Cape Town in 1798. The Glasgow Missionary Society, later absorbed by the Missions of the United Free Church of Scotland in South Africa (loosely, the Presbyterians), established its first mission in South Africa in 1824. After 175 years of ministering to Dutch settlers, the Dutch Reformed Church established a mission to the Khoikhoi in 1827, and a missionary society in 1857. The Paris Evangelical Missionary Society established its Basutoland (Lesotho) Mission in 1833. A relative latecomer to the South African mission field, the Anglicans (the Church of the Province of South Africa), established their first missions in the Ciskei in 1854. Taylor, *Christianity and the Natives*, 202, 205, 229, 236, 245, 248.

18. Whiteside, *Wesleyan Methodist Church*, 35–36; De Gruchy, *Church Struggle in South Africa*, 14.

19. De Gruchy, *Church Struggle in South Africa*, 14; W. D. Hammond-Tooke, ed., *The Journal of William Shaw* (Cape Town, 1972), 7–10. William Shaw (1798–1872) was the son of a noncommissioned officer in the North York Militia. He served the Wesleyan Missionary Society in South Africa from 1820 to 1856. (Hammond-Tooke, 2–3, 5, 14.)

20. De Gruchy, *Church Struggle in South Africa*, 14; D. D. T. Jabavu drew his 1923 figures for African members of the Wesleyan Methodist Church membership from the official 1921 census: "In point of numbers it stands an easy first of all religious missionary bodies in South Africa, being followed in order (according to the latest census figures of attenders) by the Dutch Reformed 88,956; Anglican 82,044; Presbyterians 35,580; Congregational 32,191; Roman Catholic 22,288; Baptist 8,043. Wesleyans have 137,041 attenders" (D. D. T. Jabavu, *What Methodism Has Done*, 4). Kuper quoted much higher figures for Methodist Church membership: 451,746 (11.2% of the total) in 1911, 795,369 (12.1%) in 1936, and 1,313,129 (12.0%) in 1960. The discrepancy is accounted for by Jabavu's stress on regular church attenders, rather than on those professing a particular religious affiliation. Leo Kuper, "African Nationalism in South Africa, 1910–1964," *The Oxford History of South Africa*, ed. Monica Wilson and Leonard Thompson (New York, 1971), 2:475.

21. Comaroff and Comaroff, *Of Revelation and Revolution*, 231–34; Kuper, *African Bourgeoisie*, 73–74.

22. Tengo Jabavu's brother, Jonathon James Jabavu (1865–1927), was ordained a Methodist minister in 1890. Wesleyan Methodist Church of South Africa, *Minutes of the Forty-Fifth Annual Conference* (1927), 13.

23. D. D. T. Jabavu, "Pilgrim Hall, January 8, 1932," Speech to the Department of Woman's Work, Massachusetts Congregational Conference and Missionary Society, 1, ABC: Biographical Collection: Individuals: Jabavu, Mr. and Mrs. David Dan [*sic*] Tengo, American Board of Commissioners for Foreign Missions Archive, Houghton Library, Harvard University, Cambridge, Massachusetts (hereafter Houghton Library, HU); D. D. T. Jabavu, "After Three Generations," 42.

24. D. D. T. Jabavu, *E-Indiya nase East Africa* (In India and East Africa), trans. Cecil Wele Manona [unpub.] (Lovedale, 1951), 61. Had he followed African naming practices, which did not include passing on a surname from generation to generation, John Tengo Jabavu would have been (John) Tengo-ka-Ntwanambi (Tengo, son of Ntwanambi). To avoid confusion with his father, Davidson Don Tengo would not have been given the name Tengo. Soga, *Ama-Xosa*, 294, 324–25; idem, *South-Eastern Bantu*, 61–69.

25. Gitywa, "Male Initiation in the Ciskei," 203. Gitywa's thesis examines Xhosa-speaking societies, including the Mfengu. See also Mills, "Role of African Clergy," 83. Mills's focus is the Xhosa, though he extends his generalizations to include other Xhosa-speaking peoples, including the Mfengu.

26. By Mills's account, *intonjane* for girls carried far less social and religious significance than did circumcision for boys. Although it usually took place at puberty, it could be delayed until marriage, and the custom itself "did not involve instruction in sexual matters and techniques, or even in the duties of wife and mother." It did entail some rather expensive feasting and slaughter of beasts, paid for by the girl's father. Missionary objections to *intonjane* focused on what they perceived as the "lewd dancing" that accompanied *intonjane*, and the fact that the girls appeared in public nude. Missionaries did succeed in having the Cape parliament ban *intonjane* in 1891, and by the 1920s it was rarely practiced. Mills, "Role of the African Clergy," 63–65, 72.

27. Mills has cautioned against overstating the religious aspect of initiation, observing that it "was largely inherent rather than explicit and overt," an argument corroborated by Gitywa. Mills, "Role of African Clergy," 83–84, 107 n1, 2, 4; Gitywa, "Male Initiation in the Ciskei," 213–17. There is some debate about whether circumcision was a religious or a social practice. The Rev. Tiyo Soga, who was not circumcised and encountered serious prejudice from the people he was meant to serve insisted it was "a civil not a religious rite." John A. Chalmers, *Tiyo Soga: A Page of South African Mission Work* (Edinburgh, 1877), 264; see also Gitywa, "Male Initiation in the Ciskei," 220–22.

28. Mills, "Role of the African Clergy," 85–86; Gitywa, "Male Initiation in the Ciskei," 203–4. Mills recorded only minor differences separating the initiation rites followed by the various Xhosa-speaking peoples: "The Xhosa proper, who perform the operation in the afternoon, are taken from the feast to the river for a washing and the operation [is] performed. The Mfengu do not perform the operation until the following morning before dawn" (p. 84).

29. Mills, "Role of African Clergy," 91, 93.

30. Ibid., 89.

31. Ibid., 96.

32. Ibid., 97–98.

33. Ibid., 96. A circuit was the Methodist equivalent of a parish.

34. Missionaries did not advocate the suppression of the circumcision schools, only their supervision. "General Missionary Conference, Johannesburg, June 30th to July 3rd, 1925," *South African Outlook*, August 1, 1925, 180.

35. "A Reply to the General Missionary Conference Resolution," *South African Outlook*, December 1, 1926, 272.

36. See "The Prime Minister's Reply to the Resolutions of the General Missionary Conference," *South African Outlook*, April 1, 1926, 83–85.

37. Gitywa, "Male Initiation in the Ciskei," 221–22; Mills, "Role of the African Clergy," 89–90.

38. Chalmers, *Tiyo Soga*, 264.

39. Interview with Sipo Makalima, Alice, Ciskei, August 16, 1988. Chief Burns Ncamashe (a Xhosa) insisted that neither Tengo nor D. D. T. Jabavu was circumcised, an assertion rejected by other informants. Interview with Chief Burns Ncamashe, Alice, Ciskei, August 9, 1988; interview with Violet Jabavu (widow of Wilson Weir Jabavu's son Matthew) and Mr. G. Soya Mama, New Brighton (Port Elizabeth), Cape, August 12, 1988; interview with Vincent Gitywa, Bisho, Ciskei, August 16, 1988; interview with Benjamin Mbete, Healdtown, Ciskei, August 17, 1988. See also Gitywa, "Male Initiation in the Ciskei," 203–4; Johns, *Protest and Hope*, 296; Mills, "Role of the African Clergy," 82; Odendaal, "African Political Mobilisation," 45. Benjamin L. Mbete was born in Healdtown and attended the South African Native College at Fort Hare in the late 1940s. He spent his career as a teacher in and around Healdtown. Vincent Gitywa attended Fort Hare in the 1950s and earned his Ph.D. there in 1976 for his thesis, "Male Initiation in the Ciskei."

40. Interview with Benjamin Mbete, Healdtown, Ciskei, August 17, 1988. Mbete told me: "It happened behind that hill; I can't take you there because you are a woman." See also Noni Jabavu, *Ochre People*, 47–49.

41. "Davidson Don Tengo Jabavu" [curriculum vitae], Jabavu Crosfield Collection.

42. Gitywa, "Male Initiation in the Ciskei," 221–22; Mills, "Role of the African Clergy," 96.

43. *Imvo Zabantsundu*, August 22, 1916; *Alice Times, Seymour and Peddie Gazette*, August 17, 1916.

44. Florence Tandiswa Makiwane was born in the village of Tyumie, near Alice, in September 1895. Estate of Florence Tandiswa Jabavu, Master of the Supreme Court, Cape Town, MOOC no. 4334/51.

45. Florence Makiwane had enrolled in Lovedale's College Department in 1908, graduating with a Third Class Certificate (T3) in teaching in 1911, which qualified her to teach in elementary schools. In addition to standard coursework in reading, writing, and arithmetic, she also taught needlework and music. By the time D. D. T. Jabavu returned to South Africa in 1914, she had been teaching at Lovedale for almost three years. Lovedale Missionary Institution, South Africa, *Report for 1911* (Lovedale, 1912), 5; *Report for 1913* (Lovedale, 1914), 9; *Report for 1914* (Lovedale, 1915), 3; Department of

Public Education, "Teachers' Inspection Schedule, Victoria East, Lovedale Elementary School, November 24, 1913," Lovedale Papers, UFH.

A student had to have passed standard seven (grade nine) before enrolling for the three-year course leading to the Third Class Certificate in teaching, which was the lowest diploma a certified teacher could hold. Candidates for the Second Class Certificate (T2) had to have a University Matriculation Certificate and candidates for the First Class Certificate (T1) had to have passed the B.A. examination and completed eighteen months of university coursework. Malherbe, *Education in South Africa*, 1:151–53.

46. Davis, "School vs. Blanket," 17–19.

47. Interviews with Noni Jabavu, Harare, Zimbabwe, August 2 and August 3, 1987 ; Davis, "School vs. Blanket," 19. Tengo Jabavu's marriage to Elda Sakuba had also been arranged. D. D. T. Jabavu, *John Tengo Jabavu*, 16.

48. Nozipo Jabavu was born in 1917 and died in 1919, a victim of the influenza epidemic. Helen Nontando (Noni) was born in 1919; Alexandra Kerr was born in 1926, and Tengo Max, the couple's only son, was born in 1928. Jabavu Collection, UNISA, files 4.3, 4.4; "In Memoriam. On the death of little Nozipo," *S.A.N.C. Magazine* 1, no.4 (November 1919): 19; interviews with Noni Jabavu, Harare, Zimbabwe, August 2 and August 3, 1987; interview with Alexandra Jabavu-Mulira, Port St. John's, Transkei, August 14, 1988. See also H. Philips, "South Africa's Worst Demographic Disaster: The Spanish Influenza Epidemic of 1918," *South African Historical Journal* 20 (1988): 57–73.

49. Daisy Makiwane Majombozi was also the first African woman in the Cape to earn a matriculation certificate. Noni Jabavu, *Ochre People*, 103–4.

50. See Rebecca Reyher, "Philosophy of Great Bantu Feminist: Mrs. Jabavu's Message to African Women," *Cape Times*, July 9, 1951; Ntantala, *Life's Mosaic*, 69, 230.

51. James Henderson to Alfred B. Fox, April 26, 1913, Henderson Papers, MS14,851, Cory Library; Rich, "Appeals of Tuskegee," 277.

52. Noni Jabavu, *Ochre People*, 252.

53. Williams, *Umfundisi*, 26. The Sogas did encounter prejudice on their return to South Africa; of the reaction of whites to him and his wife, Tiyo Soga observed: "I would not be surprised if, to some, there was something absurd in the fact of a black man walking side by side with a white lady" (p. 32).

54. For D. D. T. Jabavu's opinion of "mixed" marriages, see D. D. T. Jabavu, *Segregation Fallacy*, 113, and "Christianity and the Bantu," *Thinking with Africa: Chapters by a Group of Nationals Interpreting the Christian Movement*, ed. Milton Stauffer (New York, 1927), 125.

55. D. D. T. Jabavu, *John Tengo Jabavu*, 99, 101; Interviews with Noni Jabavu, Harare, Zimbabwe, August 2 and August 3, 1987. Florence Jabavu's marriage name (the name given to her on her marriage) was Nolwandle—"Mother of the [over]seas"—that is, mother of the children of a man who had been educated overseas. Interview with Sipo Makalima and Ethel N. Mzamane, Middledrift, Ciskei, February 12, 1988.

56. Noni Jabavu, *Ochre People*, 72. Florence Jabavu arrived at Kingsmead College for the spring 1922 term and left after the summer 1923 term. *Kingsmead College Year Book* (1926), 20; *Kingsmead Letter* (autumn term 1923), 11; Class photographs (uncatalogued

collection), Kingsmead College, Birmingham, United Kingdom; J. M. Howard to Alexander Kerr, October 2, 1923, Kerr Papers, Cory Library.

57. *Alice Times,* August 17, 1916. Judging by the list of wedding gifts and the surviving photographs, the ceremony itself was a well-attended and impressive (if not lavish) affair. *Imvo Zabantsundu,* August 22, 1916; Jabavu Collection, UNISA, fol. 4.3, fol. 4.4.

58. D. D. T. Jabavu, *Black Problem,* 144–45. In 1925 he served on the General Missionary Conference-sponsored investigation into the debilitating effects of *lobola* in Natal. "General Missionary Conference," *South African Outlook,* August 1, 1925, 180.

59. Delegates to the 1925 meeting of the Wesleyan Native Synod of the Clarkebury district resolved that the *lobola* "system was by no means an ideal one and should not be encouraged by the Christian Church as it has evil tendencies." *South African Outlook,* April 1, 1925, 79; Adam Kuper, *Wives for Cattle: Bridewealth and Marriage in Southern Africa* (London, 1982), 112, 162–63. See also Mills, "Role of the African Clergy," 112–45.

60. D. D. T. Jabavu, *Black Problem,* 146. Soga indicated that twelve cattle were exchanged among the Mfengu. Soga, *Ama-Xosa,* 267.

61. Noni Jabavu, *Ochre People,* 252.

62. King William's Town Deeds Office, Deed of Transfer #208/1902. On the Mfengu custom of relatives assisting a young man in raising *lobola,* see Soga, *Ama-Xosa,* 267. D. D. T. Jabavu may have covered the *lobola* himself. His starting salary at the South African Native College, where he had been employed since February, was £250 a year. Draft of Advertisement, August 24, 1914, Kerr Papers, Cory Library, PR4088.

63. D. D. T. Jabavu, *John Tengo Jabavu,* 123; Noni Jabavu, *Ochre People,* 255–56.

64. D. D. T. Jabavu, *John Tengo Jabavu,* 110.

65. Ibid., 111.

66. Ibid., 114, 118; Wesleyan Methodist Church of South Africa, *Minutes of the [nth] Annual Conference* (Cape Town, 1883–1921), Cory Library.

67. D. D. T. Jabavu, *John Tengo Jabavu,* 116.

68. See Nosipho Majeke [Dora Taylor], *The Role of the Missionaries in Conquest* (Alexandra Township [Johannesburg], n.d.), and Monica Wilson's response, *Missionaries: Conquerors or Servants of God?* (King William's Town, 1976).

69. D. D. T. Jabavu, *John Tengo Jabavu,* 112. Not all clergy of this period were so sanguine about missionary work. Nineteenth-century English wit and Anglican cleric Sydney Smith expressed a somewhat lower opinion of Methodist missionaries: "Why are we to send out little detachments of maniacs to spread over the fine regions of the world the most unjust and contemptible opinion of the Gospel?" Hesketh Pearson, *The Smith of Smiths: Being the Life, Wit and Humour of Sydney Smith* (1934; reprint, London, 1984), 68.

70. D. D. T. Jabavu, *John Tengo Jabavu,* 112.

71. Ibid., 115.

72. Brian Rose and Raymond Tunmer, eds. *Documents in South African Education* (Johannesburg, 1975), 211.

73. D. D. T. Jabavu, "The Meaning of the Cross in the Life of the World Today," *Foreign Missions Conference of North America 1932.* Report of the Thirty-Ninth Annual Meeting of the Conference of Foreign Mission Boards in Canada and in the United States,

Atlantic City, New Jersey, January 12–15, 1932, ed. Leslie B. Moss and Mabel H. Brown (New York, [1932]), 234.

74. D. D. T. Jabavu, "Pilgrim Hall, January 8, 1932," 2, ABC: Biographical Collection: Individuals: Jabavu, Houghton Library, HU.

75. D. D. T. Jabavu, "After Three Generations," 42.

76. See Elphick, "Mission Christianity," 64–80.

77. "A Settler's Centenary Meeting. Queenstown—Wesleyan Conference—Thursday 1st May 1919. Address by D. D. T. Jabavu B.A. (Lond.)," Cory Library, PR4183, 1.

78. Ibid., 2.

79. Ibid.

80. D. D. T. Jabavu, *What Methodism Has Done*, 3.

81. Wesleyan Methodist Church of South Africa, *Annual Report of the Missionary Society of the Wesleyan Methodist Church of South Africa with Lists of Contributions to the Sustentation and Mission Fund*, 1917–1941. Jabavu's donations on behalf of his family were quite generous; most dues paid by Africans were in the 5s. range.

82. D. D. T. Jabavu, "Pilgrim Hall, January 8, 1932," 8. Though Tengo Jabavu apparently supported his parents financially until their deaths, their existence was clearly a lean one. D. D. T. Jabavu, *John Tengo Jabavu*, 11.

83. D. D. T. Jabavu, *What Methodism Has Done*, 5.

84. Odendaal, *Vukani Bantu!*, 25. De Gruchy has argued that by the early 1900s black South African Christians had three ecclesiastical options: "They could be members of mission churches, whose membership was wholly black, but which were under the control of white missionaries and their mission boards, . . . they could be members of multiracial denominations, those churches largely of British origin where the line between settler and mission church had not been clearly drawn. . . . [or] They could leave the mission and the multiracial churches and initiate their own." De Gruchy, *Church Struggle*, 41.

85. See Robert Edgar, *Because They Chose the Plan of God: The Story of the Bulhoek Massacre* (Johannesburg, 1988).

86. D. D. T. Jabavu, *John Tengo Jabavu*, 118.

87. D. D. T. Jabavu, "Lessons from the Israelite Episode (part of an address to Fort Hare students by Mr. D. D. T. Jabavu, Sunday, May 29, 1921)," *Christian Express*, July 1, 1921, 105–6. (I am grateful to Rob Gordon for this reference.)

88. D. D. T. Jabavu, foreword to *The Native Separatist Church Movement in South Africa* by Allen Lea (Cape Town, [1926]), 11–12. Lea's book drew heavily from the 1925 government report on the African churches. See Union of South Africa, *Report of the Native Churches Commission*, U.G. 39–'25 (Cape Town, 1925).

89. "A Settlers' Centenary Commemoration. . . . Address by D. D. T. Jabavu," 3–4.

90. James Stewart (1831–1905) was born in Scotland and trained as a medical doctor before joining the staff of the Lovedale Institution in 1867, which was then under the direction of the Rev. William Govan. When Stewart succeeded Govan as principal in 1870, he "made it known that he felt that the education of a primitive people was best advanced, not, as Govan thought, by advanced education for the few, but by the ele-

mentary education of the many" (*DSAB*, 1:770–71). Nevertheless, he supported the establishment of the South African Native College at Fort Hare, which was in the early planning stages when he died in 1905. Robert Moffat (1795–1883) was born in Scotland and joined the London Missionary Society in 1816. He arrived in Cape Town in 1817, and in 1820 took up the London Missionary Society mission to the Tswana (first at Dithakong and then at Kuruman), returning to the United Kingdom only in 1870. *DSAB*, 1:546–50.

91. Elphick, "Mission Christianity," 78.

92. *South African Outlook*, March 1, 1923, 50. See also "The United Missionary Campaign," *South African Outlook*, February 2, 1925, 32.

93. D. D. T. Jabavu, *What Methodism Has Done*, 2. Jabavu delivered the speech, which became the basis for the pamphlet, at the Wesleyan Native Church in King William's Town on April 28, 1923.

94. Jabavu explored similar themes in "The Bantu and the Gospel," first presented to the 1925 meeting of the South African General Missionary Conference and reprinted in *The Segregation Fallacy* (106–15) in 1928.

95. D. D. T. Jabavu, *What Methodism Has Done*, 7.

96. See Couzens, *New African*.

97. Elphick has argued that the "traditional missions" had extended their interests "into the realm of social service" as early as the 1890s, largely in response to "the greatest tremor ever to shake the missionary enterprise in South Africa: the revolt of the black clergy . . . and the founding of the Independent Churches." Elphick, "Mission Christianity," 71.

98. D. D. T. Jabavu, *What Methodism Has Done*, 7.

99. Jabavu's call for an activist church in South Africa arguably reflected the broader international call to action in response to the death and devastation caused by the First World War. See for example, Milford Hall Lyon, *The Basis for Brotherhood and Kindred Themes* (New York, 1923), which is dedicated "To The Soldiers and Sailors of The Great War." See also Elphick, "Mission Christianity," 74.

100. D. D. T. Jabavu, *What Methodism Has Done*, 8.

101. Ibid. Elphick has pointed out that by the 1920s most evangelists were Africans in any event. Elphick, "Mission Christianity," 68.

102. Taylor, *Christianity and the Natives*, x–xi. The campaign excluded the Roman Catholic missions, although representatives were invited to conferences as nonvoting members. The aim of the campaign was "twofold. First, that every Christian in South Africa should have a new vision of his or her vocation, which is surely first and foremost to be a witness by life and work and word to the Lord Jesus Christ. . . . Second, that each may receive a renewed will, and inducement of the Spirit, to fulfill this splendid obligation and trust." "United Missionary Campaign," *South African Outlook*, February 2, 1925, 31.

103. "United Missionary Campaign," *South African Outlook*, August 1, 1925, 32.

104. Ironically, the end of the First World War marked the beginning of the decline in the Social Gospel movement in the United States. The theologian Robert Handy linked this decline to the undermining of the "liberal theology on which the social gospel had

rested. . . . Liberals, with their optimistic orientation and heritage of idealism, were finding it hard to deal satisfactorily with the realities of depression and the rise of totalitarianism." Robert Handy, *The Social Gospel in America 1870–1920* (New York, 1966), 14–15. Elphick has observed a similar phenomenon in South Africa: "The twenties and the thirties were an ephemeral time of influence for missionaries, not only in South Africa but throughout British Africa. . . . [but] their empire rested on a shaky foundation, and they knew it." Elphick, "Mission Christianity," 71.

105. Handy, *Social Gospel in America*, 3–4. For a discussion of the parallel Roman Catholic movement, see Aaron I. Abell, *American Catholicism and Social Action: A Search for Social Justice, 1865–1950* (Garden City, N.Y., 1960).

106. Elphick, "Mission Christianity," 74.

107. Handy, *Social Gospel in America*, 5.

108. Others who brought the Social Gospel to South Africa included the Gold Coast educator J. E. K. Aggrey and Thomas Jesse Jones of the New York-based Phelps-Stokes Fund (which funded African education). Elphick, "Mission Christianity," 74.

109. See for example "The Africa Conference," *South African Outlook*, October 1, 1926, 223 and March 1, 1923, 53; Alexander Kerr, "Extracts from Report on Some American Institutions," *South African Outlook*, September 1, 1923, 201–3; *South African Outlook*, April 1, 1926, 79 and September 1, 1927, 164–65.

110. Elphick, "Mission Christianity," 74–75.

111. *The South African Outlook* was the unofficial journal of the Conference. "The General Missionary Conference of South Africa," Methodist Missionary Society Archives, Record Group 69. Special Collections, Yale Divinity School Library, New Haven, Connecticut, 1.

112. Elphick, "Mission Christianity," 75; International Missionary Council, *Addresses on General Subjects*, vol. 8 of *The Jerusalem Meeting of the International Missionary Council, March 24-April 8, 1928* (New York, 1928), 1.

113. A. C. Headlam, *The Doctrine of the Church and Christian Reunion: Being the Bampton Lectures for the Year 1920*, 2d ed. (London, 1920), 315; "The Reunion of Christendom.—II," *South African Outlook*, May 1, 1925, 110.

114. Support for church reunion came from a variety of sources. J. L. Komane of Phoqoane, writing to the editor of *The South African Outlook*, suggested that church officials consult Africans, many of whom were in favor of the idea. The Swedish minister Hans Nilson suggested that the missionaries were responsible for the rapid growth of separatist churches and were insincere in their statements about reunion, trends which he hoped to see reversed. "Towards Reunion" and "A United Native Church," *South African Outlook*, March 1, 1926, 70–71. See also *South African Outlook*, April 1, 1925, 75–76.

115. J. Scott Lidgett, "Reunion of Non-Episcopal Churches from the Standpoint of Methodism," *South African Outlook*, February 1, 1926, 44–47. The model for reunion was the United Church of Canada, which had absorbed the Presbyterian, Methodist, and Congregational churches. The Methodist missions in South Africa included two episcopal churches, the Methodist Episcopal Church and the African Methodist Episcopal

Church, and three nonepiscopal churches, the Wesleyan Methodist Church of South Africa, the Free Methodist Mission in Africa (American), and the Primitive Methodist Churches of South Africa. Taylor, *Christianity and the Natives*, x–xi.

116. "United Missionary Campaign," *South African Outlook*, February 1, 1925, 31–32.

117. D. D. T. Jabavu, "Christianity and the Bantu," 110–34.

118. Ibid., 116–17; see also Kuper, *African Bourgeoisie*, 193–94.

119. D. D. T. Jabavu, "Christianity and the Bantu," 117. In the early 1930s, this charge remained of great concern to missionaries. In 1931 three branches of the Methodist Church—the Wesleyan Methodist Church of South Africa, the Transvaal and Swaziland District of the Wesleyan Methodist Church of Great Britain, and the Primitive Methodist Missions in the Union of South Africa—addressed the issue of fragmentation by uniting as the Wesleyan Methodist Church in South Africa. Allen Lea, *The Story of the Methodist Union in South Africa: Being an Account of the Unification of Methodism in South Africa* (Cape Town, [1932]), 13–14. The Congregational and Presbyterian churches merged in 1933. "Church Union in South Africa," *South African Outlook*, June 1, 1933, 103–4. The ecumenical movement gained further strength with the establishment of the Christian Council of South Africa, embracing the English-speaking churches and the Dutch Reformed Churches in 1936. This latter union did not last long; the Transvaal Synod of the DRC broke with the Christian Council in 1941. De Gruchy, *Church Struggle*, 39. Despite all these efforts to reach out to African communities, there were by 1932 more than 300 African separatist churches. See Brookes, *Colour Problems of South Africa*, 34, 193–201.

120. D. D. T. Jabavu, Addresses [1923–1957], Jabavu Collection, UNISA. The Order of Ethiopia was founded in 1899, the Bantu Presbyterian Church in 1923, and the Bantu Baptist Church in 1927. D. D. T. Jabavu, *African Indigenous Church*, 3; Odendaal, *Vukani Bantu!*, 27.

121. Walshe, *Rise of African Nationalism*, 252.

122. Zaccheus Richard Mahabane (1881–1970) was born in the Orange Free State and studied at Morija in Basutoland with D. D. T. Jabavu. Mahabane qualified as a teacher in 1901, and became a Methodist minister in 1914. He was elected president of the Cape Congress in 1919 and served two terms as president-general of the national ANC—from 1924 to 1927, and 1937 to 1940. He joined the All African Convention in 1935, and was active in the Non-European Unity Movement in the 1940s. Gerhart and Karis, *Political Profiles*, 65.

123. Walshe, *Rise of African Nationalism*, 252–53; Gerhart and Karis, *Political Profiles*, 65.

124. D. D. T. Jabavu, "Christianity and the Bantu," 118–19.

125. Ibid., 117.

126. "Ciskei Missionary Council. Report on the Economic Condition of the Native People," *South African Outlook*, March 1, 1928, 47–50. The Ciskeian Missionary Council (affiliated with the General Missionary Conference at the national level) was established in 1925, reviving the long-lapsed Kaffrarian Missionary Conference, originally founded in 1862. Interracial and interdenominational, it included all the churches active in the

Ciskei. "1925 A Retrospect," *South African Outlook*, January 1, 1926, 7; "The Ciskeian Missionary Council," *South African Outlook*, December 1, 1925, 277–79.

127. "Ciskei Missionary Council," *South African Outlook*, March 1, 1928, 48. The most accurate figures were collected for the Victoria East district, where 1,076 of 2,776 African men resident had no access to land.

128. Ibid., 49.

129. Ibid., 50.

130. De Gruchy has asserted that "few scholars, if any, would disagree with George Ladd's assertion that 'the Kingdom is the reign of God, not merely in the human heart but dynamically active in the person of Jesus and in human history.'" De Gruchy, *Church Struggle*, 197.

131. Rufus M. Jones, "Secular Civilization and the Christian Task," *The Christian Life and Message in Relation to Non-Christian Systems of Thought and Life*, vol. 1 of *The Jerusalem Meeting of the International Missionary Council, March 24–April 8, 1928* (New York, 1928), 230, 272–73.

132. D. D. T. Jabavu, "After Three Generations," 46. See below, n145.

133. David H. Anthony III, "Max Yergan in South Africa: From Evangelical Pan-Africanist to Revolutionary Socialist," *African Studies Review* 34, no. 2 (September 1991): 31, 43, 45–46. Yergan embraced communism in the early 1930s and left South Africa in 1936, unable to accept the impending passage of the Hertzog bills.

134. International Missionary Council, *Addresses on General Subjects*, vol. 8 of *Jerusalem Meeting of the International Missionary Council*, 165. (Nyasaland is modern-day Malawi.)

135. Earlier meetings included those held in the United States and Great Britain in 1854, in Liverpool in 1860, in London in 1878 and 1888, in New York in 1900, and in Edinburgh in 1910. *Addresses on General Subjects*, vol. 8 of *Jerusalem Meeting of the International Missionary Council*, 1–2, 4, 159–70.

136. Ibid., 6.

137. Ibid., 165; *Imvo Zabantsundu*, November 1, 1927.

138. D. D. T. Jabavu, *E-Jerusalem* (In Jerusalem), 4th ed., trans. Cecil Wele Manona [unpub.] (Lovedale, 1948), 8; interview with J. M. Mohapeloa, Maseru, Lesotho, March 30, 1988; interview with Sipo Makalima, Alice, Ciskei, November 23, 1987.

139. D. D. T. Jabavu, *E-Jerusalem*, 22.

140. Ibid., 27.

141. Ibid., 23.

142. Noni Jabavu, *Ochre People*, 10–11.

143. International Missionary Council, *Addresses on General Subjects*, vol. 8 of *Jerusalem Meeting of the International Missionary Council*, 8.

144. International Missionary Council, *The Christian Mission in the Light of Race Conflict*, vol. 4 of *Jerusalem Meeting of the International Missionary Council*; William Paton, "The Jerusalem Meeting of the International Missionary Council," *International Review of Missions* 17 (1928): 9.

145. International Missionary Council, *The Christian Mission in the Light of Race Conflict*, vol. 4 of *Jerusalem Meeting of the International Missionary Council*, 184. Continent-wide, Islam was clearly the dominant religion. In 1932 Jabavu estimated there were ten million Christians, sixty million Muslims, and sixty million "heathens" on the African continent. D. D. T. Jabavu, "After Three Generations," 46. In South Africa, Jabavu's concern about the Muslim "threat" (while widely held) appeared to be largely groundless. According to the 1921 census, 1,605,356 of 4,607,813 Africans professed to be Christians; only 453 identified themselves as Muslims. *South African Outlook*, January 2, 1925, 3–4; "General Missionary Conference, Johannnesburg," *South African Outlook*, August 1, 1925, 178; Richard Gray, *Black Christians and White Missionaries* (New Haven, 1990), 79; Houghton and Dagut, *South African Economy*, 3:80.

146. The Mines and Works (Amendment) Act (the Colour Bar Act) was passed in May 1926 and barred blacks from holding skilled positions in the mining industry. Max Yergan, "The Race Problem in Africa," *The Christian Mission in the Light of Race Conflict*, vol. 4 of *Jerusalem Meeting of the International Missionary Council*, 181; Johns, *Protest and Hope*, 352; Davenport, *South Africa*, 3d ed., 287.

147. The Dutch Reformed Churches (DRC) sponsored two "Bantu-European" Conferences in September 1923 and February 1927. Yergan, "Race Problem in Africa," 181; Johns, *Protest and Hope*, 352.

148. Yergan, "Race Problem in Africa," 180.

149. J. Dexter Taylor, "Relations between the Black and White Races in South Africa," *The Christian Mission in the Light of Race Conflict*, vol. 4 of *Jerusalem Meeting of the International Missionary Council*, 79–117.

150. Ibid., 87. See also J. H. Oldham, *Christianity and the Race Problem* (London, 1925). Oldham was a secretary of the International Missionary Council. Elphick, "Mission Christianity," 75.

151. D. D. T. Jabavu, "Christianity and the Bantu," 134.

152. "The Race Problem. Lecture by Professor Jabavu. Jerusalem Conference and Segregation," *Cape Mercury*, August 27, 1928, reprinted in *Imvo Zabantsundu*, September 4, 1928.

153. Gerhart and Karis, *Political Profiles*, 1.

154. Johns, *Protest and Hope*, 151.

155. D. D. T. Jabavu, *'Native Disabilities' in South Africa* (Lovedale, 1932), 5; D. D. T. Jabavu, *E-Amerika* (In America), trans. Cecil Wele Manona [unpub.] (Lovedale, 1932), 16.

156. D. D. T. Jabavu, *'Native Disabilities,'* 6–7, 16–17; *Imvo Zabantsundu*, December 22, 1931.

157. D. D. T. Jabavu, *E-Amerika*, 12.

158. Hertzog's policies were the subject of a series of lectures Jabavu gave during a brief trip to Canada after the Buffalo convention. See "Native Reviews Africa's Problems. Noted Professor Gives Address at Trinity United Church Service. Says Injustice Shown," *Globe* (Toronto), January 5, 1932; "Describes Life African People. Don Davidson [*sic*] Tengo Jabavu Addresses Gathering at Chalmers," *Ottawa Journal*, January 6, 1932; "Problems of Race at Prayer Rally. . . . Professor Jabavu, of Bantu Tribe Indicts Union Government for Repression of Native," *Gazette* (Montreal), January 7, 1932.

159. A. Keppel-Jones, *South Africa*, 5th ed. (London, 1975), 164, 180.

160. The American Board established its American Zulu Mission in 1835. Taylor, *Christianity and the Natives*, 229.

161. Odendaal, *Vukani Bantu!*, 25; J. Mutero Chirenje, *Ethiopianism and Afro-Americans in Southern Africa, 1883–1916* (Baton Rouge, 1987), 3; Walter L. Williams, *Black Americans and the Evangelization of Africa 1877–1900* (Madison, Wis., 1982), 54–58.

162. The historian Carol Page has observed that white missionaries were also disappointed by the arrival of African-American missionaries, fearing that their color would place them at a competitive advantage, especially in the denominationally overcrowded Cape Colony. Carol A. Page, "Colonial Reaction to AME Missionaries in South Africa, 1898–1910," *Black Americans and the Missionary Movement in Africa*, ed. Sylvia M. Jacobs (Westport, Conn., 1982), 177.

163. Odendaal, *Vukani Bantu!*, 27.

164. D. D. T. Jabavu, "Christianity and the Bantu," 119.

165. D. D. T. Jabavu, *E-Amerika*, 16, 27; *Dictionary of American Biography*, supplement 5, 1951–1955 (1977), 506–8; D. D. T. Jabavu to J. R. Mott, May 7, 1928, John R. Mott Papers, Special Collections, Yale Divinity School Library, Manuscript Group no. 45, Box 44, Folder 813 (hereafter Mott Papers, YDSL). See also C. Howard Hopkins, *John R. Mott, 1865–1955: A Biography* (Grand Rapids, Mich., 1979).

166. Hopkins, *John R. Mott*, 676–77; "Dr. John R. Mott. Auspicious Opening to South African Visit," *South African Outlook*, May 1, 1934, 91. When Mott was nominated for the Nobel Peace Prize in 1934, Jabavu wrote to congratulate him: "my prayer is that . . . [you] . . . be granted many more years of life in order to enable you to see the fruition of some of the efforts you have engaged in for the furtherance of the Kingdom of God here on common earth." D. D. T. Jabavu to J. R. Mott, September 1, 1934, Mott Papers, YDSL.

167. *Buffalo Courier-Express*, December 30, 1931.

168. Writing a synopsis of a discussion on race in South Africa, Jabavu observed: "Remarkable enthusiasm was displayed in all our sessions, especially because there were many coloured delegates, who evinced a lively consciousness of grievance from cases of ill-treatment in their various areas." D. D. T. Jabavu, "White and Black in South Africa," *The Christian Mission in the World Today*, Report of the Eleventh Quadrennial Convention of the Student Volunteer Movement for Foreign Missions, Buffalo, New York, December 30, 1931, to January 3, 1932, ed. Raymond P. Currier (New York, 1932), 238.

169. D. D. T. Jabavu, "After Three Generations," 43.

170. Ibid.

171. See Wilson, *Interpreters*.

172. The roundtable drew representatives from East Africa, India, Rhodesia, West Africa, Canada, and the United States. D. D. T. Jabavu, "White and Black in South Africa," 238.

173. Ibid.

174. D. D. T. Jabavu, "Christian Service," 64–65.

175. Ibid., 70.

176. D. D. T. Jabavu, "Pilgrim Hall, January 8, 1932," ABC: Biographical Files: Individuals: Jabavu, Houghton Library, HU, 4.

177. Elphick, "Mission Christianity," 72.

178. In her autobiography the writer Phyllis Ntantala, who attended the South African Native College in the 1930s, offered stinging criticism of Yergan and his family, who were based at Fort Hare:

> They had no contact whatsoever with the black students on campus. No students and few black staff were ever invited to their place. . . . The Yergans stayed in South Africa for twenty-two years, eighteen of which were spent at Fort Hare. I wondered if by the time they left they could say 'Good Morning' in Xhosa. Dr. Yergan was supposed to be working among the people, but he never learnt their language. Puzzled, we would ask each other: 'Why did America send the Yergans here? For what purpose?' In the end we concluded it was to show us, blacks and whites in South Africa, that a black American can live as a white man. [Ntantala, *Life's Mosaic*, 70]

179. D. D. T. Jabavu, "Christian Service," 66, 72–73.

180. Ibid., 72. Ray E. Phillips was an American Board missionary whose book *The Bantu Are Coming: Phases of South Africa's Race Problem* (London, [1930]) urged the acceptance of Africans as a permanent urban community. Gerhart and Karis, *Political Profiles*, 126.

181. The Phelps-Stokes Fund was established in 1909 under the terms of the will of Caroline Phelps Stokes and administered a one-million-dollar grant to be used for "the education of Negroes, both in Africa and the United States, North American Indians and deserving white students." In March 1921 Thomas Jesse Jones, Director of Education for the fund, and African educator James E. K. Aggrey (who was born in the Gold Coast but educated largely in the United States) toured South Africa as representatives of the first Phelps-Stokes Commission on Education in British Africa. Jones and Aggrey met the Jabavus when they visited the South African Native College. *Phelps-Stokes Reports on Education in Africa*, abridged, with an introduction by L. J. Lewis (London, 1962), 1; Edwin W. Smith, *Aggrey of Africa: A Study in Black and White* (New York, 1929), xi, 165.

182. Ibid., 66, 71–72; Linda Ntuli, "Zenzele Women's Self-Improvement Association," trans. Cecil Wele Manona (typescript, n.d.), author's private collection; "The African Women's Self-Improvement Association: Constitution" (typescript, n.d.), author's private collection. See also [Florence] Jabavu, "Bantu Home Life," *Christianity and the Natives of South Africa: A Year Book of South African Missions*, ed. J. Dexter Taylor (Lovedale, [1928]), 164–76. Max Yergan's wife, Susie Wiseman Yergan, founded a rival organization, the Unity Home Makers' Club, in 1929—much to the chagrin of Florence Jabavu, who regarded her as a foreign interloper. Anthony, "Max Yergan in South Africa," 32, 55; [Susie W.] Yergan, "The Unity Home-Makers' Club. African Women's Self-Help Effort," *South African Outlook*, April 1, 1933, 78–79; interview with Joel and Bernice Mohapeloa, Mafeteng, Lesotho, August 22, 1988. Bernice Morolong Mohapeloa studied at Fort Hare in the early 1920s and then taught in Natal. She married Joel

Mohapeloa in 1929. He taught commerce at Fort Hare from 1931 to 1935, after which the couple settled in Basutoland.

183. D. D. T. Jabavu, "Christian Service," 66.

184. D. D. T. Jabavu, "Pilgrim Hall, January 8, 1932," 8. ABC: Biographical Files: Individuals: Jabavu, Houghton Library, HU.

185. "Students Focus Their Attention upon Hot Dogs. Foreign Delegates to Convention Give Time to This Phase of American Life," *Buffalo Courier-Express,* January 3, 1932.

186. "Africa's Hope Lies in Youth: Prof Jabavu Tells of Inter-Racial Hatred," *Boston Globe,* January 8, 1932; "Prof. Jabavu Talks in Two Churches: South African Educator also Tendered Dinner," *Boston Globe,* January 9, 1932; press release from D. P. Cushing, News Editor, American Board of Commissioners for Foreign Missions (n.d.), 1, ABC: Biographical Files: Individuals: Jabavu, Houghton Library, HU; D. D. T. Jabavu, *E-Amerika,* 32.

187. Writing to Jabavu in mid-1932, Cushing noted, "As you have doubtless heard, the American Board is being forced to make heavy cuts in its work because of lack of income this year." Dorothy P. Cushing to D. D. T. Jabavu, May 25, 1932. ABC: Biographical Collection: Individuals: Jabavu, Houghton Library, HU. For a discussion of the impact of the depression in the United States in the 1930s, see William E. Leuchtenburg, *Franklin D. Roosevelt and the New Deal 1932–1940* (New York, 1963), chaps. 1, 3. See also D. D. T. Jabavu, 'Native Disabilities,' 6.

188. Dorothy P. Cushing, "Jabavu Comes—Sees—and Conquers," *Missionary Herald,* March, 1932, 93, ABC: Biographical Collection: Individuals: Jabavu, Houghton Library, HU.

189. Ibid., 98 (emphasis in original).

190. Leslie B. Moss and Mabel H. Brown, eds., *Report of the Thirty-Ninth Annual Meeting of the Conference of Foreign Mission Boards in Canada and the United States, Atlantic City, New Jersey, January 12–15, 1932* (New York, 1932), 1, 280–82.

191. D. D. T. Jabavu, "Meaning of the Cross," 239.

192. Ibid., 232.

193. Ibid., 235–36.

194. Ibid., 237.

195. D. D. T. Jabavu, *E-Amerika,* i.

196. Ibid., 22–23.

197. Ibid., 23.

198. Walshe, *African National Congress,* 253. An Anglican priest, James Arthur Calata was born at Debe Nek, near King William's Town, in 1895. He joined the ANC in 1930, served as secretary-general from 1936 to 1949, and was president of the Cape African Congress from 1930 to 1949. Gerhart and Karis, *Political Profiles,* 16–17.

199. "The Separatist Churches of South Africa," letter to the editor from James A. Calata, *South African Outlook,* April 1, 1938, 93. See also S. Grosskopf, "Indigenous Churches (Reflections Suggested by the Adams Conference)," *South African Outlook,* October 1, 1938, 225–27.

200. Grosskopf, "Indigenous Churches," *South African Outlook,* October 1, 1938, 225–27. Moroka ultimately served as president of the ANC from 1949 to 1952; Mosaka broke

with the ANC to found the African Democratic Party in 1943; and Nhlapo withdrew from politics, becoming the editor of *The Bantu World* in the mid-1950s. Gerhart and Karis, *Political Profiles*, 97–100, 116. *The Bantu World* was established in Johannesburg in 1932 by B. F. G. Paver, with the backing of J. D. Rheinallt Jones, Howard Pim, and the Pretoria businessman Charles Magg. According to Switzer and Switzer, the newspaper "was virtually unique in striving to be a newspaper of record for the African community," although "mining and commercial interests" did manage "to squash both more radical liberal ideology plus black commercial interests and 'Africanism.'" Switzer and Switzer, *Black Press*, 122.

201. Walshe, *African National Congress*, 253; "The Separatist Churches of South Africa," *South African Outlook*, April 1, 1938, 92; D. D. T. Jabavu, *African Indigenous Church*, 5.

202. This was the interpretation of I. B. Tabata in a letter to T. I. N. Sondlo, the secretary of the AAC. Tabata was a member of the AAC executive for its Cape Town-based Western Province branch and Jabavu's strongest critic within the AAC. I. B. Tabata to T. I. N. Sondlo, November 3, 1943, and T. I. N. Sondlo to the editor, the "Torch," October 1946, Unity Movement Papers, J. W. Jagger Library, University of Cape Town Libraries, Cape Town, BC925 (hereafter Unity Movement Papers, UCT). *The Torch* was founded in Cape Town as the official organ of the Non-European Unity Movement (NEUM). Switzer and Switzer have described it as "one of the more significant efforts to coordinate black protest groups prior to 1960." Switzer and Switzer, *Black Press*, 61.

203. D. D. T. Jabavu, *African Indigenous Church*, 4.

204. Alan Palmer, *The Penguin Dictionary of Modern History 1789–1945*, 2d ed. (New York, 1983), s.v. "Atlantic Charter."

205. D. D. T. Jabavu, *African Indigenous Church*, 3, 15.

206. A. L. Warnshuis, "Major Issues in the Relations of the Younger and the Older Churches," *The Relation between the Younger and the Older Churches*, vol.3 of *Jerusalem Meeting of the International Missionary Council*, 7, 34; D. D. T. Jabavu, *African Indigenous Church*, 2.

207. D. D. T. Jabavu, *African Indigenous Church*, 3. The distinction between *indigenous* and *independent* could be confusing—in a bibliography Monica Wilson cited Jabavu's pamphlet as *An African Independent Church*. Monica Wilson, *Religion and the Transformation of Society: A Study in Social Change in Africa* (Cambridge, 1971), 154.

208. D. D. T. Jabavu, *African Indigenous Church*, 15–16.

209. Walshe, *Rise of African Nationalism*, 253.

210. D. D. T. Jabavu, *African Indigenous Church*, 12–13, 16.

211. Ibid., 14. Z. K. Matthews was appointed the headmaster of Adams College (an American Board Mission school) in 1925. Adams College had been founded in 1853 as the Amanzimtoti Institute, and like other early mission schools, its goal was to train teachers and ministers. By the early twentieth century it had expanded its offerings to include industrial training in addition to teacher training and secondary education. Z. K. Matthews, *Freedom for My People*, 83–85; Marks, *Not Either an Experimental Doll*, 19.

212. D. D. T. Jabavu, *African Indigenous Church*, 14.

213. The section title is from Psalms 127:1; quoted in D. D. T. Jabavu, *African Indigenous Church*, 15.

214. Ibid.

215. D. D. T. Jabavu, "After Three Generations," 45.

216. D. D. T. Jabavu, Addresses [1923–1957], Jabavu Collection, UNISA.

217. Ibid. Out of approximately 300 sermons and lessons, Jabavu spoke about the Good Samaritan twenty-eight times. Ibid.; Luke 10:30.

4 The Rise of an African Politician, 1920–1936

1. *Politician* is used here in the broad sense to describe an individual who "actively engaged in politics," since most African political activity was by necessity extraparliamentary. *Webster's New Universal Dictionary*, deluxe 2d ed. (1983), s.v. "politician."

2. Davenport, *South Africa*, 3d ed., 257, 262; Trapido, "'Friends of the Natives,'" 252–53; Willan, *Sol Plaatje*, 166.

3. D. D. T. Jabavu, *John Tengo Jabavu*, 48.

4. Willan, *Sol Plaatje*, 166.

5. Switzer and Switzer, *Black Press*, 40; Willan, *Sol Plaatje*, 165–66.

6. Gerhart and Karis, *Political Profiles*, 42, 128. By contrast, the SANNC founders counted among their number Plaatje (Tswana), John Dube (Zulu), Walter Rubusana (Xhosa), and Pixley ka I. Seme (Tonga). Gerhart and Karis, 24, 134, 137.

7. Davenport, *South Africa*, 3d ed., 259–60.

8. Plaatje, *Native Life*, 78–99; Davenport, *South Africa*, 3d ed., 259.

9. Plaatje, *Native Life*, 192–98; Willan, *Sol Plaatje*, 166.

10. See above, chap. 1.

11. D. D. T. Jabavu, *John Tengo Jabavu*, 48.

12. Ibid., 18, 48; Roux, *Time Longer than Rope*, 2d ed., 84; Ngcongco, "John Tengo Jabavu," 152–53; Manona, "Ethnic Relations in the Ciskei," 105; Peires, "Lovedale Press," 162.

13. *Imvo Zabantsundu*, January 23, 1917; Davenport, *South Africa*, 3d ed., 262.

14. D. D. T. Jabavu, *John Tengo Jabavu*, 51–52. Tengo Jabavu did serve as a member of the provincial commission on African education in 1919. Cape of Good Hope, *Report of Commission on Native Education, 1919*.

15. Switzer, *Power and Resistance*, 243; Philips, "South Africa's Worst Demographic Disaster."

16. Helen Bradford, *A Taste of Freedom: The ICU in Rural South Africa, 1924–1930* (Johannesburg, 1987), 2; see also Philip Bonner, "The Transvaal Native Congress, 1917–1920: The Radicalisation of the Black Petty Bourgeoisie on the Rand," *Industrialisation and Social Change in South Africa: African Class Formation, Culture, and Consciousness, 1870–1930*, ed. Shula Marks and Richard Rathbone (London, 1982), 270–313.

17. Bradford, *Taste of Freedom*, 3. In 1921 the ICU combined with the Industrial and Commercial Coloured and Native Workers' (Amalgamated) Union of South Africa (ICWU), which had been founded in 1920. The new organization's name became the Industrial and Commercial Workers' Union (shortened to ICU) (p. 6). Clements Kadalie (ca. 1896–1951) was born in Nyasaland (modern-day Malawi) and moved to Cape Town in 1918. He remained a prominent figure in the ICU even as it collapsed into competing factions in the late 1920s. He established the Independent ICU in 1929, but was banned from speaking in public by the government in 1930. He eventually joined the ANC and participated in the protest against Hertzog's Native Bills in 1935 and 1936. Gerhart and Karis, *Political Profiles*, 45–47.

18. Jack Simons and Ray Simons, *Class and Colour in South Africa, 1850–1950* ([London], 1983), 193–98, 203, 207–16; Robert A. Hill and Gregory A. Pirio, "'Africa for the Africans': The Garvey Movement in South Africa, 1920–1940," *The Politics of Race, Class and Nationalism in Twentieth-Century South Africa*, ed. Shula Marks and Stanley Trapido (London, 1987), 232. See also Edward Roux, *S. P. Bunting: A Political Biography*, rev. ed. (Bellville, South Africa, 1993).

19. D. D. T. Jabavu, *Black Problem*, 1.

20. Ibid., 15.

21. Ibid., 10, 16.

22. Alexander Jabavu identified this division in the late 1920s. Bradford, *Taste of Freedom*, 86.

23. D. D. T. Jabavu, *Black Problem*, 7.

24. Davenport, *South Africa*, 3d ed., 260.

25. Ingham, *Jan Christian Smuts*, 121.

26. John Langalibelele Dube (1871–1946) was born in Inanda in the Natal Province. He studied at Oberlin College in Ohio in the late 1880s, and established the Tuskegee-style Ohlange Institute in Natal in 1901. He was elected the first president of the SANNC (ANC) in 1912. He resigned as president of the national SANNC in 1917, but remained as head of the Natal branch until 1945. Gerhart and Karis, *Political Profiles*, 25.

27. Dubow, *Racial Segregation*, 108–9.

28. Ibid., 108. See also Martin Legassick, "The Making of South African 'Native Policy,' 1903–1923: The Origins of 'Segregation,'" paper presented to the postgraduate seminar on Ideology and Social Structure in Twentieth Century South Africa, Institute of Commonwealth Studies, University of London, 1972, 8.

29. Hancock, *Smuts: Sanguine Years*, 3, 33; Ingham, *Jan Christian Smuts*, 5–6; Davenport, *South Africa*, 3d ed., 585.

30. D. D. T. Jabavu, "Native Affairs Bill: Views of Natives," *Black Problem*, 22.

31. Ibid., 25.

32. Ingham, *Jan Christian Smuts*, 167; see also Letters of General Smuts, 1930, April 8, 1930 (642/201), J. C. Smuts Papers, A1, vol. 230, CAD (hereafter Smuts Papers, CAD).

33. The historian W. K. Hancock has argued that Smuts's motive in supporting the retention of the Cape franchise in the 1909 South Africa Act was a pragmatic one. In agreeing to maintain the Cape franchise, Smuts was refusing "to attempt the politically

impossible task of sponsoring a revolutionary alteration of the time-honoured franchise of the Transvaal." Hancock, *Smuts: Fields of Force*, 115. See also Thompson, *Unification of South Africa*, 118–20.

34. Hancock, *Smuts: Fields of Force*, 213; Davenport, *South Africa*, 3d. ed., 295–96.

35. Davenport, *South Africa*, 3d ed., 258–60; Hancock, *Smuts: Fields of Force*, 113–14, 225, 251; Ingham, *Jan Christian Smuts*, 167.

36. D. D. T. Jabavu, "Native Affairs Bill: Views of the Natives," *Black Problem*, 24.

37. John Cell, *The Highest Stage of White Supremacy: The Origins of Segregation in South Africa and the American South* (Cambridge, 1982), 3. See also Davenport, *South Africa*, 3d ed., 293–94; Dubow, *Racial Segregation*, 3.

38. D. D. T. Jabavu, "Native Affairs Bill: Views of the Natives," *Black Problem*, 24.

39. Dubow, *Racial Segregation*, 15; Hancock, *Smuts: Fields of Force*, 127; Davenport, *South Africa*, 3d ed., 257, 273–74, 585. Hertzog established the National Party in 1914 after breaking with the South African Party in 1912.

40. Dubow, *Racial Segregation*, 15, 172; Hancock, *Smuts: Fields of Force*, 213, 225.

41. Jabavu was not the only one seduced by Smuts's liberal segregationism—Martin Legassick has argued that white liberals also regarded Smuts as the great hope of liberalism in government, abandoning him in 1928 in favor of J. H. Hofmeyr only after Smuts had appeared to acquiesce to Hertzog's Native Bills. Legassick, "Modern South African Liberalism," 29. (Regarding Hofmeyr, see below, n166.)

42. Born in the Gold Coast (modern-day Ghana) in 1875, Aggrey was recruited by a visiting minister of the African Methodist Episcopal Zion Church (who hoped to make a missionary of him) to attend the church's school. Livingstone College in Salisbury, North Carolina, had been established in 1882 to educate freed slaves; Aggrey enrolled there in 1898 and graduated with a B.A. in 1902. He was appointed a professor at the college the same year and lectured in (among other things) New Testament Greek and exegesis, Christian sociology, and economics. The Livingstone-affiliated Hood Theological Seminary conferred a Doctor of Divinity degree on him in 1912. Smith, *Aggrey of Africa*, xi, 57–58, 61–62, 105, 109.

43. Thomas Jesse Jones was born in Wales in 1873, and immigrated to the United States with his parents in 1884. He did his undergraduate work at Washington and Lee University in Virginia, and earned his M.A., B.D., and Ph.D. at Columbia University. He taught sociology at the Hampton Institute in Virginia and worked for the U.S. Census Bureau before joining the Phelps Stokes Fund. Kenneth James King, *Pan-Africanism and Education: A Study of Race Philanthropy and Education in the Southern States of America and East Africa* (Oxford, 1971), 21–22, 28; Smith, *Aggrey of Africa*, 68–69. For an "expert" on African-American issues, Jones was not particularly sympathetic. He dismissed calls for "Negro Independence" as "a shibboleth used by a certain number of Negroes to persuade the race into their own power and away from the influence of whites" (p. 24).

44. King, *Pan-Africanism and Education*, 232.

45. Dubow, *Racial Segregation*, 155–56.

46. The Council on Interracial Cooperation was established in Atlanta in 1919, and sought "to bring 'the best' whites and blacks together . . . in an effort to ameliorate racial

tension growing out of World War I." Approximately 800 state and local interracial councils were established throughout the South in the 1920s. Ann Wells Ellis, "Commission on Interracial Cooperation (CIC)," *Encyclopedia of Southern Culture*, ed. Charles Reagan Wilson, William Ferris, Ann J. Abadie, and Mary L. Hart (Chapel Hill, 1989), 204. For a further discussion of the CIC, see Morton Sosna, *In Search of the Silent South: Southern Liberals and the Race Issue* (New York, 1977), chap. 2.

47. Baruch Hirson, "Tuskegee, the Joint Councils, and the All African Convention," *Collected Seminar Papers on the Societies of Southern Africa in the Nineteenth and Twentieth Centuries*, University of London, Institute of Commonwealth Studies, vol. 10 (October 1978–June 1979), 68.

48. Dubow, *Racial Segregation*, 156.

49. Ibid.

50. King, *Pan-Africanism and Education*, 232.

51. Hill and Pirio, "'Africa for the Africans,'" 227.

52. Smith, *Aggrey of Africa*, 123.

53. Ibid., 122. Garvey had established the United Negro Improvement Association in his native Jamaica in 1914. He moved to New York City in 1916 and opened a branch of the UNIA there in 1917. He was convicted of mail fraud in 1924. On his release from prison in 1927, he was deported to Jamaica. E. David Cronin, *Black Moses: The Story of Marcus Garvey and the Universal Negro Improvement Association* (Madison, Wis., 1955, 1969), 3, 16, 42, 133, 142.

54. The SANNC changed its name to the ANC in 1923. Davenport, *South Africa*, 3d ed., 284.

55. Hill and Pirio, "'Africa for the Africans,'" 215, 231–32, 235. James Thaele (1888–1948) was born in Basutoland and attended Lovedale from 1906 to 1910. In 1913 he went to the United States, where he studied at Lincoln University (a historically black college), and earned a B.A. and a bachelor's degree in theology. He returned to South Africa in 1923, according to Gerhart, "strongly affected by the Garveyist movement." He became president of the western Cape ANC in the 1920s. Gerhart and Karis, *Political Profiles*, 154–55.

56. Hill and Pirio, "'Africa for the Africans,'" 226–28.

57. Quoted in King, *Pan-Africanism and Education*, 98. So impressed was the Governing Council of the South African Native College by Aggrey and his message of racial harmony, that they offered him a professorship in sociology and education, which he declined. Smith, *Aggrey of Africa*, 123. See also Frederickson, *Black Liberation*, 146–49.

58. Though his political philosophy was much more radical, Garvey had in fact been heavily influenced by Washington; one of his first goals when he arrived in New York in 1916 was to set up a Tuskegee-style industrial school. Cronin, *Black Moses*, 18–19, 42.

59. The political scientists Thomas Karis and Gwendolen Carter identified Jabavu as the author of the article in their collection of political documents, and it is written in his style. [D. D. T. Jabavu], *Black Peril and Colour Bar* (Lovedale, 1923), Carter-Karis Collection Microfilm, Yale University Library Manuscripts and Archives, New Haven, Connecticut, 2:XJ2:84/3 (hereafter Carter-Karis Collection Microfilm, YUL).

60. Though the pages of *The South African Outlook* were often filled with letters to the editor addressing the contents of earlier issues, there was no response to Jabavu's article, and he published it shortly thereafter, though still anonymously, in pamphlet form. *South African Outlook*, January 1, 1923, 3.

61. "Black Peril and Colour Bar—I," *South African Outlook*, December 1, 1922, 260.

62. Ibid., 261.

63. Ibid., 260. For a discussion of the resurgence of academic economic liberalism in the 1930s, see Legassick, "Modern South African Liberalism," 23–27.

64. "Black Peril and Colour Bar—I," *South African Outlook*, December 1, 1922, 261.

65. "Black Peril and Colour Bar—II," *South African Outlook*, January 1, 1923, 8–9.

66. Legassick, "Modern South African Liberalism," 3, 5; Dubow, *Racial Segregation*, 156–57.

67. "Black Peril and Colour Bar—II," *South African Outlook*, January 1, 1923, 8.

68. Dubow, *Racial Segregation*, 157–58. Members of the Joint Council movement were prominent among the delegates to the conference.

69. De Gruchy, *Church Struggle*, 19.

70. Taylor, *Christianity and the Natives*, 205. As Elphick has noted, Calvinist ecclesiology meant that clergymen at the Cape were "responsible first for a European congregation and only second for converting non-Christians" (Elphick, "Africans and the Christian Campaign," 278–79). The Dutch Reformed Churches included the Nederduitse Gereformeerde Kerk (NGK), founded originally in the Cape, the Nederduitsch Herformde Kerk (NHK), which had broken away from the NGK in the Transvaal in 1853, the Gereformeerde ("Dopper") Kerk, which broke with the NHK in 1859, and the Verenigde Kerk, established in the 1880s in opposition to the amalgamation of the NGK and NHK churches in the Transvaal. Davenport, *South Africa*, 3d ed., 77, 89–91, 93.

71. De Gruchy, *Church Struggle*, 69–70; Davenport, *South Africa*, 3d ed., 584–85.

72. Federal Council of Dutch Reformed Churches of South Africa, *European and Bantu: Being Papers and Addresses Read at the Conference on Native Affairs, Held under the Auspices of the Federal Council of the D.R. Churches at Johannesburg on 27th to 29th September, 1923* (Cape Town, [1923]), 10.

73. During the 1924 election campaign, Hertzog would claim that he had been thinking about a comprehensive scheme of segregation since 1912. Dubow, *Racial Segregation*, 136. After winning the 1924 election, however, he claimed, "This Government has no native policy at this moment." Davenport, *South Africa*, 3d ed., 257, 293.

74. Federal Council of Dutch Reformed Churches, *European and Bantu*, 38.

75. Ibid., 39. Mahabane explored similar themes in "Exclusion of the Bantu," his 1921 presidential address to the Cape Province Native Congress, and in his 1922 presidential address, "The Evil Nature of the Colour Bar." Gwendolen M. Carter and Sheridan W. Johns III, eds., *The Good Fight: Selected Speeches of Rev. Zaccheus R. Mahabane*, (Evanston, Ill., [1965]), 13–30.

76. Federal Council of Dutch Reformed Churches, *European and Bantu*, 40. Conference delegates similarly proclaimed themselves in favor of Edgar Brookes's "principle of

differential development of the Bantu, so far as such differentiation is based on Bantu traditions and requirements, and is not used as a means of repression," again adding a qualifier: "so far as this general differential development can be described as 'Segregation,' the Conference is in favor of segregation." Federal Council of Dutch Reformed Churches, *European and Bantu*, 44; Dubow, *Racial Segregation*, 158.

77. Hertzog and F. H. P. Creswell (the leader of the Labour Party), condemned Smuts's SAP as a "tool of 'big finance,'" following the 1922 strikes on the Witwatersrand. Ideologically at odds (Nationalists suspected Labour of "Bolshevism"; Labour questioned the National Party's loyalty to the British Crown), they were united largely by their opposition to Smuts. For a discussion of the pact, see Davenport, *South Africa*, 3d ed., 283–85.

78. J. B. M. Hertzog, *The Segregation Problem* (Cape Town, 1925).

79. Davenport, *South Africa*, 3d ed., 258, 286; see also T. R. H. Davenport, *The Beginnings of Urban Segregation in South Africa: The Natives (Urban Areas) Act of 1923 and Its Background* (Grahamstown, 1971); and Union of South Africa, *First Report of the Select Committee on Native Affairs*, S.C. 3-'23 (Cape Town, 1923); Thompson, *Unification of South Africa*, 118–20, 125–26, 429–30.

80. Dubow, *Racial Segregation*, 136.

81. Davenport, *South Africa*, 3d ed., 247.

82. Willan, *Sol Plaatje*, 309; C. M. Tatz, *Shadow and Substance in South Africa: A Study in Land and Franchise Policies Affecting Africans, 1910–1960* (Pietermaritzburg, 1962), 46–47, 53; Davenport, *South Africa*, 3d ed., 293–94; "Premier's Native Policy," *Cape Times*, November 14, 1925; see also Richard John Haines, "The Opposition to General J. B. M. Hertzog's Segregation Bills, 1925–1936: A Study in Extra-Parliamentary Protest" (M.A. thesis, University of Natal, 1978).

83. D. D. T. Jabavu, "The South African Problem," *International Review of Missions* 15 (July 1926): 384, reprinted as "Crossroads of Native Policy" in *The Segregation Fallacy*, 88–105. The political scientist Marian Lacey quoted Jabavu in support of her assertion that Hertzog's primary concern was not the protection of European civilization, but rather the abolition of the "Cape vote . . . so that all Africans could be reduced to a super-exploitable condition. Cape African voters had access to political power and property and union rights. Clearly they were less vulnerable to exploitation" (Marian Lacey, *Working for Boroko: The Origins of a Coercive Labour System in South Africa* [Johannesburg, 1981], 5, 46, 50). Jabavu, however, was willing to acknowledge the reality if not the legitimacy of white fears ("South African Problem," 379), which Dubow has also acknowledged in *Racial Segregation*, 9.

84. *Imvo Zabantsundu*, December 29, 1925.

85. D. D. T. Jabavu, "South African Problem," 380.

86. Ibid., 383.

87. Ibid., 383–84.

88. Ibid., 384.

89. Ibid.

90. Ibid., 386.

91. Tatz, *Shadow and Substance*, 46, 53 n18.

92. A farmer and businessman, Charles Kwelemtini Sakwe (1886–1964) was an active member of the South African Native Farmers' Congress. He joined the Cape Native Voters' Convention and in 1935 attended the first conference of the AAC. He was elected to the Natives' Representative Council (NRC) in 1937 and sat as a member of the Transkei Territories General Council for forty years. Gerhart and Karis, *Political Profiles*, 135; "S.A. Native Farmers' Congress," CMT, ref. 43/c, vol. 3/1485, CA.

93. Union of South Africa, *Report of the NAC for 1925–26*, U.G. 17-'27, 61–62; Willan, *Sol Plaatje*, 311.

94. Union of South Africa, *Report of the NAC for 1925–26*, U.G. 17-'27; Gerhart and Karis, *Political Profiles*, 155–57.

95. Union of South Africa, *Report of the NAC for 1925–26*, U.G. 17-'27, 73; D. D. T. Jabavu, "The Government Native Conference," *Cape Times*, November 19, 1926; reprinted in *Imvo Zabantsundu* as a four-part series on December 7, 14, 21, 28, 1926.

96. D. D. T. Jabavu, *U-Kayakulu*, 1, 15–16.

97. Union of South Africa, *Report of the NAC for 1925–26*, U.G. 17-'27, 74.

98. The number of white voters in the Cape had increased from 121,346 to 156,531. In 1910 the ratio of African to white voters had been 1:18; by 1926 it was 1:11. D. D. T. Jabavu, *Segregation Fallacy*, 39.

99. D. D. T. Jabavu, "The Cape Native Franchise: Representation Bill Discussed," *Cape Times*, January 29, 1927, and "Cape Native Franchise: Eight Arguments," *Cape Times*, January 31, 1927; reprinted as a three-part series in *Imvo Zabantsundu* on February 15 and 22, and March 1, 1927, and in *South African Outlook*, March 1, 1927, 46–50, and in *The Segregation Fallacy* (1928) as "The Disfranchisement of the Cape Native," 29–45.

100. D. D. T. Jabavu, "Cape Native Franchise," *Cape Times*, January 29, 1927.

101. Ibid.

102. D. D. T. Jabavu to A. Abdurahman, April 18, 1927, A. Abdurahman Papers, J. W. Jagger Library, University of Cape Town, Cape Town, BCZA 85/21–3 (hereafter Abdurahman Papers, UCT). Jacob Daniël Krige (1896–1959) was born in Stellenbosch and first practiced law in the late 1920s before retraining as an anthropologist and joining the faculty at Rhodes University in 1940. *DSAB*, 4:292–93. (Arthur Francis) Thomas William Smartt (1858–1929) was born in Ireland and qualified as a surgeon before settling in the Cape Colony in 1880. He was elected to the Cape Colony parliament in 1894, and joined the Unionist Party (which was later absorbed by the South African Party) at Union in 1910. He was a lifelong supporter of the Cape nonracial franchise and favored its extension throughout South Africa. *DSAB*, 1:725–27.

103. A. Abdurahman to D. D. T. Jabavu, April 22, 1927, Abdurahman Papers, UCT.

104. "Minutes of Evidence Taken before the Select Committee on Subject of Native Bills [Prof. D. D. T. Jabavu]," Union of South Africa, *Report of the Select Committee on the Subject of the Native Council Bill, Coloured Persons Rights Bill, Representation of Natives in Parliament Bill, and Natives Land (Amendment) Bill*, S.C.10-'27 (Cape Town, [1928]), 239–253, 262, 270, 273, 289.

105. "Testimony of Professor D. D. T. Jabavu, Walter Rubusana, and the Rev. Abner Mtimkulu of the Cape Native Voters' Convention and Meshach Pelem of the Bantu

Union, before the Select Committee on Subject of the Native Bills," quoted in Karis, *Hope and Challenge*, 211. See also D. D. T. Jabavu, "The Disfranchisement of the Cape Native," *Segregation Fallacy*, 29–45.

106. Union of South Africa, *Report of the Select Committee*, S.C. 10-'27, 250. The only new material he included were the resolutions of the Wesleyan Methodist Conference held in Bloemfontein in early May. Though he had not attended the conference, he took the opportunity to air its resolution, so similar to his own assertions: "We claim for the Bantu the right to live in the land of their birth in contentment and peace, the right to physical, intellectual and moral freedom, the right to the economic and political privileges of full citizenship in the Union." He testified before the Select Committee as a representative of the Wesleyan Methodist Conference of South Africa, the European-Bantu Conference, the Cape Native Voters' Convention, the Ciskei Native Convention, the government Native Conference, the South African Native Farmers' Congress, the South African Native Teachers' Federation, and the South African Native and Coloured Health Society.

107. Non-European Conference, *Minutes of the First Non-European Conference. Kimberley, 23rd, 24th and 25th June, 1927*, Carter-Karis Collection Microfilm, YUL, 2:DN1:30/1, 40.

108. C. Kadalie to A. Abdurahman, April 16, 1927, Abdurahman Papers, UCT.

109. A. Abdurahman to D. D. T. Jabavu, April 22, 1927, Abdurahman Papers, UCT.

110. D. D. T. Jabavu to A. Abdurahman, April 26, 1927, Abdurahman Papers, UCT. Helen Bradford, focusing on rural areas, did not refer to the conflict between the ICU and the Non-European Conference. Bradford, *Taste of Freedom*.

111. Bradford, *Taste of Freedom*, 86.

112. Quoted in Switzer, *Power and Resistance*, 255–56.

113. Ibid.

114. D. D. T. Jabavu to A. Abdurahman, May 20, June 6, 1927, Abdurahman Papers, UCT.

115. Non-European Conference, *Minutes of the First Non-European Conference*, 2; *Cape Times*, June 24, 1927.

116. D. D. T. Jabavu, "The Non-European Conference," *South African Outlook*, September 1, 1927, 172.

117. Non-European Conference, *Minutes of the First Non-European Conference*, 10.

118. D. D. T. Jabavu, "Non-European Conference," *South African Outlook*, September 1, 1927, 172; D. D. T. Jabavu to A. Abdurahman, June 6, 1927, Abdurahman Papers, UCT.

119. Non-European Conference, *Minutes of the First Non-European Conference*, 16.

120. Allison Wessels George Champion (1893–1975) was born in Natal and attended the Amanzimtoti Training Institute (later Adams College). After being suspended for "rebelliousness" in 1913, he worked as a policeman and then as a mine clerk before joining the ICU in 1925 as the secretary for the Transvaal. After the collapse of the ICU in the late 1920s, he became a leading member of the Natal ANC in the late 1930s, and served on the Natives' Representative Council in the 1940s. Gerhart and Karis, *Political Profiles*, 18–19.

121. Dubow, *Racial Segregation*, 155.

122. Non-European Conference, *Minutes of the First Non-European Conference*, 17, 23; *Cape Times*, February 1, 3, 1927.

123. Non-European Conference, *Minutes of the First Non-European Conference*, 10.

124. Ibid., 63.

125. Ibid., 53.

126. Ibid., 19; *Cape Times*, June 25, 1927.

127. Dubow, *Racial Segregation*, 156.

128. Ibid., 157–58.

129. "The Native Franchise," *South African Outlook*, June 1, 1928, 105.

130. Ibid., 106.

131. "The Native Franchise," letter to the editor from D. D. T. Jabavu, *South African Outlook*, July 2, 1928, 140.

132. D. D. T. Jabavu, *Segregation Fallacy*, vi.

133. National European-Bantu Conference, *Report of the National European-Bantu Conference. Cape Town, February 6–9, 1929* (Lovedale, [1929]), Carter-Karis Collection Microfilm, YUL, 2:FN2:30/1, i.

134. "Inter-Racial Council of South Africa," Records of the Joint Council Movement of Europeans and Africans, Historical and Literary Papers, University of the Witwatersrand Library, Johannesburg, AD1433, Aa3.2 (hereafter Joint Council Records, UWL). James Wellwood Mushet (1881–1954) was born in Scotland and immigrated to South Africa in 1899. He established "J. W. Mushet and Co., general merchants of Cape Town, Johannesburg, and Durban," before winning election as a South African Party MP in 1920. He retired from politics in 1953. *DSAB*, 4:384. The Rev. Abner Mtimkulu was ordained a minister in the Wesleyan Methodist Church, but he eventually joined the independent Bantu Methodist Church. He attended the first conference of the All African Convention in 1935, and was a leading member of the Natal ANC from the 1920s through the 1940s. Gerhart and Karis, *Political Profiles*, 106.

135. "Inter-Racial Council of South Africa," Joint Council Records, UWL, Aa3.2. See also Paul Rich, "The South African Institute of Race Relations and the Debate on 'Race Relations,' 1929–1958," *Collected Seminar Papers on the Societies of Southern Africa in the Nineteenth and Twentieth Centuries*, University of London, Institute of Commonwealth Studies, vol. 12 (1981), 77–90; Catherine Higgs, "The Founding of the South African Institute of Race Relations," Southern African Research Program, Yale University, 1985, 24–25.

136. Interview with Leo Sihlali, Mount Frere, Transkei, March 22, 1988. Sihlali earned a Diploma in Education from the South African Native College in 1940. He was active in both the All African Convention and the Non-European Unity Movement. South African Native College, *Calendar for 1944*, 52.

137. "European-Bantu Conference," *South African Outlook*, March 1, 1929, 54.

138. Ibid., 55.

139. Dubow, *Racial Segregation*, 159; Ingham, *Jan Christian Smuts*, 162.

140. South African Institute of Race Relations, *Second Annual Report 1931* (Johannesburg, [1931]), 99. A few changes in the executive had been made: Pim became treasurer, while Rheinallt Jones took on the roles of secretary, convener and adviser on Race

Relations at a salary of £1,000 a year. Loram was elected chairman and managed, no doubt through his influence over the institute's purse strings, to have the nonpolitical, research-oriented nature of the organization confirmed. Jabavu remained a vice president. See also Rich, "South African Institute of Race Relations."

141. Dubow, *Racial Segregation*, 159.

142. Tatz, *Shadow and Substance*, 60–61.

143. Dubow, *Racial Segregation*, 140–41; Hancock, *Smuts: Fields of Force*, 213–17; Krikler, "South African Party and the Cape Franchise," 71–77.

144. Davenport, *South Africa*, 3d ed., 297.

145. Dubow, *Racial Segregation*, 142; Krikler, "South African Party and the Cape Franchise," 64.

146. Johns, *Protest and Hope*, 354; Davenport, *South Africa*, 3d ed., 297–98; 587.

147. Margery Perham, *African Apprenticeship: An Autobiographical Journey in Southern Africa 1929* (London, 1974), 11.

148. Ibid., 10. Perham visited the Belgian Congo (modern-day Zaire), Northern and Southern Rhodesia (Zambia and Zimbabwe), Mozambique, Bechuanaland (Botswana), and South Africa.

149. Ibid., 53–54.

150. D. D. T. Jabavu, *Izithuko* (Praise poems), trans. Cecil Wele Manona [unpub.] (Lovedale, 1954), no. 16. M. M. Sihele remains an anonymous figure—in one praise poem (no. 15) he described himself as "the man of Thembu."

151. "Hai abant'Abamnyama," Cory Library, Rhodes University, MS16,396; Dierdre D. Hansen, "The Life and Work of Benjamin Tyamzashe: A Contemporary Xhosa Composer," Occasional Paper no. 11, Institute of Social and Economic Research, Rhodes University, Grahamstown, 1968, 22.

152. "Report on Meeting Held by Cape Native Voters Association at Queenstown on the 16/12/1929," NTS vol. 7215, ref. no. 59/326, CAD. See also *Imvo Zabantsundu*, January 7, 1930.

153. Perham, *African Apprenticeship*, 133; *Imvo Zabantsundu*, January 14, 1930.

154. Beinart, "Soil Erosion;" Redding, "African Middle Class," 524–25.

155. Perham, *African Apprenticeship*, 132–33.

156. Ibid., 133.

157. *Cape Times*, April 8, 1930.

158. D. D. T. Jabavu, "Native Voting Rights. Why Leaders Will Not Compromise. The Thin End of the Stick. Some Questions for the Government," *Cape Times*, April 8, 1930.

159. Ibid.

160. *Cape Times*, April 16, 1930.

161. *Imvo Zabantsundu*, December 16, 23, 1930.

162. D. D. T. Jabavu to Howard Pim, February 18, 1931, J. Howard Pim Papers, Historical and Literary Papers, University of the Witwatersrand Library, Johannesburg, A881, BL 1 (hereafter Pim Papers, UWL). Dubow, *Racial Segregation*, 163. White men in Natal and the Cape were exempted from the property and salary qualifications in 1931. Davenport, *South Africa*, 3d ed., 311.

163. Johns, *Protest and Hope*, 354.

164. Dubow, *Racial Segregation*, 141; Davenport, *South Africa*, 3d ed., 310–13. On the differing histories of the franchise in Natal and the Cape, see Davenport, *South Africa*, 3d ed., 118–20.

165. Writing to his wife, Ruby, Nicholls worried that his independent stand on the Select Committee on the Native Bills was making him "more and more an enemy of Smuts." In 1932 Smuts would publicly sanction Nicholls for his advocacy of separatism for the Natal Province. Dubow, *Racial Segregation*, 146.

166. Dubow, *Racial Segregation*, 163; Legassick, "Modern South African Liberalism," 29. Jan Frederik Hendrik Hofmeyr (1894–1948) was born in Cape Town and earned a B.A. from the South African College (later the University of Cape Town) at the age of fifteen in 1909. He earned a B.A. in science in 1910 and an M.A. in classics in 1911 before attending Oxford University on a Rhodes Scholarship in 1913. In 1929 he was elected to parliament as a member of the South African Party, and became a key adviser to Smuts. Hofmeyr's biographer, the historian Alan Paton, observed that at the beginning of his parliamentary career Hofmeyr "regarded total segregation of the races as morally defensible but doubted its practicality." In 1933 Hertzog as prime minister appointed Hofmeyr Minister of Education, of the Interior, and of Public Health, but he would ultimately reject Hertzog's Native Bills in 1936. *DSAB*, 2:309–11. See also Alan Paton, *Hofmeyr* (London, 1964); see above, n41.

167. [J. D. Rheinallt Jones] to D. D. T. Jabavu, March 28, 1931; D. D. T. Jabavu to J. D. Rheinallt Jones, April 8, 1931; J. D. Rheinallt Jones to J. H. Hofmeyr, April 18, 1931; Records of the South African Institute of Race Relations, part 2, Historical and Literary Papers, University of the Witwatersrand Library, Johannesburg, AD 843/RJ, KB17.1 (hereafter Records of the SAIRR, part 2, UWL). (I am grateful to Anna Cunningham for these references.) Dubow offers an excellent synopsis of this correspondence in *Racial Segregation*, 162–63.

168. Quoted in Dubow, *Racial Segregation*, 163; see also D. D. T. Jabavu to J. H. Hofmeyr, April 8, 1931, J. H. Hofmeyr Papers, Historical and Literary Papers, University of the Witwatersrand Library, Johannesburg, A1, Aa448.

169. Dubow, *Racial Segregation*, 163.

170. D. D. T. Jabavu to J. D. Rheinallt Jones, Records of the SAIRR, part 2, UWL, KB17.1 (emphasis in original).

171. Non-European Conference, *Minutes of the Third Conference Held at Bloemfontein. January 5th, 6th, and 7th, 1931* (Lovedale, [1931]), 4. J. Mancoe attended representing the ICU; A. W. G. Champion represented the ICU Yase Natal; and C. Kadalie, H. D. Tyamzashe, S. Elias, and A. Mnika represented the Independent ICU.

172. Ibid., 6.

173. *Imvo Zabantsundu*, January 13, 1931.

174. *Imvo Zabantsundu*, January 13, 1931.

175. Hill and Pirio, "'Africa for the Africans,'" 238. Garveyism did continue to attract followers in the Transkei through the 1930s (pp. 238–42).

176. A Riotous Assemblies Bill was introduced in the House of Assembly in 1914, "which prohibited recruitment to unions by force, banned violent picketing and any

strikes in the public utility services, permitted magistrates to prohibit meetings thought likely to endanger public peace, and greatly enforced police powers of law enforcement." The law was strengthened in 1930 to tighten control over African labor. Davenport, *South Africa*, 3d ed., 269, 295.

177. D. D. T. Jabavu to Howard Pim, February 18, 1931, Pim Papers, UWL, BL1. The Student Volunteer Movement provided Jabavu with a grant of £100. D. D. T. Jabavu, *E-Amerika*, 1.

178. D. D. T. Jabavu, "Native Disabilities," 6.

179. D. D. T. Jabavu, *E-Amerika*, 11. I was unable to locate any records of Jabavu's meeting with MacDonald at the Public Records Office in London.

180. National European-Bantu Conference, *Fifth National European-Bantu Conference, Bloemfontein, July 5, 6, 7, 1933. Report. Minutes, Findings, Addresses* (Johannesburg, 1933), 26.

181. Quoted in Johns, *Protest and Hope*, doc. 43b, 252.

182. Hertzog abandoned the gold standard in 1932; by 1933 the worldwide price for gold had doubled, and the South African economy was on the road to recovery. David Yudelman, *The Emergence of Modern South Africa: State, Capital, and the Incorporation of Organized Labor on the South African Gold Fields, 1902–1939* (Westport, Conn., 1983), 41–42.

183. Dubow, *Racial Segregation*, 146–47; Davenport, *South Africa*, 3d ed., 298, 306.

184. Johns, *Protest and Hope*, 158. For a discussion of the politics of coalition and fusion, see Davenport, *South Africa*, 3d ed., 303–8; Hancock, *Smuts: Fields of Force*, 252–58.

185. Ingham, *Jan Christian Smuts*, 178.

186. Davenport, *South Africa*, 3d ed., 305.

187. Dubow, *Racial Segregation*, 147–48.

188. Walshe, *Rise of African Nationalism*, 118. The Transkeian Territories, the Cape Province, and Natal would each get one senator; a fourth senator would be shared by the Transvaal and Orange Free State.

189. Tatz, *Shadow and Substance*, 56, 71; Walshe, *Rise of African Nationalism*, 118.

190. Tatz, *Shadow and Substance*, 99; Walshe, *Rise of African Nationalism*, 112, 118; Karis, *Hope and Challenge*, 4.

191. D. D. T. Jabavu to J. D. Rheinallt Jones, Records of the South African Institute of Race Relations, Microfilm, Yale University Library, B100.1 (file 1) (hereafter Records of the SAIRR, YUL). In March 1935, before the bills were published, Jabavu had written to Smuts: "When your cabinet considers future policy with regard to the Native question, I hope you will persuade your *confrères* to leave the vote or franchise question severely alone." D. D. T. Jabavu to J. C. Smuts [March 1935], *Selections from the Smuts Papers*, vol. 6, *December 1934-August 1945*, ed. Jean Van Der Poel (Cambridge, 1973), 12–13.

192. D. D. T. Jabavu, *Criticisms of the Native Bills* (Lovedale, 1935), Carter-Karis Collection Microfilm, YUL, 2:XJ2:84/5, 5.

193. Ibid., 6.

194. Dubow, *Racial Segregation*, 131–32.

195. Ibid., 165; Rich, *White Power*, 64.

196. D. D. T. Jabavu, comp., *Native Views on the Native Bills* (Lovedale, 1935). See especially Jabavu's own article, "The Segregationists Answered," which was a response to Nicholls's pamphlet on the Native Bills: G. Heaton Nicholls, *The Native Bills: Being an Address Delivered before the Bantu Study Group of the University of the Witwatersrand* (Durban, 1935).

197. E. J. Evans to J. D. Rheinallt Jones, September 21, 1935; J. D. Rheinallt Jones to E. J. Evans, September 30, 1935; D. D. T. Jabavu to E. J. Evans, October 26, 1935; R. A. Steer to J. D. Rheinallt Jones, October 28, 1935; D. D. T. Jabavu to J. D. Rheinallt Jones, October 30, 1935; J. D. Rheinallt Jones to E. J. Evans, November 7, 1935, Records of the SAIRR, YUL, B100.1.

198. Haines, "Opposition to Hertzog's Segregation Bills," 293.

199. Alfred Bitini Xuma (1893–1962) was born near Engcobo in the Transkei, and attended the Clarkebury Institute. He qualified as a teacher in 1911, and in 1913 enrolled at the Tuskegee Institute. He spent fourteen years in the United States, eventually qualifying as a medical doctor at Northwestern University. He set up his practice in Johannesburg in 1928, but did not become politically active until 1935, when he joined the All African Convention. He left the AAC in 1940 and served as president of the ANC from 1940 to 1949. Gerhart and Karis, *Political Profiles*, 164–65; Steven D. Gish, "Alfred B. Xuma: African, American, South African" (Ph.D. diss., Stanford University, 1994), 133.

200. Walshe, *Rise of African Nationalism*, 119, 254–55; see also I. B. Tabata, *The All African Convention: The Awakening of a People* (Johannesburg, 1950), 16.

201. Gish, "Alfred B. Xuma," 133.

202. Switzer, *Power and Resistance*, 288; interview with Sipo Makalima, Alice, Ciskei, November 23, 1987; interview with Cadoc Kobus, Tsolo, Transkei, March 24, 1988; interview with A. P. Mda, Mafeteng, Lesotho, August 22, 1988. Cadoc Kobus earned a B.A. from the South African Native College and worked as a teacher before qualifying as a lawyer. He was a founding member of the NEUM in 1943. After retiring from practicing law, he returned to teaching. Gerhart and Karis, *Political Profiles*, 50.

203. [Notes of an interview with James A. Calata], Carter-Karis Collection Microfilm, YUL, 2:XJ2:96/2. This was not an entirely fair assessment of Jabavu; knowing his limitations, he served as secretary of the South African Native Farmers' Congress.

204. As William Beinart and Colin Bundy have noted, there was always some fluidity to ethnic identifications. Beinart, "*Amafelandawonye*," 225; Colin Bundy, "Conflict in Qumbu: Rural Consciousness, Ethnicity and Violence in Colonial Transkei," *Hidden Struggles in Rural South Africa: Politics and Popular Movements in the Transkei and Eastern Cape 1890–1930*, ed. William Beinart and Colin Bundy, 111. Gish has observed that when Xuma's parents relocated to a Thembu area of the Transkei in the 1870s, they identified themselves as Thembu. Gish, "Alfred B. Xuma," 21. Gerhart and Karis, *Political Profiles*, 16–17, 65, 155.

205. D. D. T. Jabavu, *I-Nkulungwane yama Mfengu*, 11–12.

206. Gish, "Alfred B. Xuma," 133.

207. All African Convention, *The Findings of the All African Convention* (n.p., [1935]), Carter-Karis Collection Microfilm, YUL, 2:DA13:84/7, 21; Dubow, *Racial Segregation*, 164.

208. Ibid., 3.

209. All African Convention, *Findings of the AAC* [1935], 12–14; *Imvo Zabantsundu*, December 29, 1935.

210. All African Convention, *Findings of the AAC* [1935], 3.

211. Ibid., 25–26. In a 1929 article Jabavu noted that "over 60 black Africans," including seven doctors and seven lawyers, had obtained "various university degrees overseas." D. D. T. Jabavu, "Higher Education and the Professional Training of the Bantu," *South African Journal of Science* 26 (1929): 934, 936. By the end of 1935, fifty-one students had graduated with bachelor's degrees from the South African Native College. South African Native College, *Calendar for 1937*, 78–79.

212.. All African Convention, *Findings of the AAC* [1935], 6; Dubow, *Racial Segregation*, 164.

213. All African Convention, *Findings of the AAC* [1935], 7–9; *Imvo Zabantsundu*, December 29, 1935.

214. Union of South Africa, *Joint Sitting of Both Houses of Parliament on Representation of Natives Bill*, 13th February to 7th April 1936, J.S. 1-'36 and J.S. 2-'36 (Cape Town, 1936), col. 19. Heaton Nicholls quoted Dube's article during his opening remarks in the joint session. Nicholls argued that Dube supported his own position that the Cape African franchise was a sham. Dube founded *Ilanga lase Natal* in 1903 at the Ohlange Institute. Switzer and Switzer, *Black Press*, 138.

215. All African Convention, *Findings of the AAC* [1935], 9. Born in Cape Town, John Gomas worked as a tailor. He joined the Garment Workers' Union and the ICU, but was expelled from the latter organization in 1926 when it fell out with the Communist Party of South Africa (CPSA). Gomas was a regular contributor to the CPSA newspaper *Umsebenzi*, whose pages he used in an attempt to encourage a broad-based protest movement. Fellow communist Edward Roux acknowledged, however, that the CPSA's protest meetings were poorly attended, and their calls for strikes and demonstrations went unheeded. (Subtitled *The South African Worker*, *Umsebenzi* was founded in 1915 as the *International* and ceased publication in 1950. Switzer and Switzer, *Black Press*, 77–79.) *Umsebenzi*, April 25, 1936; Roux, *Time Longer than Rope*, 2d ed., 289; Simons and Simons, *Class and Colour in South Africa*, 482–83, 495–501; see also Musson, *Johnny Gomas: Voice of the Working Class*.

216. All African Convention, *Findings of the AAC* [1935], 9.

217. Walshe, *Rise of African Nationalism*, 119.

218. Roux, *Time Longer than Rope*, 2d ed., 289. A. P. Mda made a similar observation in 1988. Interview with A. P. Mda, Mafeteng, Lesotho, August 22, 1988.

219. All African Convention, *Findings of the AAC* [1935], 7; Dubow, *Racial Segregation*, 166.

5   The Fall of an African Politician, 1936–1948

1. Letters of General Smuts, 1936, January 24, 1936, Smuts Papers, A1, vol. 240, 251/207, CAD.

2. S. J. Mvambo, J. M. Dippa, and H. S. Kekane were also members of the delegation. All African Convention, *Minutes of the All African Convention, June 1936* (Lovedale,

1936), Carter-Karis Collection Microfilm, YUL, 2:DA13:30/1, 33. H. Selby Msimang was born near Pietermaritzburg in 1886 and educated at the Kilnerton Training Institute in Pretoria and at Healdtown, where he qualified as a teacher in 1907. He worked as a labor controller in Johannesburg before joining the SANNC (ANC) in 1912, and he was active in the ICU in the early 1920s. R. H. Godlo (1899–1972) worked as a reporter for the East London *Daily Dispatch*. He was active in the AAC in the 1930s, and in the ANC in the 1940s, and served on the Natives' Representative Council until it was dissolved in 1951. Gerhart and Karis, *Political Profiles*, 31–32, 104–5.

3. *Cape Times*, February 11, 1936, 13; Hancock, *Smuts: Fields of Force*, 265–66; J. C. Smuts to M. C. Gillet, January 24, 1936, *Selections from the Smuts Papers*, vol. 6, *December 1934-August 1945*, 31–32; Tatz, *Shadow and Substance*, 76.

4. Walshe, *Rise of African Nationalism*, 130; Hancock, *Smuts: Fields of Force*, 266.

5. Letters of General Smuts 1935, September 23, 1935, Smuts Papers, vol. 238, 937/228, CAD.

6. Native Legislation 1932–1939, vol. 63, General J. B. M. Hertzog Collection, A32, Central Archives Depot, Pretoria (hereafter Hertzog Collection). See especially "Sy Edele die Minister van Naturellesake," an invitation to the Minister of Native Affairs to Hertzog's meeting with Jabavu and the AAC delegation on February 3, 1936.

7. Tatz, *Shadow and Substance*, 91 n47; Walshe, *Rise of African Nationalism*, 130; Dubow, *Racial Segregation*, 167.

8. *Cape Times*, February 15, 1936.

9. *Umteteli wa Bantu*, February 15, 1936. *Umteteli wa Bantu* (The mouthpiece of the African peoples) was published in Johannesburg by the Native Recruiting Corporation for the Transvaal Chamber of Mines. Though the paper avoided criticism of the mining industry, it did serve as a forum for black opinion on a wide variety of political, social, and cultural issues. Switzer and Switzer, *Black Press*, 110.

10. *Umteteli wa Bantu*, February 15, 1936; *Cape Times*, February 17, 1936.

11. Walshe, *Rise of African Nationalism*, 123; Tatz, *Shadow and Substance*, 76, 91 n47.

12. Gerhart and Karis, *Political Profiles*, 165; "A. B. Xuma's Autobiography" (typescript, [1954]), A. B. Xuma Papers, Historical and Literary Papers, University of the Witwatersrand Library, Johannesburg, ABX, box P, 44–45 (hereafter Xuma Papers, UWL); see also A. B. Xuma to Max Yergan, November 27, 1936, Xuma Papers, UWL, ABX361127c.

13. Tabata, *All African Convention*, 29–36. Isaac Bangani Tabata (1909–1990) was born near Queenstown in the Cape Province, and attended Lovedale and Fort Hare, though he left before graduating. He joined the multiracial Lorry Driver's Union in Cape Town in 1931, and educated himself by reading Marx and Trotsky. He joined the Cape Native Voters' Convention and the AAC before helping to found the Non-European Unity Movement (NEUM) in 1943. Gerhart and Karis, *Political Profiles*, 150; *Sunday Mail* (Harare, Zimbabwe), October 14, 1990. (I am grateful to Noni Jabavu for this reference.)

14. Maurice Webb to Edgar Brookes, February 26, 1936, Records of the SAIRR, YUL, 100.1 (file 2). The Rev. E. W. Grant was active in the Joint Council movement.

15. See Rich, *White Power*. Rich offers a more sympathetic analysis of white and, more broadly, English-speaking liberals in *Hope and Despair: English-Speaking Intellectuals and South African Politics 1896–1976* (London, 1993).

16. Dubow, *Racial Segregation*, 171; Elphick, "Mission Christianity," 72; see also Legassick, "Modern South African Liberalism."

17. [A. E. W.] Ramsbottom to J. B. M. Hertzog, February 22, 1936, Hertzog Collection, A32, CAD. Hertzog's private secretary replied with a form letter thanking her for her interest. Private secretary to A. E. W. Ramsbottom, March 4, 1936.

18. Davenport, *South Africa*, 3d ed., 308.

19. *Umteteli wa Bantu*, February 22, 1936. Walshe supports this interpretation. Walshe, *Rise of African Nationalism*, 130.

20. Hancock, *Smuts: Fields of Force*, 266.

21. Interview with Wycliffe M. Tsotsi, Maseru, Lesotho, March 30, 1988.

22. All African Convention, *Findings of the AAC* [1935], 21–22.

23. [Statement by D. D. T. Jabavu, March 1936?], Records of the SAIRR, YUL, 91.1.1. See also *Daily Dispatch*, March 12, 13, 1936; *Cape Mercury*, March 16, 1936. The Communist Party of South Africa's newspaper *Umsebenzi* (March 7, 1936) rejected any suggestion that the AAC had supported the Compromise Bill as did *Imvo Zabantsundu* (April 11, 1936). *Imvo* had passed out of the financial control of the Jabavu family in 1935, but Alexander Jabavu remained its understandably partisan editor until 1940. Switzer and Switzer, *Black Press*, 40, 43–44.

24. Quoted in Tatz, *Shadow and Substance*, 82–83. Hofmeyr's speech earned him a place in the pantheon of South African liberalism, but Dubow has questioned the "mythologization" of Hofmeyr, arguing that he still favored a program of "constructive segregation" in 1936, and abandoned the bills only when he became convinced that whites were unwilling to give up enough land to make segregation work. Dubow, *Racial Segregation*, 170. Alan Paton, Hofmeyr's more sympathetic biographer, nevertheless acknowledged that Hofmeyr's position on segregation remained contradictory in the late 1930s. Paton, *Hofmeyr*, 269.

25. D. D. T. Jabavu to J. H. Hofmeyr, April 13, 1936, Hofmeyr Papers, UWL, Aa680; Paton, *Hofmeyr*, 232; Smuts Papers, CAD.

26. Krikler, "South African Party and the Cape Franchise," 131.

27. Tatz, *Shadow and Substance*, 86.

28. *Umteteli wa Bantu*, July 4, 1936; *Umsebenzi*, June 6, 13, 27, July 11, 1936; All African Convention, *Minutes of the All African Convention, December 1940* (n.p., n.d.), 22; All African Convention, *Minutes of the All African Convention, December 1944* [1943] (n.p., n.d.), 12, Carter-Karis Collection Microfilm, YUL, 2:DA13:30/5 (although the title page of the pamphlet refers to the 1944 conference, the contents refer to the December 1943 meeting of the AAC); Simons and Simons, *Class and Colour in South Africa*, 495–98, 545. The conference minutes were printed in English, Sesuto, and Zulu. D. D. T. Jabavu to A. B. Xuma, September 23, 1936, Xuma Papers, UWL, ABX360923.

29. All African Convention, *Minutes of the All African Convention, June 1936* (Lovedale, 1936), 46.

30. For a discussion of Pan-Africanism see P. Olisanwuche Esedebe, *Pan-Africanism: The Idea and the Movement 1776–1963* (Washington, D.C., 1982); Robert Hill and Barbara Bair, eds., *Marcus Garvey: Life and Lessons* (Berkeley, 1987); Appiah, *In My Father's House*; Cronin, *Black Moses*; Mudimbe, *Invention of Africa*.

31. All African Convention, *Minutes of the AAC, June 1936*, 36; *Imvo Zabantsundu*, July 4, 1936.

32. *Natal Advertiser*, June 29, 1936, newsbook 10, Killie Campbell Library, Durban, 131; *Cape Mercury*, June 30, 1936.

33. H. Selby Msimang, *The Crisis* (n.p., [1936]), Carter-Karis Collection Microfilm, YUL, 2:DA13:84/2, 12. Alexander Kerr, writing to Rheinallt Jones, described Msimang's position as "left-wing," but given its essential conservatism, it could just as easily have been described as right-wing. Alexander Kerr to Rheinallt Jones, June 18, 1936, Records of the SAIRR, part 1, UWL, 3.5. (I am grateful to Richard Haines for this reference.)

34. "Programme of Action" [1936], Records of the SAIRR, part 1, UWL, 3.5.

35. D. D. T. Jabavu to J. D. Rheinallt Jones, June 13, 1936, Records of the SAIRR, part 1, UWL, 3.5.

36. Interview with Leo Sihlali, Mount Frere, Transkei, March 22, 1988.

37. All African Convention, *Minutes of the AAC, June 1936*, 43.

38. D. D. T. Jabavu to J. D. Rheinallt Jones, [July] 1936, Records of the SAIRR, part 1, UWL, 3.5.

39. Msimang left the AAC and joined the ANC in Natal in 1941. Gerhart and Karis, *Political Profiles*, 105; *Inkundla ya Bantu*, February 1941.

40. All African Covention, *Minutes of the AAC, June 1936*, 13–14. Delegates were also critical of the government's expenditure of £3,500 on five regional conferences on the Native Bills in 1935, the findings of which they felt had been completely ignored.

41. Ibid., 32.

42. Friends World Conference, *Official Report, Held at Swarthmore and Haverford Colleges near Philadelphia, Pennsylvania September 1st to 8th 1937* (Philadelphia, 1937), 3, 126.

43. Ibid., 74, 76.

44. D. D. T. Jabavu, Addresses [1923–57], Jabavu Collection, UNISA.

45. Max Yergan to Beatrice Shipley, July 26, 1937, Friends House Library Record Group 1 (FHL RG1), Friends World Conference, 1937, Swarthmore College, Swarthmore, Pennsylvania, box 2, folder Visitation, J-K-L; All African Convention, *Minutes of the AAC, December 1937* (n.p., n.d.), 39; Max Yergan to A. B. Xuma, February 4 and March 10, 1937, Xuma Papers, UWL, ABX 370204, ABX370310c; Anthony, "Max Yergan in South Africa," 46.

46. The idea was promoted in a short biographical sketch of Jabavu by an unknown author that was sent to the American Board of Commissioners. Their response is not on file. "Professor Jabavu an Accomplished Leader of the Bantu" (1937), ABC: Biographical Collection: Individuals: Jabavu, Houghton Library, HU.

47. All African Convention, *Minutes of the AAC, December 1937*, 37–41.

48. Ibid., 43. The National Negro Congress (NNC) was founded at Howard University in Washington, D.C., in 1935. The NNC was a coalition of religious, labor and fraternal

organizations, all interested "in the economic betterment of Afro-Americans." In addition, the NNC was interested in fostering "improved relations among blacks around the world." Among its leaders was Ralph Bunche. W. Augustus Low and Virgil A. Clift, eds., *Encyclopedia of Black America* (New York, 1981), 634.

49. "Changes in South Africa: Report of a Speech by Prof. D. D. T. Jabavu," *Keys* 5, no. 2 (October-December 1937): 57.

50. "An interview with Professor D. D. T. Jabavu, broadcast in 'Picture Page' on 15th September 1937," Transcript and Tape Unit, British Broadcasting Corporation, London, 1–2.

51. All African Convention, *Minutes of the AAC, December 1937*, 29.

52. Bunche's two-year trip—which included three months in South Africa—had been funded by the Social Science Research Council. Bunche earned a Ph.D. in political science from Harvard University in 1934, and was awarded the Nobel Peace Prize in 1950 after serving as a United Nations negotiator in the Middle East. Robert R. Edgar, ed., *An African American in South Africa: The Travel Notes of Ralph J. Bunche, 28 September 1937–1 January 1938* (Athens, Ohio, 1992), 1, 5.

53. Z. K. Matthews, *Freedom for My People*, 96–97.

54. Edgar, *African American*, 130. A survey of the South African *Hansard* did not turn up the white MP who so flattered Jabavu.

55. Switzer, *Power and Resistance*, 289; Z. K. Matthews, *Freedom for My People*, 124.

56. Edgar, *African American*, 135.

57. Ibid., 161.

58. Frieda Matthews, *Remembrances*, 13; Z. K. Matthews, *Freedom for My People*, 96–98. Z. K. Matthews earned an M.A. from Yale University in 1934 for his thesis, "Bantu Law and Western Civilization in South Africa: A Study in the Clash of Cultures."

59. Z. K. Matthews, *Freedom for My People*, 138–57.

60. Walshe, *Rise of African Nationalism*, 124; see also Karis, *Hope and Challenge*, 69.

61. Interview with A. P. Mda, Mafeteng, Lesotho, August 22, 1988.

62. Gerhart, *Black Power*, 126.

63. All African Convention, *Minutes of the AAC, December 1937*, 47; *Bantu World*, January 2, 1937. Ironically, Xuma would be accused of doing precisely that. See *Inkundla ya Bantu*, March 17, 1944 (letter to the editor).

64. All African Convention, *Minutes of the AAC December 1937*, 18.

65. Karis, *Hope and Challenge*, 93; Gerhart and Karis, *Political Profiles*, 165.

66. Gish, "Alfred B. Xuma," 138.

67. Writing to a friend in December 1937, Smuts noted that the NRC "contains all the most prominent Native leaders except David Jabavu who would or could not stand (his brother is a member)." J. C. Smuts to M. C. Gillet, December 6, 1937, *Selections from the Smuts Papers*, vol. 6, *December 1934–August 1945*, 107–8.

68. Gerhart and Karis, *Political Profiles*, 39; *Imvo Zabantsundu*, February 27, 1937.

69. "Constitution of the AAC, December 1937," Karis, *Hope and Challenge*, doc. 15, 64.

70. Thompson, *History of South Africa*, 162.

71. Karis, *Hope and Challenge*, 73-74.

72. All African Convention, *Minutes of the AAC, December 1940*, 25-26.

73. Ibid., 8.

74. Hancock, *Smuts: Fields of Force*, 371-72.

75. Karis, *Hope and Challenge*, 73-74; All African Convention, *Minutes of the AAC, December 1940*, ii.

76. All African Convention, *Minutes of the AAC, December 1940*, 9.

77. Ibid., 25-26.

78. *Inkundla ya Bantu*, February 1942. The newspaper ran both favorable and critical articles about the ANC, the AAC, and, after 1943, the African Democratic Party (ADP) and the Non-European Unity Movement (NEUM). (See, for example, *Inkundla ya Bantu*, January 30, July 28, 1943.) See also Karis, *Hope and Challenge*, 72.

79. All African Convention, *Minutes of the AAC, December 1940*, 5.

80. Rich, *White Power*, 81.

81. All African Convention, *Minutes of the AAC, December 1940*, 6; Davenport, *South Africa*, 3d ed., 338-40.

82. All African Convention, *Minutes of the AAC, December 1940*, 7.

83. Karis, *Hope and Challenge*, doc. 62, 345.

84. Ibid., 344.

85. Ibid., 340.

86. Ibid., 341.

87. Ibid., 173. The ANC conference took place from December 14 to December 16, 1941; Tabata addressed the AAC on December 16, 1941.

88. Ibid., 343.

89. Ibid., 344; see also *Inkundla ya Bantu*, December 1941.

90. All African Convention, *Minutes of the AAC, December 1941*, 6.

91. Bill Nasson, "The Unity Movement Tradition: Its Legacy in Historical Consciousness," *History from South Africa: Alternative Visions and Practices*, ed. Joshua Brown et al. (Philadelphia, 1991), 146; Gerhart and Karis, *Political Profiles*, 150.

92. Gerhart and Karis, *Political Profiles*, 65, 150.

93. Karis, *Hope and Challenge*, doc. 62, 346.

94. Ibid., 345-46.

95. D. D. T. Jabavu, "Some Criticisms of the Act and Its Results," *Political Representation of Africans in the Union*, New Africa Pamphlet no. 4 (Johannesburg, 1942), 22-23.

96. Karis, *Hope and Challenge*, doc. 63, 347.

97. Paton, *Hofmeyr*, 353. For a discussion of the Atlantic Charter, see Theodore A. Wilson, *The First Summit: Roosevelt and Churchill at Placentia Bay, 1941*, rev. ed. (Lawrence, Kans., 1991), 149-75.

98. Paton, *Hofmeyr*, 353; J. C. Smuts to L. S. Amery, September 9, 1941, *Selections from the Smuts Papers*, vol. 6, 317.

99. Davenport, *South Africa*, 3d ed., 339, 338-40; Paton, *Hofmeyr*, 353-55; Hancock, *Smuts: Fields of Force*, 370-71; *Inkundla ya Bantu*, February 28, 1942 and March 25, 1943; Karis, *Hope and Challenge*, 73-74.

100. Karis, *Hope and Challenge*, 347.

101. The All-African Convention Committee (Western Province), "Calling All Africans" (June 1943), Unity Movement of South Africa Papers, J. W. Jagger Library, University of Cape Town, BC925 (uncatalogued collection, hereafter Unity Movement Papers, UCT); Karis, *Hope and Challenge*, 112. Members of the Non-European United Front (NEUF) had attended the 1941 AAC conference. All African Convention, *Minutes of the AAC, December 1941*, 10. The NEUF was founded in Cape Town in 1938 by members of the National Liberation League, a radical Coloured organization; the NEUF participated in the Anti-CAD (Anti-Coloured Affairs Department) movement in 1943 and was ultimately absorbed into the NEUM. Simons and Simons, *Class and Colour in South Africa*, 501, 541–42.

102. "Manifesto of the All African Convention" (July 1943), Unity Movement Papers, UCT.

103. Karis, *Hope and Challenge*, doc. 62, 343.

104. I. B. Tabata to D. D. T. Jabavu, July 6, 1943, Unity Movement Papers, UCT.

105. D. D. T. Jabavu to J. D. Rheinallt Jones, September 28, 1943, J. D. Rheinallt Jones Papers, Historical and Literary Papers, University of the Witwatersrand Library, Johannesburg, A394, C6/3 (hereafter Rheinallt Jones Papers, UWL).

106. Non-European Unity Movement, *Proceedings of the 2nd Unity Conference Held on Saturday, 8th July, 1944, at Kholvad House, Market Street, Johannesburg* (Cape Town, 1944), addendum 1 (1), Dr. J. S. Moroka Collection, UNISA Documentation Centre for African Studies, University of South Africa, Pretoria, Acc. 46, A6.1 (hereafter Moroka Collection, UNISA); Karis, *Hope and Challenge*, doc. 64, 347–52.

107. Karis, *Hope and Challenge*, doc. 64, 348.

108. Ibid., 350.

109. Ibid., 113, 351. The government introduced legislation in April 1943 (the Pegging Act) that suspended all property dealings between whites and Indians in Natal and the Transvaal for a period of three years. Davenport, *South Africa*, 3d ed., 267, 351.

110. Karis, *Hope and Challenge*, doc. 65, 353.

111. Ibid., 113.

112. Ibid., doc. 65, 356 (emphasis in original); Simons and Simons, *Class and Colour in South Africa*, 543.

113. Archibald Campbell Jordan (1906–1968) was a founding member of the AAC and the NEUM. Educated at St. John's College, Lovedale, Fort Hare, and UNISA, he earned a Ph.D. from the University of Cape Town in 1956, where he also taught African languages. He left South Africa in 1961 for a post at the University of Wisconsin. In 1973 his estate published *Tales from Southern Africa* and *Towards an African Literature: The Emergence of Literary Form in Xhosa*. Gerhart and Karis, *Political Profiles*, 44.

114. Library of the South African Institute of Race Relations, Johannesburg. A survey of the files of the SAIRR revealed that Jabavu regularly attended the institute's yearly meetings throughout the 1940s, but appears to have contributed little to the discussions. He remained a member until his death in 1959.

115. D. D. T. Jabavu to J. D. Rheinallt Jones, September 28, 1943, Rheinallt Jones Papers, UWL, C6/3.

116. Jabavu wrote a brief obituary of Rheinallt Jones on his death in 1953 in which he described him as "a man growing progressively greater in mental stature than any position to which he could be formally attached. . . . He was, as it were, among the historical personages so vividly outlined in Holy Scriptures as those who 'endure,' in the sublime sense of having been courageously more than equal to the responsibilities imposed on them." D. D. T. Jabavu, "John David Rheinallt Jones" (typescript), Carter-Karis Collection Microfilm, YUL, 2:XJ2:77, 1. Rheinallt Jones retired from the Senate in 1942 and resigned as secretary of the SAIRR in 1947. *DSAB*, 5:640.

117. J. D. Rheinallt Jones to D. D. T. Jabavu, October 22 and November 1, 1943, Rheinallt Jones Papers, UWL, C6/13, C6/17.

118. D. D. T. Jabavu to J. D. Rheinallt Jones, October 25, 1943, Rheinallt Jones Papers, UWL, C6/15. The African Democratic Party was founded in 1943. Karis, *Hope and Challenge*, 511. See below, n121.

119. I. B. Tabata to Joe [A. C. Jordan], October 27, 1943, Unity Movement Papers, UCT.

120. *DSAB*, 5:516–17.

121. Karis, *Hope and Challenge*, 90. Basner was elected to the Senate as Natives' Representative for the Transvaal in 1942. Rich, *White Power*, 81. According to Gerhart, younger members of the ANC admired Mosaka for "his brilliance and the militancy of his statements" in the NRC, but Mosaka himself "looked on the ANC and the staid A. B. Xuma as obstacles to progress, both for the African cause and for himself." Gerhart and Karis, *Political Profiles*, 99–100; *Inkundla ya Bantu*, September 18, 1944.

122. Davenport, *South Africa*, 3d ed., 340; Gerhart and Karis, *Political Profiles*, 4–5.

123. For a discussion of these distinctions, see Joshua N. Lazerson, *Against the Tide: Whites in the Struggle against Apartheid* (Boulder, 1994), 18–19.

124. Tabata to Jordan, October 27, 1943, Unity Movement Papers, UCT.

125. D. D. T. Jabavu to A. B. Xuma, November 11, 1943, A. B. Xuma Papers, UWL, ABX431121a.

126. All African Convention, *Minutes of the AAC, December 1944* [1943], 12–13. Communist Party members, who had attended AAC meetings regularly since 1935, found themselves unwelcome after 1943 when the Anti-CAD—which tended to see the CPSA as a rival—joined the AAC and the NEUM. Simons and Simons, *Class and Colour in South Africa*, 495–98, 545.

127. Janub (Jane) Gool was active in the AAC and was a founding member of the anti-CAD and the NEUM. She left South Africa for Zambia in 1963 with I. B. Tabata; when he died in 1990 they were living in Zimbabwe. Gerhart and Karis, *Political Profiles*, 33–34; *Sunday Mail* (Harare, Zimbabwe), October 14, 1990.

128. All African Convention, *Minutes of the AAC, December 1944* [1943], 5–6; *Imvo Zabantsundu*, January 1, 1944.

129. Jordan Kush Ngubane was born in Natal in 1917 and educated at Adams College. He spent his career working as a journalist, first for John Dube's newspaper *Ilanga lase Natal*, then for *The Bantu World*, and finally for *Inkundla ya Bantu*, which he edited from 1944 to 1951. Gerhart and Karis, *Political Profiles*, 114–15; Switzer and Switzer, *Black Press*, 44.

130. Ngubane's assessment of Jabavu became ironic when, unable to accept the Communist Party's influence in the ANC, he left and joined the Liberal Party (founded by white liberals in 1953). He was elected national vice-chairman in the late 1950s, but ultimately left and joined the Pan Africanist Congress (PAC). Gerhart and Karis, *Political Profiles*, 115; Davenport, *South Africa*, 3d ed., 366. For an assessment of the Liberal Party, see Janet Robertson, *Liberalism in South Africa 1948–1963* (Oxford, 1971).

131. *Inkundla ya Bantu*, December 30, 1943. In January 1944 *Inkundla* took this argument one step further, asserting that making the AAC a permanent body in 1936 was a "blunder." *Inkundla ya Bantu*, January 31, 1944. The newspaper did, however, give equal time to the AAC and to the NEUM. It had published an article supportive of the idea of Non-European unity in its July 28, 1943, issue, and it published the AAC's "Calling All Africans" on August 28, 1943, and "Along the New Road" on August 31, 1944. It also regularly published the minutes of Tabata's AAC (WP). See, for example, *Inkundla ya Bantu*, April 20, 1942; May 22, 1943; April 17, 1944.

132. Non-European Unity Movement, *2nd Unity Conference*, addendum 1 (1), Moroka Collection, UNISA.

133. Ibid., 1–2.

134. Karis, *Hope and Challenge*, 109.

135. Interview with Leo Sihlali, Mount Frere, Transkei, March 22, 1988; interview with Cadoc Kobus, Tsolo, Transkei, March 24, 1988; interview with A. P. Mda, Mafeteng, Lesotho, August 22, 1988.

136. Abdulla Ismail Kajee (ca. 1896–1947) was a prominent Muslim businessman and a leading figure in the Natal Indian Congress from the mid-1930s until shortly before his death. Gerhart and Karis, *Political Profiles*, 48. A. Ismail was a member of the SAIC executive. Surendra Bhana and Bridglal Pachai, eds., *A Documentary History of Indian South Africans* (Cape Town, 1984), 157.

137. I. B. Tabata to D. D. T. Jabavu, Unity Movement Papers, UCT.

138. Ibid.

139. "Along the New Road," All African Convention Executive Committee's Statement 7th July, 1944, Unity Movement Papers, UCT; Karis, *Hope and Challenge*, 113.

140. "Along the New Road," Unity Movement Papers, UCT, 1 (emphasis in original).

141. Karis, *Hope and Challenge*, 72, 510–11; Simons and Simons, *Class and Colour in South Africa*, 546–47; Davenport, *South Africa*, 3d ed., 340. See also *Inkundla ya Bantu*, January 30 and February 25, 1943.

142. "Along the New Road," Unity Movement Papers, UCT, 2.

143. Ironically, the NEUM had held aloof from the Communist Party–sponsored, ANC-endorsed Anti-Pass campaign, which began in May 1944, in part because of political rivalries, but also because for the teachers who dominated the NEUM, participation in strikes and demonstrations could cost them their jobs. Simons and Simons, *Class and Colour in South Africa*, 543–45.

144. Non-European Unity Movement, *2nd Unity Conference*, 2.

145. I. B. Tabata to Wycliffe Tsotsi, May 6, 1944, Unity Movement Papers, UCT; Karis, *Hope and Challenge*, 88.

146. Switzer, *Power and Resistance*, 288; Gish, "Alfred B. Xuma," 187–88.

147. Karis, *Hope and Challenge*, vol. 2 of *From Hope to Challenge*, 90; Z. K. Matthews, *Freedom for My People*, 124–25, 223; Switzer, *Power and Resistance*, 289. Matthews was elected to the NRC in 1942 (replacing A. M. Jabavu), and resigned in 1946.

148. Gish, "Alfred B. Xuma," 202–6.

149. Switzer, *Power and Resistance*, 290; Walshe, *Rise of African Nationalism*, 350–51. For a discussion of the ANCYL, see Gerhart, *Black Power*, chaps. 3, 4.

150. Karis, *Hope and Challenge*, 99–100.

151. Anton Muziwakhe Lembede (1914–1947) was born in Natal and educated at Adams College. He later earned a B.A. and an LL.B. by correspondence from the University of South Africa. Walter Max Ulyate Sisulu was born in the Transkei in 1912. Unlike many of his contemporaries, he was a working man. Before becoming a real estate agent in 1940 (the same year he joined the ANC), he worked as a gold miner and a factory worker. Gerhart and Karis, *Political Profiles*, 55–56, 143–44.

152. Mandela was expelled from the South African Native College in 1941 after a student food strike; Tambo graduated with a B.Sc. in 1941. Gerhart and Karis, *Political Profiles*, 72, 151.

153. Karis, *Hope and Challenge*, 100, 102.

154. Non-European Unity Movement, *2nd Unity Conference*, 4.

155. Ibid.

156. Ibid., 4, 5.

157. Ibid., 5. Benjamin Kies was born in Cape Town in 1917. He earned a B.A. and an M.A. from the University of Cape Town, and worked as a teacher before becoming a lawyer. Gerhart and Karis, *Political Profiles*, 50.

158. Non-European Unity Movement, *2nd Unity Conference*, 10.

159. Non-European Unity Movement, *Report of the 3rd Unity Conference Held in the Banqueting Hall, Cape Town on 4th and 5th January, 1945* (Cape Town, 1945), Carter-Karis Collection Microfilm, YUL, 2:DN3:30/4, 2.

160. Karis, *Hope and Challenge*, 114.

161. Gerhart and Karis, *Political Profiles*, 65.

162. Non-European Unity Movement, *Minutes of the Fourth Unity Conference* (n.p., [December 1945]), Carter-Karis Collection Microfilm, YUL, 2:DN3:30/1, 14.

163. Non-European Unity Movement, *Fourth Unity Conference*, 8; Karis, *Hope and Challenge*, 357–61. Goolam H. Gool was a physician and the son-in-law of APO founder Abdul Abdurahman. He challenged Abdurahman's leadership unsuccessfully in the 1930s and later joined the AAC and the Anti-CAD, and served as vice-chairman of the NEUM. Gerhart and Karis, *Political Profiles*, 33. E. C. Roberts was a teacher and a founding member of the Anti-CAD in 1943. Gavin Lewis, *Between the Wire and the Wall: A History of South African "Coloured" Politics* (New York, 1987), 213.

164. Karis, *Hope and Challenge*, doc. 66, 358.

165. Ibid., 359, 361.

166. Non-European Unity Movement, *Proceedings of 5th Unity Conference Held on 20th and 21st December, 1946 at City Hall, Kimberley* (Cape Town, n.d.), Carter-Karis Collection Microfilm, YUL, 2:DN3:30/5, 1–2; Davenport, *South Africa*, 3d ed., 351.

167. Non-European Unity Movement, *5th Unity Conference*, 6.

168. Ibid., 8.

169. Ibid., 12.

170. Ibid., 13.

171. [D. B. Molteno] to D. D. T. Jabavu, September 16, 1947, D. B. Molteno Papers, J. W. Jagger Library, University of Cape Town, Cape Town, BC579, C6.141 (hereafter Molteno Papers, UCT). See also D. D. T. Jabavu to A. B. Xuma and H. Selby Msimang, September 28, 1936, Xuma Papers, UWL, ABX360928.

172. D. D. T. Jabavu to [D. B.] Molteno, September 23, 1947, Molteno Papers, UCT, C6.142.

173. Ibid.

174. I. B. Tabata to Z. R. Mahabane, October 22, 1947, Unity Movement Papers, UCT.

175. I have been unable to locate any AAC minutes for December 1947. Karis, *Hope and Challenge*, 115, 129 n90.

176. Non-European Unity Movement, *Proceedings of the Sixth Unity Conference of the Non-European Unity Movement, Held on 28th, 29th and 30th March, 1948, in Rondebosch Town Hall*, Carter-Karis Collection Microfilm, YUL, 2:DN3:30/7; *Torch*, March 29, 1948, and April 5, 1948. See above, n125.

177. Davenport, *South Africa*, 3d ed., 344; Union of South Africa, *Report of the Native Laws Commission 1946–48*, U.G. 28-'48 (Pretoria, 1948); Karis, *Hope and Challenge*, 512.

178. Davenport, *South Africa*, 3d ed., 344.

179. Ibid., 344, 345; Thompson, *History of South Africa*, 185–86.

180. For the details of the election see Davenport, *South Africa*, 3d ed., 350–53.

181. D. D. T. Jabavu to J. C. Smuts, April 28, 1948, Smuts Papers, vol. 275, no. 58, CAD.

182. Thompson, *History of South Africa*, 186.

183. Karis, *Hope and Challenge*, doc. 67, 364, 366.

184. Mandela made the comment in 1956. Nelson Mandela, *No Easy Walk to Freedom*, rev. ed. (Oxford, 1990), 46. In a 1988 interview, Leo Sihlali said that Mandela in fact had great respect for Tabata's intellectual gifts. Interview with Leo Sihlali, Mount Frere, Transkei, March 22, 1988.

185. Karis, *Hope and Challenge*, doc. 68, 368. Richard Baloyi was an Alexandra businessman who served as treasurer-general of the ANC from 1938 to 1949 and as a member of the NRC from 1937 to 1942; Roseberry Bokwe (son of John Knox Bokwe) was a physician and an official of the ANC; and Logan Ntalbati was a teacher and member of the ANC executive. Gerhart and Karis, *Political Profiles*, 5, 9, 122.

186. Karis, *Hope and Challenge*, doc. 68, 369.

187. Davenport, *South Africa*, 3d ed., 367. Moroka, Matthews, Champion, Mosaka, Thema, and Godlo all served on the NRC. Gerhart and Karis, *Political Profiles*, 98, 80, 19, 99, 156, 31.

188. Moroka was already far beyond the pale. He had joined the AAC in 1936 as its treasurer, and stood for the NRC in 1942, believing, according to Gerhart, "that the way to expose the hypocrisy of the Natives' Representative Council was to get on it and then denounce it." He ignored the AAC's call to boycott the NRC in 1944, but denounced it in 1946, even though he did not ultimately resign until 1950. In 1949 Moroka left the AAC and became president of the ANC. Gerhart and Karis, *Political Profiles*, 98.

189. Karis, *Hope and Challenge*, 118, doc. 69, 370–71.

190. Ibid., doc. 69, 372–73.

191. Ibid., 373.

192. Ibid., 374, 376. Moses Kotane was born in the western Transvaal in 1905 to a Christian Tswana family. He worked as a domestic servant, a miner, and a baker before joining the CPSA in 1929. He went to work for the CPSA full-time in 1931. He was elected to the ANC national executive in 1946, took part in the 1952 Defiance Campaign, and in 1963 went into exile in Tanzania. Gerhart and Karis, *Political Profiles*, 50–52.

193. Karis, *Hope and Challenge*, 377.

194. Ibid., 119.

195. Gerhart and Karis, *Political Profiles*, 160. Tsotsi served as president of the AAC until 1959.

196. Interview with Leo Sihlali, Mount Frere, Transkei, March 22, 1988.

197. D. D. T. Jabavu to A. B. Xuma, November 21, 1943, Xuma Papers, UWL, ABX431121a.

6 Final Years, 1948–1959

1. D. D. T. Jabavu to Nonny and Lexie [Jabavu], April 20, 1948, Jabavu Crosfield Collection. Lexie (Alexandra) was studying nursing. Interview with Alexandra Jabavu-Mulira, Port St. John's, Transkei, August 14, 1988.

2. Paton, *Hofmeyr*, 509, 512, 525.

3. Ibid., 520. I thank Leonard Thompson for pointing out this analogy.

4. D. D. T. Jabavu, "Hofmeyr and the Africans," *Jan Hendrik Hofmeyr: A Tribute* (Johannesburg, 1949).

5. World Pacifist Meeting, *The Task of Peace-Making: Reports of the World Pacifist Meeting, Santiniketan and Sevagram 1949* (Calcutta, [1949]), xi.

6. Ibid., 87.

7. See Lewsen, "Cape Liberal Tradition," 69.

8. Mahatma Gandhi, *Mahatma Gandhi: His Own Story*, ed. C. F. Andrews (New York: 1930), 98. For a discussion of Gandhi's career in South Africa, see R. A. Huttenback, *Gandhi in South Africa* (Ithaca, New York, 1971); Maureen Swann, *Gandhi: The South African Experience* (Johannesburg, 1985).

9. Gandhi's philosophy was inspired by sources as diverse as the Christian New Testament's Sermon on the Mount, the Hindu *Bhagavad Gita,* and Tolstoy's *Kingdom of God Is within You.* S. Bhana, "The Tolstoy Farm: Gandhi's Experiment in 'Co-operative

Commonwealth,'" *South African Historical Journal*, no. 7 (1975): 89; World Pacifist Meeting, *Task of Peace-Making*, 76. See also Ved Mehta, *Mahatma Gandhi and His Apostles* (New Haven, 1993).

10. D. D. T. Jabavu to J. C. Smuts, April 28, 1948, Smuts Papers, vol. 275, no. 58, CAD.

11. World Pacifist Meeting, *Task of Peace-Making*, 40, 88–92.

12. The Immorality (Amendment) Act also passed in 1950. The act made "extramarital intercourse a more serious offence if indulged in across racial frontiers." Davenport, *South Africa*, 3d ed., 362.

13. World Pacifist Meeting, *Task of Peace-Making*, 26.

14. Elizabeth S. Landis, "South African Apartheid Legislation," reprinted from the *Yale Law Journal* 71, no. 1 (November 1961): 2 n7.

15. World Pacifist Meeting, *Task of Peace-Making*, 27. Manilal Gandhi (1892–1956) was the editor of the South African newspaper *Indian Opinion* (founded by Mahatma Gandhi in 1904) from 1918 until his death. Gerhart and Karis, *Political Profiles*, 30.

16. See above, chap. 2, n167.

17. Jabavu estimated Kenya's population at just over 5.2 million people, including 90,000 Indians. D. D. T. Jabavu, *E-Indiya*, 51–52. In 1952 Mau Mau freedom fighters opposed to British rule began attacking white settler farms; in 1961 Britain granted Kenya its independence. Kevin Shillington, *History of Africa*, rev. ed. (New York, 1995), 388–89. For a discussion of the rebellion, see Robert B. Edgerton, *Mau Mau: An African Crucible* (New York, 1989).

18. Ibid., 51, 58, 60. (Jabavu placed Uganda's population at just under 5 million, including 36,000 Indians.)

19. Shillington, *History of Africa*, 387.

20. D. D. T. Jabavu, "South African Problem," 380.

21. *Fort Hare Graduation Ceremony, 27th April 1951*, 9.

22. Ibid., 13.

23. Ibid.

24. Ibid., 16.

25. D. D. T. Jabavu, *Imbumba*, 8–11, 14–19, 21–23. *Imbumba* was revised and expanded in 1953 and in 1957. D. D. T. Jabavu, *IziDungulwana*, 27. Conversation with Cecil Wele Manona, August 1, 1988, Grahamstown, South Africa. See also Noni Jabavu, *Drawn in Colour*, 28.

26. D. D. T. Jabavu, *Imbumba*, 21–22.

27. D. D. T. Jabavu, *Izithuko*.

28. *Imvo Zabantsundu*, August 1, 1942. See also *Imvo Zabantsundu*, May 24, 1941; May 1, 1943; October 14, 1944.

29. D. D. T. Jabavu, *Izithuko*, 4, 5,

30. Switzer and Switzer, *Black Press*, 47.

31. D. D. T. Jabavu, *John Tengo Jabavu*, 125–26.

32. D. D. T. Jabavu, *Imbumba*, 6. See also Noni Jabavu, *Ochre People*, 61.

33. Omer-Cooper, *Zulu Aftermath*, 167.

34. D. D. T. Jabavu, *Imbumba*, 37.

35. Ibid., 38–9.

36. D. D. T. Jabavu, *I-Nkulungwane yama Mfengu*, 5–6.

37. While the historians Les Switzer and Anne Mager have suggested that Jabavu did participate in the Defiance Campaign in Middledrift, there is no hard evidence to support the claim. Mager has asserted that Jabavu joined the ANC in the 1950s, a misinterpretation based on a misreading of Noni Jabavu's *Ochre People*, for which Mager did not provide a page reference. Anne Mager, "'The People Get Fenced': Gender, Rehabilitation and African Nationalism in the Ciskei and Border Region, 1945–1955," *Journal of Southern African Studies* 18, no. 4 (December 1992): 775 n83. (I am grateful to Karin Shapiro for this reference.) Using Mager as his source, Switzer mistakenly claimed that Jabavu participated in the 1952 Defiance Campaign. Switzer, *Power and Resistance*, 306.

38. Frederickson, *Black Liberation*, 246–49.

39. Davenport, *South Africa*, 3d ed., 370.

40. D. D. T. Jabavu to Alexander Kerr, August 4, 1952, Cory Library, PR4159.

41. A. Kerr to the Registrar, Rhodes University, December 15, 1952, Cory Library, PR4159.

42. Davenport, *South Africa*, 3d ed., 370.

43. D. D. T. Jabavu to Alexander Kerr, July 27, 1953; Acting Registrar, Rhodes University, to Alexander Kerr, July 19, 1953; Cory Library, PR4159; *Fort Hare Graduation Ceremony, 23rd April, 1954*, 3–7.

44. Davenport, *South Africa*, 3d ed., 374.

45. Paton, *Hofmeyr*, 507.

46. J. R. Swartland and D. C. Taylor, "Community Support for Schooling in Botswana Past and Present," *Boleswa Educational Research Journal* 5 (1987): 3; B. C. Thema, "Moeng College—A Product of 'Self-Help,'" *Botswana Notes and Records* 2 (1970): 71–74. (I am grateful to Don Taylor for these references.) See also Bamangwato College, Bechuanaland Protectorate, *Prospectus* (n.d.); Diana Wylie, *A Little God: The Twilight of Patriarchy in a Southern African Chiefdom* (Hanover, Mass., 1990).

47. D. D. T. Jabavu, *IziDungulwana*, 5. Jabavu was replaced by I. D. Mkize, who had founded the Langa High School in Cape Town. Mkize held a B.A. from the University of London and an M.Ed. from the University of South Africa. Though Jabavu praised Mkize in *IziDungulwana*, in her autobiography Phyllis Ntantala dismissed Mkize as a collaborator who "had, at the instigation of the Native Affairs Department, launched his Cape African Teachers' Union" in opposition to the Cape African Teachers' Association (which Jabavu had helped found). "The excuse" Mkize used, Ntantala asserted, "was that CATA had affiliated to the All-African Convention which, according to their reasoning, did not represent all African organisations." Ntantala, *Life's Mosaic*, 153.

48. D. D. T. Jabavu, *IziDungulwana*, 5.

49. Ibid., 8, 10.

50. Ibid., 7.

51. *Bantu World*, March 12, 1955; *Zonk!* 7, no. 4, (April 1955): 12–13; *Cape Mercury*, March 10, 1955. *Zonk!* was founded by Isaac Brooks in Johannesburg in 1949 as a

nonpolitical entertainment magazine, and ceased publication in 1964. Switzer and Switzer, *Black Press*, 124.

52. *Drum*, April 1955, 19. *Drum* was established in Cape Town in March 1951 but relocated to Johannesburg shortly thereafter. *Drum* mixed political news, crime reporting, "personality profiles, local news and gossip columns," with "quality fiction" and features on music and sports. Though its editors were white until 1969, it trained many notable black journalists, including Ezekiel Mphahlele, Can Themba, and Bloke Modisane. Switzer and Switzer, *Black Press*, 102–3.

53. *Bantu World*, June 4, 1955.

54. *Bantu World*, April 9, 1955; interview with Alexandra Jabavu-Mulira, Port St. John's, Transkei, August 14, 1988.

55. Noni Jabavu, *Drawn in Colour*, 18. Estate of Florence Tandiswa Jabavu, Master of the Supreme Court, Cape Town, MOOC, File no. 4334/51. Nozipo Ntshona Lebentlele, who boarded with the Jabavus when she was a student at Fort Hare in the late 1920s, recalled Florence Jabavu suffering from severe stomach pains after eating. Noni Jabavu identified her mother's illness as gall bladder disease. Interview with Nozipo Ntshona Lebentlele, Maseru, Lesotho, August 23, 1988; interview with Noni Jabavu, Harare, Zimbabwe, August 2 and 3, 1987.

56. *Drum*, no. 103 (October 1959): 65; Kerr, *Fort Hare*, 276; interview with Ethel N. Mzamane, Middledrift, Ciskei, August 3, 1988; Noni Jabavu, *Drawn in Colour*, 31–34.

57. Noni Jabavu, *Ochre People*, 51–54, 108; interview with Benjamin Mbete, Healdtown, Ciskei, August 17, 1988; interview with Ethel Mzamane, Middledrift, Ciskei, August 3, 1988.

58. The Royal African Society was founded in 1901 with the purpose of "investigating the usages, institutions, customs, religions, antiquities, history, and languages of the native races of Africa; of facilitating the commercial and industrial development of the continent in the manner best fitted to secure the welfare of its inhabitants; and as a central institution in England for the study of African subjects." *Journal of the Royal African Society* 1 (October 1901): xxi. The Royal African Society medals "'for dedicated service to Africa'" were "awarded annually between 1953 and 1972." Kenneth Robinson, "The Society's Medals," *African Affairs: Journal of the Royal African Society* 85, no. 338 (January 1986): 3.

59. D. D. T. Jabavu, Addresses [1923–1957], Jabavu Collection, UNISA; *Lovedale Bulletin*, no. 31 (October 25, 1957); Kenneth Robinson and Tom Soper, "Medals Awarded by the Royal African Society" and "Medals Correspondence: Names and Citations (Bronze)," Royal African Society, London; Robinson, "Society's Medals," 10.

60. Davenport, *South Africa*, 3d ed., 387–88; Frederickson, *Black Liberation*, 282; Mandela, *No Easy Walk to Freedom*, 39.

61. Cronin, *Black Moses*, 65; Davenport, *South Africa*, 3d ed., 388.

62. Davenport, *South Africa*, 3d ed., 388; Frederickson, *Black Liberation*, 283.

63. Frederickson, *Black Liberation*, 283.

64. The Communist Party of South Africa had been disbanded after the passage of the Suppression of Communism Act in 1950, and many of its members found refuge in the

Marxist-leaning Congress of Democrats. Davenport, *South Africa*, 3d ed., 368–69; Lazerson, *Against the Tide*, 69–71.

65. Frederickson, *Black Liberation*, 283; Davenport, *South Africa*, 3d ed., 387.

66. Davenport, *South Africa*, 3d ed., 388. Robert Mangaliso Sobukwe was born in Graaf Reinet in the Cape Province in 1924, and graduated from the Healdtown Institution in 1947 and from the South African Native College in 1949. He founded a branch of the ANC Youth League at Fort Hare in 1948, and helped draft the ANC's 1949 Program of Action. He became a language instructor at the University of the Witwatersrand, and in the late 1950s took up the editorship of *The Africanist*. Gerhart and Karis, *Political Profiles*, 147–49; Gerhart, *Black Power*, 190–98.

67. Davenport, *South Africa*, 3d ed., 386–87; Lazerson, *Against the Tide*, 161–87.

68. D. D. T. Jabavu, *IziDungulwana*, 25.

69. D. D. T. Jabavu to Helen Crosfield (Noni Jabavu), May 13, 1959, Jabavu Crosfield Collection.

70. "Death Notice. Davidson Don Tengo Jabavu," Master of the Supreme Court, Grahamstown, no. 1080/59. The official cause of death was listed as "Senile My[o]cardial Dege[neration], Senile Trophic Ulcer—R Leg."

71. Benson Dyantyi, "Drum's Last Tribute to a Leader," *Drum*, no. 103 (October 1959): 64.

72. *Cape Argus*, August 10, 1959.

73. "The Man Dr. Jabavu Was: Dr. Kerr's Notable Tribute at Memorial Unveiling," *South African Outlook*, August 1, 1963, 116, 118; "Jabavu Memorial Fund," James Arthur Calata Papers, Historical and Literary Papers, University of the Witwatersrand Library, Johannesburg, A1729, F.2.

74. See above, chap. 1, n168.

75. Karis and Gerhart, *Challenge and Violence*, 803–6; Davenport, *South Africa*, 3d ed., 389–405. The Pan Africanist Congress established its own military wing—Poqo—in 1962. Frederickson has argued that "the difference between the more controlled and less lethal violence of the ANC's military arm, Umkhonto we Sizwe, and the out-and-out terrorism of Poqo highlighted the contrast between the ANC's political astuteness and ideological eclecticism and the PAC's rashness and rigidity." Frederickson, *Black Liberation*, 286.

76. "Medals Correspondence. Names and Citations (Bronze)," Royal African Society, London; Robinson, "Society's Medals," 10.

77. *Lovedale Bulletin*, no. 31 (October 25, 1957).

Selected Bibliography

ARCHIVAL AND MANUSCRIPT COLLECTIONS

Cape Archives Depot (CA), Cape Town
    Chief Magistrate Transkei (CMT)
    Keiskammahoek (KHK)
    Master of the Supreme Court (MOOC)

Central Archives Depot (CAD), Pretoria
    J. B. M. Hertzog Collection
    Native Affairs (NTS)
    J. C. Smuts Papers

Cory Library for Historical Research (Cory Library), Rhodes University, Grahamstown
    Alexander Kerr Papers

Documentation Centre for African Studies, University of South Africa (UNISA), Pretoria
    D. D. T. Jabavu Collection
    Z. K. Matthews Papers
    Dr. J. S. Moroka Collection

Historical and Literary Papers, University of the Witwatersrand Library (UWL), Johannesburg
    William and Margaret Ballinger Papers
    James Arthur Calata Papers
    J. H. Hofmeyr Papers
    J. Howard Pim Papers
    Records of the Joint Council Movement of Europeans and Africans
    Records of the South African Institute of Race Relations
    J. D. Rheinallt Jones Papers
    A. B. Xuma Papers

Houghton Library, Harvard University (HU), Cambridge, Massachusetts
    American Board of Commissioners for Foreign Missions Archives (ABC)

Howard Pim Library of Rare Books, University of Fort Hare (UFH), Alice
    J. Lennox Papers (uncatalogued)
    Lovedale Institution Papers (uncatalogued)

J. W. Jagger Library, University of Cape Town (UCT)
    A. Abdurahman Papers
    D. B. Molteno Papers
    Unity Movement of South Africa Papers (uncatalogued)

King William's Town Deeds Office
    Deeds of Transfer

Library of Congress (LC), Washington, D.C.
    Booker T. Washington Papers

Master of the Supreme Court
    Cape Town
    Grahamstown

Rhodes House Library, Oxford University
    Aborigines' and Anti-Slavery Protection Society

Society of Friends, United Kingdom
    Westminster and Longford Meeting
    Warwickshire North Monthly Meeting

Swarthmore College, Swarthmore, Pennsylvania
    Friends House Library, Record Group 1, Friends World Conference
    Helen Nontando Jabavu Crosfield Collection, in the care of Harrison M. Wright, Professor Emeritus of History

Transvaal Archives Depot (TAD), Pretoria
    Government Native Labour Bureau (GNLB)

University of London, University College
    Records of Davidson Don Tengo Jabavu (629)

Walsall Grammar School for Boys, United Kingdom
    Archives of Queen Mary's Grammar School, Walsall

Yale Divinity School Library (YDSL), Special Collections, New Haven, Connecticut
    John R. Mott Papers

Yale University Library (YUL), Manuscripts and Archives, New Haven, Connecticut
    Carter-Karis Collection (Microfilm)
    Records of the South African Institute of Race Relations (Microfilm)

GOVERNMENT PUBLICATIONS

Cape of Good Hope. Commission on Native Education. *Report of Commission on Native Education, 1919.* Cape Town: Cape Times Limited, Government Printers, 1920.

South Africa. *South African Native Affairs Commission 1903–5. Minutes of Evidence.* 4 vols. Cape Town: Cape Times Limited, Government Printers, 1904-[1906].

Union of South Africa. *First Report of the Select Committee on Native Affairs.* S.C. 3-'23. Cape Town: Cape Times Limited, Government Printers, 1923.

————. *Joint Sitting of Both Houses of Parliament on Representation of Natives Bills,* 13th February to 7th April 1936. J.S. 1-'36 and J.S. 2-'36. Cape Town: Cape Times Limited, Government Printers, [1936].

————. *Report of the Department of Native Affairs for the Years 1913 to 1918.* U.G. 7-'19. Cape Town: Cape Times Limited, Government Printers, 1919.

———. *Report of the Interdepartmental Committee on Native Education 1935–1936.* U.G. 29-'36. Pretoria: Government Printer, 1936.

———. *Report of the Native Affairs Commission for the Years 1925–26.* U.G. 17-'27. Cape Town: Cape Times Limited, 1927.

———. *Report of the Native Affairs Department for the Years 1922 to 1926.* U.G. 14-'27. Cape Town: Cape Times Limited, Government Printers, 1927.

———. *Report of the Native Churches Commission.* U.G. 39-'25. Cape Town: Cape Times Limited, Government Printers, 1925.

———. *Report of the Natives Land Commission.* U.G. 19-'16. Cape Town: Cape Times Limited, Government Printers, 1916.

———. *Report of the Native Laws Commission 1946–48.* U.G. 28-'48. Pretoria: Government Printer, 1948.

———. *Report of the Select Committee on the Subject of the Native Council Bill, Coloured Persons Rights Bill, Representation of Natives in Parliament Bill, and Natives Land (Amendment) Bill.* S.C. 10-'27. Cape Town: Cape Times Limited, Government Printers, [1928].

PUBLICATIONS OF THE ALL AFRICAN CONVENTION, THE EUROPEAN-AFRICAN CONFERENCES, THE NON-EUROPEAN CONFERENCES, AND THE NON-EUROPEAN UNITY MOVEMENT

All African Convention. *The Findings of the All African Convention.* N.p., [1935].

———. *Minutes of the All African Convention, June 1936.* Lovedale: Lovedale Press, 1936.

———. *Minutes of the All African Convention, December 1937.* N.p., n.d.

———. *Minutes of the All African Convention, December 1940.* N.p., n.d.

———. *Minutes of the All African Convention, December 1941.* Lovedale: Lovedale Press, n.d.

———. *Minutes of the All African Convention, December 1944* [1943]. N.p., n.d.

Federal Council of the Dutch Reformed Churches of South Africa. *European and Bantu: Being Papers and Addresses at the Conference on Native Affairs, Held under the Auspices of the Federal Council of the D.R. Churches at Johannesburg on 27th to 29th September, 1923.* Cape Town: Published for the Federal Council of the D.R. Churches, [1923].

National European-Bantu Conference. *Fifth National European-Bantu Conference, Bloemfontein, July 5, 6, 7, 1933. Report. Minutes, Findings, Addresses.* Johannesburg: Published for the South African Institute of Race Relations by the Lovedale Press, 1933.

———. *Report of the National European-Bantu Conference. Cape Town, February 6–9, 1929.* Lovedale: Lovedale Institution Press, 1929.

Non-European Conference. *Minutes of the First Non-European Conference. Kimberley, 23rd, 24th and 25th June, 1927.* N.p., n.d.

———. *Minutes of the Third Conference Held at Bloemfontein, January 5th, 6th, and 7th, 1931.* Lovedale: Lovedale Press, [1931].

Non-European Unity Movement. *Minutes of the Fourth Unity Conference.* N.p., [December 1945].

———. *Proceedings of 5th Unity Conference Held on 20th and 21st December, 1946 at City Hall, Kimberley.* Cape Town: Non-European Unity Movement, n.d.

———. *Proceedings of the 2nd Unity Conference Held on Saturday, 8th July, 1944, at Kholvad House, Market Street, Johannesburg.* Cape Town: Non-European Unity Movement, 1944.

———. *Proceedings of the Sixth Unity Conference of the Non-European Unity Movement, Held on 28th, 29th and 30th March, 1948, in Rondebosch Town Hall.* N.p., n.d.

———. *Report of the 3rd Unity Conference Held in the Banqueting Hall, Cape Town on 4th and 5th January, 1945.* Cape Town: Non-European Unity Committee, 1945.

NEWSPAPERS

The Alice Times
The Bantu World
The Cape Argus
The Cape Mercury
The Cape Times
The Christian Express (renamed *The South African Outlook*)
Daily Dispatch (East London)
Drum
The Eastern Province Herald (Port Elizabeth)
Imvo Zabantsundu
Inkundla ya Bantu
Kensington Express
Kent Messenger
The Manchester Guardian
The Times (London)
The Torch
Umsebenzi
Umteteli wa Bantu
Zonk!

SELECTED WRITINGS OF D. D. T. JABAVU

"The African Child and What the School Makes of Him." In *Educational Adaptations in a Changing Society.* Report of the South African Education Conference Held in Cape Town and Johannesburg in July, 1934, under the Auspices of the New Education Fellowship, ed. E. G. Malherbe, 432–35. Cape Town: Juta, 1937.

An African Indigenous Church: A Plea for Its Establishment in South Africa. Lovedale: Lovedale Press, 1942.

"After Three Generations." In *The Christian Mission in the World Today*. Report of the Eleventh Quadrennial Convention of the Student Volunteer Movement for Foreign Missions, Buffalo, New York, December 30, 1931 to January 3, 1932, ed. Raymond P. Currier, 42–47. New York: Student Volunteer Movement for Foreign Missions, 1932.

Afterword to *Nkosi Sikelel' I Africa* (The Bantu national anthem), by Enoch Sontonga. Lovedale Sol-fa Leaflets, no. 17, 1934.

"Bantu Grievances." In *Western Civilization and the Natives of South Africa: Studies in Culture Contact*, ed. I. Schapera, 285–99. London: George Routledge and Sons, 1934.

Black Peril and Colour Bar. Lovedale: Lovedale Press, 1923.

The Black Problem: Papers and Addresses on Various Native Problems. Lovedale: Lovedale Institution Press, 1920.

"Christian Service in Rural and Industrial South Africa." In *The Christian Mission in the World Today*. Report of the Eleventh Quadrennial Convention of the Student Volunteer Movement for Foreign Missions, Buffalo, New York, December 30, 1931 to January 3, 1932, ed. Raymond P. Currier, 65–74. New York: Student Volunteer Movement for Foreign Missions, 1932.

"Christianity and the Bantu." In *Thinking with Africa: Chapters by a Group of Nationals Interpreting the Christian Movement*, ed. Milton Stauffer, 11–34. New York: Published for the Student Volunteer Movement for Foreign Missions by the Missionary Education Movement of the United States and Canada, 1927.

"The Claims of the Bantu." *The Eastern Province Herald* (Port Elizabeth), *Educational Review* [supplement], October 12, 1932.

Criticisms of the Native Bills. Lovedale: Lovedale Press, 1935.

E-Amerika (In America). Trans. Cecil Wele Manona. [unpub.] Lovedale: Lovedale Press, 1932.

E-Indiya nase East Africa (In India and East Africa). Trans. Cecil Wele Manona. [unpub.] Lovedale: Lovedale Press for the publisher, Prof. D. D. T. Jabavu, 1951.

E-Jerusalem (In Jerusalem). 4th ed. Trans. Cecil Wele Manona. [unpub.] Lovedale: Lovedale Press, 1948.

Foreword to *The Native Separatist Church Movement in South Africa*, by Allen Lea. Cape Town: Juta, 1926.

"Higher Education and the Professional Training of the Bantu." *South African Journal of Science* 26 (December 1929): 934–36.

"Hofmeyr and the Africans." In *Jan Hendrik Hofmeyr: A Tribute*, ed. Donald B. Molteno. Johannesburg: South African Institute of Race Relations, 1949.

Imbumba yamaNyama. (Unity is strength). Trans. Cecil Wele Manona. [unpub.] Lovedale: By the author, 1952.

The Influence of English on Bantu Literature. Lovedale: Lovedale Press, 1943.

Comp. *I-Nkulungwane yama Mfengu 1835–1936 ne si-vivane: Fingo Centenary 1835–1935 and Centenary Fund*. Trans. Cecil Wele Manona. [unpub.] Lovedale: Lovedale Press, [1935].

IziDungulwana (Tidbits). Trans. Cecil Wele Manona. [unpub.] Cape Town: Maskew Miller, 1958.

Iziganeko Zamabali (Dates and incidents). Trans. Cecil Wele Manona. [unpub.] Lovedale: By the author, 1935.

Izithuko (Praise poems). Trans. Cecil Wele Manona. [unpub.] Lovedale: By the author, 1954.

The Life of John Tengo Jabavu, Editor of Imvo Zabantsundu, 1884–1921. Lovedale: Lovedale Institution Press, 1922.

"The Meaning of the Cross in the Life of the World Today." In *Foreign Missions Conference of North America 1932.* Report of the Thirty-Ninth Annual Meeting of the Conference of Foreign Mission Boards in Canada and the United States, Atlantic City, New Jersey, January 12–15, 1932, ed. Leslie B. Moss and Mabel H. Brown, 232–40. New York: Foreign Missions Conference of North America, [1932].

'Native Disabilities' in South Africa. Lovedale: Lovedale Press, 1932.

Native Taxation: A Comparison between What the Natives Pay Directly and Indirectly to the State and What They Should Reasonably Receive in Direct Benefit. Lovedale: Lovedale Press, 1931.

The Segregation Fallacy and Other Papers: A Native View of Some South African Inter-Racial Problems. Lovedale: Lovedale Institution Press, 1928.

"Some Criticisms of the Act and Its Results." In *Political Representation of South Africans in the Union.* New Africa Pamphlet no. 4. Johannesburg: South African Institute of Race Relations, 1942.

"The South African Problem." *International Review of Missions* 15 (July 1926): 376–89.

U-Kayakulu: Umhlaba otengwa e Rustenberg ngu Nkosi Shadrack F. Zibi (Great home: The land bought in Rustenberg by Chief Shadrack F. Zibi). Trans. Cecil Wele Manona. [unpub.] Lovedale: By the author, 1930.

Umsebenzi wama Wesile ku Bantsundu (The work of the Methodists among blacks). Trans. Cecil Wele Manona. [unpub.] N.p., [1923].

What Methodism Has Done for the Natives. Lovedale: Lovedale Press, [1923].

"White and Black in South Africa." In *The Christian Mission in the World Today.* Report of the Eleventh Quadrennial Convention of the Student Volunteer Movement for Foreign Missions, Buffalo, New York, December 30, 1931, to January 3, 1932, ed. Raymond P. Currier, 238–39. New York: Student Volunteer Movement for Foreign Missions, 1932.

BOOKS, PAMPHLETS, AND REPORTS

Abel, Richard L. *The Legal Profession in England and Wales.* Oxford: Basil Blackwell, 1988.

Abell, Aaron I. *American Catholicism and Social Action: A Search for Social Justice, 1865–1950.* Garden City, N.Y.: Hanover House, 1960.

Anderson, James D. *The Education of Blacks in the South, 1860–1935.* Chapel Hill: University of North Carolina Press, 1988.

Appiah, Kwame Anthony. *In My Father's House: Africa in the Philosophy of Culture.* New York: Oxford University Press, 1992.

Ayliff, John, and Joseph Whiteside. *History of the Abambo Generally Known as Fingos.* 1912. Reprint. Willem Hiddigh Reprint Series, no. 17. Cape Town: C. Struik, 1962.

Beinart, William. *Twentieth-Century South Africa.* Oxford: Oxford University Press, 1994.

Bhana, Surendra, and Bridglal Pachai, eds. *A Documentary History of Indian South Africans.* Cape Town: David Philip, 1984.

Bradford, Helen. *A Taste of Freedom: The ICU in Rural South Africa, 1924–1930.* Johannesburg: Ravan Press, 1987.

Brookes, Edgar H. *The Colour Problems of South Africa: Being the Phelps-Stokes Lectures, 1933, Delivered at the University of Cape Town.* Lovedale: Lovedale Press, 1934.

———. *The History of Native Policy in South Africa from 1830 to the Present Day.* Cape Town: Nasionale Pers, 1924.

———. *A South African Pilgrimage.* Johannesburg: Ravan Press, 1977.

———. *White Rule in South Africa 1830–1910: Varieties in Governmental Policies Affecting Africans.* Pietermaritzburg: University of Natal Press, 1974.

Bundy, Colin. *The Rise and Fall of the South African Peasantry.* Berkeley: University of California Press, 1979.

Burrows, H. R. *A Short Pictorial History of the University College of Fort Hare 1916–1959.* Lovedale: Lovedale Press, 1961.

Carter, Gwendolen M., and Sheridan W. Johns III, eds. *The Good Fight: Selected Speeches of Rev. Zaccheus R. Mahabane.* Program of African Studies. Evanston, Ill.: Northwestern University, [1965].

Cell, John. *The Highest Stage of White Supremacy: The Origins of Segregation in South Africa and the American South.* Cambridge: Cambridge University Press, 1982.

Chalmers, John A. *Tiyo Soga: A Page of South African Mission Work.* Edinburgh: Andrew Elliot, 1877.

Chapman, J. Vincent. *Professional Roots: The College of Preceptors in British Society.* Epping, England: Theydon Bois Publications, 1985.

Chirenje, J. Mutero. *Ethiopianism and Afro-Americans in Southern Africa, 1883–1916.* Baton Rouge: Louisiana State University Press, 1987.

Comaroff, Jean, and John L. Comaroff. *Of Revelation and Revolution: Christianity, Colonialism, and Consciousness in South Africa.* Vol. 1. Chicago: University of Chicago Press, 1991.

Couzens, Tim. *The New African: A Study of the Life and Work of H. I. E. Dhlomo.* Johannesburg: Ravan Press, 1985.

Cronin, E. David. *Black Moses: The Story of Marcus Garvey and the Universal Negro Improvement Association.* Madison: University of Wisconsin Press, 1955, 1969.

Curtin, Philip, Steven Feierman, Leonard Thompson, and Jan Vansina. *African History.* Boston: Little, Brown, 1978.

Davenport, T. R. H. *The Afrikaner Bond: The History of a South African Political Party, 1880–1911.* Cape Town: Oxford University Press, 1966.

———. *The Beginnings of Urban Segregation in South Africa: The Natives (Urban Areas) Act of 1923 and Its Background.* Grahamstown: Institute of Social and Economic Research, Rhodes University, 1971.

———. *South Africa: A Modern History.* 2d ed. Toronto: University of Toronto Press, 1978.

———. *South Africa: A Modern History.* 3d ed. Toronto: University of Toronto Press, 1987.

Debrunner, Hans Werner. *Presence and Prestige: Africans in Europe: A History of Africans in Europe before 1918.* Basel: Basler Afrika Bibliographien, 1979.

De Gruchy, John W. *The Church Struggle in South Africa.* 2d ed. London: Collins Liturgical Publications, 1986.

Dictionary of South African Biography. Editor in chief W. J. de Kock. 5 vols. Cape Town: Tafelberg-Uitgewers for the Human Sciences Research Council, 1968–87.

Dubow, Saul. *Racial Segregation and the Origins of Apartheid in South Africa, 1919–36.* Houndmills, England: Macmillan Press in association with St. Antony's College, Oxford, 1989.

Edgar, Robert R. *An African American in South Africa: The Travel Notes of Ralph J. Bunche 28 September 1937–1 January 1938.* Athens: Ohio University Press, 1992.

———. *Because They Chose the Plan of God: The Story of the Bulhoek Massacre.* Johannesburg: Ravan Press, 1988.

Esedebe, P. Olisanwuche. *Pan-Africanism: The Idea and the Movement 1776–1963.* Washington, D.C.: Howard University Press, 1982.

Etherington, Norman. *Preachers, Peasants and Politics in Southeast Africa, 1835–1880: African Christian Communities in Natal, Pondoland, and Zululand.* London: Royal Historical Society, 1978.

Frederickson, George M. *Black Liberation: A Comparative History of Black Ideologies in the United States and South Africa.* New York: Oxford University Press, 1995.

Friends Service Council. *Kingsmead, Selly Oak, Birmingham: What It Offers to Friends To-day.* London: Friends Service Council, March 1928.

Friends World Conference. *Official Report. Held at Swarthmore and Haverford Colleges near Philadelphia, Pennsylvania September 1st to 8th 1937.* Philadelphia, 1937.

Fryer, Peter. *Staying Power: The History of Black People in Britain.* London: Pluto Press, 1984.

Gandhi, Mahatma. *Mahatma Gandhi: His Own Story.* Ed. C. F. Andrews. New York: Macmillan, 1930.

Garvey, Marcus. *Marcus Garvey: Life and Lessons.* A Centennial Companion to the Marcus Garvey and Universal Negro Improvement Association Papers. Ed. Robert Hill and Barbara Bair. Berkeley: University of California Press, 1987.

Gerhart, Gail M. *Black Power in South Africa: The Evolution of an Ideology.* Berkeley: University of California Press, 1978.

Gerhart, Gail M., and Thomas Karis. *Political Profiles 1882–1964.* Vol. 4 of *From Protest to Challenge: A Documentary History of African Politics in South Africa 1882–1964,* ed. Thomas Karis and Gwendolen M. Carter. 4 vols. Stanford, Calif.: Hoover Institution Press, Stanford University, 1972–77, 1987.

Gray, Richard. *Black Christians and White Missionaries.* New Haven: Yale University Press, 1990.

Hammond-Tooke, W. D., ed. *The Journal of William Shaw.* Cape Town: A. A. Balkema for Rhodes University, Grahamstown, 1972.

Hancock, William Keith. *Smuts.* Vol. 2, *The Fields of Force 1919–1950.* Cambridge: Cambridge University Press, 1968.

———. *Smuts.* Vol. 1, *The Sanguine Years, 1870–1919.* Cambridge: Cambridge University Press, 1962.

Handy, Robert. *The Social Gospel in America 1870–1920.* New York: Oxford University Press, 1966.

Harlan, Louis R. *Booker T. Washington.* Vol. 1, *The Making of a Black Leader 1856–1901.* New York: Oxford University Press, 1972.

———. *Booker T. Washington.* Vol. 2, *The Wizard of Tuskegee 1901–1915.* New York: Oxford University Press, 1983.

———. *Booker T. Washington in Perspective: Essays of Louis R. Harlan.* Ed. Raymond W. Smock. Jackson: University of Mississippi Press, 1988.

Headlam, A. C. *The Doctrine of the Church and Christian Reunion: Being the Bampton Lectures for the Year 1920.* 2d ed. London: John Murray, 1920.

Hertzog, J. B. M. *The Segregation Problem.* Cape Town: Nasionale Pers, 1925.

Hewison, Hope Hay. *Hedge of Wild Almonds: South Africa, the Pro-Boers and the Quaker Conscience, 1890–1910.* Portsmouth, N.H.: Heinemann, 1979.

Hodgson, Janet. *Ntsikana's Great Hymn: A Xhosa Expression of Christianity in the Early Nineteenth Century Eastern Cape.* Communications no. 4. University of Cape Town, Centre for African Studies, 1980.

Hoernlé, R. F. Alfred. *South African Native Policy and the Liberal Spirit: Being the Phelps-Stokes Lectures, Delivered before the University of Cape Town, May, 1939.* Cape Town: Published on Behalf of the Phelps-Stokes Fund of the University of Cape Town, 1939.

Hofmeyr, J. W., and K. E. Cross, eds. *History of the Church in Southern Africa: A Select Bibliography of Published Material to 1980.* Vol. 1. Pretoria: University of South Africa, 1980.

Holden, W. Clifford. *A Brief History of Methodism and of Methodist Missions in South Africa.* London: Wesleyan Conference Office, 1877.

Hopkins, C. Howard. *John R. Mott, 1865–1955: A Biography.* Grand Rapids, Mich.: William B. Eerdmans, 1979.

Houghton, D. Hobart. *Life in the Ciskei: A Summary of the Findings of the Keiskammahoek Rural Survey, 1947–1951.* Johannesburg: South African Institute of Race Relations, 1955.

Houghton, D. Hobart, and Jenifer Dagut, eds. *Source Material on the South African Economy: 1860–1970.* 3 vols. Cape Town: Oxford University Press, 1972–73.

Hughes, W. *Dark Africa and the Way Out; or, A Scheme for Civilizing and Evangelizing the Dark Continent.* London: Sampson Low, Marston, 1892.

Ingham, Kenneth. *Jan Christian Smuts: The Conscience of a South African.* Johannesburg: Jonathan Ball, in association with Weidenfeld and Nicolson, London, 1986.

Innes, Sir James Rose. *Sir James Rose Innes: Selected Correspondence (1884–1902).* Ed. Harrison Wright. Second series, no.3. Cape Town: Van Riebeeck Society, 1972.

International Missionary Council. *The Jerusalem Meeting of the International Missionary Council, March 24-April 8, 1928.* 8 vols. London: International Missionary Council, 1928.

Jabavu, Noni. *Drawn in Colour: African Contrasts.* London: John Murray, 1960.

———. *The Ochre People: Scenes from a South African Life.* London: John Murray, 1963.

Johns, Sheridan, III. *Protest and Hope 1882–1934.* Vol. 1 of *From Protest to Challenge: A Documentary History of African Politics in South Africa 1882–1964,* ed. Thomas Karis and Gwendolen M. Carter. 4 vols. Stanford, Calif.: Hoover Institution Press, Stanford University, 1972–77, 1987.

Joint Council of Europeans and Natives, Johannesburg. *General Hertzog's Solution of the Native Question.* Memorandum no. 1. Supplement to *South African Outlook,* December 1, 1926.

Jones, Lucy M., and Ivor Wynne Jones. *H. M. Stanley and Wales.* St. Asaph, Wales: H. M. Stanley Exhibition Committee, 1972.

Jones, Stuart, and André Müller. *The South African Economy, 1910–1990.* Houndmills, England: Macmillan, 1992.

Karis, Thomas. *Hope and Challenge 1935–1952.* Vol. 2 of *From Protest to Challenge: A Documentary History of African Politics in South Africa 1882–1964,* ed. Thomas Karis and Gwendolen M. Carter. 4 vols. Stanford, Calif.: Hoover Institution Press, Stanford University, 1972–77, 1987.

Karis, Thomas, and Gail M. Gerhart. *Challenge and Violence 1953–1964.* Vol. 3 of *From Protest to Challenge: A Documentary History of African Politics in South Africa 1882–1964,* ed. Thomas Karis and Gwendolen M. Carter. 4 vols. Stanford, Calif.: Hoover Institution Press, 1972–77, 1987.

Keiskammahoek Rural Survey. 4 vols. Pietermaritzburg: Shuter and Shooter, 1952.

Keppel-Jones, A. M. *South Africa: A Short History.* 5th ed. London: Hutchinson University Library, 1975.

Kerr, Alexander. *Fort Hare 1915–48: The Evolution of an African College.* Pietermaritzburg: Shuter and Shooter, in association with C. Hurst, 1968.

King, Kenneth James. *Pan-Africanism and Education: A Study of Race Philanthropy and Education in the Southern States of America and East Africa.* Oxford: Clarendon Press, 1971.

King William's Town. *A Documentary History of King William's Town.* King William's Town: Kaffrarian Museum, n.d.

King William's Town Chamber of Commerce. *Minutes of a Conference of Representatives of the Money Guaranteed towards the Founding of the Inter-State Native College.* N.p., 1907.

Kuper, Adam. *Wives for Cattle: Bridewealth and Marriage in Southern Africa.* London: Routledge and Kegan Paul, 1982.

Kuper, Leo. *An African Bourgeoisie: Race, Class and Politics in South Africa.* New Haven: Yale University Press, 1965.

Lacey, Marian. *Working For Boroko: The Origins of a Coercive Labour System in South Africa.* Johannesburg: Ravan Press, 1981.

Lazerson, Joshua N. *Against the Tide: Whites in the Struggle against Apartheid.* Boulder: Westview Press, 1994.

Lea, Allen. *The Story of Methodist Union in South Africa: Being an Account of the Unification of Methodism in the Union of South Africa.* Cape Town: Methodist Book Depot, 1931.

Leuchtenburg, William E. *Franklin D. Roosevelt and the New Deal 1932–1940.* New York: Harper and Row, 1963.

Lewis, David Levering. *W. E. B. Du Bois: Biography of a Race, 1868–1919.* New York: Henry Holt, 1993.

Lewis, Gavin. *Between the Wire and the Wall: A History of South African "Coloured" Politics.* New York: St. Martin's Press, 1987.

Lewsen, Phyllis. *John X. Merriman: Paradoxical South African Statesman.* New Haven: Yale University Press, 1982.

A List of South African Newspapers 1800–1982. Pretoria: State Library, 1983.

Little, K. L. *Negroes in Britain: A Study of Racial Relations in English Society.* London: Keagan Paul, Trench, Trubner, 1947.

Loram, Charles T. *The Education of the South African Native.* London: Longmans, Green, 1917. Reprint. New York: Negro Universities Press, 1969.

Lovedale Missionary Institution. *Report.* 1900–1947.

Luthuli, Albert. *Let My People Go: An Autobiography.* Albert Luthuli, 1962. Reprint. Fount Paperbacks, 1982.

Lynch, Hollis R. *Edward Wilmot Blyden: Pan-Negro Patriot 1832–1912.* London: Oxford University Press, 1967.

Lyon, Milford Hall. *The Basis for Brotherhood and Kindred Themes.* New York: Fleming H. Revell, 1923.

Majeke, Nosipho [Dora Taylor]. *The Role of the Missionaries in Conquest.* Alexandra Township (Johannesburg): Society of Young Africa, n.d.

Malherbe, E. G. *Education in South Africa.* 2 vols. Cape Town: Juta, 1925, 1975–77.

Mandela, Nelson. *Long Walk to Freedom: The Autobiography of Nelson Mandela.* Boston: Little, Brown, 1994.

———. *No Easy Walk to Freedom.* Rev. ed. Oxford: Heinemann International, 1990.

Marks, Shula. *The Ambiguities of Dependence in South Africa: Class, Nationalism, and the State in Twentieth-Century Natal.* Johannesburg: Ravan Press, 1986.

———, ed. *Not Either An Experimental Doll: The Separate Worlds of Three South African Women.* Bloomington: University of Indiana Press, 1987.

Mashinini, Emma. *Strikes Have Followed Me All My Life: A South African Autobiography.* New York: Routledge, 1991.

Mathabane, Mark. *Kaffir Boy: The True Story of a Black Youth's Coming of Age in Apartheid South Africa.* New York: Macmillan, 1986. Reprint. New York: New American Library, 1989.

Mather, Frank Lincoln. *Who's Who of the Coloured Race: A General Biographical Dictionary of Men and Women of African Descent.* Vol. 1. 1915. Reprint. Detroit: Gale Research, 1976.

Matthews, Frieda. *Remembrances.* Bellville, South Africa: Mayibuye Books, 1995.

Matthews, Z. K. *Freedom for My People: The Autobiography of Z. K. Matthews, Southern Africa 1901 to 1968.* Memoir by Monica Wilson. Cape Town: David Philip, 1981.

Meer, Fatima. *Higher than Hope: The Authorized Biography of Nelson Mandela.* Johannesburg: Skotaville, 1988. Reprint. New York: Harper Collins, 1990.

Mehta, Ved. *Mahatma Gandhi and His Apostles.* New York: Viking Press, 1977. Reprint. New Haven: Yale University Press, 1993.

Merriman, John X. *Selections from the Correspondence of John X. Merriman 1899–1905.* Ed. Phyllis Lewsen. 4 vols. Cape Town: Van Riebeeck Society, 1960–69.

Missionary Society of the Wesleyan Church of South Africa. *Annual Report of the Missionary Society of the Wesleyan Methodist Church of South Africa with Lists of Contributions to the Sustentation and Mission Fund,* 1917–1941.

Mokgatle, Naboth. *The Autobiography of an Unknown South African.* Berkeley: University of California Press, 1971.

Mostert, Noël. *Frontiers: The Epic of South Africa's Creation and the Tragedy of the Xhosa People.* New York: Alfred A. Knopf, 1992.

Mphahlele, Ezekiel. *Down Second Avenue.* Garden City, N.Y.: Doubleday, 1971.

Msimang, H. Selby. *The Crisis.* N.p., [1936].

Mudimbe, V. Y. *The Invention of Africa: Gnosis, Philosophy, and the Order of Knowledge.* Bloomington: Indiana University Press, 1988.

Musson, Doreen. *Johnny Gomas, Voice of the Working Class: A Political Biography.* Cape Town: Buchu Books, 1989.

Nicholls, G. Heaton. *The Native Bills: Being an Address Delivered before the Bantu Study Group of the University of the Witwatersrand.* Durban: Home Journal Press, September 1935.

Ntantala, Phyllis. *A Life's Mosaic: The Autobiography of Phyllis Ntantala.* Berkeley: University of California Press, 1992.

Odendaal, André. *Vukani Bantu!: The Beginnings of Black Protest Politics in South Africa to 1912.* Cape Town: David Philip, 1984.

Oldham, J. H. *Christianity and the Race Problem.* 4th ed. London: Student Christian Movement, 1925.

Omer-Cooper, J. D. *The Zulu Aftermath: A Nineteenth-Century Revolution in Bantu Africa.* London: Longmans, 1966.

Palmer, Alan. *The Penguin Dictionary of Modern History 1789–1945.* 2d ed. New York: Penguin, 1983.

Paton, Alan. *Hofmeyr.* London: Oxford University Press, 1964.

Pearson, Hesketh. *The Smith of Smiths: Being the Life, Wit and Humour of Sydney Smith.* London: Hamish Hamilton, 1934. Reprint. London: Hogarth Press, 1984.

Peires, J. B. *The Dead Will Arise: Nongqawuse and the Great Xhosa Cattle-Killing Movement of 1856–7.* Bloomington: Indiana University Press, 1989.

———. *The House of Phalo: A History of the Xhosa People in the Days of Their Independence.* Berkeley: University of California Press, 1982.

Perham, Margery. *African Apprenticeship: An Autobiographical Journey in Southern Africa, 1929.* London: Faber and Faber, 1974.

Peteni, Randall L. *Towards Tomorrow: The Story of the African Teachers' Associations of South Africa.* Morges, Switzerland: World Confederation of Organizations of the Teaching Profession, 1978.

Peters, M. A., and C. P. Bothma, comps. *IBhibliyografi yolwimi olusisiXhosa ukuya kutsho kunyaka we-1990* (Bibliography of the Xhosa language to the year 1990). Xhosa text ed. G. T. Sirayi. Pretoria: State Library, 1992.

Phelps-Stokes Reports on Education in Africa. Abridged, with an introduction by L. J. Lewis. London: Oxford University Press, 1962.

Phillips, Ray. *The Bantu Are Coming: Phases of South Africa's Race Problem.* London: Student Christian Movement Press, [1930].

Plaatje, Sol T. *Native Life in South Africa: Before and since the European War and the Boer Rebellion.* London: P. S. King and Son, 1916. Rev. ed. Athens: Ohio University Press by arrangement with Ravan Press, Johannesburg, 1991.

Porter, Andrew N. *The Origins of the South African War: Joseph Chamberlain and the Diplomacy of Imperialism, 1895–1899.* Manchester: Manchester University Press, 1980.

Rich, Paul. *Hope and Despair: English-Speaking Intellectuals and South African Politics 1896–1976.* London: British Academic Press, 1993.

———. *White Power and the Liberal Conscience: Racial Segregation and South African Liberalism 1921–1960.* Manchester: Manchester University Press, 1984.

Rive, Richard, and Tim Couzens. *Seme: The Founder of the ANC.* Trenton: Africa World Press, 1993.

Roberts, Brian. *Cecil Rhodes: Flawed Colossus.* New York: W. W. Norton, 1988.

Rose, Brian, and Raymond Tunmer, eds. *Documents in South African Education.* Johannesburg: A. D. Donker, 1975.

Rotberg, Robert I. *The Founder: Cecil Rhodes and the Pursuit of Power.* New York: Oxford University Press, 1988.

Roux, Edward. *S. P. Bunting: A Political Biography.* Rev. ed. Bellville, South Africa: Mayibuye Books, 1993.

———. *Time Longer than Rope: A History of the Black Man's Struggle for Freedom in South Africa.* 2d ed. Madison: University of Wisconsin Press, 1964.

Scobie, Edward. *Black Britannia: A History of Blacks in Britain.* Chicago: Johnson Publishing, 1972.

Shepherd, Robert H. W. *Lovedale South Africa, 1824–1955.* Alice: Lovedale Press, 1971.

————. *Lovedale South Africa: The Story of a Century, 1841–1941.* Lovedale: Lovedale Press, 1940.

Shillington, Kevin. *History of Africa.* Rev. ed. New York: St. Martin's Press, 1995.

Simons, Jack, and Ray Simons. *Class and Colour in South Africa 1850–1950.* [London]: International Defence and Aid Fund for Southern Africa, 1983.

Smith, Edwin W. *Aggrey of Africa: A Study in Black and White.* New York: Friendship Press, 1929.

Smuts, Jan Christian. *Selections from the Smuts Papers.* Ed. Jean Van Der Poel. 7 vols. Cambridge: Cambridge University Press, 1973.

Soga, J. Henderson. *The Ama-Xosa: Life and Customs.* Lovedale: Lovedale Press, [1931].

————. *The South-Eastern Bantu (Abe-Nguni, Aba-Mbo, Ama-Lala).* Johannesburg: Witwatersrand University Press, 1930.

Sosna, Morton. *In Search of the Silent South: Southern Liberals and the Race Issue.* New York: Columbia University Press, 1977.

South African Institute of Race Relations. *Second Annual Report 1931.* Johannesburg: South African Institute of Race Relations, [1931].

South African Native College. *Report of the Opening of the College 8th-9th February 1916.* Lovedale: Lovedale Mission Press, [1916].

South African Native Races Committee. *The South African Natives: Their Progress and Present Condition.* 1908. Reprint. New York: Negro University Press, 1969.

Southern, Eileen. *The Music of Black Americans: A History.* 2d ed. New York: W. W. Norton, 1983.

Stanford, Sir Walter. *The Reminiscences of Sir Walter Stanford,* ed. J. W. Macquarrie. 2 vols. Cape Town: Van Riebeeck Society, 1962.

Switzer, Les. *Power and Resistance in an African Society: The Ciskei Xhosa and the Making of South Africa.* Madison: University of Wisconsin Press, 1993.

Switzer, Les, and Donna Switzer. *The Black Press in South Africa and Lesotho: A Descriptive Bibliographic Guide to African, Coloured, and Indian Newspapers, Newsletters, and Magazines, 1836–1976.* Boston: G. K. Hall, 1979.

Tabata, I. B. *The All African Convention: The Awakening of a People.* Johannesburg: People's Press, 1950.

Tatz, Colin M. *Shadow and Substance in South Africa: A Study in Land and Franchise Policies Affecting Africans, 1910–1960.* Pietermaritzburg: University of Natal Press, 1962.

Taylor, J. Dexter, ed. *Christianity and the Natives of South Africa: A Year Book of South African Missions.* Lovedale: Lovedale Institution Press, 1929.

Thompson, Leonard. *A History of South Africa.* New Haven: Yale University Press, 1990.

————. *The Unification of South Africa, 1902–1910.* Oxford: Clarendon Press, 1960.

Universal Races Congress. *Papers on Inter-Racial Problems Communicated to the First Universal Races Congress.* Held at the University of London, July 26–29, 1911. Ed. G. Spiller. London: P. S. King and Son, 1911.

————. *Record of the Proceedings of the First Universal Races Congress.* Held at the University of London, July 26–29, 1911. London: P. S. King and Son, 1911.

University of London. *The Historical Record (1836–1912)*. London: Hodder and Stoughton, 1912.

Vail, Leroy, ed. *The Creation of Tribalism in Southern Africa*. Berkeley: University of California Press, 1989.

Walshe, Peter. *The Rise of African Nationalism in South Africa: The African National Congress, 1912–1952*. London: C. Hurst, 1970.

Warwick, Peter. *Black People and the South African War, 1899–1902*. Johannesburg: Ravan Press, 1983.

———, ed. *The South African War: The Anglo-Boer War, 1899–1902*. London: Longman, 1980.

Wells, James. *Stewart of Lovedale: The Life of James Stewart*. 3d ed. London: Hodder and Stoughton, 1909.

Wesleyan Methodist Church of South Africa. *Minutes of the Annual Conference*. 1883–1921. Cape Town: Methodist Publishing House.

Whiteside, Joseph. *History of the Wesleyan Methodist Church of South Africa*. London: Elliott Stock, 1906.

Willan, Brian. *Sol Plaatje: South African Nationalist, 1876–1932*. Berkeley: University of California Press, 1984.

Williams, Donovan. *Umfundisi: A Biography of Tiyo Soga, 1829–1871*. Lovedale: Lovedale Press, 1978.

Williams, Walter L. *Black Americans and the Evangelization of Africa, 1877–1900*. Madison: University of Wisconsin Press, 1982.

Williamson, Joel. *The Crucible of Race: Black-White Relations in the American South since Emancipation*. New York: Oxford University Press, 1984.

Wilson, Monica. *The Interpreters*. Third Dugmore Memorial Lecture. Grahamstown: 1820 Settlers National Monument Foundation, September 1, 1972.

———. *Missionaries: Conquerors or Servants of God?* King William's Town: South African Missionary Museum, 1976.

———. *Religion and the Transformation of Society: A Study in Social Change in Africa*. Cambridge: Cambridge University Press, 1971.

Woloch, Isser. *Eighteenth-Century Europe: Tradition and Progress, 1715–1789*. New York: W. W. Norton, 1982.

Woodward, C. Vann. *The Strange Career of Jim Crow*. 2d rev. ed. New York: Oxford University Press, 1966.

World Pacifist Meeting. *The Task of Peace-Making: Reports of the World Pacifist Meeting, Santiniketan and Sevagram, 1949*. Calcutta: Visva-Bharati for the World Pacifist Meeting Committee, 1951.

Yudelman, David. *The Emergence of Modern South Africa: State, Capital, and the Incorporation of Organized Labor on the South African Gold Fields, 1902–1939*. Westport, Conn.: Greenwood Press, 1983.

Zell, Hans M., ed. *The African Book World and Press: A Directory*. 4th ed. London: Hans Zell Publishers, 1989.

Zinsser, William, ed. *Extraordinary Lives: The Art and Craft of American Biography*. New York: American Heritage, 1986.

ARTICLES, PAPERS, AND DISSERTATIONS

"The African Women's Self-Improvement Association: Constitution." N.p., n.d. Author's private collection. Typescript.

Anthony, David H., III. "Max Yergan in South Africa: From Evangelical Pan-Africanist to Revolutionary Socialist." *African Studies Review* 34, no. 2 (September 1991): 27–55.

Beinart, William. "*Amafelandawonye* (The Die-hards): Popular Protest and Women's Movements in Herschel District in the 1920s." In *Hidden Struggles in Rural South Africa: Politics and Popular Movements in the Transkei and Eastern Cape 1890–1930*, ed. William Beinart and Colin Bundy, 222–69. London: James Currey, 1987.

————. "Soil Erosion, Conservationism and Ideas about Development: A Southern African Exploration, 1900–1960." *Journal of Southern African Studies* 11, no. 1 (October 1984): 52–83.

Bhana, Surendra. "The Tolstoy Farm: Gandhi's Experiment in 'Co-operative Commonwealth.'" *South African Historical Journal*, no. 7 (1975): 88–100.

Bonner, Philip. "The Transvaal Native Congress, 1917–1920: The Radicalisation of the Black Petty Bourgeoisie on the Rand." In *Industrialisation and Social Change in South Africa: African Class Formation, Culture, and Consciousness, 1870–1930*, ed. Shula Marks and Richard Rathbone, 270–313. London: Longman, 1982.

Bouch, Richard. "The Mfengu Revisited: The Nineteenth Century Experience of One Mfengu Community through the Eyes of Historians and Contemporaries." In *Collected Seminar Papers of the Societies of Southern Africa in the Nineteenth and Twentieth Centuries*. University of London, Institute of Commonwealth Studies, vol. 17 (October 1989-June 1990), 81–89.

Brandon, Laverne. "Booker T. Washington and D. D. T. Jabavu: Interaction between an Afro-American and a Black South African." In *A Current Bibliography on African Affairs*, vol. 5, series 2 (1972), 509–15.

Brandon, Mattye Laverne. "The Interaction of Afro-Americans and South Africans, 1898–1940." M.A. thesis, Howard University, 1971.

"A Brief History of the Lesotho Training College." *Basutoland Witness* (Lesotho Evangelical Church, P.E.M.S.), no. 71 (November 1969): 1–18.

Bundy, Colin. "Conflict in Qumbu: Rural Consciousness, Ethnicity and Violence in the Colonial Transkei." In *Hidden Struggles in Rural South Africa: Politics and Popular Movements in the Transkei and Eastern Cape 1890–1930*, ed. William Beinart and Colin Bundy, 106–37. London: James Currey, 1987.

Burchell, D. E. "African Higher Education and the Establishment of the South African Native College, Fort Hare." *South African Historical Journal*, no. 8 (November 1976): 60–83.

Cobbing, Julian. "The Mfecane as Alibi: Thoughts on Dithakong and Mbolompo." *Journal of African History* 29 (1988): 487–519.

The Crisis: A Record of the Darker Races. 47 vols. The Black Experience in America: Negro Periodicals in the United States, 1840-1960. Reprint. New York: Negro Universities Press, 1969.

Davenport, T. R. H. "The Cape Liberal Tradition to 1910." In *Democratic Liberalism in South Africa: Its History and Prospect,* ed. Jeffrey Butler, Richard Elphick, and David Welsh, 21-34. Middletown, Conn.: Wesleyan University Press, 1987.

Davis, R. Hunt. "The Administration and Financing of African Education in South Africa 1910-1953." In *Apartheid and Education: The Education of Black South Africans,* ed. Peter Kallaway, 127-38. Johannesburg: Ravan Press, 1984.

————. "Charles T. Loram and the American Model for African Education in South Africa." In *Apartheid and Education: The Education of Black South Africans,* ed. Peter Kallaway, 108-26. Johannesburg: Ravan Press, 1984.

————. "John L. Dube: A South African Exponent of Booker T. Washington." *Journal of African Studies* 2, no. 4 (1975-76): 497-528.

————. "School vs. Blanket and Settler: Elijah Makiwane and the Leadership of the Cape School Community." *African Affairs: Journal of the Royal African Society* 78, no. 310 (January 1979): 12-31.

Eldredge, Elizabeth. "Sources of Conflict in Southern Africa, c. 1800-1830: The 'Mfecane' Reconsidered." *Journal of African History* 33 (1992): 1-35.

Elphick, Richard. "Africans and the Christian Campaign in Southern Africa." In *The Frontier in History: North America and Southern Africa Compared,* ed. Howard Lamar and Leonard Thompson, 270-307. New Haven: Yale University Press, 1981.

————. "Mission Christianity and Interwar Liberalism." In *Democratic Liberalism in South Africa: Its History and Prospect,* ed. Jeffrey Butler, Richard Elphick and David Welsh, 64-80. Middletown, Conn.: Wesleyan University Press, 1987.

Erlmann, Veit. "A Feeling of Prejudice: Orpheus M. McAdoo and the Virginia Jubilee Singers in South Africa 1890-1898." *Journal of Southern African Studies* 4, no. 13 (April 1989): 331-50.

Gentle, Roy. "The NEUM in Perspective." B.Soc.Sc. hons. thesis, University of Cape Town, 1978.

Gish, Steven D. "Alfred B. Xuma, 1893-1962: African, American, South African." Ph.D. diss., Stanford University, 1994.

Gitywa, Vincent Zanoxolo. "Male Initiation in the Ciskei: Formal Incorporation into Bantu Society." Ph.D. diss., University of Fort Hare, 1976.

Green, Jeffrey P. "A Black Community? — London, 1919." *Immigrants and Minorities* 5, no. 1 (March 1986): 107-16.

————. "*In Dahomey* in London in 1903." *Black Perspective in Music* 11, no. 1 (Spring 1983): 23-40.

Grove, Richard. "Early Themes in African Conservation: The Cape in the Nineteenth Century." In *Conservation in Africa: People, Policies and Practice,* ed. David Anderson and Richard Grove, 21-39. Cambridge: Cambridge University Press, 1987.

Haines, Richard John. "The Opposition to General J. B. M. Hertzog's Segregation Bills, 1925-1936: A Study in Extra-Parliamentary Protest." M.A. thesis, University of Natal, 1978.

Hansen, Deirdre D. "The Life and Work of Benjamin Tyamzashe: A Contemporary Xhosa Composer." Occasional Paper no. 11. Institute of Social and Economic Research, Rhodes University, Grahamstown, 1968.

Harms, Robert. "The End of Red Rubber: A Reassessment." *Journal of African History* 16, no. 1 (1975): 73-88.

Higgs, Catherine. "The Founding of the South African Institute of Race Relations." Southern African Research Program, Yale University, 1985. Typescript.

————. "The Political Thought and Career of Edgar H. Brookes." B.A. hons. thesis, Queen's University at Kingston, 1984. Typescript.

Hill, Robert A., and Gregory A. Pirio. "'Africa for the Africans': The Garvey Movement in South Africa, 1920-1940." In *The Politics of Race, Class and Nationalism in Twentieth-Century South Africa*, ed. Shula Marks and Stanley Trapido, 209-53. London: Longman, 1987.

Hirson, Baruch. "Tuskegee, the Joint Councils and the All African Convention." In *Collected Seminar Papers on the Societies of Southern Africa in the Nineteenth and Twentieth Centuries*. University of London, Institute of Commonwealth Studies, vol. 10 (October 1978 -June 1979), 65-76.

Hogan, Neville. "The Posthumous Vindication of Zachariah Gqishela: Reflections on the Politics of Dependence at the Cape in the Nineteenth Century." In *Economy and Society in Pre-Industrial South Africa*, ed. Shula Marks and Anthony Atmore, 275-95. Burnt Mill, England: Longman, 1980.

Holroyd, Michael. "How I Fell into Biography." In *The Troubled Face of Biography*, ed. Eric Homberger and John Charmley, 94-103. New York: St. Martin's Press, 1988.

Jabavu, [Florence]. "Bantu Home Life." In *Christianity and the Natives of South Africa: A Year Book of South African Missions*, ed. J. Dexter Taylor, 164-76. Lovedale: Lovedale Institution Press, [1928].

Jones, Rufus M. "Secular Civilization and the Christian Task." In *The Christian Life and Message in Relation to Non-Christian Systems of Thought and Life*. Vol. 1 of *The Jerusalem Meeting of the International Missionary Council, March 24-April 8, 1928*. New York: International Missionary Council, 1928, 230-73.

The Keys: The Official Organ of The League of Coloured Peoples. 7 vols. 1933-1939. Reprint. Millwood, N.Y.: Kraus-Thompson, 1976.

"King William's Town: Its Rise and Progress." In *King William's Town Directory, Visitor's Guide and Resident's Handbook.* N.p., 1902.

Krikler, J. M. "The South African Party and the Cape African Franchise, 1926-1936." B.A. hons. thesis, University of Cape Town, 1980.

Kuper, Leo. "African Nationalism in South Africa, 1910-1964." In *The Oxford History of South Africa*, ed. Monica Wilson and Leonard Thompson, 2:424-76. New York: Oxford University Press, 1971.

Lea, Allen. "The Wesleyan Methodist Church of South Africa." In *Christianity and the Natives of South Africa: A Year Book of South African Missions*, ed. J. Dexter Taylor, 210–15. Lovedale: Lovedale Institution Press, [1928].

Legassick, Martin. "The Making of South African 'Native Policy,' 1903–1923: The Origins of 'Segregation.'" Paper presented to the postgraduate seminar on Ideology and Social Structure in Twentieth Century South Africa. Institute of Commonwealth Studies, University of London, 1972.

———. "Race, Industrialization and Social Change in South Africa: The Case of R. F. A. Hoernlé." *African Affairs: Journal of the Royal African Society* 75 (1976): 225–39.

———. "The Rise of Modern South African Liberalism: Its Assumptions and Social Base." Paper presented to the postgraduate seminar on Ideology and Social Structure in Twentieth Century South Africa. Institute of Commonwealth Studies, University of London, 1972.

Lewsen, Phyllis. "The Cape Liberal Tradition—Myth or Reality?" *Race: Journal of the Institute of Race Relations* 12, no. 1 (July 1971): 65–79.

Mager, Anne. "'The People Get Fenced': Gender, Rehabilitation and African Nationalism in the Ciskei and Border Region, 1945–1955." *Journal of Southern African Studies* 18, no. 4 (December 1992): 761–82.

Manona, Cecil W. "Ethnic Relations in the Ciskei." In *Ciskei: Economics and Politics of Dependence in a South African Homeland*, ed. Nancy Charton, 97–121. London: Croom Helm, 1980.

The Mermaid (University of Birmingham) 10, no. 2 (December 1913).

Mills, Wallace George. "The Role of African Clergy in the Reorientation of Xhosa Society to the Plural Society in the Cape Colony, 1850–1915." Ph.D. diss., University of California at Los Angeles, 1975.

Molteno, Frank. "The Historical Foundations of the Schooling of Black South Africans." In *Apartheid and Education: The Education of Black South Africans*, ed. Peter Kallaway, 45–107. Johannesburg: Ravan Press, 1984.

Moyer, Richard A. "A History of the Mfengu of the Eastern Cape 1815–1865." Ph.D. diss., University of London, 1976.

———. "The Mfengu, Self-Defence and the Cape Frontier Wars." In *Beyond the Cape Frontier: Studies in the History of the Transkei and Ciskei*, ed. C. Saunders and R. Derricourt, 101–26. London: Longman, 1974.

Nasson, Bill. "The Unity Movement Tradition: Its Legacy in Historical Consciousness." In *History from South Africa: Alternative Visions and Practices*, ed. Joshua Brown, Patrick Manning, Karin Shapiro, and Jon Wiener, 144–64. Philadelphia: Temple University Press, 1991.

Ngcongco, Leonard D. "*Imvo Zabantsundu* and Cape 'Native' Policy, 1884–1902." M.A. thesis, University of South Africa, 1974.

———. "Jabavu and the Anglo-Boer War." *Kleio Bulletin*, no. 2 (October 1970): 6–18.

———. "John Tengo Jabavu, 1859–1921." In *Black Leaders in Southern African History*, ed. Christopher Saunders, 142–56. London: Heinemann Educational Books, 1979.

Ntuli, Linda. "Zenzele Women's Self-Improvement Association." Trans. Cecil Wele Manona. [unpub.] Author's private collection. Typescript.

Odendaal, André. "African Political Mobilisation in the Eastern Cape, 1880–1910." Ph.D. diss., Cambridge University, 1983.

———. "South Africa's Black Victorians: Sport, Race and Class in South Africa before Union." In *Collected Seminar Papers on the Societies of Southern Africa in the Nineteenth and Twentieth Centuries*. University of London, Institute of Commonwealth Studies, vol. 15 (October 1986-June 1988), 13–28.

Page, Carol A. "Colonial Reaction to AME Missionaries in South Africa, 1898–1910." In *Black Americans and the Missionary Movement in Africa*, ed. Sylvia M. Jacobs, 177–96. Westport, Conn.: Greenwood Press, 1982.

Paton, William. "The Jerusalem Meeting of the International Missionary Council." *International Review of Missions* 17 (1928): 3–10.

[Peires, J. B.] "Ethnicity and Pseudo-Ethnicity in the Ciskei." In *The Creation of Tribalism in Southern Africa*, ed. Leroy Vail, 395–413. Berkeley: University of California Press, 1989.

———. "The Lovedale Press: Literature for the Bantu Revisited." *History in Africa* 6 (1979): 155–75.

Philips, H. "South Africa's Worst Demographic Disaster: The Spanish Influenza Epidemic of 1918." *South African Historical Journal* 20 (1988): 57–73.

Radcliffe-Brown, Alfred R. "Science and Native Problems: How to Understand the Bantu." 1924. Reprinted, with an introduction by Adam Kuper, in *Anthropology Today* 2, no. 4 (1986): 17–21.

Redding, Sean. "Peasants and the Creation of an African Middle Class in Umtata, 1880–1950." *International Journal of African Historical Studies* 26, no. 3 (1993): 513–39.

———. "A South African Town in Black and White: Umtata 1870-1955." Amherst, Mass., 1991. Typescript.

Rich, Paul B. "The Appeals of Tuskegee: James Henderson, Lovedale, and the Fortunes of South African Liberalism, 1906-1930." *International Journal of African Historical Studies* 20, no. 2 (1987): 271–92.

———. "Segregation and the Cape Liberal Tradition." In *Collected Seminar Papers on the Societies of Southern Africa in the Nineteenth and Twentieth Centuries*. University of London, Institute of Commonwealth Studies, vol. 10 (October 1978-June 1979), 31–41.

———. "The South African Institute of Race Relations and the Debate on 'Race Relations', 1929-1958." In *Collected Seminar Papers on the Societies of Southern Africa in the Nineteenth and Twentieth Centuries*. University of London, Institute of Commonwealth Studies, vol. 12 (1981), 77–90.

Robinson, Kenneth. "The Society's Medals." *African Affairs: Journal of the Royal African Society* 85, no. 338 (January 1986): 3–11.

Shingler, John David. "Education and Political Order in South Africa, 1902-1961." Ph.D. diss., Yale University, 1973.

Skidelsky, Robert. "Only Connect: Biography and Truth." In *The Troubled Face of Biography*, ed. Eric Homberger and John Charmley, 1–16. New York: St. Martin's Press, 1988.

Starfield, Jane. "'Not Quite History': The Autobiographies of H. Selby Msimang and R. V. Selope Thema and the Writing of South African History." *Social Dynamics* 14, no. 2 (1988): 16–35.

Swartland, J. R., and D. C. Taylor. "Community Support for Schooling in Botswana Past and Present." *Boleswa Educational Research Journal* 5 (1987): 1–11.

Taylor, J. Dexter. "Relations between the Black and White Races in South Africa." In *The Christian Mission in the Light of Race Conflict*, vol.4 of *The Jerusalem Meeting of the International Missionary Council, March 24-April 8, 1928*. New York: International Missionary Council, 1928, 79–117.

Thema, B. C. "Moeng College—A Product of 'Self-Help.'" *Botswana Notes and Records* 2 (1970): 71–74.

Trapido, Stanley. "African Divisional Politics in the Cape Colony, 1884–1910." *Journal of African History* 9, no. 1 (1968): 79–98.

———. "'The Friends of the Natives': Merchants, Peasants and the Political and Ideological Structure of Liberalism in the Cape, 1854–1910." In *Economy and Society in Pre-Industrial Africa*, ed. Shula Marks and Anthony Atmore, 247–74. Burnt Mill, England: Longman, 1980.

———. "Liberalism in the Cape in the Nineteenth and Twentieth Centuries." In *Collected Seminar Papers on the Societies of Southern Africa in the Nineteenth and Twentieth Centuries*. University of London, Institute of Commonwealth Studies, vol. 4 (October 1972 -June 1973), 53–66.

———. "The Origins of the Cape Franchise Qualifications of 1853." *Journal of African History* 5, no. 1 (1964): 37–54.

Warnshuis, A. L. "Major Issues in the Relations of the Younger and the Older Churches." In *The Relation Between the Younger and the Older Churches*, Vol. 3 of *The Jerusalem Meeting of the International Missionary Council: March 24-April 8, 1928*. New York: International Missionary Council, 1928, 3–104.

Wilson, Monica. "Cooperation and Conflict: The Eastern Cape Frontier." In *A History of South Africa to 1870*. 2d ed., ed. Monica Wilson and Leonard Thompson, 233–72. Beckenham, England: Croom Helm, 1982.

———. "The Nguni Peoples." In *A History of South Africa to 1870*. 2d ed., ed. Monica Wilson and Leonard Thompson, 75–130. Beckenham, England: Croom Helm, 1982.

Yergan, Max. "The Race Problem in Africa." In *The Christian Mission in the Light of Race Conflict*, vol. 4 of *The Jerusalem Meeting of the International Missionary Council, March 24-April 8, 1928*. New York: International Missionary Council, 1928, 179–81.

UNIVERSITY AND COLLEGE CALENDARS

South African Native College, Fort Hare, 1916–1945.
University of Birmingham, 1913–1914.
University of London, University College, 1903–1913.

INTERVIEWS

Bam, Villiers, and Edna Bam. Maseru, Lesotho. March 31, 1988.

Bom, Jemima. Alice, Ciskei. December 10, 1987.

Danana, John M. Umtata, Transkei. March 24, 1988.

Davidson, James Taylor, and Sipo Makalima. Alice, Ciskei. October 27, 1987.

Denalane, Eunice. Mamelodi (Pretoria), Transvaal. February 8, 1988.

Dudley, Robert O. Cape Town, Cape. April 21, 1988.*

Gelderbloem, Stanley. Great Brak River, Cape. July 18, 1988.

Gitywa, Vincent. Bisho, Ciskei. August 16, 1988.***

Gugushe, Richard N. Soweto, Transvaal. February 16, 1988.

Jabavu, Violet, and G. Soya Mama. New Brighton (Port Elizabeth), Cape. August 12, 1988.

Jabavu Crosfield, Helen Nontando (Noni Jabavu). Harare, Zimbabwe. August 2 and August 3, 1987.

Jabavu-Mulira, Alexandra. Port St. John's, Transkei. August 14, 1988.

Jolobe, Jeannie. Port St. John's, Transkei. April, 6, 1988.*

Kerr, Beatrice Tooke. Grahamstown, Cape. November 29, 1987.

Khaketla, Caroline N. Ramolahloane, and Nozipo Ntshona Lebentlele. Maseru, Lesotho. March 30, 1988.

Kobus, Cadoc. Tsolo, Transkei. March 24, 1988.

Lazarus, Arthur D. Reservoir Hills, Natal. March 15, 1988.

Lebentlele, Nozipo Ntshona. Maseru, Lesotho. March 31, 1988 and August 23, 1988.**

Lewis, Patrick R. B. Johannesburg, Transvaal. October 8, 1988.

Majombozi, Jessie C. N., Evelyn Somtunzi, Margaret Majombozi, and Kraai Madlala. Soweto, Transvaal. September 26, 1988.

Makalima, Sipo. Alice, Ciskei. November 23, 1987, and August 16, 1988.***

Makalima, Sipo, and Ethel N. Mzamane. Middledrift, Ciskei. February 12, 1988.

Matthews, Frieda Bokwe. Gaborone, Botswana. August 30, 1988.

Mbete, Benjamin. Healdtown, Ciskei. August 17, 1988.

McQuarrie, John, and Irene McQuarrie. Somerset West, Cape. April 11, 1988.

Mda, A. P. [Ashby Peter]. Mafeteng, Lesotho. August 22, 1988.

Mdlele, H. H. Zwelitsha (King William's Town), Cape. December 14, 1987.

Moerane, Manasseh T. Durban, Natal. April 4, 1988.

Mohapeloa, Joel, and Bernice Mohapeloa. Mafeteng, Lesotho. April 1, 1988, and August 22, 1988.

Mohapeloa, Josias Makibinyane. Maseru, Lesotho. March 30, 1988.

Mtimkulu, Donald. London, Ontario, Canada. November 29, 1988.

Mvusi, C. B. Harare, Zimbabwe. January 12, 1988.

Mzamane, Ethel N. Middledrift, Ciskei. August 3, 1988.

Name, Hobson. Alice, Ciskei. August 17, 1988.

Ncamashe, Chief Burns. Alice, Ciskei. August 9, 1988.

Nkamana, Dora. Pretoria, Transvaal. February 9, 1988.

Ntloko, C. S. Durban, Natal. March 19, 1988.

Ntloko, William. Umtata, Transkei. March 21, 1988.

Ntshona, Penny. Alice, Ciskei. August 3, 1988.

Ntuli, Zulu. Bisho, Ciskei. August 16, 1988.

Nyembezi, C. L. S. Pietermaritzburg, Natal. March 14, 1988.

Peteni, Randall L. Soweto, Transvaal. March 2, 1988.

Phahlane, Mike Mazurki. Johannesburg, Transvaal. October 1, 1988.

Phahle, Ambrose. Manchester, England. October 30, 1988.

Pitje, Godfrey M. Johannesburg, Transvaal. February 24, 1988.

Rajuili, Benjamin S. Johannesburg, Transvaal. February 24, 1988.

Searle, Alan. Somerset West, Cape. June 15, 1988.

Sihlali, Leo L. Mount Frere, Transkei. March 22, 1988.

Tremeer, Rhodes. Alice, Ciskei. December 8, 1987.

Tsotsi, Wycliffe M. Maseru, Lesotho. March 30, 1988.

Van der Ross, David. Wynberg, Cape. July 9, 1988.

Van der Ross, Richard E. Erica, Cape. May 12, 1988.

Zim, J. Khayaletu, Ciskei. December 10, 1987.

Zita, Mavis N., and Albertina N. Tyibilika. Peddie, Ciskei. December 18, 1987.

* Telephone interview, no tape.

** Informant declined to be taped.

*** Written notes only.

INDEX